LEGISLATING THE WAR ON TERROR

Legislating the War on Terror
An Agenda for Reform

Benjamin Wittes

Editor

Brookings Institution Press
Washington, D.C.

Copyright © 2009
GEORGETOWN UNIVERSITY LAW CENTER and
THE BROOKINGS INSTITUTION
1775 Massachusetts Avenue, N.W., Washington, DC 20036.
www.brookings.edu

Library of Congress Cataloging-in-Publication data
Legislating the war on terror : an agenda for reform / Benjamin Wittes, editor.
     p.   cm.
   Includes bibliographical references and index.
   Summary: "Tackles some of the most challenging dilemmas and the new post-9/11 realities
confronting Congress as it legislates the new ground rules for the war on terror. Presents an
agenda for reforming statutory laws governing this new battle that balances need for security,
rule of law, and constitutional rights of freedom"—Provided by publisher.
   ISBN 978-0-8157-0310-5 (hardcover : alk. paper)
   1. War on Terrorism, 2001—Law and legislation—United States. 2. Terrorism—United
States. I. Wittes, Benjamin. II. Title.
   KF9430.L434 2009
   345.73'02--dc22   2009038910

9 8 7 6 5 4 3 2 1

Printed on acid-free paper

Typeset in Minion

Composition by Cynthia Stock
Silver Spring, Maryland

Printed by R. R. Donnelley
Harrisonburg, Virginia

Contents

Acknowledgments

This volume reflects the work of a great many people, only some of whose names appear as authors on the chapters that make it up. It emerges out of a collaboration between the Brookings Institution and two other research organizations—the Hoover Institution and the Georgetown Center on National Security and the Law—which teamed up in 2007 to produce a series of papers on improving the statutory architecture of U.S. counterterrorism operations. The collaboration represents the latest joint effort between the Brookings Governance Studies program and Hoover and the first of what I hope will be many joint projects with the Georgetown center.

A few people within these institutions deserve special recognition. Within Brookings, two directors of Governance Studies have offered at different times unstinting support for the project. Pietro Nivola was instrumental in bringing me to Brookings and helped me get my program on counterterrorism and law off the ground. Darrell West, since taking the reins at Governance Studies, has been a constant source of support for my work. In addition to Hoover's direct support for the series of papers, David Brady and Peter Berkowitz have provided through Hoover's Task Force on National Security and Law a remarkable forum for the non-ideological discussion of legal issues and counterterrorism. Several of the chapters in this volume were produced by task force members and benefited from early comments in the crucible of the task force's regular meetings. At Georgetown, Neal Katyal (before returning to government) was instrumental in helping me launch the paper series, and he also helped to identify ideal authors for some of the papers. I am deeply grateful for the work of all of these people, without which the current volume would never have been born.

I owe a special word of thanks to Mike Quinn, Sean O'Brien, and Jen Patja and the rest of the staff at the Montpelier Center for the Constitution, which hosted two multiday seminars at which the authors of the chapters in this volume had the opportunity to discuss and present their work both to each other and to an outstanding group of journalists.

Several individuals played essential roles as well. My research assistant, Zaahira Wyne, helped edit the papers and coordinated their web publication. Governance Studies interns Jennifer Gaudette and Joshua Roselman helped harmonize the papers stylistically and prevented any number of embarrassing errors from reaching readers. Whether in Washington, in the Bahamas, or in London, Georgina Druce labored mightily on research related both to foreign counterterrorism law and to domestic covert action. Janet Walker and Eileen Hughes of the Brookings Institution Press helped bring the various parts of the manuscript together into a book. And last but certainly not least, nothing at Governance Studies would get done without the dedicated band of staffers—Bethany Hase, Ellen Higgins, Gladys Arrisueno, John Seo, and Courtney Dunakin—who make this particular ship sail every day and keep it whole and sound.

Finally, a word of particular thanks to the many individuals of all political stripes who have labored at the often thankless task of imagining a better statutory environment in which to conduct counterterrorism operations. Those on the left and the right alike tend to view this project with suspicion— the left because it sometimes sees legislation as a legitimizing agent for policy that it prefers to confront and the right because it sees legislation as encroaching on presidential prerogatives. This volume has sought to highlight some of the scholars and practitioners who work in this area. But there are many others whose combined intellectual labor will, I am confident, over time place the confrontation of the United States with global jihadist terrorism on a sounder intellectual and legal basis. To all of them this book is dedicated.

LEGISLATING THE WAR ON TERROR

BENJAMIN WITTES

Introduction

The war on terror has entered a new phase, the phase of institutional-ization. What began as a series of responses to a crisis and then triggered backlashes from the courts, the political system, and the international com-munity now gropes toward the creation of more durable structures to both legitimize and control strong action against global terrorism. The current phase is, at one level, a period of instability, as the old certitudes that coun-terterrorism is warfare or that it is law enforcement dissolve. It is also a phase of considerable opportunity, for institutionalization of the confrontation with international terrorist organizations gives the United States the chance to design the structures that will govern it for the long term.

This new phase does not come as any more of surprise than did its prede-cessors. In fact, the phases immediately following the September 11 attack followed precisely the script that one might have written for them. The exec-utive branch acted boldly—sometimes with wisdom, sometimes foolishly—subject to limited legal constraint. It treated the conflict through legal and ana-lytical lenses that maximized its own latitude to respond flexibly. It resisted efforts by other institutions to assert themselves in ways that might encum-ber its struggle. It concerned itself more with the exercise of power than with the legitimacy of power, much less with the perception of the legitimacy of power. And for a while, particularly in the absence of further attacks, the exec-utive branch succeeded in maintaining that ground.

But just as predictable as the assertion of executive authority during the cri-sis was the waning over time of society's willingness to tolerate unrestrained executive leadership. Within a few years of the advent of the war, the courts and Congress had begun insisting upon the imposition of legal rules—and rejecting the executive's instinct to make up and change the rules on its own

1

and for its own convenience. That phase of reaction saw a raft of Supreme Court decisions on detention of terrorist suspects; it saw new legislative restrictions on interrogation; and it saw a great deal of intellectual ferment in favor of a return to a criminal justice approach to terrorism.

But now the second phase is giving way to a third, one characterized by the attempt to synthesize the insights of the first two phases and to develop more durable law that reflects that synthesis. Broadly speaking, the synthesis recognizes that global counterterrorism is neither pure law enforcement nor pure warfare but draws on the key elements, authorities, and limits of both. It acknowledges that executive authority to prosecute the conflict must be robust, yet it insists also that executive powers must be constrained by law and oversight mechanisms. In any number of areas—detention and surveillance, for example—the law has already moved in that direction, sometimes as a consequence of judicial action, sometimes as a consequence of legislation. Indeed, the process of institutionalization is not new; it began under the Bush administration. That said, the Bush administration did not midwife the process but engaged in it reluctantly, fitfully. It brought to the table too much residual commitment to the propositions that it had all the authority that it needed, that warfare provided the appropriate model for the project at hand, and that the other branches of government could only get in the way.

A new administration now confronts the same hard problems that plagued its ideologically opposite predecessor, and its very efforts to turn the page on the past make acute the problems of institutionalization. For while the new administration can promise to close the detention facility at Guantánamo Bay and can talk about its desire to prosecute suspects criminally, for example, it cannot so easily forswear noncriminal detention. While it can eschew the term "global war on terror," it cannot forswear those uses of force—Predator strikes, for example—that law enforcement powers would never countenance. Nor is it hastening to give back the surveillance powers that Congress finally gave the Bush administration. In other words, its very efforts to avoid the Bush administration's vocabulary have only emphasized the conflict's hybrid nature—indeed, emphasized that the United States is building something new here, not merely applying something old.

That point should not provoke controversy. The evidence that the United States is fumbling toward the creation of hybrid institutions to handle terrorism cases is everywhere around us. U.S. law, for example, now contemplates extensive, probing judicial review of detentions under the laws of war—a naked marriage of criminal justice and wartime traditions. It also contemplates warrantless wiretapping with judicial oversight of surveillance targeting procedures—thereby mingling the traditional judicial role in reviewing domestic surveillance with the vacuum cleaner–type acquisition of intelligence typical of overseas intelligence gathering. Slowly but surely, through an unpredictable combination of litigation, legislation, and evolutionary developments within executive branch policy, the nation is creating novel institutional arrangements to authorize and regulate the war on terror.

The real question is not whether institutionalization will take place but whether it will take place deliberately or haphazardly, whether the United States will create through legislation the institutions with which it wishes to govern itself or whether it will allow an endless sequence of common law adjudications to shape them.

The authors of the chapters in this book disagree about a great many things. They span a considerable swath of the U.S. political spectrum, and they would no doubt object to some of one another's policy prescriptions. Indeed, some of the proposals are arguably inconsistent with one another, and it will be the very rare reader who reads this entire volume and wishes to see all of its ideas implemented in legislation. What binds these authors together is not the programmatic aspects of their policy prescriptions but the belief in the value of legislative action to help shape the contours of the continuing U.S. confrontation with terrorism. That is, the authors all believe that Congress has a significant role to play in the process of institutionalization—and they have all attempted to describe that role with reference to one of the policy areas over which Americans have sparred these past several years and will likely continue sparring over the next several.

The essays are organized around the major tools that the United States has deployed against al Qaeda, as well as some of the major legal problems that have arisen as a result of their use. Those tools—detention, criminal process, surveillance, targeted strikes against terrorist leaders, interrogation, deportation, and border control—differ significantly from one another in the controversy that they engender. In some cases—for example, targeted killing and detention—many people doubt the propriety of their use per se. In others, such as interrogation, criminal process, and immigration enforcement, their use is a given; the controversy surrounds the mode of use. In general, it is not the purpose of these chapters to convince the skeptical reader of the necessity or propriety of the use of these tools. The book starts, rather, with the observation that they existed under the previous administration—with at least the tacit consent of Congress—and that, with the exception of aggressive interrogation, the current administration has not forsworn them. The question, therefore, becomes how Congress should authorize, regulate, and limit their use and under what circumstances it should permit and encourage their use. There is, to lay a bias squarely on the table, a methodological assumption here that a genuine conflict exists and that, rhetoric aside, a certain degree of political consensus exists among those who have to prosecute that conflict about the legal tools in the U.S. arsenal. The authors share a commitment to pushing a reluctant Congress to play a more active role than it has to date in writing the rules of the road concerning the use of those tools.

The chapters range a great deal in the specificity of their calls for legislative action. Some, like Robert Chesney's proposals for optimizing criminal law as a counterterrorism tool and David Martin's suggestions for refinements to immigration law, give detailed road maps for legislative reforms. Others, like Matthew Waxman's discussion of the strategic purposes of detention policy, describe higher-altitude considerations for Congress to take into account. Still others, like Kenneth Anderson's arguments for congressional defense of targeted killing, involve a largely hortatory and oversight role for the legislature—not one of defining rules as such.

The chapters, however, are all designed to focus discussion on what Congress can and should do to answer some of the fundamental legal policy questions that the country faces in its fight against terrorism. Collectively, they represent a set of ideas—useful in isolation from one another as well as in various possible combinations—that the national legislature could seek to implement in the course of institutionalizing the war on terror.

The chapters are grouped thematically. Chapter 1 presents Mark Gitenstein's survey of the approaches taken by other democracies to some of the major issues with which the United States has struggled—looking in particular at the strategies those countries have employed with respect to detention, interrogation, and surveillance. This chapter highlights the diversity of practice among democracies in certain areas and the commonality of practice and law in others. It opens the book with a broad sense of the lay of the democratic land in the counterterrorism arena.

Following this come two chapters on detention policy, Matthew Waxman's study of the possible strategic purposes for administrative detention (chapter 2) and Jack Goldsmith's examination of how to refine the U.S. system of judicial review of detentions (chapter 3). Waxman challenges policymakers to think about the strategic purpose of detaining people without charging them criminally. He cautions against jumping too quickly to questions of how and under what rules to allow administrative detention but emphasizes that careful consideration of detention's strategic purpose should guide the design elements of any detention system that Congress might create. Goldsmith, in contrast, focuses on the design elements, imagining the broad contours of a system of judicially reviewed law of war detention to replace the current raft of Guantánamo Bay habeas corpus litigation.

Two chapters follow on the vexing problem of how to bring to trial those terrorist suspects that the government wishes to charge with crimes. In chapter 4, Robert Chesney suggests a series of refinements to U.S. criminal law designed to make criminal law a maximally powerful instrument against terrorism. In chapter 5, Robert Litt and Wells Bennett propose the statutory creation of a bar of defense counsel cleared to receive classified material as a way of facilitating criminal prosecution in national security cases. Both Chesney and Litt and Bennett emerged from their studies of the policy options surrounding criminal trials impressed by the capacity of the contemporary civilian justice system to handle terrorism cases. Their primary interest is in building on the system that currently exists, rather than either establishing a new tribunal or making military commissions the tribunal of choice for terrorism cases.

In chapter 6, David Martin reminds readers that it was immigration law that provided the government with robust domestic detention powers during the initial response to September 11 and that in the next crisis, any administration will likely find those tools attractive as well. He suggests a series of adjustments designed to keep that power focused on its core purposes and effective in achieving those purposes.

David Kris then examines U.S. surveillance law, arguing in chapter 7 that Congress's efforts to modernize the Foreign Intelligence Surveillance Act are probably an interim step in a much broader, longer-term rewrite of laws governing wiretapping and domestic electronic intelligence collection; he sketches a legislative program designed to simplify the mind-numbingly complicated laws that govern domestic and international spying.

In chapter 8, the only one that does not address a tool used by the executive branch against terrorism per se, Justin Florence and Matthew Gerke take on the problem of civil litigation in the national security arena. They suggest reform of the state secrets privilege to make the privilege less of a blunt instrument and more of a scalpel in litigation against the government and third parties.

In chapter 9, Stuart Taylor Jr. and I suggest a statutory framework for high-stakes interrogation, one that attempts to break with the sins of the past while preserving flexibility for interrogators in the most wrenching emergency situations. This chapter suggests both broadening the current legal prohibition of torture to make it correspond more closely to the colloquial understanding of the word "torture" and enacting legislation that affirmatively authorizes judicious use of certain forms of coercion by the CIA that are forbidden by the military.

Finally, in chapter 10, Kenneth Anderson studies the question of targeted killing, arguing that Congress must act boldly to preserve the shrinking space for a species of covert action whose use has become a matter of near consensus between the political parties. Anderson traces the strategic logic that has made targeted killing an ever-growing feature of U.S. counterterrorism and also examines the trends in international law that militate strongly against the legitimacy of the tool. He concludes that absent strong—albeit mostly rhetorical—legislative moves to defend this activity, the United States will grow increasingly isolated and will ultimately face a reckoning with instruments of international justice such as prosecution for war crimes in international tribunals or in the courts of nations asserting universal jurisdiction over such crimes.

The chapters are intended to be stand-alone essays, and the reader should feel free to treat them in isolation, as guides to specific policy problems. At the same time, their selection was not accidental; they were chosen to make a larger argument as well: Congress has a lot of work to do in refining U.S. counterterrorism law. That work is not confined to any one issue; it is broad-based and multifaceted. As a society, the United States has not yet written the basic rules under which it will confront an enemy that does not play by its old rules. The nation has not decided where and how it should be constrained and where it should be unconstrained, when it should take risks in the name of its values and where the threat is so great that it prefers to take risks *with* its values. This volume is intended both to highlight how much work there is to be done and to offer a set of ideas for how to begin.

MARK H. GITENSTEIN

1

Nine Democracies and the Problems of Detention, Surveillance, and Interrogation

The United States faces vexing questions concerning how to safeguard civil liberties and human rights in the face of threats to its national security, and its experience has resulted in a unique balancing of those concerns. But the threats against the United States are not unique; other nations have faced—and still face—terrorist threats. Those nations have confronted the same type of threats in light of their own civil libertarian and democratic traditions. As the United States considers the long-term legal architecture for its confrontation with terrorism, it is instructive for the country to look beyond its borders to examine the successes and failures of international efforts to combat similar—though not identical—threats. Without abandoning either U.S. ideals in the pursuit of a hermetic sort of security or U.S. safety in the pursuit of unbridled personal autonomy, the country can learn from the experiences of other nations—from the similarities and differences in their approaches and those that the United States has taken. While some of the choices of other states reflect the particular concerns of their unique local democratic cultures, others reflect wisdom from which Americans might learn.

This chapter surveys the responses among a number of democratic countries around the world to three fundamental problems with which the United

This research effort was undertaken by me and several colleagues—Caroline Brown, Raj De, Michael Paisner, Shiek Pal, Michael Passaportis, Brian Netter, and Georgina Druce—based on our review of publicly available information and, in many cases, of excellent secondary sources. Amos N. Guiora provided valuable assistance by reviewing the factual assertions contained in this chapter; however, he did not review any of the opinions expressed here, and his participation should not be viewed as an endorsement thereof. All substantive work on this chapter was completed by the time I became ambassador to Romania in the summer of 2009. The opinions expressed are my own and do not reflect the views or policies of the United States government or of any other entity or person.

States has struggled since the September 11 attacks: the circumstances under which a government may detain individuals without criminal process; the proper limits on interrogation techniques; and the circumstances under which a government may subject persons whom it does not detain to domestic electronic surveillance.

My purpose in these pages is not to advocate any particular policy. It is to set up the discussion in the chapters that follow concerning the details of policy trade-offs by comparing the U.S. response so far in these three areas with those of eight other democracies: Australia, France, Germany, India, Israel, Spain, South Africa, and the United Kingdom. Three of these countries—Australia, India, and the United Kingdom—share the common law tradition of the U.S. judiciary. Three others—France, Germany, and Spain—come from a civil law tradition. The remaining two—Israel and South Africa—exhibit aspects of both traditions. Each of the countries is party to major international agreements such as the Geneva Conventions and the Convention against Torture and Other Cruel, Inhuman, or Degrading Treatment or Punishment.[1]

While it is common to discuss the U.S. response to terrorism since September 11 as excessive in comparison with the responses of other countries, the survey reveals a more complicated picture. For while U.S. law, particularly as interpreted by the Bush administration, is indeed more permissive in some respects than the laws of some other democracies, it is also significantly more restrictive in other respects. Indeed, in such areas as surveillance and detention, the survey is striking for the remarkable diversity of approaches that recognizably democratic countries have taken. By contrast, the democratic world has converged toward an increasingly uniform rejection of harsh interrogation tactics—which perhaps explains the world's horrified reaction to the Bush administration's interrogation policies, which deviated substantially from the emerging consensus.

One striking feature of the survey is that no other democracy has proceeded under the executive power model advanced by the Bush administration. Where foreign counterterrorism powers are broader than comparable U.S. powers, they are broad by statute, not by asserted inherent authority. That fact to some degree reflects the uniqueness of the U.S. constitutional system, in which the executive branch does not depend on the legislature for its powers. But that observation also has important process implications. For it means that foreign prime ministers and leaders are much less likely to be operating in stark tension with the legislature in pursuing even robust counterterrorism measures than was the Bush administration.

The Countries

To draw suitable comparisons, it is necessary to be mindful of the threats that each country faces and how its terrorism defenses have been altered by past attacks. The countries surveyed here differ from the United States both in terms of the threats that they face and in terms of their legal systems and civil libertarian traditions. The United States is blessed to have such a deep and storied civil libertarian tradition as well as a vigilant and independent judicial system. The United States also faces a more recent and more manageable domestic threat than that faced by some other countries. What's more, no country in history has ever had to project force abroad the way that the United States has had to in order to confront its terrorism problems at home. The laws of other democracies, in other words, are designed for confronting terrorists locally, not globally.

Australia

Australia has a federal system of courts like that of the United States. However, Australia lacks both a constitutional and a statutory bill of rights. Unlike that of the other nations studied here, Australia's exposure to terrorism is recent—there has been no terrorist attack on Australian soil, although numerous Australian citizens were killed in the Bali bombings of 2002 and 2005 and Australian officials have worried about attacks within Australia itself.[2] In the aftermath of September 11, Australia instituted a variety of legal measures to combat terrorism, notably by criminalizing "terrorist acts"[3] and derivative crimes[4] and authorizing the Australian Security Intelligence Organization (ASIO) to adopt special investigative measures; it also expanded ASIO's power to detain suspects in terrorism-related investigations.[5]

France

France has long faced threats of terrorism stemming both from the importation of foreign conflicts and from domestic terrorist groups. In the 1950s and 1960s, as a consequence of the bitter war in Algeria, mainland France experienced a wave of terrorism. After a lull of more than a decade, terrorism reemerged as a problem in the late 1970s, with attacks by foreign organizations such as the Palestine Liberation Organization, political extremist groups, and separatist movements. During the mid-1980s, France was subjected to the rapid and intense succession of more than twenty deadly attacks that likely were sponsored by Iran and Syria. In the mid-1990s, Algerian Muslim fundamentalists were responsible for several attacks. Since then, France has foiled several attacks linked to Islamic extremists, such as a 2005 plot by Salafi militants to attack targets in Paris.[6] Islamic extremists—most notably transnational groups such as the Algerian Groupe Islamique Armée (GIA), which has links to al Qaeda—continue to pose a serious threat to France. In addition, however, France's large and dissatisfied Muslim community forms 10 percent of its population.[7]

To confront France's long-standing, if constantly morphing, threat of terrorism, French authorities wielded preemptive and intrusive powers long before the September 11 attacks. A system of centralized and specialized investigative magistrates dates back to the attacks of the mid-1980s, and additional legislation enacted in 1996 to prohibit conspiracy to commit terrorism was used in the aftermath of September 11 for preventive arrests and investigations. Those legislative measures have undergone careful scrutiny by legal institutions to determine their compatibility with the rights of individuals protected by France's 1958 constitution.[8] In the wake of September 11 and the London bombings of 2005, the scope of terrorism crimes has expanded still further, penalties have been stiffened, and new investigative techniques have been authorized.[9]

Germany

Germany traditionally has perceived its terrorist threat as largely domestic, although that changed to some degree following the September 11 attacks. The most significant terrorist actions occurred in the mid-1970s, when the left-wing Red Army Faction mounted a series of violent attacks against prominent figures. Although international terrorists have sporadically attacked Germany, terrorism has largely been addressed as a matter of criminal law enforcement.[10] September 11 was particularly shocking to Germans because the planning for the attacks took place in Hamburg, raising concerns that the country had become a safe harbor for transnational networks of Islamic extremists planning and initiating terrorism. Two major bomb plots since 2006—one aimed at German trains, the other at U.S. interests in Germany— have further intensified scrutiny of the nature of the terrorist threat and Germany's approach to terrorism.[11]

In response to September 11, the German legislature enacted two broad antiterrorism packages. They were intended to expand existing legal authority to pursue individuals and entities involved in terrorism, enhance the investigative authority of the government agencies charged with combating terrorism, and increase the resources devoted to identifying and prosecuting terrorists. The federal government's response has been necessarily constrained by Germany's constitution—the Basic Law.[12] The German federalist system divides governing authority between the federal government and the sixteen states, resulting in a decentralized security apparatus. Despite Germany's decentralization of power and civil liberty protections, German security authorities have pursued antiterrorism efforts with vigor, detecting a number of extremist cells and possibly thwarting some attacks.[13]

India

India faces a multitude of internal and external threats. The most visible sources of terrorist activity are external groups in or supported by Pakistan, internal separatists in the northern states of Jammu and Kashmir, and domestic religious extremists. India has experienced terrorist activities aimed against its government, the assassinations of prime ministers Indira Gandhi in 1984 and Rajiv Gandhi in 1991, and, most prominent, an armed attack on Parliament in 2001. It has seen attacks aimed against religious groups and communities—for example, a 2002 attack on a train of Hindu pilgrims, the ensuing pogroms against Muslims, and a 1984 mass attack against Sikhs following the assassination of Indira Gandhi. Moreover, it has seen attacks against the establishment by fringe groups such as the Naxalites (Communists). Most recently, it suffered the devastating 2008 Mumbai attacks against tourist and other infrastructure in India's financial capital. Given the variety and complexity of threats facing India, it is difficult to characterize them in a general manner conducive to supporting broad legislation.

In response to the December 2001 terrorist attack on the Indian parliament, India passed the Prevention of Terrorism Act (POTA).[14] POTA restored and refined numerous counterterrorism measures that had been enacted under the Terrorist and Disruptive Activities (Prevention) Act (TADA),[15] which was passed in response to the assassination of Indira Gandhi in 1984 but had lapsed in 1995. POTA shared many features with TADA, such as a broad definition of terrorism offenses. Following widespread domestic and international condemnation of POTA, the government of Manmohan Singh made good on a campaign pledge to repeal it in 2004.

In response to the Mumbai terrorist attacks on November 26, 2008, however, the Indian parliament introduced two pieces of legislation, both of which became law within a few days of their introduction. The Unlawful Activities (Prevention) Amendment of 2008 (UAPA) focused more specifically on terrorism than an earlier law, the Unlawful Activities (Prevention) Act of 1967, by introducing a definition of "terrorist act" that was missing from the 1967 legislation and introducing numerous new terrorist offenses.[16]

Offenses included raising funds for terrorist acts, organizing terrorist camps, and recruiting anyone for a terrorist act. In addition, the bill extended the maximum period of detention without bail to 180 days. The act also amended the presumption of innocence for terrorist acts to a presumption of guilt if the prosecution shows that substances specified under the definition of "terrorist act" were recovered from the accused or that there is reason to believe that such substances were used in commission of a terrorist act or if expert evidence places the accused's fingerprints anywhere at the site of the offense.[17]

In important respects, the UAPA goes further in its provisions than did the POTA. For example, the POTA's definition of "terrorist act" was almost identical to that of the UAPA; however, the UAPA includes as terrorist acts those that are "likely to" threaten the unity and sovereignty of society, whereas the POTA had been limited to those acts specifically intended to threaten society. The UAPA also does not limit the effects of a terrorist act to Indians but specifically provides that a terrorist act can include striking terror in people of a foreign country or acts intended to induce the government of a foreign country to act. The POTA, by contrast, had not specifically mentioned the people or government of foreign countries. The POTA also had not included the additional terrorist offenses criminalized in the UAPA (such as organizing terrorist camps or recruiting persons for terrorist acts) unless the accused was a member of a prescribed terrorist organization and was recruiting members for that organization.

The second piece of legislation, the National Investigation Agency (NIA) Act of 2008, established a national agency to investigate terrorism offenses and to coordinate with various state and local law enforcement agencies. That is the first time that such an agency had been proposed.

Israel

Israel faces threats from surrounding Arab nations and the Palestinian territories, the most immediate coming from militant and extremist groups within the Gaza Strip and West Bank. The second intifada—characterized by the Israeli government as an "armed conflict short of war"—presents the most constant and visible threat, and there is tension between political and military/security efforts to resolve or ameliorate the situation. Hezbollah, based in southern Lebanon, also presents a prominent threat. In addition, Israeli society has had difficulty in assessing and addressing potential threats from Israeli Arabs who reside within Israel, although there have been few proven instances of terrorist attacks involving Israeli Arabs.

The Knesset passed no legislation in specific response to September 11, but Israeli law has developed in response to the two intifadas. Given its history and geographic location, Israel's experience with terrorism is deep. Many of the specific antiterror measures in place now were implemented in response to the first intifada (1987–94) and the second intifada (2000 onward). Other antiterror legislation and administrative detention laws predated the first intifada,[18] as did emergency legislation carried over from the pre-state British Mandate,[19] which is still used in dealing with terrorism. Following international momentum in the wake of September 11, Israel adopted terrorist financing legislation in 2004.[20] As a hybrid of common law and civil law, Israel's independent judiciary enjoys wide judicial discretion, including the judicial power to create case law.

Spain

Spain has a long history of terrorist attacks on its own soil—largely perpetrated, at least until recently, by Euskadi Ta Askatasuna (ETA), the armed Basque separatist organization. According to Spanish government figures, ETA has killed more than 800 people in terrorist attacks since 1968.[21] ETA attacks have fallen off sharply recently, although the organization was responsible for the Madrid airport bombing in 2006[22] and the assassination of an ex-politician in 2008.[23] In recent years, Spain also has faced the threat of terrorist attacks from Spanish citizens of North African descent and illegal immigrants from that part of the world; the individuals tried for the devastating 2004 Madrid train bombings, which killed 191 people, were mostly Moroccan citizens.[24]

Because of the earlier ETA activity, Spain already had in place special sections of the criminal code relating to terrorism crimes and special procedures for their investigation and prosecution; the government therefore elected to use the existing legal infrastructure instead of passing new laws to deal with terrorist threats in the wake of September 11.[25] New legislation was limited to a 2002 act permitting the legislature to declare a political party illegal if it fails to respect democratic principles and values. Even that act was aimed chiefly at the political wing of ETA, not at jihadist terrorists.[26] Spain continued this approach in the wake of the Madrid train bombings in 2004.[27] As a general matter, Spain treats terrorism as an aggravated form of crime.[28]

South Africa

South Africa has not experienced significant terrorist threats since the end of the apartheid era, but concern has been growing that the nation, while not a target itself, may be used increasingly for terrorist support activities. Analysts believe that al Qaeda and other Islamist terrorist groups may have at least some presence there. That concern was intensified by the 2004 arrest of two South African militants with Khalfan Ghailani in Pakistan. Ghailani, a well-known al Qaeda figure on the FBI's Most Wanted List, is thought to have been a participant in the 1998 U.S. embassy bombings and was one of four-teen high-value detainees transferred in 2006 to Guantánamo Bay from secret detention facilities abroad.

In November 2004, South Africa passed the Protection of Constitutional Democracy against Terrorist and Related Activities Act, its most significant counterterrorism legislation of the post-apartheid era.[29] The act codifies ter-rorism as a distinct criminal offense, provides for extensive liability of accom-plices for terrorist activities, and criminalizes specific terrorist activities by way of implementing South Africa's international obligations. Those activities include financing terrorist activity, hijacking, and hostage taking.[30] The law was in development prior to September 11 and was shaped more by the coun-try's apartheid legacy than by the events of that day. Indeed, the very term "ter-rorism" has a complicated legacy in South Africa, because the apartheid gov-ernment used it to suppress political opposition. As a result, the act specifically exempts acts of advocacy, protest, and dissent and labor organizing, as well as acts committed during armed struggle in the exercise of one's legitimate right of self-determination.[31] Notably, after consideration of a series of controver-sial provisions that would have given the country's executive the unreviewable authority to detain suspected terrorists, the legislature ultimately dropped those provisions.

The United Kingdom

The United Kingdom of Great Britain and Northern Ireland consists of four countries—England, Wales, Scotland, and Northern Ireland—that include three distinct jurisdictions with distinct court systems and legal professions. The United Kingdom has no written constitution, and it has experienced ter-rorist activities of one sort or another for more than a century. The British Empire faced campaigns of political violence in anticolonial conflicts in Pales-tine, India, Kenya, Malaysia, Cyprus, and Aden. Its laws also reflect the legal impact of campaigns by the Irish Republican Army and other paramilitary Irish organizations, such as the Irish National Liberation Army and the Ulster Volunteer Force. Most recently, Britain has faced serious Islamist violence. In the aftermath of September 11, al Qaeda sought to bomb a flight from Britain to the United States. The London transit system was targeted in 2005, when the United Kingdom hosted the G-8 summit; two weeks later, four more bombs were planted in the transit system, although there were no casualties. And British officials famously foiled plans to use liquid explosives to bring down numerous transatlantic flights.

The main British legislative response to September 11 was the Antiterrorism, Crime, and Security Act of 2001 (ATCSA),[32] which Parliament passed after just sixteen hours of debate with strong support from the main opposition party in the House of Commons and the overwhelming backing of members generally. The bill partially abrogated habeas corpus by permitting the detention of suspected international terrorists when their "removal or departure from the United Kingdom is prevented" by law or practical considerations.[33] It thereby made the United Kingdom the only country in Europe in the wake of September 11 to derogate from Article 5 of the European Convention on Human Rights (ECHR) by authorizing indefinite detention without criminal charge. However, the act applied only to foreigners subject to immigration control, since a prerequisite for detention is that the accused must be liable for detention under certain sections of the Immigration Act 1971.[34] In 2005 Parliament passed the Prevention of Terrorism Act 2005, which replaced the regime of detention without trial under the 2001 act with restriction by way of a control order—a kind of system of house arrest.[35] Following the 2005 London bombings, Parliament passed the Terrorism Act 2006,[36] which extended police powers of detention after arrest and limited free speech by making it a criminal offense to incite or encourage others to commit acts of terrorism.[37] In an especially controversial provision, publishers may be held accountable if they recklessly publish statements likely to be understood by their audience as a direct or indirect encouragement for the commission, preparation of, or instigation of acts of terrorism.[38]

The American Exception

The architecture of the U.S. response to September 11 has roots both in the unusual nature of the U.S. confrontation with terrorism—which involves confronting an enemy that seeks to mount domestic attacks but is based halfway around the world—and in the structure of U.S. democracy itself. Democracy in the United States is quite distinct from that in the other states in this survey, none of which share the full panoply of U.S. civil libertarian bulwarks. Only South Africa, for example, has an enumerated bill of rights insulated from majoritarian interference and enforceable through an independent judiciary. None of the other democracies shares the U.S. commitment to freedom of speech nor to the rights against self incrimination, cruel and unusual punishment, and freedom from search and seizure. In the United States, the independent judiciary is further fortified by the life tenure of its judges, and constitutional violations may be remedied by excluding tainted evidence from court proceedings. In addition, the United States is unique in authorizing private causes of action, allowing individual citizens to enforce fundamental rights in court. Most of the nations studied here have centralized systems of intelligence gathering and criminal law enforcement, whereas in the United States the intelligence and criminal investigative functions are mostly distinct at the national level and further decentralized among the states. Germany has some of the U.S. features as a legacy of its reaction to the Nazi era, and South Africa has adopted some as a reaction to apartheid, but they are far from all the protections that citizens of the United States enjoy. France and the United Kingdom attempt to draw some of the distinctions between intelligence collection and criminal prosecution that U.S. law draws, but neither country has the precise limitations contained, for example, in the U.S. Foreign Intelligence Surveillance Act (FISA).

In other words, the United States moved toward the use of military process to deal with terrorists in part because its civilian criminal justice process is quite restrictive and because the enemy, in any event, tends to reside in areas where application of U.S. law is difficult. Fellow democracies, for better or for worse, find their terrorists closer to home and have more robust criminal investigative powers; therefore they have felt less need to resort to military process.

The Power to Detain

Under U.S. law, a citizen or permanent resident may be detained in the absence of a specific criminal charge only in limited situations. Outside the context of mental illness or communicable disease, the U.S. government may hold a person without charge for an extended period of time only if that person is a material witness to a criminal investigation whose testimony prosecutors need but cannot secure by subpoena. In the context of the war on terrorism, the absence of any generalized preventative or investigative detention authority placed great pressure on detention authorities created to address other needs. For present purposes, two authorities played an especially significant role: authority to detain under the material witness statute and authority to detain under the laws of war. (For a discussion of detention under immigration law, which also played a significant role after September 11, see chapter 6.) Specifically, the Bush administration construed the definition of "material witness" broadly in the war on terror—and for enemy combatants captured abroad, the naval outpost at Guantánamo Bay, Cuba, offered a starkly different approach.

The material witness law allows for the detention of witnesses in criminal proceedings under a limited set of circumstances—for example, for a grand jury investigation or for trial—and it can last for a "reasonable period of time."[39] Civil liberties groups have reported that at least seventy men were detained as material witnesses in the aftermath of the September 11 attacks in order to investigate potential suspects. Of those men, seven were ultimately charged with terrorism-related offenses, but another thirty never even testified before a grand jury. One-third were incarcerated for at least two months, and at least one material witness was jailed for more than a year.[40]

Detention under the laws of war involved a much larger cohort of detainees, almost all of them seized abroad. The United States has not had a stable statutory policy governing such detentions. Instead, in a series of post–September 11 executive actions, the Bush administration created special detention procedures and facilities, including the detention center at Guantánamo Bay, prompting rebukes by the Supreme Court. That in turn has led to additional rounds of legislation and executive policymaking—the latest round of which is now under way in the Obama administration. In both the Detainee Treatment Act of 2005 and the Military Commissions Act of 2006, Congress attempted to deny federal courts the authority to entertain habeas corpus petitions with respect to the detainees, but the Supreme Court has repeatedly rejected attempts to define Guantánamo Bay as being beyond judicial oversight. In its 2008 decision in *Boumediene* v. *Bush,* the Court held that detainees must be allowed to petition for a writ of habeas corpus, although the Court has not provided details as to the contours of the habeas corpus right. In the course of the discourse among the executive, legislative, and judicial branches of government on the rights of alleged enemy combatants, more questions have arisen than answers, concerning both the definition of an "unlawful enemy combatant"—a term that the Obama administration now chooses to avoid—and the rights of the individual detained as such. (For a more detailed discussion of U.S. detention law and policy, see chapters 3 and 4.)

Such profoundly difficult questions have not arisen in most other countries, which simply have not claimed the authority to seize terrorist suspects on foreign soil and hold them as unlawful enemy combatants either within their own territory or on off-shore military bases. The notable exception to that rule is Israel, which does claim the right to administratively detain foreign terrorists as unlawful enemy combatants. Under a 2002 law that was upheld in 2008 by the Israeli Supreme Court, a person may be detained for membership in a terrorist organization. The Israeli Supreme Court construed that to require active—as opposed to nominal—membership.[41] The Israeli authorization for detention of terrorist suspects as enemy combatants, however, is the exception among democracies, most of which eschew the kind of detentions that the United States has undertaken since September 11.

That said, it is quite wrong to confuse those countries' rejection of *military* detention with a broader rejection of preventative detention of their own citizens within their own borders. Indeed, while the other democracies do not authorize indefinite detention of the sort characterized by the U.S. detention of enemy combatants at Guantánamo Bay, they generally do authorize domestic preventative detention of terrorist suspects (including their own citizens) by other means. Most other democracies do not tie preventative detention of terrorist suspects to purported enemy belligerence or to whether a person of interest has witnessed a particular crime. Preventive detention, rather, takes a variety of different forms, from simple administrative detention to detention for purposes of facilitating an investigation.

Many countries permit periods of detention without charge while an investigation is proceeding. Australia, for example, has an especially elaborate regime of detentions of varying lengths authorized for different purposes. Under the Crimes Act, the Australian Federal Police (AFP)—the equivalent of the U.S. Federal Bureau of Investigation—may detain and question a suspect for the purpose of investigating whether he or she committed a terrorism offense. Such a detention may last for only a "reasonable" period of up to four hours unless extended by a judicial officer to a total of twenty-four hours. Notably, the time limitations are for *questioning* time, so accounting for "dead time"—such as breaks for meals, sleep, or translation—can extend detention to days or even weeks, the twenty-four-hour limit notwithstanding. In practice, twelve days appears to be the outer limit.[42]

In addition, special antiterrorism legislation provides for two types of warrants (questioning warrants and detention warrants) and two forms of detention orders not requiring criminal charges (preventative detention orders and control orders). A *questioning warrant* permits the Australian Security Intelligence Organisation to bring a person for questioning before a former judge appointed by the attorney general. To secure such a warrant, the ASIO must obtain the attorney general's consent and then satisfy a federal magistrate or judge that there are reasonable grounds for believing that the warrant "will substantially assist the collection of intelligence that is important in relation to a terrorism offense." The subject of the warrant need not be suspected of prohibited activities, nor do criminal proceedings against the subject need to be anticipated. A questioning warrant can last up to twenty-eight days with periods of questioning of up to twenty-four hours, in eight-hour blocks—with the court permitted to extend questioning under certain circumstances.[43] A *detention warrant* permits ASIO to take a person into custody for questioning for up to seven days. The procedure for obtaining this warrant is similar to that for obtaining a questioning warrant, although there must also be a showing of exigent circumstances.[44]

A *preventative detention order,* known in Australia as a PDO, allows the physical restraint of a person. PDOs are sought by the Australian Federal Police instead of the ASIO. Temporary PDOs lasting up to twenty-four hours may be issued with the assent of a high-ranking member of the AFP. Further detention, up to an additional twenty-four hours, requires the assent of a serving or retired federal judge who has agreed to act in this capacity. PDOs can be issued for two basic purposes—to prevent realization of an imminent threat and to preserve evidence of a recent terrorist act.[45]

Persons subjected to questioning and detention warrants are entitled to their choice of lawyer, though that right may be suspended if it is shown that access may tip off others involved in the suspected activities or lead to the destruction of evidence. Once a lawyer is present, the detainee may communicate with the lawyer, but their communications may be monitored. In the case of a questioning warrant, the lawyer may not interrupt the questioning except to seek clarification of an ambiguous question. The person questioned may not refuse to answer and may not give misleading information, on penalty of up to five years imprisonment. "Derivative use" immunity applies, however, meaning that neither the detainee's statement nor any information derived from it can be used against the detainee. For preventative detention orders, no questioning is permitted unless the ASIO seeks and obtains a questioning warrant for that purpose.[46]

For longer-term incapacitation of terrorists, Australian law authorizes the use of *control orders,* which impose various restrictions on the subject's movements and activities. To obtain a control order, the AFP must show that detention would "substantially assist in preventing a terrorist act" or that the detainee "has provided training to, or received training from, a listed terrorist organization." Law enforcement must justify the restrictions proposed, which can range from restricting movement, to prohibiting contact with specified people, to banning access to certain communications media, to wearing a tracking device. An AFP application for a control order requires the written assent of the attorney general before being made to a federal court. An interim control order may then be sought ex parte from a serving federal judge. A confirmation hearing before the court must then occur as soon as reasonably practicable, but not less than seventy-two hours after the issuing of the interim order, and the detainee has the right to present evidence.[47] Control orders last a maximum of one year, although the law theoretically permits successive control orders on the same person.

The United Kingdom employs control orders in a similar manner, distinguishing between control orders that derogate from the European Court of Human Rights and those that do not.[48] For those that require derogation from the ECHR, the secretary of state must file an application to the High Court, which then holds a preliminary hearing, which may occur ex parte without notifying the named individual. The secretary of state is required to prepare a report every three months concerning his or her use of control orders and to appoint an individual to review the operation of the act.[49] Control orders that do not derogate from the ECHR last a maximum of twelve months, while those that do are restricted to a maximum of six months—although as in Australia, in Britain control orders can theoretically be renewed as many times as need be. The secretary of state and the court can impose at their discretion any restriction on an individual that they consider "necessary for purposes connected with preventing or restricting involvement by that individual in terrorism-related activity."[50] As of February 4, 2009, thirty-eight people had been made the subject of nonderogating control orders; of those, a total of seven have absconded, including one man who allegedly was approached to become a suicide bomber on the London Underground and has been linked to a number of the men who plotted to bomb the Ministry of Sound nightclub in London.[51]

Other countries have built into their criminal justice apparatus the ability to detain suspects for long periods in the absence of a criminal conviction. In France, for example, the detention system is built around the extraordinary power of the investigative magistrates, which is characteristic of France's civil law heritage.[52] For terrorism-related offenses, the police may detain suspects up to six days—as opposed to a maximum of two days for other offenses—although extensions beyond two days must be approved by a magistrate. The purpose of police detention is to gather information confirming the initial information or intelligence and decide whether an investigation is warranted. After the police detention period has ended, the suspect is released with no further action or charged before the investigating magistrate. If charges are brought, the magistrate directs the ensuing investigation, with some judicial supervision. French law provides that for the most serious terrorism cases, pretrial detention of the suspect may last for up to four years. In France, an individual has no right to see a lawyer for the initial seventy-two hours of detention if charged with a terrorism offense. The detainee's dwelling may be searched and seized at any time without the authorization of the owner.[53]

During the post-charge period, the magistrate can question a suspect with the suspect's lawyer present. Thus, in practice, the six-day limit is far from a ceiling on detention.[54] An example is the detention of Christian Ganczarski, a German national and alleged al Qaeda operative whom the French suspected of organizing a bombing in Tunisia. After he was apprehended by Saudi officials and sent to Paris, he was detained for questioning during an investigation that lasted at least seventeen months.[55]

India likewise allows lengthy periods of investigative detention, even in the absence of charges. Such detention can last for up to 120 days, encompassing thirty days of police custody followed by ninety days of judicial custody. A total of 180 days of detention is permitted upon notice to the court of the need for additional time to complete an investigation. Thus, police have up to 180 days before filing charges, although after the initial thirty days there is some measure of judicial supervision.[56] Although preventative detention was nominally prohibited under the POTA in response to criticism of the practice under TADA, the liberal standards for investigative detention outlined above, which allow for extended periods of detention, have important collateral preventative uses.

The German and South African systems operate most like the U.S. criminal justice system. Anybody arrested in Germany must be brought before a judge by the "termination of the day following the arrest." This forty-eight-hour period of provisional police custody is the closest German counterpart to precharge detention in the U.S. justice system. On presentation of the suspect, the judge may issue an arrest warrant—analogous to a "charge"—and remand the suspect into custody while the criminal investigation and prosecution are still under way.[57] A judge may order such a "detention in remand" if there are strong grounds to suspect that the suspect committed the crime, if there is a risk of flight, or if there is danger of interference with witnesses or evidence and the length of detention is proportionate to the possible sentence. The detention must be reviewed by a judge at the request of the person detained or at intervals that do not exceed six months each; at each stage, the prosecuting authorities need to satisfy the judge that the evidence still warrants the suspect's detention.[58] Provisions of the German Criminal Procedure Code prohibit courts from considering ex parte presentations of evidence in determining whether to continue detention.[59] German law also allows the detention of individuals if there is an imminent risk that a crime will be committed, even if no formal criminal investigation is pending. The length of such detention for public safety reasons is controlled by the individual *länder,* for a maximum of two weeks.[60]

There is no provision for preventative detention in South Africa. Section 12 of the Bill of Rights guarantees the right not to be detained without trial, and section 35 states several express guarantees for those who are arrested or detained, including the right to challenge the lawfulness of the detention in person in court.[61] Under section 35, arrested individuals must be charged or released within forty-eight hours.[62] An extremely controversial—and likely unconstitutional—provision of the antiterrorism bill that would have allowed for detention without trial of both suspects and witnesses for purposes of interrogation was dropped prior to enactment. Much of the controversy that surrounded that provision and led to its deletion stemmed from the relatively fresh memories of apartheid-era illegal detention and other abuses.

Unsurprisingly, given the high and constant threat of terrorism that it faces, the country with the broadest detention authority is Israel. And while Israeli law authorizes the detention of foreign terrorists as unlawful enemy combatants, that is not the principal source of the country's detention authority. Rather, the 1979 Administrative Detention Law allows administrative detention under a state of emergency—a status Israel invoked in 1949 and has lived under continuously ever since.[63] Administrative detention is predicated on intelligence—which would not be admissible in criminal proceedings and could not be declassified without jeopardizing intelligence gathering activities—suggesting that the individual in question would be involved in a future terrorist attack.

The procedure for detention differs depending on whether the detainee is an Israeli—Jewish or Arab—or a Palestinian resident of the Occupied Territories.[64] Administrative detention of Israelis must be authorized by the minister of defense, and a detainee must be brought before a civilian court within forty-eight hours of detention or released. The civilian courts provide oversight, first by confirming, annulling, or shortening the initial detention order and then by reviewing the status of each detainee at least every three months, overlapping with review every six months by the minister of defense.

For Palestinian residents of occupied areas, oversight is conducted not by civilian courts but by two different levels of military courts, subject to the same requirement for an initial hearing within forty-eight hours, followed by review every six months.[65] Although detention thus can be enforced without regard to the detainee's nationality or residence, in practice it is very rarely used against Israelis but frequently used against Palestinians living in the West Bank. In the latter case, detentions under these procedures have extended up to several years. Under Israeli law, detainees have the right to an attorney and the right to be present at their detention review hearing and at all subsequent judicial proceedings—although in the Occupied Territories that right may be postponed by decision of the General Security Services.

In short, almost all countries examined had both broader domestic detention authorities than those in the United States and narrower military detention authorities—or no military detention authorities at all. While the powers available vary considerably, judicial review of detentions and significant procedural protections for detainees are a common thread.

The Limits of Appropriate Interrogation

A principal purpose in detaining a terrorism suspect is to extract information that can be used to thwart pending plots. In the post–September 11 era, certain interrogation techniques have come under fire for violating the rights of detainees and producing unreliable intelligence, either because they constitute "torture" or because they constitute cruel, degrading, and inhuman treatment short of torture. The world's democracies have shown a remarkable convergence concerning appropriate legal restraints on interrogation, in contrast to their views regarding detention.

Like the other countries under study here, the United States is a party to the Convention against Torture and Other Cruel, Inhuman, or Degrading Treatment or Punishment (CAT), which defines torture as "any act by which severe pain or suffering, whether physical or mental, is intentionally inflicted on a person for such purposes as obtaining from him or a third person information or a confession, punishing him for an act he or a third person has committed or is suspected of having committed, or intimidating or coercing him or a third person, or for any reason based on discrimination of any kind, when such pain or suffering is inflicted by or at the instigation of or with the consent or acquiescence of a public official or other person acting in an official capacity."

Beginning in 2002, the Bush administration took the position that the various Geneva Conventions did not apply to terrorism suspects held at Guantánamo Bay or in U.S. military custody elsewhere, although it held that the precepts of the conventions should generally be respected as a matter of policy. When the Supreme Court repudiated that position in 2006 in the *Hamdan* case, the administration agreed to comply with the ruling and began applying Common Article 3 of the conventions, which prohibits "outrages upon personal dignity, in particular humiliating and degrading treatment." Nonetheless, the administration repeatedly asserted that extreme interrogation techniques such as waterboarding did not constitute "torture" or violate other restrictions in all circumstances. The Obama administration, in one of its first actions, repudiated that position.

In the Detainee Treatment Act of 2005, Congress enacted a restriction proposed by Senator John McCain that requires military (as opposed to CIA) interrogators to follow the Army Field Manual, which prohibits harsh interrogation tactics. When Congress later proposed similar language designed to cover the CIA and other intelligence interrogators, Bush objected, arguing that the CIA needed greater latitude, and his veto was sustained. (For a more detailed discussion of U.S. interrogation policy and law, see chapter 9.)

None of the countries under study here has taken anything like the Bush administration's position. Rather, there exists a strong and ever-strengthening consensus against coercive interrogation. While some diversity in practice remains, there is significantly less diversity than in the past. To begin, Israel and the United States are the only countries that have not signed the Optional Protocol to the CAT, which allows outside parties to ensure compliance with the CAT. Australia, which had held out for a long time, announced plans to join the Optional Protocol in 2008. The United Kingdom was one of the first states to ratify the Optional Protocol, in December 2003. The protocol, which entered into force on June 22, 2006, creates an international system to monitor places of detention worldwide and a parallel domestic monitoring system in each country that ratifies it. The British government has been active in lobbying other governments to ratify the protocol.

In recent years even Israel has moved decisively away from the position that the Bush administration embraced. Back in the late 1980s, a state commission investigated the death of a Palestinian terrorist in Israeli custody and included in its final report a specific listing of the types and extent of moderate physical interrogation techniques that the security services were permitted to use.[66] Yet the use of "moderate physical pressure" in interrogations when "necessary" to prevent a terrorist act has not survived. A subsequent decision by the High Court of Justice in 1999 famously barred all forms of physical interrogation beyond the most basic forms of restraint.[67] Considering that methods such as shaking a person, forcing a person to maintain a stress position, and depriving a person of sensory stimulation were excluded, it would certainly appear that techniques as extreme as waterboarding would not be allowed under that ruling—although no specific discussion of waterboarding (a tactic Israeli authorities have not used) appears in the decision. Some discussion continues in the popular press of the use of torture by Israeli forces, particularly by the Israel Defense Forces and its associated border police, who have the authority to question suspects in the field (although not in custody) suspected of illegal entry at the Israeli border. But highly coercive interrogation tactics are no longer a matter of policy. Although several parliamentarians wanted the General Security Service Law, enacted by the Knesset in 2002, to contain an explicit authorization for the use of "moderate physical pressure," the law did not contain any such measure.[68]

Other countries likewise eschew any formal authorization for aggressive interrogation—although they often leave open important questions concerning what tactics are off limits. Section 12 of South Africa's bill of rights, for example, expressly provides, among other things, that everyone has the right "to be free from all forms of violence from either public or private sources," the right "not to be tortured in any way," and the right "not to be treated or punished in a cruel, inhuman, or degrading way."[69] What's more, developing South African case law suggests that its courts will bar evidence obtained by coercion from criminal proceedings. In April 2008, the Supreme Court of Appeal—second only to the Constitutional Court—held that evidence obtained from an accomplice through the use of torture was inadmissible, even when the evidence was reliable and necessary to secure the conviction of a person facing serious charges.[70] In reaching its conclusion, the court relied in part on section 35(5) of the bill of rights, which provides that evidence obtained in violation of any right guaranteed by the bill of rights "must be excluded if the admission of that evidence would render the trial unfair or otherwise be detrimental to the administration of justice."[71]

Yet while South Africa has clearly embraced a policy against torture, including through the establishment of its Policy on the Prevention of Torture and Treatment of Persons in Custody of the South African Police Service, there is neither a definition of torture nor a specific offense addressing torture in the criminal code. South Africa has reported to the UN Committee on Torture that a bill to explicitly prohibit torture has been prepared and is being considered by parliament.

Moreover, the experience of France suggests that prohibiting torture may ultimately afford somewhat less protection than it initially appears to. Torture is banned by French law and the French constitution. However, France has a checkered history on this score, stemming from the conduct of its military in the Algerian war. Over the last decade, the European Court of Human rights has found that individuals in French custody have been subjected to mistreatment, including torture.[72] And French interrogation law generally permits a great deal of nonviolent behavior that U.S. law would not tolerate. For example, during precharge custody (*garde à vue*), police may interrogate detainees at will, without their lawyers present and at any time of the day or night, a practice that, according to Human Rights Watch, can lead to "oppressive questioning."[73] Human Rights Watch gives the example of a terrorism suspect questioned for a total of forty-three hours during his four days of *garde à vue*. In addition, detainees in France do not need to be notified of their right to remain silent, and all statements made under interrogation are admissible in court. Recently, a reform to commence audio and video recording of all police interrogations explicitly excluded terrorism cases.[74]

Indeed, even countries that have stringent rules sometimes have trouble enforcing them. Germany's Basic Law provides that "persons in custody must not be subjected to mental or physical mistreatment." The issue of torture is taken very seriously in Germany because of the country's history and because Germany's most fundamental constitutional right is the right to human dignity. Law enforcement officials who violate the ban on torture face a potential ten-year prison sentence.[75] Yet over the last several years, there have been a number of allegations that the German military, border police, and law enforcement officials have engaged in unauthorized use of force or threats of force against individuals in their custody. For example, a report published by the Council of Europe charged members of the German border police with using unnecessary force when deporting foreigners, and it also alleged that German military officers tortured recruits during basic training while pretending to be Arab terrorists.[76]

What's more, Germany has seen some debate over how illicitly obtained information should be handled. The president of the Federal Office for the Protection of the Constitution has publicly declared that information obtained through coercive techniques should be usable in the campaign against terror.[77] However, there is no concrete proof that such information has been used.

This diversity of views, however, occurs within the context of societies that have resolutely set themselves against the use of physical pressure in interrogation. The broad point is that the diversity of approaches that exists among democratic nations with respect to detention is nowhere apparent with respect to interrogation—which is perhaps why the outrage at U.S. interrogation policy under the Bush administration was so uniform. The United States is clearly moving back toward the consensus position. Congress pushed during the Bush administration to restrain aggressive interrogation, and almost immediately upon taking office, the Obama administration shifted gears considerably. The new president rescinded the lenient legal guidance of his predecessor concerning the application of the torture statute, the McCain amendment, and Common Article 3 to interrogations. And he has applied the Army Field Manual to CIA interrogations—effectuating precisely the policy shift by executive order that Bush vetoed when Congress sought to place it in statute.

What Rules Govern Domestic Electronic Surveillance?

Since the enactment in 1978 of the Foreign Intelligence Surveillance Act, domestic surveillance of U.S. citizens and resident aliens—referred to collectively as "U.S. persons"—has been subject to a process whereby a special court issues a judicial warrant authorizing surveillance. Although the governing law contains limitations,[78] it was considered to be the exclusive source of surveillance powers in the ordinary course of intelligence gathering until the Bush administration challenged that premise claiming that the president has inherent surveillance powers as commander-in-chief under Article II of the Constitution. Previous presidents—including Jimmy Carter—had gestured to the commander-in-chief power as a means to circumvent FISA in extraordinary circumstances, but no president before President Bush had actually sought to exercise that authority.

In 2005 the *New York Times* revealed that immediately after September 11, President Bush authorized warrantless electronic surveillance of persons inside the United States in cases in which another party to the communication was outside the United States and there was reason to believe that one party to the communication was associated with al Qaeda. That executive action, which led to revisions to FISA designed to relax the legal requirements governing such surveillance, has been the subject of intense controversy. The debate over FISA has raised questions in the United States about the power of government to conduct surveillance of its own citizens and the appropriate level of judicial involvement in that process. (For a more detailed discussion of U.S. domestic surveillance, see chapter 7.) But in other nations, the striking feature of surveillance law—in stark contrast to interrogation rules—is how permissive it is compared with U.S. law. Indeed, while other countries have developed different oversight mechanisms, they generally do not require advance judicial authorization for intelligence-gathering wiretaps. The political fight over the Bush administration's warrantless surveillance program would likely not have taken place in many countries abroad, where the laws often do not restrict intelligence gathering activities to the same degree that U.S. law did in 2001.

While a number of other countries use judicial warrants for surveillance, the warrant requirements of only one, South Africa, even remotely approach the stringent requirements of FISA. South Africa has perhaps the strictest warrant requirement of any of the countries under study here. Section 14 of the country's bill of rights guarantees everyone the right to privacy, including the right not to have "the privacy of their communications infringed."[79] Domestic surveillance is governed by a comprehensive statutory framework enacted pursuant to the Regulation of Interception of Communications and Provision of Communication-Related Information Act of 2002.[80] As with South Africa's antiterrorism bill, the surveillance bill had been in development prior to the attacks of September 11 and was shaped largely by the country's past abuses under the apartheid-era regime.

The act prohibits all interception of communications other than those authorized pursuant to its expressed terms.[81] Wiretaps and other electronic surveillance are allowed only upon judicial issuance of an "interception direction," which can be issued only after consideration of a proper application, which must be made in writing. The order cannot provide authorization for a period exceeding three months at a time.[82] An interception direction generally may be issued only when there are reasonable grounds to believe that a serious offense, defined to include terrorism, is being committed or probably will be committed and surveillance is necessary to gather information concerning an actual or potential threat to national security or public health and safety; surveillance also is authorized to assist foreign governments with respect to communications that relate to organized crime or terrorism offenses.[83] The act also requires that the interception be capable of producing the necessary information and that other investigative procedures have been tried and have failed to do so.[84] It also permits lawfully intercepted communications to be used as evidence in criminal trials.[85] And as noted above, South Africa's constitution requires that evidence obtained in violation of an individual's constitutional rights be excluded if admission would render his or her trial unfair—a standard that seems to be interpreted much as the exclusionary rule is in the United States.[86] An important consideration is that South Africa's National Intelligence Agency (NIA), the entity that gathers and provides the government with intelligence regarding domestic threats and that is charged with responsibility for domestic counterintelligence, is subject to the act's comprehensive judicial approval controls.[87]

The only other country in this study that requires prior judicial involvement in intelligence wiretapping is Spain, although Spanish law permits that requirement to be circumvented in terrorism cases and in exigent circumstances.[88] And while Spanish law requires a judicial warrant for searches of domiciles, postal or electronic communications may be monitored for three days based only on a rational belief that terrorist activities are occurring. After that, an application must be made to a judicial officer or the surveillance must cease.

Much more common is a warrant requirement for criminal cases, with greater latitude in intelligence matters. Australia, for example, has a judicial warrant requirement for its equivalent of FISA electronic surveillance, but those warrants are issued by retired judges appointed by the attorney general. While the Australian Security Intelligence Organization makes a request with the assent of the attorney general, the attorney general is essentially a political appointee of the prime minister.[89] Under a 1979 law, ASIO's director general can issue a request to the attorney general to collect intelligence by entering and searching premises; inspecting, removing, and retaining records; frisk-searching a person; and accessing a computer or other electronic equipment and copying data from it. If the attorney general is satisfied that a person is, or is reasonably suspected of being, engaged in activities that would prejudice national security and that surveillance will aid the procurement of security-related intelligence, the attorney general can also issue a warrant allowing ASIO to monitor the person's communications, use a tracking device on the person, or inspect the person's mail. Communications warrants are issued for a limited time, up to six months.[90] The Australian parliament amended the 1979 law in 2006 to expand ASIO's powers. It now permits the agency to request a warrant from the attorney general to intercept the telecommunications of people not suspected of any wrongdoing when doing so might "assist [ASIO] in carrying out its function of obtaining intelligence relating to security."[91]

French law, similarly, makes electronic intelligence gathering a nonjudicial affair. The law provides for two different types of intercepts: intercepts pursuant to a judicial warrant and security intercepts. Investigative magistrates may authorize judicial warrant intercepts, which may be used as evidence in criminal proceedings.[92] By contrast, the government can use security intercepts only for intelligence purposes and must wall off from law enforcement and the courts the intelligence that it collects under them. These intercepts, however, are authorized in writing by the prime minister in accordance with proposals submitted by three other ministers. The motives must be precise, the information must be destroyed as soon as it is no longer useful, and the decision to proceed with the intercept is applicable for a period limited to four months, with one renewal possible.

In an interesting twist on U.S. judicial supervision of intelligence wiretaps, oversight of security intercepts in France takes place not in the courts but in the legislature, which has charged a special commission with supervising and determining the legality of each intercept. The commission has the power to investigate how the government conducted the intercept, and it can recommend that the intercept be halted. The commission publishes an annual report on its activities.[93] Although not directly involved in the security intercept process, magistrates also become involved as security investigations morph into judicial investigations. If intelligence agents think that they have information that warrants a judicial investigation, they have the option of approaching an investigative magistrate directly, who can then authorize the opening of the investigation. The investigative magistrates and the intelligence agencies work together closely in such circumstances.

German law also designates the legislature, not the judiciary, as the key body for oversight of intelligence surveillance, but in a different manner. German law normally permits electronic surveillance only if it is based on a judicial warrant.[94] However, the Basic Law tolerates exceptions for certain circumstances involving foreign intelligence and security, and Germany's criminal procedure law does not regulate "preventive" police operations and the operations of the intelligence agencies.[95] Accordingly, Germany's Foreign Intelligence Service may engage in certain types of foreign intelligence surveillance without obtaining a judicial warrant so long as it obtains a warrant from a commission selected by a special parliamentary committee. The commission reviews the legality of each individual domestic communications intercept and has the authority to suspend an individual intercept if it appears that the evidence sustaining it is weak or if it infringes any law. Citizens who fear that they may have had their communications intercepted illegally have the right to apply directly to the commission to investigate.[96] Interestingly, under German law, surveillance of a subject's domicile is subject to entirely different treatment than surveillance elsewhere. In particular, the Federal Constitutional Court has prohibited the planting of bugs in the home—a practice that FISA does permit.[97]

In India, interception of wire, electronic, or oral communications was permitted under POTA upon application to relevant authorities. The application required a description of the terrorist act that had been or was about to be committed, with supporting facts and a description of the types of communication to be intercepted. Such monitoring was limited to a maximum period of sixty days.[98] Under POTA a police officer of at least superintendent rank applied in writing to the court for an order to intercept if he believed that interception would provide, or had provided, evidence of any offense involving a terrorist act. In deciding whether to issue the order, the court considered whether there was probable cause to support the belief that a terrorist offense had been or might be committed, that communication concerning an offense might be intercepted, and that the facilities from which the communication was to be intercepted were involved or used in connection with commission of an offense. The maximum duration of such an order was sixty days.

The two pieces of legislation enacted following the Mumbai attack do not cover surveillance procedures, but even in the absence of POTA, Indian authorities retain broad wiretapping powers. The preexisting law governing wiretaps permits the government to intercept information from computers to investigate any offense, if the central government certifies that interception is in the interests of "the sovereignty or integrity of India, defence of India, security of the State, friendly relations with foreign States or public order or for preventing incitement to the commission of any cognizable offence relating to above or for investigation of any offence." The only procedural requirement is that the central government must give the reasons for the interception in writing. On doing so, the government may direct "any agency of the Government to intercept or monitor or decrypt or cause to be intercepted or monitored or decrypted any information transmitted through any computer resource."[99] In addition, the Indian Telegraph Act 1885 permits the central or a state government to "direct that any message or class of messages to or from any person or class of persons, or relating to any particular subject, brought for transmission by or transmitted or received by any telegraph, . . . shall be intercepted or . . . disclosed to the Government." Such interceptions can take place on "the occurrence of any public emergency, or in the interest of the public safety" as long as the government is satisfied that "it is necessary or expedient so to do in the interests of the sovereignty and integrity of India, the security of the State, friendly relations with foreign States or public order or for preventing incitement to the commission of an offence."[100]

Israeli law permits extensive electronic surveillance. While wiretaps on phone calls originating in Israel require a court order and are subject to regular judicial review, no such court order is required for calls originating in Gaza and the West Bank.

The Secret Monitoring Law of 1979, as later amended, governs the interception of communications.[101] Under its terms, the supervising and authorizing bodies for surveillance differ depending on the purpose of the surveillance. For criminal cases, the police must receive permission from the president of the district court to intercept any form of wire or electronic communication or to plant a microphone, for a renewable three-month period. Although courts weigh privacy concerns against law enforcement needs before authorizing wiretaps, authorization is, in practice, generally given on request. The police inspector general must file a monthly report to the attorney general regarding the eavesdropping permits issued under the law and the terms of the permits. The number of permits in the late 1990s averaged between 1,000 and 1,100 annually, roughly half of which concerned drug-related offenses. The inspector general also must file an annual report to the Constitution, Law, and Justice Committee of the Knesset regarding the number of requests and permits issued during the reporting period, as well as the number of persons, telephone lines, and telecommunications devices covered by the permits. In addition, the inspector general may authorize a wiretap for up to forty-eight hours if it is deemed urgently necessary to prevent a crime or to apprehend perpetrators and if a permit cannot be issued quickly enough. In such cases the attorney general, who can cancel the permit at his or her discretion, must be notified immediately.

By contrast, intelligence agencies may wiretap people suspected of endangering national security without receiving advance judicial permission. Such wiretaps can proceed on written approval from the prime minister or the defense minister. As with the police wiretap permits, the permits are valid for up to three months, after which they are reviewed by a court, which may renew them. The law also permits emergency forty-eight-hour wiretaps with only the authorization of the head of the security agency involved.

The chief military censor may also intercept international conversations to or from Israel in order to censor them as well as to eavesdrop on police or military communications. In all cases, irrespective of the authorizing body or agency conducting the surveillance, there are procedures for periodic review by the authorizing body to ensure that the need for surveillance is ongoing. In cases involving the intelligence agencies, the authorizing minister must review the request every six months, overlapping with the three-month judicial review.

The Knesset amended the law in 1995 following a finding that the police were abusing wiretap procedures.[102] The 1995 amendments also were aimed at controlling the burgeoning phenomenon of unauthorized surveillance by private investigators. Although the amendments sought to tighten the rules, they also expanded the Secret Monitoring Law to cover new technologies, such as mobile phones, faxes, satellite transmissions, and e-mail. In addition, the amendments increased penalties for illegal taps while allowing interception of privileged communications, such as those between a person and his or her lawyer, psychologist, doctor, or clergy member. Under the law, the president of a district court (a chief judge in U.S. parlance) may permit a recording or other surveillance of such conversations if the judge is convinced that there is a reasonable suspicion that the professional is personally involved in murder, manslaughter, a drug transaction, or a felony involving harm to state security and that the wiretap is essential for preventing or investigating the offense.

The United Kingdom has likewise explicitly rejected the judicial warrant requirement in electronic surveillance of terrorists—and even crime more generally.[103] The Regulation of Investigatory Powers Act 2000 (RIPA) outlines who must authorize warrants for various types of surveillance. In addition to RIPA, interception of communications, electronic data, and forms of surveillance are covered by the Police Act 1997 and the Intelligence Services Act 1994.[104] An administrative warrant is required for the lawful interception of communications in most circumstances in Britain, although exceptions do exist.[105] Warrants to intercept communications must be personally issued by the secretary of state upon receipt of an application by designated persons.[106] Except for warrants issued in response to requests under a mutual assistance agreement or in urgent cases, a warrant must be personally signed by the secretary of state. In emergency cases, a senior official designated by RIPA can sign a warrant, although the secretary of state still must personally authorize the warrant. A warrant for electronic surveillance can apply to either one person or one premises for three months. For warrants issued on the grounds of prevention and detection of serious crimes, the period can be extended for an additional three months; warrants issued on the grounds of national security of the United Kingdom can be renewed for an additional six months.[107]

An important subsidiary issue concerning electronic surveillance is whether and under what circumstances information gathered in a national security investigation can be introduced in court in support of a criminal prosecution or offered to police personnel to assist in a criminal investigation. In the United States, information learned in the course of FISA surveillance traditionally was shielded under many circumstances from use in a criminal prosecution—although that "wall" broke down for the most part with the passage of the Patriot Act and in subsequent litigation. Several countries created similar barriers, but those barriers too have sometimes proven porous.

For example, in France, sensitive intelligence material that normally would not be admissible in court can be "judicialized" to render it admissible. The intelligence is produced in a summary form as a police statement, and the magistrate includes the report in the dossier of evidence during an investigation. It can then be introduced at trial, although it is not possible to secure a conviction based on such a report alone. Because even the magistrate may not probe into how the intelligence was obtained, this procedure demonstrates the high level of trust between magistrates and the intelligence agencies.[108]

In the United Kingdom, none of the information obtained through interception of communications may be used as evidence in a court of law, even if every legal requirement has been met. There are a few exceptions, however. Section 18(4) of RIPA permits the use of intercepted communication as evidence if one party consents to the intercept.[109] And the courts have interpreted the prohibition on using intercept evidence narrowly, holding that it applies only to communications intercepted in the United Kingdom itself, thereby permitting the admission of intercepted communications legally obtained abroad.[110]

Despite the wide variety of approaches to surveillance surveyed above, they have one factor in common: no executive has the authority to bypass the relevant statutory scheme, as President Bush claimed to have in the United States. As noted above, that reflects both the fact that the requirements for obtaining warrants in most of these countries are less demanding than those of FISA and the fact that the U.S. executive branch is an unusually powerful actor. That said, the consistency of agreement on this point across democracies cautions against further unilateral presidential efforts to deal with inadequacies in U.S. surveillance statutes by questioning their applicability. At the same time, the diversity of approaches in other democracies cautions against too rigid an insistence on the precise lines that FISA draws. I see no reason why the executive branch and Congress should not agree on a comprehensive statutory scheme that would bind future presidents in every respect. The recent relaxation in FISA requirements covering conversations with individuals outside the United States shows that legitimate compromise is possible. Even with the relaxation, U.S. law is still stringent compared with, for example, the law in Britain or Israel, where authorities have unusually strong powers but derive them through legislative grants, not from claims of inherent authority.

The preceding survey also suggests the possibility of another approach to oversight of surveillance that the United States has not to date adopted. Both France and Germany have powerful parliamentary committees with very specific responsibilities for overseeing individual surveillance decisions. The commissions receive detailed briefings on specific targets and are responsible for hearing and resolving complaints from individuals who allege illegal surveillance. Congress has considerable expertise in conducting oversight, though typically at a more general level. It is worth exploring whether and under what circumstances legislative oversight mechanisms might complement judicial ones in protecting U.S. Fourth Amendment rights.

Conclusions

As this brief survey reveals, considerable differences exist between the policies of the United States and those of nations that are, in many other respects, quite similar. To a certain extent, the value of drawing comparisons lies in acknowledging that the U.S. situation is unique. Although imperfections exist, the United States enjoys robust civil liberties despite the threats that it faces. However, there remain lessons to be learned for policymakers with respect to each of the issues discussed above. Other chapters in this volume discuss in depth how U.S. law should treat surveillance, detention, and interrogation in the future. The broad lesson from the democracies surveyed here, however, is twofold.

First, the United States has a lot of latitude in policymaking with respect to both detention and surveillance, which it can take advantage of without straying far from the mean of democratic countries—particularly in the extent to which it weaves detention authority into the fabric of its criminal justice system. That is not to suggest that doing so is necessarily a wise or even constitutional course. It has far less latitude with respect to interrogation and detention under *military,* as opposed to civilian, authorities. In these areas, U.S. policy under the Bush administration genuinely exceeded what other countries have empowered their executives to do.

Second, perhaps the biggest U.S. deviation from the norm lies in the extraordinary manner in which the previous administration made U.S. counterterrorism rules, giving rise to the possibility of virtually unlimited executive authority with respect to detention, surveillance, and even torture. No other country, however permissive the authority that it grants its security services, comes even close. Bringing the United States into line with other democracies, in other words, will involve a strange combination of tightening rules, relaxing rules, and insisting on the conventional order in which rules get made.

Reform on those fronts will help to restore the moral credibility of the United States with regard to human rights. U.S. alliances with each of the eight nations surveyed here will prove essential as the country continues to combat jihadist terrorism. To be sure, there will be many situations in which U.S. rules protect civil liberties more robustly than do those in other democracies, as well as some situations in which the unique U.S. counterterrorism effort—which operates throughout the world as a kind of hybrid encompassing military action, covert operations, and criminal justice procedures—requires powers that many countries do not need or claim for themselves. That's okay. Democracies can take different approaches without being less democratic.

Notes

1. These treaties contain Optional Protocols as well. All but the United States, India, and Israel are parties to the Additional Protocol to the Geneva Convention, which permits outside inspection by independent third parties. Only the United Kingdom has further signed the Optional Protocol to the Convention against Torture.

2. In 2004 the Australian government published an analysis of the terrorist threat to Australia. Within that analysis the government states that Osama bin Laden referred to Australia in six separate statements and specifically explored Australian targets in 2000. In addition, Jack Roche, a British immigrant to Australia who had converted to Islam and was associated with the terrorist group Jemaah Islamiyah, pled guilty in May 2004 to conspiracy to commit offenses by undertaking acts preparatory to a future bombing of the Israeli embassy in Canberra and the Israeli consulate in Sydney in June 2002. Commonwealth of Australia, Department of Foreign Affairs and Trade, *Transnational Terrorism: The Threat to Australia* (Canberra, 2004), pp. 66, 73 (www.dfat.gov. au/publications/terrorism/transnational_terrorism.pdf).

3. A "terrorist act" is defined to include an action or threat done with the intention of "advancing a political, religious or ideological cause" and "coercing, or influencing by intimidation" a government or "intimidating the public," although specific exemptions, such as for union organizing, are provided. Commission of a terrorist act is subject to stiff punishment, up to life imprisonment. See Andrew Lynch and George Williams, *What Price Security? Taking Stock of Australia's Anti-Terror Laws* (Sydney, Australia: UNSW Press, 2006), pp. 14–17.

4. For instance, a person may not "collect or make a document" that is "connected with preparation for, the engagement of a person in, or assistance in a terrorist act." In addition, new criminal provisions prohibit membership in or association with a terrorist organization and the funding of terrorist organizations or activities. Lynch and Williams, *What Price Security?* pp. 18, 24.

5. Ibid., pp. 29–40.

6. Yonah Alexander, *Counterterrorism Strategies: Successes and Failures of Six Nations* (Dulles, Va.: Potomac Books, 2006), pp. 45–49, 52. Over the last decade there

has, however, been some terrorist violence in Brittany and Corsica linked to independence movements in those regions.

7. Ibid., pp. 51–54.

8. Reuel Marc Gerecht and Gary Schmitt, American Enterprise Institute for Public Policy Research, "France: Europe's Counterterrorist Powerhouse," *European Outlook* 4, no. 3 (November 2007); Jeremy Shapiro and Benedicte Suzan, "The French Experience of Counterterrorism," *Survival* 45 (Spring 2003), pp. 1, 76–86, 88–93.

9. Alexander, *Counterterrorism Strategies,* p. 69.

10. Ibid., pp. 72, 82; Kim Scheppele, "Other People's Patriot Acts: Europe's Response to September 11," *Loyola Law Review* 50 (2004), p. 102.

11. Christoph J. M. Safferling, "Terror and Law: German Responses to 9/11," *Journal of International Criminal Justice* 4, no. 5 (2006), p. 2; Gerecht and Schmitt, "France: Europe's Counterterrorist Powerhouse," p. 1.

12. The material on these legislative enactments is derived from Oliver Lepsius, "Liberty, Security, and Terrorism: The Legal Position in Germany," *German Law Journal* 5 (2004), pp. 435, 439–40; Shawn Boyne, "The Future of Liberal Democracies in a Time of Terror," *Tulsa Journal of Comparative and International Law* 11 (2003), pp. 111, 118, 120–21, 155–56, 174; Shawn Boyne, "Preserving the Role of Law in a Time of Terror: Germany's Response to Terrorism," in *Law Versus War: Competing Approaches To Fighting Terrorism* (Carlisle, Pa.: U.S. Army War College Strategic Studies Institute, 2005), p. 18; Safferling, "Terror and Law," pp. 3–4; Scheppele, "Other People's Patriot Acts," p. 113; Christian Walter, *Submission to the Eminent Panel on Terrorism, Counter-Terrorism, and Human Rights, European Union Sub-Regional Hearing,* Eminent Jurists Panel on Terrorism, Counter-Terrorism, and Human Rights, July 2007, pp. 5–6, 9; Alexander, *Counterterrorism Strategies,* 86–88.

13. Alexander, *Counterterrorism Strategies,* pp. 72, 79.

14. Parliament of India, Prevention of Terrorism Act, 2002, no. 15.

15. Parliament of India, Terrorist and Disruptive Activities (Prevention) Act, 1987, no. 28.

16. The Unlawful Activities (Prevention) Amendment Bill of 2008 defines a terrorist act as follows: "Whoever does any act with intent to threaten or likely to threaten the unity, integrity, security or sovereignty of India or with intent to strike terror or likely to strike terror in the people or any section of the people in India or in any foreign country,—

(a) by using bombs, dynamite or other explosive substances or inflammable substances or firearms or other lethal weapons or poisons or noxious gases or other chemicals or by any other substances (whether biological, radioactive, nuclear or otherwise) of a hazardous nature or by any other means of whatever nature to cause or likely to cause—

(i) death of, or injuries to, any person or persons; or

(ii) loss of, or damage to, or destruction of, property; or

(iii) disruption of any supplies or services essential to the life of the community in India or in any foreign country; or

(iv) damage or destruction of any property in India or in a foreign country used or intended to be used for the defence of India or in connection with any other purposes of the Government of India, any State Government or any of their agencies; or

(b) overawes by means of criminal force or the show of criminal force or attempts to do so or causes death of any public functionary or attempts to cause death of any public functionary; or

(c) detains, kidnaps or abducts any person and threatens to kill or injure such person or does any other act in order to compel the Government of India, any State Government or the Government of a foreign country or any other person to do or abstain from doing any act, commits a terrorist act." *Infra,* § 4.

17. Parliament of India, The Unlawful Activities (Prevention) Amendment Act 2008, no. 76, § 43E(a)-(b).

18. Prevention of Terrorism Ordinance, 1948, 1 L.S.I. 76.

19. "Defence (Emergency) Regulations," *Palestine Gazette,* no. 1442 (published by the British Government, Palestine, 1945).

20 Prohibition on Terrorist Financing Law, 5765–2004.

21. See Amos N. Guiora, *Global Perspectives on Counterterrorism* (New York: Aspen Publishers, 2007), p. 44, n. 125.

22. See *El País,* "ETA Cargó la Bomba de Barajas con al Menos 200 Kilos de Explosivo" [ETA Loaded the Barajas Bomb with at least 200 Kilos of Explosive], December 30, 2006.

23. See *El Mundo,* "ETA Irrumpe en la Campaña Electoral y Asesina a un ex Concejal del PSE en Mondragón" [ETA Bursts into the Election Campaign and Assassinates an Ex-PSE Councilman in Mondragón], March 7, 2008.

24. See James Sturcke, "Madrid Bombings: The Defendants," *The Guardian,* October 31, 2007.

25. See Guiora, *Global Perspectives,* pp. 44–45.

26. See Amos N. Guiora, "Legislative and Policy Responses to Terrorism," *San Diego International Law Journal* 7 (2005), pp. 125, 164.

27. See Guiora, *Global Perspectives,* p. 35.

28. Ibid., p. 133.

29. Protection of Constitutional Democracy against Terrorist and Related Activities Act, 2004, no. 33.

30. Ibid., ch. 2, pt. I–II, §§ 2–10.

31. Ibid., ch. 1, §§ 1(3)-(4).

32. Antiterrorism, Crime, and Security Act, 2001, c. 24.

33. Ibid., § 23(1).

34. Two sections of the Immigration Act apply to the ATCSA. The first is schedule 2(16), which concerns persons who are "required to submit to examination" (to determine whether they are U.K. citizens or permitted to enter the United Kingdom without leave); they can be detained for the duration of the examination and pending the

decision. The second is schedule 3(2), which concerns persons who are subject to recommendation of deportation by a court; they are permitted to be detained pending the making of a deportation order.

35. Prevention of Terrorism Act 2005, c. 2, §§ 1–9.

36. Terrorism Act 2006, c. 11.

37. Ibid., §§ 1–4, 23–25.

38. Ibid., § 2.

39. See 18 U.S.C. § 3144.

40. See "Witness to Abuse: Human Rights Abuses under the Material Witness Law since September 11," *Human Rights Watch* 17, no. 2 (G) (June 2005), pp. 2, 3, 16, 33 (www.aclu.org/FilesPDFs/materialwitnessreport.pdf).

41. *Anonymous v. State of Israel,* Cr. App. 6659/06 (S. Ct. Israel, June 11, 2008). See also Kevin Jon Heller, "Israeli Supreme Court Upholds Unlawful Combatants Law," *Opinio Juris,* posted June 12, 2008 (http://opiniojuris.org/2008/06/12/israeli-supreme-court-upholds-unlawful-combatants-law/).

42. See Lynch and Williams, *What Price Security?* p. 40. The statute does not prescribe a maximum time limit for detention during questioning; since the statute's enactment there has only been one instance of a magistrate extending "dead time," and that was for twelve days. After that authorization the courts reconsidered their interpretation of a "reasonable time" of detention and determined that thereafter they would interpret detention as being subject to a "limited time" instead of a "reasonable time." There also were calls to impose a forty-eight-hour limit on such detentions. While that has not been done, the level of unease of the courts with detaining someone for twelve days indicates that that length of time is likely to remain the limit.

43. See Lynch and Williams, *What Price Security?* pp. 35–39.

44. Ibid.

45. See ibid., pp. 47–54.

46. Lynch and Williams, *What Price Security?* pp. 38, 52–53.

47. See ibid., pp. 42–46.

48. Prevention of Terrorism Act 2005, § 1(2).

49. Ibid., §§ 1(2)(b), 14(1), 14(2).

50. Ibid., § 1(3).

51. See Natalie Hanman, "Explainer: Control Orders," *The Guardian,* February 4, 2009.

52. Alexander, *Counterterrorism Strategies,* p. 70; Shapiro and Suzan, "The French Experience," p. 84.

53. Home Office, *Terrorist Investigations and the French Examining Magistrates System* (London, 2007) pp. 3–7; Alexander, *Counterterrorism Strategies,* p. 57.

54. Alexander, *Counterterrorism Strategies,* p. 57; Home Office, *Terrorist Investigations,* pp. 3–7.

55. Craig Whitlock, "French Push Limits in Fight on Terrorism: Wide Prosecutorial Powers Draw Scant Public Dissent," *Washington Post,* November 2, 2004, p. A01.

56. See Parliament of India, Unlawful Activities (Prevention) Amendment Act, above.

57. Jago Russel, *Terrorism Pre-Charge Detention: Comparative Law Study* (National Council for Civil Liberties, November 2007), hereafter cited as *Liberty Study* (www.liberty-human-rights.org.uk/issues/pdfs/pre-charge-detention-comparative-law-study.pdf).

58. Bundestag, *Strafprozessordnung* (StPO) [Code of Criminal Procedure], art. 112–130.

59. See Shawn Boyne, "Law, Terrorism, and Social Movements: The Tension between Politics and Security in Germany's Anti-Terrorism Legislation," *Cardozo Journal of International and Comparative Law* 12 (2004), pp. 41, 79; Boyne, "The Future of Liberal Democracies," p. 161.

60. *Liberty Study,* 43.

61. Republic of South Africa Constitution, ch. 2, §§ 12(1)(b), 35(1)-(2).

62. Ibid., §§ 35(1)(d)-(e).

63. Thomas F. Powers, "When to Hold 'Em," *Legal Affairs* (September-October 2004).

64. Guiora, *Global Perspectives,* pp. 332, n. 55.

65. Ibid., pp. 332–36.

66. Ibid., p. 291, n. 30.

67. See *Public Committee against Torture in Israel* v. *Israel,* HCJ 5100/94 (S. Ct. Israel, December 11, 2005).

68. Guiora, *Global Perspectives,* pp. 288–91.

69. Republic of South Africa Constitution, ch. 2, §§ 12(1)(c)-(e).

70. *Mthembu* v. *The State,* SCA 379/2007 (South Africa Sup. Ct. App., April 10, 2008), 51.

71. Ibid., par. 25–27.

72. See *Selmouni* v. *France,* Eur. Ct. H.R. 25809/94 (July 28, 1999).

73. Human Rights Watch, *Universal Periodic Review of France,* submission to the Human Rights Council, May 4, 2008 (www.hrw.org/en/news/2008/05/04/universal-periodic-review-france).

74. Ibid.

75. Boyne, "Preserving the Role of Law," p. 19; Scheppele, "Other People's Patriot Acts," p. 103.

76. Boyne, "Preserving the Role of Law," p. 20.

77. Simon Koschut, "Germany and the USA in the 'War against Terror:' Is Extraordinary Rendition Putting Transatlantic Cooperation under Strain?" *International Politics and Society* (March 2007), p. 45.

78. For example, FISA does not cover purely foreign targets in the United States and permits a seventy-two-hour emergency exception.

79. Republic of South Africa Constitution, ch. 2, § 14(d).

80. Regulation of Interception of Communications and Provision of Communication-Related Information Act, 2002, no. 70.

81. Ibid., ch. 2, pt. I, § 2.

82. Ibid., ch. 3, § 16(6).

83. Ibid., ch. 3, § 16(5).

84. Regulation of Interception of Communications and Provision of Communication-Related Information Act, § 16(5)(c).

85. Ibid., ch. 9, § 47.

86. Republic of South Africa Constitution, ch. 2, § 35(5).

87. In late 2005, however, the NIA was exposed as having engaged in unauthorized physical and electronic surveillance as part of a legal domestic intelligence operation entitled Project Avani, which was designed to assess potential threats relating to presidential succession. The scandal, detailed by an investigation and report of the inspector general, included illegal domestic surveillance of prominent business people, high-level ANC members, and the parliamentary office of the opposition party.

88. Ley Organica de Reforma de la Ley de Enjuiciamiento Criminal [Constitutional Law of Reform of the Law of Criminal Prosecution] (B.O.E. 1988, 126) (codified at L.E. CRIM. art. 553 (2004)).

89. See "The Hon Robert McClelland MP, Member for Barton (NSW)," Parliament of Australia, House of Representatives (www.aph.gov.au/house/members/biography.asp?id=JK6).

90. Lynch and Williams, *What Price Security?* p. 30.

91. Ibid., pp. 34–35.

92. Home Office, *Terrorist Investigations*, p. 2.

93. Christian Walter, *Terrorism as a Challenge for National and International Law: Security versus Liberty?* (New York: Springer, 2004), pp. 286–87.

94. Paul M. Schwartz, "German and U.S. Telecommunications Privacy Law: Legal Regulation of Domestic Law Enforcement Surveillance," *Hastings Law Journal* 54 (2003), pp. 751, 785.

95. Jacqueline Ross, "Germany's Federal Constitutional Court and the Regulation of GPS Surveillance," *German Law Journal* 6 (2005), pp. 1805, 1809–11.

96. Kim Scheppele, "We Are All Post– 9/11 Now," *Fordham Law Review* 75 (2006), pp. 607, 619–20; Francesca Bignami, "European Versus American Liberty: A Comparative Privacy Analysis Of Antiterrorism Data Mining," *Boston College Law Review* 48 (2007), pp. 609, 645.

97. Scheppele, "We Are All Post–9/11 Now," p. 621.

98. Parliament of India, Prevention of Terrorism Act, ch. 5, § 40(1).

99. Parliament of India, The Information Technology (Amendment) Bill, 2006, no. 96, § 69(1).

100. Imperial Legislative Council, Indian Telegraph Act, 1885, no. 13, § 5(2).

101. Privacy International, "State of Israel," Privacy and Human Rights 2003 (www.privacyinternational.org/survey/phr2003/countries/israel.htm).

102. Ibid.

103. Regulation of Investigatory Powers Act, 2000, c. 23, § 5 (authorizing the secretary of state to issue warrants).

104. Police Act, 1997, c. 50; Intelligence Services Act, 1994, c. 13.

105. See Regulation of Investigatory Powers Act, § 5. For exceptions, see ibid., § 3–4.
106. Ibid., § 7.
107. Ibid., § 9–10.
108. Home Office, *Terrorist Investigations,* p. 10.
109. See Regulation of Investigatory Powers Act, § 18(4).
110. See *Regina* v. *P. and Others,* EWCA Civ. 277, [2002] 1 A.C. 146.

MATTHEW C. WAXMAN

2

Administrative Detention: Integrating Strategy and Institutional Design

As the Obama administration plans the closure of Guantánamo and develops the architecture of a new terrorist detention policy going forward, it will necessarily consider whether Congress should enact administrative detention legislation.[1] To its advocates, administrative detention—detention by order of the executive branch without criminal prosecution in the courts—is an important counterterrorism tool.[2] New legislation, they argue, would more effectively and legitimately regulate detention of suspected terrorists than does the law of war as an alternative to criminal prosecution.[3] But critics warn that administrative detention is a dangerous tool, not just because it threatens liberty and entails expanding the powers of the state, but also because its likely overuse or injudicious use may be counterproductive in combating violent extremism. Opponents and skeptics of administrative detention generally argue that instead of institutionalizing and regulating detention of suspected terrorists through legislation, detention should be handled—except in foreign combat zones—through criminal prosecution, with its tight rules limiting state powers and safeguarding individual suspects' liberties.[4]

My purpose in these pages is not to convince the reader that a new administrative detention regime is necessary, nor do I mean to offer a legislative roadmap for developing one. I have argued elsewhere for "a durable, long-term framework for handling detainees—one that lets [the United States government] hold the most dangerous individuals and collect intelligence from them (including through lawful interrogation), but also (unlike Guantánamo Bay) has rules and procedures that are politically, legally and diplomatically sustainable."[5] This chapter instead examines what seem like simple questions underlying the discussion of administrative detention and the possible need for new laws: In combating terrorism, why should the government detain individuals? Whom should it detain?

The answers to those questions seem obvious at first. The government should detain individuals to *prevent* terrorism and, to that end, it should detain *terrorists*. And with those basic questions apparently settled, the administrative detention debate tends to jump quickly to the question of how to detain: What procedural protections should suspects be afforded? What rights should they be granted to challenge the evidence proffered against them? What kinds of officials will adjudicate cases?[6] Those advocating new administrative detention laws generally call for robust judicial review of what have largely been executive-only detention decisions since the early days of the Bush administration's global war on terror—perhaps by a new "national security court" charged with overseeing a process that includes adversarial process and meaningful assistance of counsel. And at that point, the discussion moves just as quickly to questions of institutional design and such procedural details as evidentiary rules, the type of judges who will hear the cases, detainee access to counsel, and counsel's own access to classified information. Administration detention critics, too, focus heavily on the procedural dynamics of administrative detention proposals: how would detention decisionmaking and, for that matter, the standards and rules governing decisions, deviate from normal criminal justice rules?

The Supreme Court similarly focused almost exclusively on procedural mechanisms in its 2006 decision in *Boumediene* v. *Bush,*[7] holding that prisoners at Guantánamo have a constitutional right to habeas corpus review of their detention by federal courts. While mandating that Guantánamo detainees receive access to U.S. federal courts empowered to correct errors after "meaningful review of both the cause for detention and the Executive's power to detain," the Court made clear that it was "not address[ing] the content of the law that governs petitioners' detention."[8]

The questions that everyone seems keen to skip over, however, are not nearly as obvious as their omission suggests. In this chapter, I therefore take a step back from the issues surrounding how to make and review detention decisions and engage the antecedent questions of why detain and whom to detain. In doing so, I mean to advance two overarching arguments that should guide the discussion of whether the United States needs administrative detention laws and, if so, of what type. First, any discussion should begin with a clear understanding of the strategic rationale for administrative detention and a sense of how detention fits within a broader counterterrorism and national security strategy. The answers to the "why detain?" question will drive the answers to the "whom to detain?" question, and those answers together will significantly affect the costs and benefits of any legal innovation.

Second, the way in which the "why" and "whom" questions are answered will, in turn, significantly determine the procedural architecture of any new administrative detention regime. That fact cautions against jumping too quickly to issues of procedural design—the "how" questions.

To whatever extent Congress decides that the United States needs a new administrative detention apparatus, this analysis points in favor of narrowing significantly the strategic flexibility and expansive operational latitude that the Bush and the Obama administrations alike have claimed through their interpretation of the law of war. It recommends that architects of proposed administrative detention schemes focus on the strategic objectives of either immediate-term disruption of terrorist plots or long-term incapacitation of suspected terrorists. As this analysis shows, it may not be as easy as it seems to design a single system that does both effectively. Only after clarifying the strategic purpose behind detention laws can Congress devise effective corresponding procedures.

The Law-of-War Approach and Calls for Reform

The Bush administration's post–September 11 approach to detention began with the notion that the United States was at war with al Qaeda and those aligned with it. The administration relied in turn on an expansive interpretation of its domestic executive war powers and the international law of war to assert that those fighting—broadly defined—on behalf of al Qaeda and its affiliates, and in some cases those supporting that fight, were enemies in an ongoing armed conflict. Therefore the United States could lawfully capture any of the constituent enemies, or "combatants," and detain them for the duration of hostilities, just as a state would be entitled in the course of a war with another state to capture and hold enemy soldiers until the end of the war.[9]

Immediately upon coming into office, the Obama administration announced its intention to close Guantánamo, but it continued to defend a broad authority to detain suspected al Qaeda and affiliated terrorists based on the law of war.[10] Specifically, it relied on the 2001 congressional Authorization for Use of Military Force to argue that it may detain "persons who were part of, or substantially supported, Taliban or Al Qaeda forces or associated forces that are engaged in hostilities against the United States or its coalition partners, including any person who has committed a belligerent act, or has directly supported hostilities, in aid of such enemy forces." The Obama administration further urged that "[i]t is neither possible nor advisable . . . to attempt to identify, in the abstract, the precise nature and degree of 'substantial support,' or the precise characteristics of 'associated forces,' that are or would be sufficient to bring persons and organizations within the foregoing framework." Rather, "the contours of the 'substantial support' and 'associated forces' bases of detention will need to be further developed in their application to concrete facts in individual cases" based on analogy to traditional armed conflicts.[11]

Of course, the war on terror is not a war between states, and some problems with relying on a direct analogy quickly become apparent. Although even in conventional warfare the notion of "enemy combatants" may defy either clear definition or easy application, members of terrorist organizations generally try to obfuscate their identities and blend indistinguishably into civilian populations. The organizations themselves lack the formalized structure of states, thereby greatly exacerbating the likelihood of misidentifying an innocent civilian as an enemy (a problem discussed in greater detail below). The stakes of such errors are magnified by the likelihood that this conflict with al Qaeda or its spin-off organizations will last for decades, raising the specter of depriving innocent people of their liberty indefinitely.[12]

Criticisms of the executive branch's reliance on this law-of-war theory to justify detentions have focused heavily on the inadequacy of the process by which detention decisions are made. Whether arguing that those detained deserve full-fledged criminal trials or that detentions should be judicially reviewed or that the government failed even to provide the minimal battlefield hearings required by the Geneva Conventions, critics have tended to focus their attacks on the "how" questions of detention.[13] Less often discussed is the "whom" question—the substantive scope of the detention class.[14]

Were Congress to consider new administrative detention laws, it would quickly confront this issue. The vast bulk of existing discussions of administrative detention, however, skips immediately back to procedural questions, the assumption being that setting the appropriate level of procedural protection can better balance security and liberty than the current approaches do. Several major elements of procedural design are most consistently and notably thought to be key to that balance: judicial review, adversarial process with lawyer representation, and transparency.[15] And, indeed, each of them—individually and in tandem—has a vital role to play in any effective administrative detention system.

Judicial review can help safeguard liberty and enhance the credibility at home and abroad of administrative detention decisions by ensuring the neutrality of the decisionmaker and publicly certifying the legality of the detention in question. Most calls for reform of existing detention laws start with a strong role for courts. Some commentators believe that a special court is needed, perhaps a "national security court" made up of designated judges who would build expertise in terrorism cases over time.[16] Others suggest that the Foreign Intelligence Surveillance Court already has judges with expertise in handling sensitive intelligence matters and mechanisms in place to ensure secrecy, so its jurisdiction ought to be expanded to handle detention cases.[17] Still others insist that specialized terrorism courts are dangerous; the legitimacy of a detention system can best be ensured by giving regular, generalist judges a say in each decision.

Adversarial process and access to attorneys can help further protect liberty and enhance the perceived legitimacy of detention systems. As with judicial review, however, proposals tend to split over how best to organize and ensure that process. Some argue that habeas corpus suits are the best check on administrative detention.[18] Others argue that administrative detention decisions should be contested at an early stage by a lawyer of the detainee's choosing.[19] Still others recognize an imperative need for secrecy and deep expertise in terrorism and intelligence matters that calls for designating a special "defense bar" operated by the government on detainees' behalf.[20]

The issue of secrecy runs in tension with a third common element of procedural and institutional reform proposals: openness and transparency. The Bush administration's approach was considered by some to be prone to error in part because of its excessive secrecy and hostility to the prying courts and Congress as well as to the press and advocacy groups. Critics and reformists argue that hearings should be open or at least partially open and that judgments should be written so that they can be scrutinized later by the public or congressional oversight committees; that, they claim, would help put pressure on the executive branch to exercise greater care in deciding which detention cases to pursue and put pressure on adjudicators to act in good faith and with more diligence.[21]

These three elements of procedural design reform—judicial review, adversarial process, and transparency—may help reduce the likelihood of mistakes and restore the credibility of detention decisionmaking. Rarely, though, do the discussions pause long on the antecedent question of what it is that the courts—however constituted—will evaluate. Judicial review of *what*? A meaningful opportunity to contest *what* with the assistance of counsel? Transparent determinations of *what*?

To answer those questions—that is, to define the class of individuals subject to administrative detention and the substantive standards by which detentions will be judged—it is necessary to step back even further, to consider carefully the strategic rationale for new proposed legal tools. Discussion of the class of individuals should begin with a clear understanding of detention's strategic purpose: what exactly is noncriminal detention for? The answer to that basic question will help determine the necessity and wisdom of administrative detention and, if it is found to be necessary, help define who should fall within the scope of an appropriately drawn regime. Only then can the precise contours of procedures be determined and the overall merits of legal innovations weighed.

Why Use Administrative Detention?

The reason that administrative detention is widely discussed at all is that its proponents believe that terrorism involves a category of individuals for whom neither criminal justice nor the laws of war—the two legal systems that generally authorize and regulate the long-term detention of dangerous terrorist threats—offer effective and just solutions. The argument generally begins with the notion that exclusive reliance on prosecution, along with its usual panoply of defendant rights and strict rules of evidence, cannot effectively, expeditiously, or exhaustively remove the threat of dangerous terrorists. Some of the concerns are practical. For example, information used to identify terrorists and their plots may include extremely sensitive intelligence sources and methods, the disclosure of which during prosecution would undermine counterterrorism operations. The conditions under which some suspected terrorists are captured (especially in faraway lawless areas or active combat zones) may make it impossible to prove criminal cases using normal evidentiary rules.[22] Other concerns are more fundamental: prosecution is designed to punish past conduct, but fighting terrorism emphasizes stopping suspects before they act; moreover, criminal justice is deliberately tilted in favor of defendants so that few if any innocent individuals are punished, but the higher stakes in terrorism cannot allow the same likelihood that some guilty individuals will go free.[23]

The concerns about relying on the criminal justice system to detain suspected terrorists are subject to much debate. Antiterrorism statutes have been expanded in recent years, making prosecution a more powerful tool.[24] In 2008 the organization Human Rights First published a study of federal prosecutions of terrorism cases since September 11 and concluded that Article III courts are generally well-equipped to handle many of the challenges just listed.[25] Administrative detention proponents, however, remain unpersuaded.

While acknowledging that prosecution is one important tool among many, they worry that it is not sufficient to deal with terrorism threats.[26]

Declaring criminal law to be inappropriate or inadequate, administrative detention proponents then usually argue that the law of war—under which individual enemy fighters can be captured and held for the duration of hostilities without trial—does not work satisfactorily either. The rules of warfare grew out of conflicts primarily between professional armies (acting as agents responsible to a state) that could be expected to last months or maybe years but that would likely end definitively. Terrorism, by contrast, involves an enemy whose fighters cannot be identified with similar precision, and it is unlikely to end soon or at all or with certainty. Applying the traditional detention rules under the law of war therefore opens the possibility of indefinite detention without trial combined with a substantial likelihood of error.[27]

The idea behind administrative detention is to free the state from the stark choice between the two systems. Rather than trying to jam the square peg of terrorist threats into the round hole of criminal law or the law of war, the United States might design a system better tailored to the special problems of terrorism. Most likely, any sensible alternative scheme will include some elements that resemble criminal law and others that resemble the law of war, for the simple reason that terrorism shares some features of crime and some features of warfare. Consequently, the U.S. government needs to think through how to define the set of cases that fall between the two existing systems and may demand an alternative. That requires first a clear notion of needs: what is it about terrorism that might necessitate a step so precipitous as creating a new detention regime?

This may sound like an obvious point, but there is remarkably little discussion in the policy or academic realms of precisely how detention fits within a broader strategy to combat terrorism or, more specifically, to combat al Qaeda. At least within the public domain there appears to be no comprehensive effort by the U.S. government to review the lessons learned to date about whom it has chosen to detain or not detain. The report of the 9/11 Commission contained only one significant recommendation with respect to detention, and that had to do with treatment standards, not the power to detain.[28] During the Bush administration, the government went to tremendous lengths to defend its detention authority at home and abroad as necessary to combat terrorism, without explaining in any public detail how its authority operated in tandem with other instruments to bring about a desired end state.[29] And while the Obama administration has appointed a task force to study future detention needs and another to review current Guantánamo cases, as of this writing those efforts are very much works in progress.

That said, it is virtually undisputed among those who advocate administrative detention that its purpose is preventive—a prophylactic measure against terrorist threats. Indeed, the term "preventive detention" is often used interchangeably with "administrative detention." Whereas criminal law also has a preventive component and some criminal liability such as conspiracy targets future conduct, it is usually retrospective in focus, in that it addresses past acts. The resulting punishment, including incarceration, serves preventive purposes insofar as it keeps a perpetrator off the street (for some period of time) and may deter both the person convicted and others in general from future crime. But at base, criminal law primarily addresses past harms.

Administrative detention proposals, by contrast, tend to be prospective in focus. They start with the notion that terrorist acts—especially major attacks—must be addressed before they occur at all. The consequences of failure to prevent terrorist attacks are too high, the argument goes, to rely on reaction alone. When it comes to crime, the mere likelihood that someone will act—even a high likelihood of even a violent crime—is typically not used to justify detention. The entire criminal justice system, including the requirement of proof beyond reasonable doubt, is tilted in favor of defendants: it is better to let ten (or a hundred) guilty people go free than to convict one innocent person. And the system tolerates high levels of recidivism in parole programs, reasoning that it is more costly to keep all convicts locked up than to accept a certain level of crime. But terrorism, according to administrative detention proponents, is different. The ability of small groups harnessing modern technology (including, especially in the future, weapons of mass destruction) to cause mass casualties, damage, panic, and threats to effective governance puts terrorism on a different plane.[30]

The notion of prevention, however, needs to be further unpacked, because it contains several subelements, each of which has its own implications for how to cast administrative detention laws and how to design institutions for adjudicating terrorism cases. Detention may serve the cause of prevention in a number of ways, including by

—incapacitating suspects

—deterring potential terrorists from joining violent extremists or undertaking violent acts

—disrupting specific, ongoing plots

—enabling the government to gather information about enemy organizations.

The most natural inclination of a government facing threats of terrorism is to *incapacitate* suspected terrorists: if someone has the will and capability to commit terrorism, then keep that person off the streets. The purpose is not punitive or retributive (though such desires might operate in the background) but protective—to put threats out of action. As Attorney General Michael B. Mukasey remarked in 2008: "[t]he United States has every right to capture and detain enemy combatants in this conflict, and need not simply release them to return to the battlefield—as indeed some have after their release from Guantánamo. We have every right to prevent them from returning to kill our troops or those fighting with us, and to target innocent civilians."[31] In May 2009 President Obama similarly remarked: "I am not going to release individuals who endanger the American people. Al Qaeda terrorists and their affiliates are at war with the United States, and those that we capture—like other prisoners of war—must be prevented from attacking us again."[32] A prevention strategy emphasizing incapacitation assumes the state's ability to assess accurately who likely poses a future danger and to devote resources to stemming their future dangerous activities.

Beyond incapacitating existing threats, the threat of detention might *deter* potential recruits from joining the terrorist cause or participating in terrorist activities. In other words, the possibility of getting caught and held by the government may dissuade terrorists from perpetrating bad acts or potential terrorists from joining the cause. The more credible the threat of capture and detention and the more severe the consequences (say, the longer the threatened period of detention), so the theory goes, the greater the deterrent pressure. Whereas an incapacitation strategy begins with the assumption that individual threats are accurately identified, a prevention strategy emphasizing deterrence assumes the state's ability to manipulate sufficiently the fears of potential perpetrators of terrorist acts.

The notion of incapacitating or deterring terrorists or potential terrorists may point to large groups of individuals and their activities. If the state can discern who has the intent and capability to commit or support terrorist acts—or the potential to develop that intent and capability—it can try to block or dissuade them. But a narrower way to formulate the preventive purpose of administrative detention might be to define its purpose as the *disruption* of terrorist plots. If a group of individuals is preparing to hijack a plane or detonate a dirty bomb, then use the detention of certain key persons to foil that plot. Whereas incapacitation focuses heavily on the characteristics of particular individuals, disruption focuses on their joint or individual activities. It is not about neutralizing dangerous people as such but about going after their imminent schemes. The critical assumption here is that the state has the ability to identify plots and their key individual enablers in advance.

All three of these preventive approaches assume substantial and accurate knowledge about terrorist network members and supporters, raising a fourth preventive reason to detain: to *gather information.* Preventing and disrupting terrorist plots requires getting inside the heads of network members to understand their intentions, capabilities, and modes of operation. Detention can facilitate such intelligence collection through, most obviously, custodial interrogation, but also perhaps through monitoring conversations among prisoners or even "turning" terrorist agents and releasing them as government informants. Governments usually justify counterterrorism detentions publicly on the grounds of incapacitation or disruption, but information gathering undoubtedly was at the forefront of the Bush administration's thinking on the issue, demonstrated by the lengths to which it has gone to defend permissive interrogation standards and programs.[33] During the early phases of the government's enemy combatant litigation against alleged al Qaeda dirty-bomber Jose Padilla, the director of the Defense Intelligence Agency attested that

> the War on Terrorism cannot be won without timely, reliable, abundant intelligence. That intelligence cannot be obtained without robust interrogation efforts. Impairment of the interrogation tool—especially with respect to enemy combatants associated with Al Qaeda—would undermine our Nation's intelligence gathering efforts, thus jeopardizing the national security of the United States.[34]

As the last point about facilitating information gathering shows, the preventive purposes of detention often work in tandem. Incapacitating individuals suspected of posing serious dangers may deter individuals from engaging in or supporting dangerous activities. Disrupting major plots and interrogating the plotters may reveal a lot about how future schemes will hatch and who among the many dangerous individuals remaining at large are most likely to play critical roles in those schemes. Any sound counterterrorism strategy will combine all of these elements to some degree.

But tensions and trade-offs among the elements of prevention also exist, in part because detention is but one among an array of tools that the government uses in implementing its counterterrorism strategy. For example, the government can monitor suspects' movements and communications, not only to foresee and forestall plots but also to gain a more complete picture of the terrorist network and its activities; the moment the government detains someone, however, those movements and communications may cease, along with its ability to track them. If more might be gained through intelligence gathering than lost through assuming the marginal risk of a captured individual's committing major violence if released, the person could be released to afford the opportunity to follow him. In other words, an aggressive incapacitation approach may sometimes undermine information-gathering activities.[35] Aside from other policy costs to detention, some of which are discussed below, the government formulates its counterterrorism detention strategy—and considers the utility of administrative detention in certain circumstances—in an environment of constrained resources. That means that it must assign priorities to the various preventive functions and sometimes sacrifice one in the service of another.

A final reason that consideration of administrative detention must begin with a clear understanding of its strategic purposes is that the ultimate policy question will not be simply whether administrative detention will effectively serve a preventive function but how it does so and how it compares with the alternatives. Even if it is not foolproof or able to cast as wide or dense a detention net, criminal law is able to serve each of the preventive functions just discussed to at least some significant degree, and the government also has an array of other tools at its disposal, including surveillance. The critical question is by what margin, if any, administrative detention might improve the effectiveness of an integrated counterterrorism strategy and at what cost.

Administrative Detention of Whom?

Answering the "why detain" question does not merely help clarify the strategic advantages of proposed administrative detention programs. It also helps guide the substantive definition of the class subject to detention—that is, it helps answer the question of "whom" to detain. It is difficult to define legislatively the factual predicate of detention decisions without knowing precisely the main strategic rationale.

If the United States were to continue to rely on the notion that it is locked in armed conflict with al Qaeda, courts might be charged with reviewing whether an individual is a "member" of a certain organization, or committed a "belligerent act," or "supported" those who are members or who have committed such acts. After all, any of those concepts has analogs in criminal law that judges apply regularly—for example, conspiracy liability in the case of membership, aiding and abetting in the case of support.[36]

In designing an administrative detention regime, however, a range exists of other possible ways to define the class of individuals subject to detention, some of them better suited to specific strategic objectives. After all, the legal notion of "combatants" or "belligerents" arose in the context of conventional warfare: participation in an enemy army could reasonably be assumed to serve as an accurate indicator of one's future threat, measured in traditional military terms. But even those who cling to a "war on terror" paradigm acknowledge that the fight against terrorism generally or al Qaeda in particular is unlike any previous war in terms of the nature of the enemy, its threat, and the way that victory is defined. Moreover, it is widely believed that since 2001 the terrorist threat to the United States and its allies has become less centralized, less hierarchical, and less formalized, complicating even further the direct application of legal standards developed for traditional warfare.[37]

One model for defining the class might be based on what are, in essence, already existing examples of administrative detention in U.S. law, which permits the long-term detention of certain categories of individuals judicially adjudged to be "dangerous." Some state laws, for example, authorize the detention of charged or convicted sex offenders who, due to a "mental abnormality," are likely to engage in certain acts of sexual violence.[38] These statutory schemes might offer a particularly apt analog because they are premised on the view that some sexual predators cannot be deterred from future violence, as is often supposed about terrorists who are religious extremists.[39] Under federal bail law, authorities can hold suspects pending trial on sufficient showing that no conditions of release would reasonably ensure community safety.[40] To be sure, it remains highly debatable whether dangerousness alone would pass constitutional muster as an administrative detention standard, at least with respect to U.S. citizens.[41] But in the context of terrorism, as in other areas of U.S. law, an administrative detention regime might include future dangerousness at least as one critical element. And, accordingly, a central inquiry for courts might be to review the executive's assessment of dangerousness.

The United Kingdom's 2005 Prevention of Terrorism Act allows for the imposition of "control orders"—which restrict an individual's movements, communications, or other freedoms—when the government "has reasonable grounds for suspecting that the individual is or has been involved in terrorism-related activity." Such activity is further defined as

(a) the commission, preparation or instigation of acts of terrorism;
(b) conduct which facilitates the commission, preparation or instigation of such acts, or which is intended to do so; (c) conduct which gives

encouragement to the commission, preparation or instigation of such acts, or which is intended to do so; (d) conduct which gives support or assistance to individuals who are known or believed to be involved in terrorism-related activity.[42]

Under this model, the critical inquiry for courts focuses not on an assessment of an individual's future dangerousness but on whether the individual committed a certain type of act. Parliament presumably selected these types of acts because it believed them to serve as good indicators of future dangerousness. But the narrow focus on acts tends to tidy the judicial inquiry considerably. Determining whether a suspect committed alleged deeds, after all, is something that courts do all the time.

Several Israeli administrative detention schemes present yet another set of models. Under one statutory scheme, the domestic Emergency Powers Law, the executive can order judicially reviewed detention based on the extremely broad standard of "reasonable cause to believe that reasons of state security or public security require that a particular person be detained."[43] This statute does not presuppose a state of war, and it contrasts with Israel's 2002 Unlawful Enemy Combatant statute. The latter statute, recently upheld by the Israeli Supreme Court, provides for detention of an individual fighting on behalf of foreign forces with which Israel regards itself as in a state of armed conflict, pursuant to strict judicial review requirements, if that individual "participated either directly or indirectly in hostile acts against the State of Israel or is a member of a force perpetrating hostile acts against the State of Israel" *and* whose "release will harm State security."[44] In other words, detention under the latter scheme requires a showing of either certain acts *or* membership *plus* dangerousness.

These examples illustrate just part of the spectrum of possible definitions of the detention class; any of them is susceptible to judicial application.[45] So which one makes sense? A broad "state security" class? A narrower membership plus public danger approach? Commission of proscribed acts? The answer depends heavily on strategic purpose.

If, for example, the principal focus of administrative detention is to incapacitate and deter individuals likely to pursue threatening terrorist activities, then the authority to detain would most naturally turn on an individual's supposed dangerousness. In that case, a suitable statutory scheme might resemble the administrative detention laws aimed at pretrial arrestees or supposedly dangerous sex offenders whose prison term has expired. Secondary questions then arise. What type of dangerous act is the individual likely to commit? Will he or she one day participate in a major terrorist attack? Attack U.S. forces or citizens? Support those who carry out terrorist attacks? What is the likelihood that the person will participate in a dangerous act? Is the likelihood substantial?

Rather than making purported dangerousness itself the test, a statute might rely on proxy indicators of future threat, such as membership in a particular terrorist organization or commission of particular acts, supposing that such membership and activities are good predictors of the likely behavior of an individual if the person is allowed to roam free. With regard to membership, consider the Alien Enemy Act, a statute enacted in 1798 and later amended. It states that during a declared war and upon presidential proclamation, "all natives, citizens, denizens, or subjects of the hostile nation or government, being of the age of fourteen years and upward, who shall be within the United States and not actually naturalized, shall be liable to be apprehended, restrained, secured, and removed as alien enemies."[46] The statute, which remains on the books today, was clearly premised on the idea that during wartime an individual's citizenship of an enemy state is a strong indicator of dangerousness.[47] With regard to past acts as a proxy for dangerousness, recall that the United Kingdom's 2005 Prevention of Terrorism Act, for example, allows for the imposition of control orders when the government "has reasonable grounds for suspecting that the individual is or has been involved in terrorism-related activity," which it then further describes. For the purposes of the U.K. law, moreover, "it is immaterial whether the acts of terrorism in question are specific acts of terrorism or acts of terrorism generally."[48]

If, by contrast, the emphasis of administrative detention is not on incapacitating individuals but on disrupting impending plots, then the authority to detain might be cast in terms of causality: *but for* detaining a particular individual, some harm would ensue. A law might authorize detention on a showing that, to quote from a 2007 Senate bill, "failure to detain . . . will result in a risk of imminent death or imminent serious bodily injury to any individual or imminent damage to or destruction of any United States facility."[49] On the one hand, in theory, authorities can disrupt specific plots by nabbing only key leaders and planners and those directly involved in those plots; even if some very dangerous but peripherally involved associates remain free, the scheme may thereby be ruined. On the other hand, detention to disrupt might justify detaining for some period of time even individuals who are not very dangerous at all when viewed in isolation—people who may not be very committed to the terrorist cause or may not be adequately trained to do much harm but who play a minor role in a particular plot or may only have information about it.[50] As explained further below, disruption detention along these lines points toward a detention period of short duration, whereas detention based on perceived dangerousness may in some cases point toward long-term detention.

Note that the key inquiry in the last example looks different from the key inquiry for incapacitation: detention to disrupt assumes a functional link between an individual and a plot (or set of plots), whereas detention to incapacitate might look to an individual's general will and capacity to do harm. A statutory regime focused on disruption might accordingly define the class on the basis of participation in plots or a showing that but for detention of a particular individual, terrorist attacks would be likely. These categories will no doubt overlap somewhat, but not completely. Take, for example, a financier who provides money to a range of terrorist organizations. Authorities may regard him as extremely dangerous and believe that his detention might reduce the likelihood and effectiveness of future terrorist attacks in general and frighten others from funding terrorism (incapacitation and deterrence). But he is unlikely to fall within the terms of a law requiring a showing that failure to detain him will substantially increase the risk of a specific, imminent attack. For a contrasting example, consider a courier believed to be carrying messages to al Qaeda members about an impending attack. Authorities assessing his future dangerousness as an individual, depending on how high the bar is set and what factors are used in the assessment, might regard him as not very threatening at all. But his personal involvement in an imminent attack, though that involvement is not in itself violent, might put him squarely within a law aimed at disruption.

If the major focus of administrative detention is information gathering, the natural definition of the detention class would look different still. Administrative detention might target individuals believed to have critical information about either terrorism threats in general or specific plots. Again, this category of individuals will often overlap with others, and a law might require a showing of membership in a terrorist organization or commission of a terrorist act as a threshold before even considering the information question. But the categories will not always overlap. Consider, for example, an al Qaeda paymaster who may not be very dangerous as an individual but who may have substantial information about associates who are. Taken to the extreme, a law authorizing detention based on suspected knowledge alone might be used to justify holding a suspected terrorist's spouse or roommate—even if not complicit—in order to question the person about the suspect's actions, communications, and intentions. Some argue that the federal government used (or abused) its material witness powers in similar ways after September 11, taking individuals into custody solely to question them about any possible knowledge of terrorist activity.[51]

In sum, the strategic focus of administrative detention proposals will bear heavily on how the law should define the substantive class.

Narrowing the Class

If the United States needs new tools to effectively combat new forms of terrorism, why not simply define the class broadly—as the Bush administration did and the Obama administration continues to do—to give the executive maximum latitude to design appropriate responses? After all, even if one rejects the full breadth of that definition, the notion is certainly correct that all the elements of prevention listed above should feature in any sensible counterterrorism strategy.

The main reason for restricting the class liable to detention is that every expansion comes at a price—one reason among many to consider the strategic priorities of detention carefully. The policy calculus must include consideration not just of the general dangers attached to enacting any new detention regime but also the marginal dangers that come from expanding the size and shape of the susceptible class. A full discussion of all such dangers is beyond the scope of this chapter, but it is worth highlighting a few because they bear on its broader thesis, namely that the ultimate policy merits of administrative detention will turn at least as much on the tough issue of defining the substantive class as it will on fashioning the right procedures. Moreover, the U.S. experience since September 11 as well as that of U.S. allies in combating terrorism in the past offers lessons in how to narrow the class.

Debates about administrative detention usually are cast in terms of liberty versus security. But administrative detention—both its use and its mere enactment—carries risks to both liberty and security. Experience since September 2001 suggests that those risks are unlikely to be mitigated even by robust procedural protections unless the substantive detention criteria are tightly constrained as well.

Opponents and skeptics of administrative detention rightly point out that creating new mechanisms for detention with procedural protections that are diluted compared with those granted criminal suspects may put liberty at risk. The most obvious concern is that innocent individuals will get swept up and imprisoned—the "false positive" problem. Civil libertarians rightly worry too that aside from the specific risk to particular individuals, any expansion of administrative detention—and I say "expansion" because, as noted earlier, it already exists in some nonterrorist contexts in U.S. law—risks eroding the checks on state power more generally. To some, the idea of administrative detention of suspected terrorists is the kind of "loaded weapon" that Justice Robert Jackson worried about at the time of Japanese internment.[52] Even if critics are satisfied that the U.S. government can use administrative detention responsibly, there are many unsavory foreign regimes that will not. The United States therefore needs to be cautious about justifying principles that might be used by less democratic regimes as a pretext to crack down, for example, on dissidents that they label "terrorists" or "national security threats."

In considering the risks to liberty, one usually thinks about the procedural protections afforded suspects, such as the opportunity to rebut evidence against them, or about the burden of proof placed on the government. But the substantive definition of the detention class is also key to managing those risks, and a narrow definition can help mitigate them. Some relatively restrictive definitions—for example, those including only individuals who commit certain acts—might generally be applied with a great degree of certainty, whereas some very broad conceptions—say, those that include individuals who are devoted to a hostile ideology—may be impossible to apply with high confidence. A broad definition of conduct or dangerousness justifying detention will also likely result in the scooping up of many individuals who would not have gone on to engage in actual terrorist conduct. Indeed, that a broad substantive definition of the detention class can overwhelm even the most robust procedural protections is reflected in criticisms that recently expanded criminal liability for providing "material support" to terrorist organizations or engaging in terrorist conspiracies has netted many individuals who were actually unlikely to engage in serious acts of terrorism.[53] Finally, with respect to international norms, a narrow set of definitional criteria—requiring, for example, a showing of commission of certain acts or a link to specific plots—stands a better chance of winning legitimacy among allies and averting over-expansive interpretation of the criteria in other countries. Although creating any new category of administrative detention risks diluting international norms that generally emphasize adherence to criminal law procedures to lock away bad actors, the more narrowly such a carve-out is defined the less prone it will be to political manipulation or to further stretching to deal with other types of public policy problems.

Besides posing risks to liberty, administrative detention can also be counterproductive from the security standpoint. Again, the substantive criteria of detention law may help mitigate the risk. Historically, detention policies—especially those viewed as overbroad by the communities in which they were implemented—have sometimes proven ill-suited to combating terrorism and radicalization of individuals or communities. The British government learned painfully that internment of suspected Northern Ireland terrorists was viewed among some communities as a form of collective punishment that fueled violent nationalism and helped dry up the supply of community informants.[54] And in Iraq and Afghanistan, though the circumstances are exceptional because combat still rages there, detention has played an important role in neutralizing threats to coalition forces, but it has also contributed to anticoalition radicalization, especially when it is perceived as being used indiscriminately.[55]

One role that well-crafted definitional criteria can play is in mitigating an executive's propensity to overuse the power to detain. Observers from both the right and the left worry correctly that in the face of terrorist threats the executive is likely to push detention powers to or even past their outer bounds in order to prevent catastrophe as well as to head off any political backlash for having failed to take sufficient action.[56] Such overbroad use of detention risks further radicalizing and alienating communities from which terrorists are likely to emerge or whose assistance is vital in identifying or penetrating extremist groups. Moreover, several important studies of counterterrorism strategy have emphasized the need to target coercive policies, including military and law enforcement efforts, narrowly precisely to avoid playing into al Qaeda propaganda efforts to aggregate local grievances into a common global movement.[57] These are fundamentally policy, not legal, problems, and they will require sound executive judgment no matter what the legal regime looks like. But once the role of detention is firmly situated in a broader counterterrorism strategy that seeks to balance the many competing policy priorities, a carefully drawn administrative detention statute can help mitigate long-term strategic damage from the propensity to overreach in the short term.

The danger that administrative detention poses to liberty and security points against emphasizing deterrence or information gathering as its primary strategic purpose. Virtually any very dangerous terrorist or supporter of terrorism that the government could hope to deter through detention would be deterred already by the threat of criminal prosecution or military attack or would be sufficiently committed to violent extremism to render the marginal deterrent threat of administrative detention negligible.[58] As for information gathering, an administrative detention law premised on detaining individuals with valuable knowledge regardless of whether they have engaged in nefarious activities sets a precedent that is too easily abused or overused at home or abroad. Information gathering, including through lawful interrogation, will undoubtedly be a strong motive for almost any administrative detention scheme, and an individual's knowledge of terrorist planning or operations could be a reason not to release the person if he or she has been validly detained on other grounds.[59] But using a person's suspected knowledge alone as the basis for detention, completely delinking detention from the individual's voluntary and purposeful actions, cuts even deeper into traditional civil liberties principles and safeguards than most other reasons for administrative detention.[60] A detention law that allows incarceration based on knowledge could also perversely deter individuals with important information from coming forward voluntarily to the government.

That leaves incapacitation and disruption as the most promising strategic drivers of administration detention reform, although, as just mentioned, information gathering is likely to be an important secondary benefit of any detention system. As noted earlier, opponents of administrative detention argue that criminal law and other nondetention tools are adequate to incapacitate or disrupt the activities of most individuals whom the government would reasonably feel compelled to target, while proponents of administrative detention insist that the use of such tools entails too-high a risk of some terrorists slipping through the net. Much of the debate comes down to differing assessments of the marginal danger posed by any terrorists who get away. But it is important to note that even opponents of new administrative schemes acknowledge that stopping an individual from carrying out a terrorist attack, as opposed to merely acquiring information or instilling fear, is a legitimate purpose of detention. The dispute is over what factual predicate should be required and what standards and processes the state must use to substantiate it.[61]

Narrowing the strategic focus of proposed new detention rules to incapacitation or disruption still leaves the question of how Congress should define the susceptible detention class. The ultimate merits of approaches based on various definitions—including a person's membership in a terrorist organization, past terrorist acts, or future dangerousness or some combination thereof—depend heavily on the processes and standards of proof used with each approach. Recent experience and some judgments about the future threat of terrorism, however, can help further narrow the range of sensible choices.

If one worries that the number of—and the danger posed by—terrorists who cannot be prosecuted in criminal trials consistent with other security imperatives is high, basing an incapacitation-oriented detention law on dangerousness makes sense. The U.S. experience at Guantánamo, however, casts considerable doubt on the ability of the government to assess dangerousness accurately. On the one hand, it brought many supposedly dangerous individuals to Guantánamo who were then released because they were believed not to pose much threat after all; on the other hand, some of those released have turned out to be quite dangerous and have reengaged in terrorist activity.[62] Central questions for Congress to probe in considering new administrative detention proposals is whether it is realistic to believe that assessments of dangerousness are accurate and what would be necessary to improve them.

If one worries that the criminal justice system or other available tools are not nimble enough to allow for emergency intervention against impending plots, a disruption-oriented detention law makes sense. Such a law could include a "but for" standard of detention: the government would have to show that unless an individual is detained, a terrorist attack is likely. This approach would limit the detainable class to individuals who are tied to specific plots or are highly central to a terrorist organization's planning, and it probably would be less prone to false positives or overbroad detention than would a more general dangerousness standard. The probability would depend, of course, on exactly how the standard is drawn, and the standard would, after all, be limited by intelligence, specifically the ability to link individuals to plotting or particular plots in advance. However, a skeptic might then ask why, if the government is so confident that it knows who is about to perpetrate a terrorist act, it cannot simply arrest and prosecute the plotters. Central questions for Congress to probe in this case include whether there exists a significantly dangerous set of individuals on whom the government is likely to have sufficient information to link them to such plotting or plots yet insufficient admissible evidence to support timely use of the criminal justice system to stop them.

Note that both of these approaches—detention based on an individual's dangerousness or on a showing that an attack is likely to occur absent detention—look very different from the one based on defining a person as an enemy combatant, certainly as the government has interpreted and used it since 2001. Indeed, past experience and the logic underlying most administrative detention proposals at least caution against applying a definition of the detainable class that is based heavily on "membership" in or "support" of a particular enemy organization or set of organizations. That would be especially important if al Qaeda and other terrorist organizations become less centralized and more dispersed.

In the end, whether it aims primarily at long-term incapacitation or immediate-term disruption, an effective definitional approach would tie the detainable class directly to a specific strategic aim by including a relatively high substantive standard of prospective or "but for" dangerousness, including proxy indicators likely to improve the accuracy of adjudications.[63]

How to Structure Administrative Detention

Along with narrowing the substantive definition of the detention class, a final reason to ground any consideration of administrative detention statutes in a careful analysis of strategy and a firm rationale for detention is that such reasoning will significantly inform the logic of institutional and procedural design.

This chapter begins with reference to the emerging consensus among advocates of administrative detention reform on a set of minimum procedural and institutional elements for most reform proposals: judicial review, adversarial process, and transparency. *Boumediene v. Bush* also made clear that robust judicial review and the opportunity to contest the legal and factual basis for detention are also constitutionally required, at least for detainees held inside the United States or at Guantánamo.[64]

Beyond identifying such minimum elements, however, it is difficult to work out the secondary details of institutional and procedural design without knowing more precisely what a new administrative detention scheme aims to achieve and whom it is built to detain. Greater strategic clarity and a sharper idea of how the substantive detention class might be defined enlightens the discussion of procedure and reveals important additional questions of institutional design.

Consider first the issue of judicial review combined with adversarial process. The U.S. legal system in general exalts those features because they are believed to promote both fairness and accuracy.[65] Whatever the test or factual predicate used to justify detention as part of a counterterrorism strategy (dangerousness? involvement in a plot? knowledge of terrorist activities? something else?), effective administrative detention ought to involve adjudicative mechanisms likely to produce accurate and fair determinations of the particular factual predicate used.

If, for example, the primary strategic purpose of detention is incapacitation and therefore the critical test is dangerousness, the government should strive for hearings designed to assess and predict future behavior accurately that involve adjudicators who have access to information relevant to the inquiry and processes that effectively test the quality of that information.[66] True, regular federal judges make similar determinations of dangerousness based on adversarial hearings all the time (take the example cited above of terms of bail while awaiting trial).[67] But assessing a terrorist's dangerousness requires an understanding not just of an individual's probable activities and the magnitude of the threat that he poses but also of how his activities relate to those of fellow terrorists. If the dangerousness test includes further inquiry into whether less restrictive means can mitigate the threat (as the British Law Lords have held in the case of recent British counterterrorism laws),[68] courts would further need to inquire into and assess the effectiveness of an array of government tools, including monitoring, surveillance, and international cooperative efforts. The latter type of inquiry seems better suited to a specialized court that would allow judges to accumulate experience and expertise in such technical and operational matters.[69] The same is probably true for detention decisions based on disruption, which would require judicial understanding of the functional links between a suspect and terrorist organizations as well as decisionmaking under extreme time pressure. The success of France's counterterrorism efforts is sometimes credited in part to its development of a specialized, centralized terrorism court that has allowed its magistrates to become "the type of expert on the subject of terrorism that is difficult to create within normal judicial institutions."[70]

If, by contrast, the substantive standard for incapacitation detention is not future dangerousness itself but whether a suspect committed certain acts or is a member of a particular group (perhaps as proxies for dangerousness), that again starts to look very much like an inquiry that regular courts ordinarily conduct, using common analytical tools and types of evidence, though perhaps with special provisions for protecting classified information. There is little reason why an act or membership inquiry could not be handled effectively by a regular generalist judge instead of a special court.

In similar ways, the different strategic imperatives behind administrative detention decisions suggest different approaches to assistance of counsel. The nature of the information used to prove or disprove the urgent need for detention in a disruption or information-gathering regime (assessment of which requires knowing a great deal about terrorist organizations as a whole) might also be better understood and handled by a dedicated bar of specialist attorneys who have been given a security clearance and access to highly sensitive intelligence, as some administrative detention advocates have proposed.[71] The need for restricting a suspect's choice of attorney in a comparatively transparent and less time-sensitive incapacitation regime would likely be significantly lower.

The strategic purpose of administrative detention and the corresponding definition of the detainable class will also guide aspects of institutional design besides judicial review and the counsel assistance mechanism, including duration of detention and whether ongoing periodic review is warranted. If administrative detention is focused on incapacitation and therefore the class is defined by dangerousness or a proxy such as past acts or membership in a group, individual detentions would logically last as long as the individual poses a danger. But whereas dangerousness itself may change over time (as events pass, plots are thwarted, or a detainee grows older or perhaps even demonstrates regret or the desire to cooperate), conditions such as past membership or past actions do not.[72] A factual assessment of dangerousness therefore probably merits periodic review,[73] while static conditions such as the latter do not (though they still may warrant limitations on length of detention).

In contrast to an incapacitation regime, which probably would include long-term detention, a disruption-based administrative detention system could be effective with very short-term detentions; indeed, merely arresting and then releasing a party to a terrorist plot might cause his collaborators to stand down.[74] And relatively short-term detentions might satisfy most information-gathering requirements too,[75] though they would create little deterrent to would-be terrorist collaborators.

Finally, the way that strategic purposes and the subject class of individuals are defined also drives the transparency of decisionmaking. An incapacitation strategy is compatible with high levels of public scrutiny, since there usually is little reason to hide—and indeed much to gain—from openly disclosing the justification for detention.[76] Some degree of transparency would be critical to a deterrence strategy as well, to the extent that locking up individuals tends to dissuade others from specific sorts of conduct.

But the transparency of disruption-based detention decisions is more problematic, because the government may not wish to tip off other collaborators or cause public panic. Some European countries, for example, have laws that allow individuals otherwise legally detained to be held incommunicado for brief periods if cutting off communications (and sometimes even access to a lawyer) is necessary to thwart terrorist attacks.[77] And information-gathering detention would require high levels of secrecy to avoid disclosing sensitive intelligence or tipping off the targets of possible stings.[78]

In any terrorist administrative detention system, sensitive intelligence will likely need to be safeguarded from public dissemination, but in the cases of detention for disruption or information gathering the very proceedings themselves might need to be at least temporarily shielded from disclosure.[79] Such administrative detention regimes might therefore have a greater need for closed or perhaps even ex parte hearings—perhaps analogous to hearings by the Foreign Intelligence Surveillance Court[80]—than would a system designed for incapacitation or deterrence.

Taken as a whole, this analysis favors very different designs for incapacitation and disruption regimes, the two most promising strategic approaches to administrative detention of those outlined above. An incapacitation regime could quite naturally feature generalist judges and lawyers conducting open and transparent hearings to regulate what often would be long-term detention. A disruption regime might require specialized courts and lawyers operating to regulate short-term detention amid some secrecy. Lawmakers therefore may need to choose between strategic approaches in fashioning a new law or consider a bifurcated system to handle the two types of detention. The broader point is that effective procedural design is not independent of strategic purpose or the substantive definition of the detention class. It is heavily driven by both.

Conclusion

The precarious step of legislating an administrative detention regime for suspected terrorists carries many risks to both liberty and, especially over the long term, security. Most of the debate over whether the risks outweigh the marginal strategic utility of administrative detention and over how to mitigate the risks moves too quickly to procedural design. That quick shift in focus overlooks a major piece of the puzzle: the scope and definition of the detention class and the substantive criteria by which any new procedural machinery will make individual decisions.

Any consideration of administrative detention legislation or, more generally, the need for legal innovation in this area should begin with a hard look at the key purposes of detention. That hard look should help guide discussion of the substantive class. From the other end of the cost-benefit matrix, the way that the substantive class is defined can exacerbate or mitigate the policy risks of administrative detention, and the U.S. experience since September 2001 supports narrowing that definition, even at the expense of the chief executive's operational flexibility. The more focused the strategic purpose and the narrower the substantive definition of the target class of individuals, the better the government can assess procedural mechanisms for achieving its goals.

There is a natural temptation for those considering new detention laws to take as a starting point existing policies on detention of enemy combatants and to build on them more robust and refined procedural protections. This analysis suggests that that temptation is misguided. Congress should first decide whether the strategic priority of proposed new administrative detention laws is incapacitation, disruption, or both; only then can the details of detention proposals be intelligently developed and evaluated.

Notes

1. For a more detailed account of the arguments contained in this chapter, see Matthew C. Waxman, "Administrative Detention of Terrorists: *Why* Detain and Detain *Whom*?" *Journal of National Security Law and Policy* 3 (2009), hereafter referred to as Waxman, "Administrative Detention." In recent congressional testimony, Secretary of Defense Robert Gates suggested that some Guantánamo detainees who could neither be prosecuted in court nor released might be moved to detention facilities inside the United States. See Elisabeth Bumiller and and William Glaberson, "Hints That Detainees May Be Held on U.S. Soil," *New York Times*, April 30, 2009.

2. See, for example, Benjamin Wittes, *Law and the Long War* (New York: Penguin Press, 2008), pp. 151–82; Jack Goldsmith and Neal Katyal, "The Terrorists' Court," *New York Times*, July 11, 2007; Andrew McCarthy and Alykhan Velshi, "We Need a National Security Court," submission for AEI book on outsourcing U.S. law, 2006 (www.defend democracy.org/images/stories/national%20security%20court.pdf); Amos N. Guiora, "Quirin to Hamdan: Creating a Hybrid Paradigm for the Detention of Terrorists," *Florida Journal of International Law* 19 (2007), p. 511.

3. Most of those proposals begin with the assumptions that criminal prosecution of suspected terrorists is the preferred option when possible and consistent with national security imperatives and that capture and detention of enemy military forces on traditional battlefields should be excluded from any new administrative detention regime because the law of war deals with those cases satisfactorily. In other words, there are categories of very threatening individuals that the existing detention frameworks serve well and any new system should not significantly disrupt their effectiveness. See, for example, Goldsmith and Katyal, *supra*; Wittes, *supra*; McCarthy and Velshi, *supra*, 6.

4. See, for example, Kenneth Roth, "After Guantánamo: The Case against Preventive Detention," *Foreign Affairs* 87, no. 2 (2008); Gabor Rona, "Legal Frameworks to Combat Terrorism: An Abundant Inventory of Existing Tools," *Chicago Journal of International Law* 5, no. 2 (2005), p. 499; Richard B. Zabel and James J. Benjamin Jr., *In Pursuit of Justice: Prosecuting Terrorism Cases in Federal Court* (New York: Human Rights First, May 2008) (www.humanrightsfirst.info/pdf/080521-USLS-pursuit-justice.pdf). According to a 2008 statement by the Constitution Project, administrative detention proposals "neglect basic and fundamental principles of American constitutional law, and they assume incorrectly that the traditional processes have proven ineffective." Steven I. Vladeck, *A Critique of "National Security Courts"* (Washington: Constitution Project, June 2008) (www.constitutionproject.org/pdf/Critique_of_the_National_Security_Courts1.pdf).

5. Matthew Waxman, "The Smart Way to Shut Gitmo Down," *Washington Post*, October 29, 2007, opinion section.

6. See Jenny S. Martinez, "Process and Substance in the 'War on Terror,'" *Columbia Law Review* 108 (2008), p. 1013, detailing how most court decisions in cases challenging

Bush administration counterterrorism detention policies have not directly addressed substantive rights but instead have focused on procedural rights.

7. *Boumediene* v. *Bush,* 128 S. Ct. 2229 (2008).

8. Ibid. at 2269.

9. See John B. Bellinger, "Legal Issues in the War on Terrorism," October 31, 2006 (www.state.gov/s/l/2006/98861.htm).

10. See Respondents' Memorandum Regarding the Government's Detention Authority Relative to Detainees Held at Guantánamo Bay, In re Guantánamo Bay Detainee Litigation, Misc. No. 08-442 (TFH) (D.D.C. March 13, 2009) (www.usdoj.gov/opa/documents/memo-re-det-auth.pdf).

11. Ibid.

12. See Matthew C. Waxman, "Detention as Targeting: Standards of Certainty and Detention of Suspected Terrorists," *Columbia Law Review* 108 (2008), hereafter Waxman, "Detention as Targeting."

13. See, for example, Lawyers Committee for Human Rights, *Imbalance of Powers: How Changes to U.S. Law and Policy since 9/11 Erode Human Rights and Civil Liberties* (Washington: Human Rights First, 2003), pp. 7–69 (www.humanrightsfirst.org/us_law/loss/imbalance/powers.pdf).

14. For an example of one of the few thorough judicial treatments of this issue, see *Al-Marri* v. *Pucciarelli,* No. 06-7427, slip op. at 25 (4th Cir. *en banc,* July 15, 2008), Motz, J., concurring in the judgment, interpreting Supreme Court precedent as supporting the conclusion that "enemy combatant status rests on an individual's affiliation during wartime with the 'military arm of the enemy government.'" On March 6, 2009, the Supreme Court vacated the Fourth Circuit's judgment in *Al-Marri* and remanded the case with instructions that it be dismissed as moot.

15. David Cole and Jules Lobel, *Less Free, Less Safe* (New York: New Press, 2008), pp. 251–52; ABA Standing Committee on Law and National Security, *Due Process and Terrorism* (Chicago: McCormick Tribune Foundation, November 2007) (www.mccormicktribune.org/publications/dueprocess.pdf).

16. Goldsmith and Katyal, *supra*; McCarthy and Velshi, *supra*; Guiora, *supra*.

17. Philip B. Heymann and Juliette N. Kayyem, *Protecting Liberty in an Age of Terror* (Cambridge: Belfer Center for Science and International Affairs, John F. Kennedy School of Government, Harvard University, 2005), pp. 18, 51–52.

18. See, for example, Alberto J. Mora and Thomas R. Pickering, "Extend Legal Rights to Guantánamo," *Washington Post,* March 4, 2007, p. B07; Senator Patrick Leahy, "On Amendment 2022, the Habeas Corpus Restoration Act of 2007," speech, U.S. Senate, Washington, September 19, 2007 (http://leahy.senate.gov/press/200709/091907.html).

19. Guiora, *supra,* at 15.

20. Goldsmith and Katyal, *supra*; McCarthy and Velshi, *supra,* at 36.

21. Goldsmith and Katyal, *supra*.

22. Andrew McBride, "We'll Rue Having Judges on the Battlefield," *Wall Street Journal*, June 21, 2008; Michael B. Mukasey, "Jose Padilla Makes Bad Law," *Wall Street Journal*, August 22, 2007.

23. See, for example, Richard A. Posner, *Not a Suicide Pact: The Constitution in a Time of National Emergency* (New York: Oxford University Press, 2006), pp. 64–65.

24. See Robert Chesney and Jack Goldsmith, "Terrorism and the Convergence of Criminal and Military Detention Models," *Stanford Law Review* 60 (2008), p. 1079.

25. See Zabel and Benjamin, *supra*. The Constitution Project's report condemning administrative detention proposals echoed those findings, concluding that "the United States government should only be permitted to detain an individual suspected of a terrorism offense if it can make a probable cause showing to a judge and it intends to prosecute that individual, or if appropriate, as part of immigration removal proceedings." Constitution Project, *supra*, at 6.

26. See Wittes, *supra*. One limitation of the Human Rights First report is that by using as its data set those cases actually prosecuted by the Justice Department, it may have excluded many of the most difficult cases, since prosecutors presumably brought forward only cases that they were confident that they would win.

27. See Waxman, "Detention as Targeting," *supra*.

28. National Commission on Terrorist Attacks upon the United States, *The 9/11 Commission Report* (Washington: Government Printing Office, 2004), pp. 379–80.

29. See National Security Council, National Strategy for Combating Terrorism (Washington: White House, September 2006), http://www.whitehouse.gov/nsc/nsct/2006.

30. See Posner, *supra*, at 64–65; Ashton B. Carter, John Deutch, and Philip Zelikow, "Catastrophic Terrorism: Tackling the New Danger," *Foreign Affairs* 77, no. 6 (November-December 1998), pp. 80.

31. Michael Mukasey, "A Speech by Attorney General Michael Mukasey," lecture, American Enterprise Institute, Washington, July 21, 2008.

32. "Remarks by the President on National Security," May 21, 2009 (www.white house.gov/the_press_office/Remarks-by-the-President-On-National-Security-5-21-09/).

33. David Johnston, James Risen, and Scott Shane, "Secret U.S. Endorsement of Severe Interrogations," *New York Times,* October 4, 2007; Sheryl Gay Stolberg, "Bush Says Interrogation Methods Aren't Torture," *New York Times,* October 6, 2007.

34. Declaration of Defense Intelligence Agency director Vice Admiral Lowell E. Jacoby at 6, *Padilla* v. *Bush*, No. 02 Civ. 4445 (S.D.N.Y. January 9, 2003). In 2006 President Bush similarly declared, in publicly disclosing the CIA detention and interrogation program, "These are dangerous men with unparalleled knowledge about terrorist networks and their plans for new attacks. . . . The security of our nation and the lives of our citizens depend on our ability to learn what these terrorists know." George W. Bush, "Creation of Military Commissions to Try Suspected Terrorists," speech, White House, Washington, September 6, 2006 (www.whitehouse.gov/news/releases/2006/09/20060906-3.html).

35. The case of the "Lackawanna 6" provides an illustration of how the tension among priorities has played out in practice. Upon discovering a possible al Qaeda sleeper cell outside Buffalo, New York, in 2002, some elements within the United States favored immediate arrest while others favored surveillance. See Robert Chesney, "The Sleeper Scenario: Terrorism-Support Laws and the Demands of Prevention," *Harvard Journal of Legislation* 42, no. 1 (2005), pp. 40–44.

36. See Robert Chesney, chapter 4 in this volume.

37. Although a major debate exists among terrorism experts as to the continuing strength of al Qaeda, even those who consider al Qaeda to be resurgent acknowledge that "informal local terrorist groups are certainly a critical part of the global terrorist network." Bruce Hoffmann, "The Myth of Grass-Roots Terrorism: Why Osama bin Laden Still Matters," *Foreign Affairs* 87, no. 3 (May-June 2008); see also Marc Sageman, *Leaderless Jihad: Terror Networks in the Twenty-First Century* (University of Pennsylvania Press, 2008), arguing that the major terrorist threat to the United States and the West now comes from loose-knit local cells.

38. See *Kansas v. Hendricks,* 521 U.S. 346 (1997).

39. See ibid at pp. 351, 362–63.

40. See *United States v. Salerno,* 481 U.S. 739 (1987).

41. The complex constitutional issues involved are beyond the scope of this chapter, but of course they are highly relevant, and any administrative detention scheme would face intense judicial challenge. Throughout this chapter I cite a number of U.S. federal and state preventive detention laws that have been upheld, though usually on very narrow grounds. In *Zadvydas* v. *Davis* the Supreme Court made clear that indefinite administrative detention of a removable alien would raise constitutional due process concerns—see *Zadvydas* v. *Davis* 533 U.S. 678 (2001)—although it noted that a statutory scheme directed at suspected terrorists might change its analysis; see ibid., at 691. For views skeptical of the constitutionality of preventive detention laws related to terrorism, see Justice Scalia's dissent in *Hamdi* v. *Rumsfeld* 542 U.S. at 554–557 (2004).

42. Ch. 2, Sec. 1, Para. 9. The U.K. statute is available at www.opsi.gov.uk/acts/acts2005/ukpga_20050002_en_1.

43. Emergency Powers Law (Detention), 1979.

44. Incarceration of Unlawful Combatants Law, 5762-2002 (2002). See *Anonymous* v. *State of Israel,* Cr. App. 6659/06 [Supreme Court, Israel] (June 11, 2008). The law passed in 2002 following the Israeli Supreme Court's concerns over detention of family members of Hezbollah fighters as bargaining chips.

45. The 2001 USA Patriot Act contains provisions authorizing the *short-term* detention of aliens on grounds similar to those discussed in the previous examples. It authorizes the attorney general to detain, among others, any alien who he has reason to believe is "likely to engage after entry in any terrorist activity," has "incited terrorist activity," is a "representative" or "member" of a terrorist organization, or "has received military-type training" from a terrorist organization. USA Patriot Act, § 412(a), 8 U.S.C.A. § 1182(a)(3)(A)-(B). Those provisions, which have never seen use,

also authorize the attorney general to detain aliens who are "engaged in any other activity that endangers the national security of the United States."

46. In *Ludecke v. Watkins,* 335 U.S. 160 (1948), the Supreme Court upheld the act's World War II implementation through a presidential directive calling for detention and removal of all alien enemies "who shall be deemed by the Attorney General to be dangerous to the public pea[c]e and safety of the United States."

47. Similarly, as mentioned, Israel's Unlawful Enemy Combatant statute requires a showing of both membership in an enemy organization as well as individual dangerousness. In upholding the statute, the Israeli Supreme Court explained its incapacitation logic: "[W]e are dealing with an administrative detention whose purpose is to . . . remov[e] from the cycle of hostilities anyone who is a member of a terrorist organization . . . in view of the threat that he represents to the security of the state and the lives of its inhabitants." *Anonymous* v. *State of Israel,* Cr. App. 6659/06 [Supreme Court, Israel] (June 11, 2008), at para. 15.

48. Prevention of Terrorism Act, Ch. 2, Sec. 2, Para. 1 (2005).

49. National Security with Justice Act, S.1876, July 25, 2007 (http://thomas.loc. gov/cgi-bin/bdquery/z?d110:s.01876:).

50. Human Rights Watch has criticized France's use of broad criminal liability for acts supporting terrorism and its use of extensive investigatory powers to disrupt terrorist plotting by casting very wide arrest nets. See *Preempting Justice: Counterterrorism Laws and Procedures in France* (New York: Human Rights Watch, July 2008) (www. hrw.org/en/reports/2008/07/01/preempting-justice), pp. 22–27.

51. An example of a similar law is the Material Witness statute, 18 U.S.C. § 3144, which under certain imperative circumstances allows arrest of an individual with information critical to a criminal proceeding. For critical accounts of its use after 9/11, see Cole and Lobel, *supra,* at 250; *Witness to Abuse: Human Rights Abuses under the Material Witness Law since September 11* (New York: Human Rights Watch, June 2005) (www.hrw.org/en/reports/2005/06/26/witness-abuse).

52. For example, Michael Ratner, president of the Center for Constitutional Rights, writes that "[p]reventive detention cuts the heart out of any concept of human liberty." "Letter to the Editor," *New York Times,* July 16, 2007, opinion section.

53. See Cole and Lobel, *supra,* at 49. Human Rights Watch has expressed similar concern that France's criminal laws against "criminal associating in relation to a terrorist undertaking" have been used to net large numbers of people who pose little threat and with little evidence against them. See *Preempting Justice, supra,* at 1.

54. See David Bonner, *Executive Measures: Terrorism and National Security* (Ashgate Publishing, 2007), pp. 87–96; Tom Parker, "Appendix A: Counterterrorism Policies in the United Kingdom," in *Protecting Liberty in an Age of Terror,* edited by Philip B. Heymann and Juliette N. Kayyem (MIT Press, 2005), pp. 125–28.

55. See Carlotta Gall, "U.S.-Afghan Foray Reveals Friction on Anti-Rebel Raids," *New York Times,* July 3, 2006; Alissa Rubin, "U.S. Remakes Jails in Iraq, but Gains Are at Risk," *New York Times,* June 2, 2008. The new U.S. military counterinsurgency

manual offers similar cautions. See Department of the Army, FM 3-24 Counterinsurgency (Washington: Department of the Army, December 2006), paras. 7-38, 7-40, 8-42.

56. See, for example, Bruce Ackerman, *Before the Next Attack: Preserving Civil Liberties in an Age of Terrorism* (Yale University Press, 2006), pp. 44–51; Jack L. Goldsmith, *The Terror Presidency: Law and Judgment Inside the Bush Administration* (New York: W.W. Norton and Company, 2007), pp. 116, 189–90.

57. See, for example, Audrey Kurth Cronin, "How al-Qaeda Ends: The Decline and Demise of Terrorist Groups," *International Security* 31, no. 1 (Summer 2006), pp. 7; David Kilcullen, "Countering Global Insurgency," *Journal of Strategic Studies* 28, no. 4 (August 2005), p. 597.

58. Also, in upholding Israel's Unlawful Enemy Combatant statute, the Israeli Supreme Court noted that deterring others from committing acts is not a legitimate purpose of administrative detention. *Anonymous* v. *State of Israel,* Cr. App. 6659/06 [Supreme Court, Israel] (June 11, 2008), at para. 18.

59. Opponents of administrative detention will argue that outside of criminal prosecution, detention, even when based on activities or threat, is still too broad and prone to abuse. See Cole and Lobel, *supra,* at 47–50.

60. Cf. *Hamdi* v. *Rumsfeld,* 542 U.S., at 521, noting that, with respect to Congress's 2001 Authorization for Use of Military Force, "[c]ertainly we agree that indefinite detention for the purpose of interrogation is not authorized."

61. An additional worry among administrative detention critics is that building a detention system outside the criminal justice system with reduced evidentiary and procedural requirements might dramatically undercut the incentive for the government to use prosecution. That concern is valid, though the benefits of justice and finality as well as bureaucratic interests might mitigate it. An administrative detention regime might also build in a requirement that the government show that prosecution is impracticable.

62. On releases from Guantánamo following later determination that an individual was not an "enemy combatant," see Gordon England, "Secretary of the Navy England Briefing on Combatant Status Review Tribunal," Washington, July 9, 2004 (www.defenselink.mil/transcripts/transcript.aspx?transcriptid=2777). For a specific example of an allegedly mistaken detention at Guantánamo, see Carol D. Leonnig, "Evidence of Innocence Rejected at Guantánamo," *Washington Post,* December 5, 2007, p. A01. On detainees released from Guantánamo who later returned to terrorism, see "Former Guantánamo Detainees Who Have Returned to the Fight," U.S. Department of Defense, July 12, 2007.

63. Besides these definitional standards themselves, there are other ways to restrict the class of individuals susceptible to new administrative laws. Detention of an individual might require an additional showing of prior terrorism-related acts, or it might require showing that less coercive means than detention could not alleviate the risk. The more such protections are added, however, the less useful administrative detention becomes compared with other legal tools like criminal prosecution.

64. See *Boumediene* v. *Bush,* 128 S.Ct. 2229 (2008).

65. See Jay Sterling Silver, "Equality of Arms and the Adversarial Process: A New Constitutional Right," *Wisconsin Law Review* (1990), p. 1008: "our system of justice is founded on the presumption that the truth is more likely to emerge from the contest between zealous advocates." This argument formed the basis of opposition to some provisions in the Detainee Treatment Act of 2005, Pub. L. No. 109-148, Title X, § 1005(e), 119 Stat. 2680, 2741-43 (2005), codified as amended at 28 U.S.C.A. § 2241(2) (West Supp. 2008), restricting habeas corpus jurisdiction at Guantánamo. See, for example, P. Sabin Willett, "Detainees Deserve Court Trials," *Washington Post,* November 14, 2005, p. A21. But others observe that adversarial process may sometimes suppress truth finding. See, for example, Marvin E. Frankel, "The Search for Truth: An Umpireal View," *University of Pennsylvania Law Review* 123 (1975), pp. 1031, 1036: "many of the rules and devices of adversary litigation as we conduct it are not geared for, but are often aptly suited to defeat, the development of the truth."

66. Procedural due process cases are illustrative here. Compare, for example, *Goldberg* v. *Kelly,* 397 U.S. 254 (1970), requiring evidentiary hearings in situations in which the veracity and credibility of claimants is key, with *Parham* v. *J.R.,* 442 U.S. 584 (1979), refusing to require judicial-style hearings for certain juvenile civil commitments because they were unlikely to improve on the practice of relying on medical expert submissions.

67. Cf. *Salerno* v. *United States,* 481 U.S. 739, 751 (1987), noting that right to counsel and adversarial process mandated in the Bail Reform Act were "specifically designed to further the accuracy of [the] determination [of the likelihood of future dangerousness]."

68. *A* v. *Sec'y of State for the Home Dep't* [2005] 2 A.C. 68, 102-111 (H.L.).

69. See Goldsmith and Katyal, *supra*; Kenneth Anderson, "Law and Terror," *Policy Review,* Oct. 2006, p. 1.

70. Jeremy Shapiro and Benedicte Suzan, "The French Experience of Counter-Terrorism," *Survival* 45 (March 2003), p. 78 (www.brookings.edu/views/articles/fellows/shapiro20030301.pdf). The Constitution Project takes issue with this view in arguing against national security courts: "unlike [with] tax and patent law, there is simply no highly specialized expertise that would form relevant selection criteria for the judges." Vladeck, *A Critique of National Security Courts,* p. 3 (www.constitutionproject.org/pdf/Critique_of_the_National_Security_Courts.pdf)

71. See, for example, Goldsmith and Katyal, *supra.*

72. Israel's Unlawful Enemy Combatant Statute, discussed at *supra* note 97 and accompanying text, requires reexamination every six months of the need for continued detention. See Incarceration of Unlawful Combatants Law, 5762-2002 www.justice.gov.il/NR/rdonlyres/7E86D098-0463-4F37-A38D-8AEBE770BDE6/0/Incarceration Lawedited140302.doc).

73. See Goldsmith and Katyal, *supra*; see also Waxman, "Detention as Targeting."

74. The Spanish government, for example, uses criminal investigatory detention powers—sometimes for very brief periods—in similar ways. See Victoria Burnett,

"After Raids, 14 Held in Spain on Suspicion of a Terror Plot," *New York Times,* January 21, 2008, p. A3. See also Human Rights Watch, *supra* note 50 at § VI (www.hrw.org/en/node/62151/section/7), detailing France's use of broad arrest powers to disrupt terrorist plotting.

75. But see Declaration of Vice Admiral Lowell E. Jacoby, *supra,* explaining that intelligence collection through interrogation may take months or years to bear fruit in some cases, especially when the suspect is trained to resist interrogation.

76. On the strategic benefits of transparency in detention decisionmaking, see Waxman, "Detention as Targeting."

77. See Anna Oehmichen, "Incommunicado Detention in Germany: An Example of Reactive Anti-Terror Legislation and Long-Term Consequences," *German Law Review* 9 (2008), p. 855 (www.germanlawjournal.com/pdf/Vol09No07/PDF_Vol_09_No_07_855-888_Articles_Oehmichen.pdf). These laws, Oehmichen goes on to explain, have come under significant scrutiny and legal challenge.

78. See "Speech by Attorney General Michael Mukasey," *supra,* emphasizing the risks of disclosing sensitive intelligence through processes to challenge detention.

79. For a view critical of secrecy in such contexts, see Stephen J. Schulhofer, *The Enemy Within: Intelligence Gathering, Law Enforcement, and Civil Liberties in the Wake of September 11* (Century Foundation Press, 2002), pp. 12–14.

80. See 50 U.S.C.A. § 1803 (West 2003 & Supp. 2008). Generally speaking, the FISC, established by the Foreign Intelligence Surveillance Act of 1978 (FISA), Pub. L. No. 95-511, 92 Stat. 1783, oversees requests for surveillance warrants against suspected foreign intelligence agents and terrorists inside the United States.

JACK GOLDSMITH

3

Long-Term Terrorist Detention and a U.S. National Security Court

For years there has been a debate about whether to create a national security court to supervise the noncriminal military detention of dangerous terrorists. The debate has many dimensions, and it often is confusing. Some opponents of a national security court are really opposed to the noncriminal military detention system that such a court would supervise; they insist that terrorists be tried in criminal court or released. Other opponents of a national security court accept the need for noncriminal military detention but do not favor institutionalizing a new, "secret" court to oversee detentions. Proponents of a national security court come in many stripes as well. They advocate different versions of the court, to which they assign different tasks, ranging from various forms of detention supervision to the conduct of criminal trials.

This chapter attempts to simplify the issues, at least a bit. It argues that the national security court debate—a debate in which I have participated[1]—is largely a canard. The fundamental issue is whether the United States should have a system of noncriminal military detention for enemy terrorists who, for many reasons, are difficult to convict in a criminal trial. If the Obama administration chooses to maintain a system of noncriminal military detention—and for reasons set forth below, I think that it should—it will also necessarily choose to have a national security court. That is because the federal courts that would constitute a "national security court" must supervise noncriminal detention under the constitutional writ of habeas corpus and a likely statutory jurisdiction conferred by Congress. Viewed that way, the United States has had

I thank Will Levi, Hagan Scotten, J. B. Tarter, and J. B. Ward for excellent research assistance and Robert Chesney and Benjamin Wittes for very helpful comments and for past collaborations on related topics.

a centralized and thinly institutionalized national security court for years in the federal courts of the District of Columbia, which have been supervising military detentions at Guantánamo Bay. The hard question about a national security court, once the need for noncriminal military detention is accepted, is not whether it should exist. The hard question concerns what its rules should be and, just as important, who should make those rules. In my view, Congress and the president, rather than the courts, must play the predominant role in crafting the rules. After explaining these points, I outline some of the issues and legal policy trade-offs that the political branches should address in doing so, including whether such a court should be an independent institution akin to the Foreign Intelligence Surveillance Court and whether it should conduct criminal trials in addition to supervising detention.

The Necessity and Legality of Long-Term Detention

The principle that a nation at war has the power to hold members of the enemy's armed forces until the cessation of hostilities is as old as warfare itself and should be uncontroversial.[2] The purpose of military detention, former Justice Sandra Day O'Connor explained in 2004, "is to prevent captured individuals from returning to the field of battle and taking up arms once again."[3] As the Nuremberg Tribunal noted, the capture and detention of enemy soldiers is "neither revenge, nor punishment, but solely protective custody, the only purpose of which is to prevent the prisoners of war from further participation in the war."[4] Military detention of enemy soldiers is the military equivalent of the long-standing practice of noncriminal administrative or preventive detention of dangerous persons such as the mentally ill, those infected with contagious diseases, or sexual predators.[5]

The wisdom of the rule of detention becomes clear as more is learned about what has happened to some of the Guantánamo detainees who have been released. Although reports about the severity of the problem differ, it is clear that a good number of the detainees released on the grounds that they were "nondangerous" have ended up back on the battlefield, shooting at Americans or non-American civilians abroad.[6] One such person, Said Ali al-Shihri, became the deputy leader of al Qaeda's Yemeni branch and is suspected of involvement in the 2008 bombing of the U.S. embassy in Yemen.[7]

Yet if the detention rule is so clear, why is the use of detention so controversial in the war against al Qaeda and its affiliates? One reason is that many observers believe that the nation is not, or cannot be, at war with nonstate actors. That is simply wrong. The United States has fought congressionally authorized wars against nonstate actors such as slave traders and pirates.[8] During the Mexican-American War, the Civil War, and the Spanish-American War, U.S. military forces engaged military opponents who had no formal connection to the state enemy.[9] Presidents also have used force against nonstate actors outside of congressionally authorized conflicts. President McKinley's use of military force to put down the Chinese Boxer Rebellion was directed primarily at nonstate actors.[10] President Wilson sent more than 7,000 U.S. troops into Mexico to pursue Pancho Villa, the leader of a band of rebels opposed to the recognized Mexican government.[11] And President Clinton authorized cruise missile strikes against al Qaeda targets in Sudan and Afghanistan.[12] In all of those instances, presidents, acting in their role as commander-in-chief, exercised full military powers against nonstate actors— sometimes with congressional authorization and sometimes without.

Consistent with those precedents, every branch of the U.S. government today agrees that the nation is in an "armed conflict" (the modern legal term for "war") with al Qaeda, its affiliates, and other Islamist militants in Afghanistan, Iraq, and elsewhere. Former president Bush took that view in September 2001, and President Obama shows no sign of adopting a different stance. Congress embraced the same view in the September 2001 Authorization for Use of Military Force (AUMF) and reaffirmed it in the Military Commissions Act of 2006 (MCA).[13] And the Supreme Court has stated or assumed that the country is at war many times.[14]

Why, then, has there been so much controversy about holding enemy soldiers in Guantánamo? Part of the reason is the suspicion of abuse of prisoners there. But even if there were no such suspicions, the war on terror has three characteristics that, taken together, make a military detention authority problematic:

—First, in most prior wars, it was easy to determine who was a member of the enemy armed forces because those people wore uniforms and usually fought for a nation-state. In this war, the enemy wears no uniforms and blends in with civilians. That unfortunate fact dramatically increases the possibility of erroneous detention.

—Second, this war, unlike any other in U.S. history, seems likely to continue indefinitely; indeed, no one knows what the end of the war will look like. That means, among other things, that mistaken detentions might result in the long-term or even indefinite detention of an innocent person.

—Third, even if mistakes are not made, indefinite detention without charge or trial strikes many as an excessive remedy for "mere" membership in an enemy terrorist organization, especially since a detainee may, after some period, no longer pose a threat to the United States.

These three concerns do nothing to eliminate the need for detention to prevent detainees from returning to the battlefield, but they do challenge the traditional detention paradigm. And while many observers believe that the country can meet that need by giving trials to everyone that it wants to detain and then incarcerating those individuals under a theory of conviction rather than of military detention, I disagree. For many reasons, it is too risky for the U.S. government to deny itself the traditional military detention power altogether and commit itself instead to trying or releasing *every* suspected terrorist.

For one thing, military detention will be necessary in Iraq and Afghanistan for the foreseeable future. For another, the country likely cannot secure convictions of all of the dangerous terrorists at Guantánamo, much less all future dangerous terrorists, who legitimately qualify for noncriminal military detention. The evidentiary and procedural standards of trials, civilian and military alike, are much higher than the analogous standards for detention. With some terrorists too menacing to set free, the standards will prove difficult to satisfy. Key evidence in a given case may come from overseas, and verifying it, understanding its provenance, or establishing its chain of custody in the manner typically required in criminal trials may be difficult. That problem is exacerbated when evidence is gathered on a battlefield or during an armed skirmish, and it only grows larger when the evidence is old and stale. And perhaps most important, the use of such evidence in a criminal process may compromise intelligence sources and methods, requiring the disclosure of the identities of confidential sources or the nature of intelligence-gathering techniques.

Opponents of noncriminal detention observe that despite these considerations, the government has successfully prosecuted some al Qaeda terrorists—in particular, Zacharias Moussaoui and Jose Padilla. That is true, but it does not follow that prosecutions are achievable in every case in which disabling a terrorist suspect is a surpassing government interest. Moreover, the Moussaoui and Padilla prosecutions highlight an underappreciated cost of trials, at least in civilian courts. Those trials were messy affairs that stretched, and some observers believe broke, ordinary U.S. criminal trial conceptions of conspiracy and the rights of the accused, among other things. The Moussaoui trial, for example, watered down the important constitutional right of the defendant to confront witnesses against him in court, and the Padilla trial rested on an unprecedentedly broad conception of conspiracy law.[15] An important cost of trying all cases is that the prosecution will invariably bend the law in ways that are unfavorable to civil liberties and due process, and those changes, in turn, will invariably spill over into nonterrorist prosecutions, thus skewing the larger criminal justice process.[16]

A final problem with using any trial system, civilian or military, as the sole lawful basis for terrorist detention is that the trials can result in short sentences (as the first military commission trial did) or even acquittal of a dangerous terrorist.[17] In criminal trials, defendants often go free because of legal technicalities, government inability to introduce probative evidence, and other factors besides the defendant's innocence. These factors are all exacerbated in terrorist trials by the difficulty of getting information from the place of capture, by restrictions on access to classified information, and by stale or tainted evidence. One way to get around the problem is to assert the authority, as the Bush administration did, to use noncriminal military detention for persons acquitted or given sentences too short to neutralize the danger that they pose. But such authority would undermine the whole purpose of trials and render them a sham. As a result, putting a suspect on trial can make it hard to detain terrorists that the government deems dangerous. For example, the government would have had little trouble defending the indefinite detention of Salim Hamdan, Osama bin Laden's driver, under a military detention rationale. Having put him on trial before a military commission, however, it was stuck with the light sentence that Hamdan has now completed at home in Yemen.

As a result of these problems, insistence on the exclusive use of criminal trials and the elimination of noncriminal detention would significantly raise the chances of releasing dangerous terrorists who would return to kill Americans or others. Since noncriminal military detention is clearly a legally available option—at least if it is expressly authorized by Congress and includes adequate procedural guarantees—that risk should be unacceptable. In past military conflicts, the release of an enemy soldier posed risks. But they were not dramatic risks, for there was only so much damage a lone actor or small group of individuals could do.[18] Today, however, that lone actor can cause far more destruction and mayhem, because technological advances are creating ever-smaller and ever-deadlier weapons. It would be astounding if the pre–9/11 U.S. legal system had struck the balance between security and liberty in a manner that precisely and adequately addressed the modern threats posed by asymmetric warfare. Today the country faces threats from individuals that are of a different magnitude than the threats posed by individuals in the past; government authorities should reflect that change.

Nonetheless, in supplementing its trial system with a detention system, the United States must design the detention system with careful attention to the three problems with detentions identified above: the possibility of detaining an innocent person, the indefinite duration of the war, and the possibility that terrorists will become less dangerous over time. While those problems do not argue for eliminating military detention, they do not argue for simply abiding by the Geneva Conventions either. A dirty little secret is that the United States already provides the Guantánamo detainees with rights that far exceed the requirements of the Geneva Conventions. That said, it does not offer enough process to overcome the anxieties that the three problems generate. The problems with indefinite detention for modern terrorists argue for a more rigorous process and for higher standards than were available for noncriminal military detention in past wars with nation-states. They argue as well for individualizing both the detention assessment and the determination of which detainees are ready for release. They argue, in short, for updating the traditional military detention model to address the novel problems presented by terrorism and to ensure that it is consistent with modern notions of due process. What the updates should look like is the subject of the remainder of this chapter.

A National Security Court Already Exists

Once one accepts the need for some system of noncriminal military detention, suddenly much less is at stake in the debate over a national security court than the heat generated by that debate would suggest. That is because any system of long-term noncriminal detention of terrorists must and will be supervised by federal judges. At a minimum, federal judges will exercise constitutional habeas corpus jurisdiction over the incarceration of suspected terrorists, thereby having the final legal say over any detention system. In addition, Congress will likely establish statutory federal court review over any detention program that it establishes, as it has already attempted to do once. So one way or another, Article III judges will be in the detention game, helping to regularize, legalize, and legitimize the detention process while reviewing the adequacy of the factual basis for each detention judgment.

In other words, once one accepts that there will be a system of long-term, noncriminal, military detention of alleged terrorists and that federal judges will supervise the process, the debate about a national security court becomes a debate about what form federal judicial supervision should take. Those favoring a national security court prefer a relatively centralized and institutionalized form of federal court supervision. Those disfavoring it prefer relatively decentralized and non-institutionalized federal court supervision.

At one extreme is the wholly decentralized and non-institutionalized system of habeas review that prevailed before the Supreme Court's initial assertion in 2004 of habeas jurisdiction in *Rasul* v. *Bush*.[19] Before then, terrorist suspects at Guantánamo could bring habeas suits in any federal district court in the country in which they could obtain jurisdiction. No special statute governed the substance of or procedure in those cases. Under this regime, the "national security court" consisted of all federal district courts in the country acting with practically no guidance from Congress, subject to appellate review in the courts of appeals and finally in the Supreme Court.

Very few people thought that this system was a good idea, and since the summer of 2004 the de facto "national security court" supervising detention has become centralized and institutionalized in two ways. First, after *Rasul* federal courts spontaneously determined that all habeas cases from Guantánamo should be brought to the federal district court of the District of Columbia, subject to appellate review in the D.C. Circuit Court.[20] Justice Anthony Kennedy confirmed the appropriateness of this judicial centralization of habeas review in 2008 in his opinion in *Boumediene* v. *Bush.*[21] Following *Boumediene,* the federal court of the District of Columbia placed Judge Thomas F. Hogan in charge of coordinating and managing most of the Guantánamo Bay cases; of ruling on procedural issues common to these cases; and of identifying substantive issues that are common to all.[22] The second centralizing and institutionalizing move came from Congress, which in 2006 required all appeals of Combatant Status Review Tribunal decisions to go to the U.S. Court of Appeals for the District of Columbia Circuit, providing minimal statutory guidance on either the substance or procedure for review. (Those appeals became a moot point after *Boumediene,* when the D.C. Circuit stopped hearing them in light of the Court's decision.)

In effect, then, the United States already has a thinly institutionalized "national security court" in the federal courts of the District of Columbia. This national security court possesses—and is further developing—some of the virtues that national security court proponents have long argued for. It is relatively centralized, it contains a limited number of judges under the procedural supervision of a single judge, it has seen many different terrorism detention cases already, and it deals with them much more efficiently than the decentralized system. The court has been developing and will continue to develop specialized expertise in the issues brought before it. It also has been developing and will continue to develop relatively coherent substantive and procedural doctrines and rules to deal with detention cases—coherent, that is, in terms of learning from the run of cases and in treating like cases alike, especially in comparison with a system in which potentially every district judge and circuit court in the country is involved.

The main problem with the national security court as it now exists is that it is almost entirely a creature of the federal courts. With respect to judicial supervision of terrorist detainees, Congress has done little more than authorize the use of force against al Qaeda and its affiliates in September 2001 and provide for undefined judicial review of Combatant Status Review Tribunal decisions in 2006, a power of review whose existence is now entirely redundant given the habeas jurisdiction being exercised by the courts and that has lapsed as a consequence. Every other question about the current national security court—involving novel issues of institutional design as well as the substantive and procedural rights of terrorist detainees—are being answered by the courts on an ad hoc basis with little guidance from precedent and even less guidance from Congress.

The real question about the national security court, therefore, is not whether the nation will have one but whether it will be designed by judges or by the political branches. The answer to that question must be the political branches. Judges should find facts and enforce basic constitutional, statutory, and treaty norms, but they should not design the national security court system from scratch and should not write the details of the law for that system. For one thing, no single branch of government should determine the entire content of the law and then apply the law, least of all the judicial branch in the area of national security and terrorism. Every single decision about the national security court will affect both the nation's security and the liberty of those in the government's custody. Any rule has the potential to push the country in the direction of excessive security or excessive liberty, with many costs in both directions. Courts lack expertise about the nature and goals of terrorism and the optimal policy responses to terrorist threats needed to make these trade-offs.[23] And they lack accountability to the people if they get it wrong, either way.

Justice O'Connor summed up those points well in a 2005 speech at West Point, responding to the criticism that the Supreme Court had done too little in making its war-on-terrorism decisions:

> The Court is only one branch of government, and it cannot, and should not, give broad answers to the difficult [war-on-terror] policy questions that face our nation today. . . . We guard the ground rules, so that the people, through their elected representatives, can run the country. . . . I think it is not too much to say that I believe some clarity from Congress and the President would be welcomed by our armed forces.[24]

Unfortunately, Justice O'Connor's words remain as relevant and true today as when she spoke them.

How to Improve the National Security Court

The United States already has a national security court, but Congress must—if it wishes to maintain noncriminal military detention generally—get involved to provide the court with the rules and institutional structures that it needs to improve its organization and ensure greater legitimacy and effectiveness for the long haul. Sensible legislation would address the following distinct issues.

Citizenship

The first and most important challenge for Congress is to define the universe of people subject to detention. I will discuss that issue presently, but whatever the definition that Congress adopts, the definition should extend to U.S citizens as well as to aliens. Detention policy to date has drawn sharp distinctions between the treatment of U.S. citizens and the treatment of aliens. That distinction should be eliminated, for two reasons.

The first was captured by Justice Robert Jackson, who wrote that "there is no more effective practical guaranty against arbitrary and unreasonable government than to require that the principles of law which officials would impose upon a minority must be imposed generally."[25] Designing detention procedures that are appropriate and legitimate in detaining dangerous U.S. citizen terrorists will ensure—and will credibly demonstrate to both domestic courts and the world in general—that the unusual detentions and the unusual procedures associated with them are legitimate and fair.

Second, there is no reason to think that the threat of terrorism is limited to noncitizens. Intelligence officials have made clear that al Qaeda and its associates are trying to recruit Westerners, including U.S. citizens, for attacks within the United States.[26] And as former attorney general Alberto Gonzales warned, "the threat of homegrown terrorist cells . . . may be as dangerous as groups like al Qaeda, if not more so."[27] The law cannot presume that the next attacker will be an alien. The system must be designed not just for the last attack, but for likely future attacks as well.

Definition of the Enemy

I turn now to the hardest question in detention policy: the definition of the enemy that will determine the universe of people subject to detention. The standard articulated by the Bush administration, based on the Authorization for Use of Military Force, is too vague and malleable. It extends the government's detention power to include an individual who was part of or supporting Taliban or Al Qaida forces, or associated forces that are engaged in hostilities against the United States or its coalition partners. This includes any person who has committed a belligerent act or has directly supported hostilities in aid of enemy armed forces.[28]

In its early court filings, the Obama administration adjusted this standard only trivially, restricting it to someone who was "part of, or *substantially* supported [emphasis added]" Taliban, al Qaeda, or associated forces.[29] The problem is that the phrase "associated forces" is indeterminate, and without further elaboration—perhaps by reference to a concept of co-belligerency[30]—it might justify sweeping up persons who lack the dangerousness that would warrant indefinite noncriminal detention. The phrase "directly supported" also is potentially quite broad.

But crafting a narrower standard that ensures detention of very dangerous terrorists is tricky. The main problem is that the group of people dangerous enough for the government reasonably to want to detain does not fit within traditional criteria for enemy combatancy. They do not fit because the terrorists blend in with civilians and do not organize themselves into traditional hierarchical commands and because the threat of terrorism is increasingly dispersed into decentralized copycat cells.

Two definitions promise more discipline than the current enemy combatant definition: terrorists who are in the command structure of al Qaeda and its co-belligerent terrorist organizations; and terrorists who directly participate in armed conflict against the United States.

Membership in the Command Structure of a Covered Terrorist Organization

Terrorist organizations have leadership and command structures, however diffuse, and persons who receive and execute orders within the command structure of an enemy terrorist group are analogous to traditional combatants. The most promising and least controversial detention criterion, therefore, is *membership in the command structure of al Qaeda and its co-belligerent terrorist organizations.*[31] This criterion would include the leadership of al Qaeda (people such as Osama bin Laden and Khalid Sheik Mohammad), subordinate al Qaeda personnel who occupy an operational role (such as Mohammed Atta), and people like Ali Saleh Kahlah al-Marri, an alleged al Qaeda operative who, in Judge Wilkinson's formulation, "knowingly plans or engages in conduct that harms or aims to harm persons or property for the purpose of further-ing the military goals of an enemy nation or organization."[32]

The command structure criterion is consistent with Congress's authoriza-tion to the president for the use of force "against those . . . organizations" responsible for "the terrorist attacks that occurred on September 11, 2001," a descriptor that expressly includes members of al Qaeda and under traditional principles of co-belligerency includes al Qaeda's affiliated terrorist organiza-tions.[33] Independent of the Authorization for Use of Military Force, the com-mand structure criterion is consistent with the traditional understanding of detention in non-international armed conflicts, which the Supreme Court has deemed the conflict with al Qaeda to be.[34] And the command structure criterion makes intuitive sense. If there is a group of people who are highly likely to be dangerous to the United States, it is the group formed by those who voluntarily associate themselves with the command structure of a terrorist organization whose aim is to kill Americans.

Direct Participation in Hostilities

The command structure criterion is useful as far as it goes. But it leaves out two important classes of terrorists that Congress might want to include. The first consists of those who fall outside the al Qaeda and co-belligerent chain of command but who nonetheless associate with terrorist organizations in ways that indicate individual dangerousness or that promote terrorists' dan-gerous goals. For example, individuals outside of the al Qaeda command structure might receive weapons training in an al Qaeda camp, give logistical support related to a particular act of violence (for example, by creating an improvised explosive device to be used by someone else), or provide more generalized logistical support (for example, by raising funds to be used for vio-lent activity). The second class consists of members of terrorist organizations inspired by al Qaeda or its jihadist principles but that are not al Qaeda co-belligerents. In other words, they do not act as agents of al Qaeda, participate with al Qaeda in acts of war against the United States, systematically provide military resources to al Qaeda, serve as fundamental communication links in the war against the United States, or systematically permit their buildings and safe houses to be used by al Qaeda in the war against the United States.

Congress could address the second class of terrorists simply by adding their organization to the list of organizations against which the United States is at war, but such organizations are so diffuse and can morph so quickly into other forms that adding them is not a stable solution. In any event, that solution does not address the problem of the first class of terrorists, who provide logistical and other non-operational support for covered terrorist organizations but who are not in the command structure. If Congress chooses to detain either class of terrorists, a status-based detention criterion like "membership in command structure" will not do. Congress will need to craft a conduct-based criterion that gets at the class of dangerous terrorists not already included in the "membership" test but that is not over-inclusive.

The best candidate for such a conduct-based criterion—best in terms of both its legal pedigree and its intuitive appeal—is the "direct participation in hostilities" standard.[35] This standard originated as a rule identifying circumstances in which a civilian—ordinarily immune from being made the object of an attack—may be targeted with lethal force.[36] But it has evolved into a more general test to distinguish those against whom military force (including detention) can be used legitimately from those against whom it cannot. The idea of detaining those who "directly participate" in hostilities captures many people's intuition about the class of terrorists who should be detained. Unfortunately, however, "direct participation" is contested in application in at least two ways.[37] First, experts disagree concerning the substance of direct participation itself. Everyone agrees that the concept applies to persons who literally engage in violence, such as by firing a rifle or setting off an explosive. But uncertainty arises as the concept moves beyond those paradigm cases to persons whose connections to violence are less direct. Does one directly participate in hostilities by ferrying ammunition to persons who are firing weapons or by constructing improvised explosive devices to be used by others? Second, experts also disagree with respect to the temporal boundaries of direct participation. When can a person be said to have ceased being a direct participant in hostilities?[38] Some have expressed concern about a revolving-door interpretation that enables civilians to contribute to violence but then immediately reacquire their protected status before facing any military consequences.[39]

There is little clear legal guidance in the laws of war—and even less clear state practice—to help Congress and the president resolve these issues and decide how to define the contours of "direct participation" as a detention criterion in a war against nonstate actors. Simply embracing the direct participation standard without more operational guidance would leave too much discretion to courts, which might interpret or apply the standard in radically over-inclusive or under-inclusive ways. In the final analysis, the proper calibration of the direct participation standard turns on how much and what kind of risk—to security and to liberty—the nation's leaders want to assume. The direct participation test provides a legitimate legal hook and general guidance, but the political branches must make the tough call about where and how to draw the line. Their choice will also, of course, be informed by the procedural safeguards associated with each substantive determination. Tighter safeguards may warrant broader detention criteria, and vice versa.

Procedural Issues

Courts have been developing procedural rules for the review of terrorist detentions on their own under the guise of some combination of due process and pragmatic justice. The following are the most important procedural questions that Congress should address:

EVIDENTIARY AND INFORMATIONAL ISSUES

There are a variety of different approaches to deciding what evidence the national security court should consider in reviewing terrorist detentions. The best approach is hard to state in the abstract—the devil is in the details. But it is clear that some deviation from ordinary criminal trial rules is necessary, especially so in four areas.

First, it will be necessary to permit introduction of hearsay and related evidence. The best approach here would be to follow the rule in international criminal courts, which have permitted evidence so long as it is relevant and "necessary for the determination of the truth."[40] The International Criminal Tribunal for the Former Yugoslavia, for example, permits the admission of hearsay and related evidence that "is relevant and has probative value, focusing on its reliability."[41]

Second, a decision will need to be made about evidence that is tainted because it was extracted in illegal or morally problematic ways. Here again international criminal tribunals might provide guidance. The International Criminal Court, for example, permits the introduction of evidence "obtained by means of a violation of this Statute or internationally recognized human rights" unless "(a) The violation casts substantial doubt on the reliability of the evidence; or (b) The admission of the evidence would be antithetical to and would seriously damage the integrity of the proceedings."[42]

Third is the question of classified information—in particular the question of whether the government should be able to establish the factual predicate for detention by presenting evidence on an ex parte basis. The ex parte approach serves the compelling government interest in preserving the secrecy of sensitive intelligence information, but it seems illegitimate to detain someone without letting him or at least his representative know about and contest the evidence. If Congress provides counsel to a detainee (as I suggest it should below), it can mediate these conflicting principles by allowing the counsel to remain during presentation of classified evidence.

The fourth and final issue concerns the government's disclosure obligations. The issue has both a substantive component (which agencies have an obligation to disclose information and what should the nature of that obligation be?) and a procedural component (who should have responsibility for enforcing disclosure obligations and what mechanism should there be, if any, for seeking to compel disclosure when necessary?). It is possible that, as with classified information, creative approaches to the use of counsel may help to finesse the tensions inherent in this issue. At a substantive minimum, however, the government should have a duty to disclose all exculpatory information and perhaps all material information reasonably within its possession.[43]

PUBLICITY

The national security court should operate with the strong presumption that its processes and decisions will receive maximum public disclosure. Particularly with a novel procedure, public knowledge of how the system operates in practice will be essential to building both domestic and international credibility. The system will need to close its proceedings when considering classified material, just as Article III courts and courts martial do. But the default option should be openness, and the government should face a burden of proof if it wishes to change that option in a given case.

REGULARIZED REVIEW

One could argue that there should be no outside limit on the time available for detention orders. England limits noncriminal detention to twenty-eight days,[44] and France limits it to six days unless someone is charged with a crime, but those limited detention periods assume that war powers are not in effect.[45] Moreover, if someone poses a very serious threat to the United States and cannot practically be tried, a single period of detention is unlikely to mitigate the threat. So there exists a legitimate need for a long-term period of detention.

At the same time, Congress should not countenance indefinite detention lightly, especially under some of the looser standards articulated above. The appropriate compromise is to limit a detention order to some period of time, say six months, subject to extension using the same processes governing the initial order. In each instance, the government will have to convince the national security court that the individual remains a threat and satisfies other detention criteria. The fact that the government will have to come back to court repeatedly to justify a detention decision will also act as a natural constraint on the expansion of preventative detention. Many government officials will dislike the continued need to justify detention and where possible will favor prosecution instead.

At some point, moreover, the periods of semiannual detention may come to look more like punishment than does detention based on dangerousness. As detention continues for years, it may be appropriate to put an escalating burden of proof on the government—perhaps from a "preponderance of the evidence" standard to something more akin to "clear and convincing evidence" or "beyond a reasonable doubt." As an alternative, it may be appropriate to insist on specialized procedures that are triggered when an individual is detained for more than a certain number of years.

Lawyers

The government should be represented in the national security court by lawyers in the Justice Department. Potential detainees should be represented by a standing pool of government-paid defense lawyers. The defense lawyers would possess security clearances, thus avoiding the problem of not providing lawyers to detainees for years. Detainees could supplement their representation by government attorneys with counsel of their own choice as long as the lawyers that they choose receive appropriate security clearances. (In chapter 5, Robert Litt and Wells Bennett propose a similar arrangement for criminal proceedings in federal court.)

Greater Institutionalization

Perhaps the most controversial issue about a national security court is whether and how it should become more institutionalized. I used to believe that this issue was more important than I now believe it to be. Once one realizes that the federal courts of the District of Columbia are a de facto national security court for detention review and that Congress can build on this court structure as it deems appropriate, the institutionalization questions become somewhat less salient. Nonetheless, three issues still dominate the debate.

Should the National Security Court Be a Stand-Alone Institution?

The national security court could continue to be staffed by the federal judges of the District of Columbia, but it could also become a new, stand-alone institution modeled on the Foreign Intelligence Surveillance Court. The arguments for such an institution are diminished by the fact that a national security court already is in operation and that Congress can simply amplify or tweak the current system. Possible benefits of a stand-alone institution are, first, that the judges of the national security court could be drawn from the hundreds of existing judges around the country rather than from the relatively homogenous federal district court in the District of Columbia; second, that such a court, having special and discrete jurisdiction, could more readily receive novel and specialized evidentiary, procedural, and classified information rules; and third, that such a court would minimize the problem of precedential spillover into the civilian justice system.

If Congress were to create such a stand-alone institution, it should not simply expand the current Foreign Intelligence Surveillance Court's jurisdiction to cover detention. The Foreign Intelligence Surveillance Act (FISA) established a court to operate in secret. By contrast, many of the issues that a national security court would deal with could appropriately be taken up in open court, as the proceedings in the current national security court of the District of Columbia have shown. To bring the FISA court into the open, even in limited settings, might hamper the work and safety of FISA jurists. And because FISA's strong default mode is to operate in secrecy, vesting that court with jurisdiction over detentions may lead to greater secrecy than is optimal in the context of detention. In addition, expanding the FISA court's duties may very well interfere with that court's ability to carry out its current functions.

First-Order Detention Determinations

The current national security court reviews the legality of detentions made by a military Combatant Status Review Tribunal (CSRT), which makes the first-order judgments of the propriety of a given detention. The CSRTs could continue to serve that function, subject to review in the national security court. As an alternative, Congress could transfer the first-order determinations to a nonmilitary or judicial body under the supervision of the national security court or to the federal judges on the national security court itself.

Trials

The national security court might also replace criminal trials by military commission, courts martial, or even ordinary criminal trials in civilian courts. It could serve either as a trial body or as an appellate body or conceivably as both. The argument here is that a national security court might be able to achieve some of the benefits of legitimacy of an Article III criminal trial while at the same time avoiding the costs of such trials. So, for example, Congress might be able to give a national security court somewhat more procedural flexibility in protecting classified information than it can an ordinary civilian criminal court. It might also be able to better protect judges and jurors in such a court. Congress also might be able to limit the court's precedents to ensure that any adjustments to substantive and procedural criminal law—as in *Moussaui* and *Padilla*—do not spill over into the ordinary criminal trial process, under which the government should bear ordinary burdens of proof.[46]

The question of whether the jurisdiction of the new court should expand beyond detention to trials is a large and complicated one that is beyond the scope of this analysis. But at a minimum, Congress must consider the design of a national security court in conjunction with the design of the trial system, for each would have profound effects on the other's effectiveness.[47]

Sunset

Any legislation related to a national security court should include a sunset provision. The United States still lacks information about its enemies and the precise threats that they pose; the nation also possesses relatively little information on how any particular national security court design would work in practice and what effect it would have on liberty and security. Those points suggest that Congress would be wise to revisit the design and operations of the national security court in a few years, after more information becomes available. Forcing Congress to reconsider a legislative scheme typically is difficult and politically costly. The ordinary problems of inertia are exacerbated by the president's veto power, which means that modifying or eliminating a poorly functioning national security court might take a supermajority rather than a simple majority.[48] Even when a majority of Congress's members want to change a law that is already on the books, it can require substantial effort, energy, and political capital to translate that wish into successful legislation. Often such efforts fail.

A good example of how sunset provisions can respond to such structural, political, and human error variables can be found in the experience with the independent counsel law.[49] The institution of independent counsel was unfamiliar to the U.S. constitutional system, and because the policy implications were so severe, Congress decided to impose a sunset. That was a wise decision. It would have been extraordinarily difficult, given the political repercussions, for members of Congress to stand up and say that they were "against independent investigations" and "against ethics in government." Yet the independent counsel law produced a constitutional monster, accountable to no one. Because of the sunset mechanism, no independent counsel law is on the books today. It was simply too difficult, in the wake of the Iran–Contra and the Whitewater–Lewinsky investigations, for members of Congress to stand up and affirmatively persuade their colleagues to vote for reauthorization of the act. But it might have been very difficult to affirmatively abrogate, had the default setting mandated its continued existence.

Similar considerations led to the sunset provision in the USA Patriot Act.[50] President Bush signed the act into law on October 26, 2001.[51] The act included December 31, 2005, sunset provisions for its most expansive and potentially controversial components.[52] Attempts to reauthorize the act began in late 2004, but Congress and the president could not agree on a single version for reauthorization, so Congress twice enacted short extensions of the soon-to-expire provisions.[53] Congress ultimately adopted two pieces of legislation that, together, increased judicial review for surveillance activities, required additional reporting by the executive branch to Congress, enhanced mandatory procedures for employing some of the Patriot Act's more controversial tools, and included further sunsets for two controversial provisions.[54] While the reauthorization made most of the provisions that were scheduled to expire permanent, it only extended the sunset for two provisions, requiring that reauthorization for them be sought again in 2009.

Advocates on both sides of the aisle praised the original Patriot Act's sunset provisions. Senator Patrick Leahy attributed both improved congressional oversight and the opportunity to improve the act to the sunset provisions.[55] Representative Martin Meehan stated that "[f]ortunately, the bill included sunset provisions, allowing Congress to revisit the law, reflect on its implementation, and fix those parts of the law that have clearly become overreaching."[56] Following reauthorization, Viet Dinh—who had authored large sections of the Patriot Act while at the Department of Justice—wrote that "[t]he reauthorization process provided a chance to fine tune, clarify, and improve upon the original provisions of the Act. It also provided an opportunity for debate about what tools law enforcement and intelligence officials need in the war on terror."[57]

Amplifications to the national security court would be appropriate candidates for a legislative sunset. Time will tell whether any such court meets the fate of the Patriot Act (renewal with some changes) or the independent counsel law (complete nonrenewal). But in the interim, the inclusion of a sunset would help forestall government abuse of detention power, because the government would know that the entire system is up for renewal and must therefore operate responsibly and with the possibility of abrogation.

Conclusion

Almost five years ago, the 9/11 Commission stated that "Americans should not settle for incremental, ad hoc adjustments to a system designed generations ago for a world that no longer exists."[58] And yet that is precisely what the country has done since the commission published those words. It is time for the president and Congress to work together to address the terrorist detention problem in a comprehensive way. If a detention system becomes part of the solution, as I believe it should, then a national security court will be part of the solution as well. It is far better to have a well-designed national security court—a court designed in a systematic way by political leaders—than to have courts making ad hoc decisions in the rough-and-tumble of high-stakes litigation.

Notes

1. See Jack Goldsmith and Neal Katyal, "The Terrorists' Court," *New York Times*, July 11, 2007, opinion section.

2. See, for example, Geneva Convention (III) Relative to the Treatment of Prisoners of War, August 12, 1949 [1955], 6 U.S.T. 3316, 3406, T.I.A.S. No. 3364, 75 U.N.T.S. 135, art. 118, stating that "[p]risoners of war shall be released and repatriated without delay after the cessation of active hostilities"; Hague Convention (II) with Respect to the Laws and Customs of War on Land, July 29, 1899, 32 Stat. 1803, art. 20 (www.icrc.org/ihl.nsf/FULL/150?opendocument), as soon as possible after "conclusion of peace."

3. *Hamdi* v. *Rumsfeld*, 542 U.S. 507, 518 (2004), plurality opinion.

4. "International Military Tribunal (Nuremberg), Judgment and Sentences," reprinted in *American Journal of International Law* 41 (1947), pp. 172, 229.

5. For critical treatments, see Paul H. Robinson, "Punishing Dangerousness: Cloaking Preventive Detention as Criminal Justice," *Harvard Law Review* 114 (2001), pp. 1429–32; Carol S. Steiker, "Foreword: The Limits of the Preventive State," *Journal of Criminal Law and Criminology* 88 (1998), pp. 771, 777–81.

6. Geoff Morell, "Department of Defense News Briefing," January 13, 2009 (www.defenselink.mil/transcripts/transcript.aspx?transcriptid=4340); Associated Press, "Report: Guantánamo Detainees Return to Battlefield," *International Herald Tribune*, January 13, 2009 (www.iht.com/articles/ap/2009/01/13/america/NA-US-Guantanamo-Detainees.php).

7. Robert F. Worth, "Freed by the U.S., Saudi Becomes al Qaeda Chief," *New York Times*, January 23, 2009 (www.nytimes.com/2009/01/23/world/middleeast/23yemen.html).

8. Curtis A. Bradley and Jack L. Goldsmith, "Congressional Authorization and the War on Terrorism," *Harvard Law Review* 118 (2005), pp. 2047, 2073–74.

9. See William E. Birkhimer, *Military Government and Martial Law,* 3rd ed., rev. (Kansas City: Franklin Hudson, 1914), pp. 123–24, 354–55; William Winthrop, *Military Law and Precedents,* 2nd ed., rev. (Boston: Little, Brown, and Co., 1896), pp. 783–84; ibid. at 832–34.

10. See, generally, Diana Preston, *Besieged in Peking: The Story of the 1900 Boxer Rising* (London: Constable, 1999), pp. 25–30; Chester C. Tan, *The Boxer Catastrophe* (New York: Columbia University Press, 1955), pp. 35–36.

11. John S.D. Eisenhower, *Intervention! The United States and the Mexican Revolution 1913–1917* (New York: W. W. Norton, 1993), pp. 231–60.

12. See National Commission on Terrorist Attacks upon the United States, *The 9/11 Commission Report* (2004) (www.9-11commission.gov/report/911Report.pdf), p. 117.

13. See Authorization for Use of Military Force, Public Law No. 107-40, 115 Stat. 224 (2001); Military Commission Act of 2006, Pub. L. No. 109-366, 120 Stat. 2600 (codified as amended at 10 U.S.C. § 948a).

14. *Hamdi* v. *Rumsfeld,* 542 U.S. 507, 518 (2004); *Hamdan* v. *Rumsfeld,* 548 U.S. 557, 568 (2006); *Boumediene* v. *Bush,* 128 S.Ct. 2229, 2240-41 (2008).

15. Robert Chesney and Jack Goldsmith, "Terrorism and the Convergence of Criminal and Military Detention Models," *Stanford Law Review* 60 (2008), pp. 1079, 1104–08.

16. See, generally, Charles Weisselberg, "Terror in the Courts: Beginning to Assess the Impact of Terrorism-Related Prosecutions on Domestic Criminal Law and Procedure in the USA," *Crime, Law, and Social Change* 50 (2008), p. 25.

17. This paragraph is drawn from Jack Goldsmith and Benjamin Wittes, "A Blueprint for the Closure of Guantánamo Bay," *Slate,* December 8, 2008 (www.slate.com/id/2206229/).

18. The exception was political assassination, which could produce substantial turmoil. Today, assassination is just one of several modern threats that can be inflicted by small groups of individuals.

19. *Rasul* v. *Bush,* 542 U.S. 466 (2004).

20. After *Padilla* and *Rasul* were decided in summer of 2004, the Supreme Court remanded *Gherebi* (a habeas petition filed in California) to the Ninth Circuit Court, which then cited *Padilla* and *Rasul* en route to concluding that it would be appropriate to transfer that petition to D.C. See *Gherebi* v. *Bush,* 374 F.3d 727, 739 (9th Cir. 2004). The court did not elaborate on why transfer was appropriate except to say that "[i]t appears to us that the proper venue for this proceeding is in the District of Columbia." Ibid. Since then all Guantánamo-related habeas petitions have been transferred to the federal district courts in Washington, D.C.

21. *Boumediene* v. *Bush,* 128 S.Ct. at 2276, concluding that "[i]f, in a future case, a detainee files a habeas petition in another judicial district in which a proper respondent can be served, the Government can move for change of venue to the court that will hear these petitioners' cases, the United States District Court for the District of Columbia." Citations eliminated.

22. See Resolution of the Executive Session of the United States District Court for the District of Columbia, July 1, 2008 (www.dcd.uscourts.gov/public-docs/system/files/Guantanamo-Resolution070108.pdf).

23. Cf. 128 S. Ct. at 2276-77, stating that "[u]nlike the President and some designated members of Congress, neither the members of this Court nor most federal judges begin the day with briefings that may describe new and serious threats to our Nation and its people."

24. Sandra Day O'Connor, "Remarks upon Receiving the Sylvanus Thayer Award," speech, United States Military Academy, West Point, N.Y., October 20, 2005 (www.westpointaog.org/NetCommunity/Page.aspx?pid=514).

25. *Railway Express Agency* v. *New York,* 336 U.S. 106, 112 (1949), J. Jackson, concurring.

26. Mark Mazetti, "Intelligence Chief Says Al Qaeda Improves Ability to Strike in U.S.," *New York Times,* February 6, 2008, world news section.

27. Alberto Gonzales, "Remarks on Stopping Terrorists before They Strike: The Justice Department's Power of Prevention," speech, World Affairs Council of Pittsburgh, Pittsburgh, August 16, 2006.

28. Deputy Secretary of Defense, "Implementation of Combat Status Review Tribunal Procedures for Enemy Combatants Detained at U.S. Naval Base Guantánamo Bay, Cuba," memorandum, July 14, 2006 (www.defenselink.mil/news/Aug2006/d20060809CSRTProcedures.pdf).

29. Respondents' Memorandum Regarding the Government's Detention Authority Relative to Detainees Held at Guantánamo Bay, Misc. No. 08-442 (TFH), U.S. District Court for the District of Columbia, March 13, 2009 (www.scotusblog.com/wp/wp-content/uploads/2009/03/doj-detain-authority-3-13-09.pdf).

30. Cf. Bradley and Goldsmith, *supra,* note 8, at 2112–13.

31. In the laws of war, a co-belligerent state is a "fully fledged belligerent fighting in association with one or more belligerent powers." Morris Greenspan, *The Modern Law of Land Warfare* (University of California Press, 1959), p. 531. As applied to non-state actor terrorist organizations, co-belligerents would include terrorist organizations that act as agents of al Qaeda, participate with al Qaeda in acts of war against the United States, systematically provide military resources to al Qaeda, or serve as fundamental communication links in the war against the United States; it would perhaps also include those that systematically permit their buildings and safe houses to be used by al Qaeda in the war against the United States. These organizations are analogous to co-belligerents in a traditional war.

32. See *al-Marri* v. *Pucciarelli,* 534 F.3d 213, 325 (4th Cir. 2008), Wilkinson, J., concurring and dissenting in part.

33. See Bradley and Goldsmith, *supra,* note 8, at 2112–13. *Hamdi* held that the authorization to use force entails authorization to detain in an international armed conflict, and the plurality's uncertainty about extending that rationale to the war against al Qaeda concerned the indefiniteness of detention and not whether "force"

entailed detention authority in that context. See *Hamdi,* 542 U.S. at 521, stating that "we understand Congress' grant of authority for the use of 'necessary and appropriate force' to include the authority to detain for the duration of the relevant conflict, and our understanding is based on longstanding law-of-war principles. If the practical circumstances of a given conflict are entirely unlike those of the conflicts that informed the development of the law of war, that understanding may unravel."

34. See Chesney and Goldsmith, *supra,* note 15, at 1121–23; *Hamdan* v. *Rumsfeld,* 548 U.S. 557, 629-31 (2006).

35. The discussion in this paragraph and the next is drawn from Chesney and Goldsmith, *supra,* note 15, at 1123–26.

36. For a thorough overview of the direct participation concept, see the trio of reports following from expert meetings on the subject jointly convened by the International Committee of the Red Cross (ICRC) and the TMC Asser Institute: Third Expert Meeting on the Notion of Direct Participation in Hostilities (2005) (www.icrc. org/Web/eng/siteeng0.nsf/htmlall/participation-hostilities-ihl-311205/$File/Direct_ participation_in_hostilities_2005_eng.pdf); Second Expert Meeting: Direct Participation in Hostilities under International Humanitarian Law (2004) (www.icrc.org/ Web/eng/siteeng0.nsf/htmlall/participation-hostilities-ihl-311205/$File/Direct_ participation_in_hostilities_2004_eng.pdf); Direct Participation in Hostilities under International Humanitarian Law (2003) (www.icrc.org/Web/eng/siteeng0.nsf/ htmlall/participation-hostilities-ihl-311205/$File/Direct%20participation%20in% 20hostilities-Sept%202003.pdf).

37. See ICRC Direct Participation studies, *supra,* note 36.

38. See, for example, Third Expert Meeting, *supra,* note 36, at 59–68, discussing the temporal component of the direct participation inquiry; HCJ 769/02 *Pub. Comm. against Torture in Israel* v. *Gov't of Israel,* para 35 [Dec. 11, 2005], broadly construing the temporal element of direct participation in the context of members of terrorist organizations (http://elyon1.court.gov.il/Files_ENG/02/690/007/a34/02007690.a34.pdf).

39. See, for example, W. Hays Parks, "Air War and the Law of War," *Air Force Law Review* 32 (1990), pp. 119–20.

40. Michael A. Newton, "The Iraqi Special Tribunal: A Human Rights Perspective," *Cornell International Law Journal* 35 (2005), pp. 863, 885.

41. *Prosecutor* v. *Tadic,* Case No. IT-94-1, Decision on the Defense Motion on Hearsay, August 5, 1996; see also Rome Statute of the International Criminal Court, art. 69(4), 2187 U.N.T.S. 90, stating that "[t]he Court may rule on the relevance or admissibility of any evidence, taking into account, inter alia, the probative value of the evidence and any prejudice that such evidence may cause to a fair trial or to a fair evaluation of the testimony of a witness."

42. Rome Statute, *supra,* note 41, art. 69(7).

43. Cf. *Parhat* v. *Gates,* 532 F. 3d 834 (D.C. Cir. 2008).

44. The Counter-Terrorism Bill of 2008 would increase the limit to forty-two days. As of October 22, 2008, it was still under debate.

45. In France, as well as in Spain, pretrial detention can last for many years without a trial. But an indictment must be made within six days of detention, and the detention process is supervised by an independent judge of liberty. The French model thus offers a different alternative worth examining—pretrial detention in which formal charges have been filed (as opposed to a preventive detention model without charge).

46. Others might want a national security court to examine other areas of law, such as those civil cases in which the "state secrets" privilege is invoked to block litigation.

47. See Goldsmith and Wittes, *supra*, note 17.

48. See U.S. Const. art. I, § 7.

49. Independent Counsel Reauthorization Act of 1994, Public Law No. 103-270, § 2, 108 Stat. 732, 732.

50. Uniting and Strengthening America by Providing Appropriate Tools Required to Intercept and Obstruct Terrorism Act of 2001, Public Law No. 107-56, 115 Stat. 272 (2001), codified as amended in scattered sections of 18, 47 and 50 U.S.C.

51. Robert E. Pierre, "Wisconsin Senator Emerges as a Maverick; Feingold, Who Did Not Back Anti-Terrorism Bill, Says He Just Votes His Conscience," *Washington Post*, October 27, 2001, p. A08.

52. American Civil Liberties Union, "The Sun Also Sets: Understanding the Patriot Act 'Sunsets'" (http://action.aclu.org/reformthepatriotact/sunsets.html).

53. Brian T. Yeh and Charles Doyle, *CRS Report for Congress, USA Patriot Improvement and Reauthorization Act of 2005: A Legal Analysis* (Congressional Research Service, 2006) (www.fas.org/sgp/crs/intel/RL33332.pdf), p. 2.

54. USA Patriot Improvement and Reauthorization Act of 2005, Public Law 109-177, 120 Stat. 177 (2006); USA Patriot Act Additional Reauthorizing Amendments Act of 2006, Public Law 109-178, 120 Stat. 278 (2006). See generally Viet D. Dinh and Wendy J. Keefer, "FISA and the Patriot Act: A Look Back and a Look Forward," *Georgetown Law Journal Annual Review of Criminal Procedure* 35 (2006), pp. iii, xxxii–iii (2006). On the two new sunsets, see Yeh and Doyle, *supra*, note 53, at 3. The two provisions are "roving wiretaps"—those that follow a given targeted individual even as he changes his communications platform—and access to certain business records under FISA. Ibid.

55. Patrick Leahy, "Patriot Bill: A Missed Opportunity to Protect Americans' Security And Civil Liberties," press release, December 8, 2005 (http://leahy.senate.gov/press/200512/120805.html).

56. 151 Cong. Rec. H11,509-10 (daily ed., December 14, 2005), remarks of Martin Meehan on reauthorization of Patriot Act, United States House of Representatives, Washington, D.C.

57. Dinh and Keefer, *supra*, note 54, at xxx.

58. National Commission on Terrorist Attacks upon the United States, *supra*, note 12, at 399.

ROBERT M. CHESNEY

4

Optimizing Criminal Prosecution as a Counterterrorism Tool

Before the September 11 attacks, the United States relied primarily on federal criminal prosecution when it sought to incarcerate suspected terrorists for an extended duration.[1] In the aftermath of September 11, however, the United States buttressed its existing options for long-term detention of terrorism suspects by asserting that some such persons are combatants subject to military detention for the duration of hostilities pursuant to the law of armed conflict, and also by establishing military commissions to oversee war crimes trials for a subset of those individuals.[2] In so doing, the government sparked intense controversy. Amid that controversy, however, an important point of consensus has emerged—namely, that there is a need for a criminal justice system that is maximally capable of trying and disabling suspected terrorists. For opponents of the new military alternatives, the criminal justice system represents the legitimate alternative to illegitimate exercises of presidential power. For proponents, the criminal justice system offers a useful additional set of tools for situations in which military options prove unavailable or unpalatable—for citizens arrested domestically, for example, or when foreign governments refuse to transfer people for extracriminal detention or trial by military commission. Whatever the merits of the military alternatives, in other words, all sides in the debate agree that the United States needs a federal criminal justice system adequate to the task of providing whatever long-term detention capacity may be required in connection with suspected terrorists.

I am grateful to Benjamin Wittes, James Benjamin, and Richard Zabel for their many constructive criticisms and suggestions. I also wish to thank participants in a conference sponsored by Brookings at the Center for the Constitution at James Madison's Montpelier and participants in the South Texas College of Law symposium "Law, Ethics, and the War on Terror."

Arguably, that need has grown more acute as a result of the 2008 election. While the Obama administration has announced that it will continue using military commissions for some war crimes trials, it clearly prefers trial in federal court when possible. And while it will likely continue holding certain people in military detention, at least for those individuals captured outside traditional combat zones it clearly prefers criminal process.[3] The result will be increased pressure on the criminal justice system—pressure that will test its capacity.

The question of whether the system is up to the task has sparked a sharp debate.[4] Some contend that it already suffices to provide whatever long-term detention authority the government requires.[5] Others contend that elimination of the military options will create an intolerable gap in detention capacity and therefore that the government should create a new, specially tailored detention system—perhaps along the lines of a national security court—in order to close that gap.[6] Few defend the status quo, though some have cited the results in the first military commission trial as proof of the system's fairness,[7] and the addition of vigorous habeas review to existing military detention practices—resulting in orders for the release of the overwhelming majority of detainees who have had their cases considered[8]—may yet generate similar arguments in support of the legitimacy of preventive military detention as it now stands after years of litigation.[9]

I do not propose to resolve this debate, but to focus on the point of consensus—that the United States needs an optimally functional criminal justice apparatus for counterterrorism cases—and to discuss how the country might move closer to that goal. To do so, I explore first the particular capacities and limitations of the federal criminal justice system as it currently stands. The chapter first identifies with precision both the substantive and procedural considerations that together define the federal criminal justice system's current capacity for conviction—and hence for long-term detention—in terrorism-related cases, with an emphasis on the scenario in which the government wishes to intervene before harm occurs.[10] This review reveals that federal criminal prosecution is far more prevention-oriented and procedurally flexible than some critics admit. At the same time, however, the review illustrates the specific ways in which hard-wired aspects of the federal criminal justice system limit its reach in comparison to at least some alternative detention systems.

Many of the system's limitations flow from constitutional law and therefore will resist any congressional attempt at reform. Others, however, do not. Optimization, in fact, involves not just the expansion of substantive criminal law, but also some carefully tailored refinements to existing federal crimes and the clarification of ambiguities associated with certain procedural questions. I suggest a series of steps that Congress could take to make the criminal justice system a more useful tool in counterterrorism cases, including the following:

—Expand the existing prohibition in federal criminal law against receiving military-style training from a terrorist organization.

—Expand the existing War Crimes Act to include attacks by noncitizens directed against civilians or civilian objects during armed conflict.

—Calibrate the maximum sentence for providing material support to designated foreign terrorist organizations so that defendants who intend harm face higher maximums, while defendants who act out of ignorance or foolishness face lesser sentences.

—Amend the 1994 law forbidding material support for terrorism so as to confine its use to scenarios actually involving terrorism.

—Hold hearings relating to the scope of conspiracy liability as it connects to terrorism in general and to the global jihad movement in particular.

—Clarify the scope of the government's obligation to search the files of the intelligence agencies for exculpatory information that the government must disclose to defendants.

—Amend the Classified Information Procedures Act, which guides the handling of classified information in criminal proceedings, to permit the appointment of "standby counsel" to act on a defendant's behalf in hearings in which the defendant has insisted upon his or her right to self-representation.

Adopting these reforms will not enable the criminal justice system to provide in every circumstance a detention option that might be within the reach of the current military detention system or some alternative detention framework. Constitutional restraints ensure that some gap will remain in that respect. Congress can, however, minimize the gap by maximizing the detention capacity of the criminal justice system.

Substantive Grounds for Prosecution in Terrorism-Related Scenarios

Substantive criminal law often is thought of as if it were largely retrospective in nature, focusing on the investigation and punishment of events that already have occurred. Certainly the post-hoc prosecution of harmful conduct lies at the core of the criminal justice system. But the center of gravity in criminal law has been gradually shifting away from that model for some time. Well before September 11, scholars were commenting on the increasing prominence of prevention of harm as a goal for the legal system in general and for criminal law in particular.[11] Today, federal criminal law relating to terrorism—particularly, the *prevention* of terrorism—is much broader than some critics have suggested. In fact, the range of circumstances in which federal criminal charges might be possible compares reasonably well with the substantive grounds currently used to justify preventive military detention and the charges possible in the military commission system.

When a government wants to recalibrate its criminal laws to enhance prevention, there are at least two variables to consider. First, society can accelerate the point at which criminal liability attaches along a continuum that runs from an individual's mere inclination to act to the action itself. Second, society can premise liability on association rather than on conduct as such. As prevention becomes a higher priority, then, the law might be expected to expand along both dimensions. And if the law already is broad on one or both dimensions, prosecutors might be expected to employ their discretion in actual cases to fully realize—or perhaps even expand—its resulting capacity to prevent harm.

Prosecutorial Options under Federal Criminal Law

Close examination reveals that federal criminal law relating to terrorism has undergone both forms of change over the past two decades. For example, Congress enacted two statutes, one in 1994 and the other in 1996, criminalizing "material support" for terrorism—both of which have an unmistakable emphasis on prevention and one of which goes so far as to criminalize active membership in designated foreign terrorist organizations.[12] More recently, Congress has enacted a prohibition on receipt of military-style training from such organizations—irrespective of membership—in direct response to a key aspect of the potentially dangerous person scenario.[13] Meanwhile, prosecutors have employed an aggressive approach to traditional conspiracy liability, thereby establishing the capacity to prosecute potential terrorists even when they have not affiliated with specific, designated groups and even in the absence of any specificity as to violent acts that they might commit. These approaches, combined with the aggressive use of the "Al Capone" charging strategy—prosecution of terrorism suspects on entirely unrelated charges that may happen to be available—provide a wide array of options for prosecutors to act.

The result of these changes is that if one sets aside questions of evidence and procedural safeguards, there are relatively few terrorism-related scenarios in which the government would be interested in detaining an individual but would lack the *substantive grounds* for prosecution. In the discussion that follows, I identify some of the most important of the statutes as they might apply to a series of prevention-oriented scenarios that tend to arise in the context of terrorism.[14] The scenarios include the prosecution of members and supporters of designated foreign terrorist organizations such as al Qaeda; persons who have been trained by such groups; and persons who cannot be linked to a specific group but who nonetheless can be shown to be part of what some have called the "global jihad movement."[15] Before discussing the rules that may apply in those settings, however, it is important to address the relatively traditional scenario in which the suspect can in fact be linked to a completed—or at least attempted—act of violence.

Suspects Linked to Specific Acts of Violence

Federal criminal law, not surprisingly, provides a broad range of charging options when a terrorism suspect allegedly has attempted or completed an act of violence. This is true most obviously with respect to such acts when they occur within the United States itself. In that context, an array of offenses may be involved depending upon the circumstances. When prosecutors can prove that a violent act involved some degree of conduct "transcending national boundaries," for example, the law provides weighty penalties up to and including the death penalty.[16] Prosecutors also might be able to draw on a number of statutes specifically addressing actions ranging from kidnapping, to hijacking, to the unlawful possession and use of explosives.[17]

A more challenging scenario involves harms or attempted harms committed overseas. When U.S. nationals are involved either as victims or perpetrators of overseas violence, prosecutors again have numerous options. The murder of U.S. nationals outside the United States is punishable by death, for example, so long as the attorney general or a designated subordinate certifies that the action was intended to "coerce, intimidate, or retaliate against a government or civilian population."[18] When explosives or certain large-caliber firearms are employed, moreover, the inaptly named "weapons of mass destruction" (WMD) statute provides the death penalty for violence causing the death of U.S. persons outside the United States.[19] The WMD statute also applies to such acts resulting in death to anyone inside the United States, subject to relatively undemanding federal jurisdictional prerequisites (such as proof that the event had an impact on interstate commerce), and it can be employed even for overseas attacks on non-U.S. nationals so long as the perpetrator is a U.S. national. And if the offender is a U.S. national or member of the U.S. armed forces whose conduct constitutes a war crime, the War Crimes Act provides comparable sanctions.[20]

When neither the perpetrators nor the victims of an overseas attack are U.S. nationals, however, charging options are quite limited. Prosecutors may bring charges against those who have committed violence overseas against "internationally protected persons" such as diplomats, so long as the defendant can be found later in the United States.[21] Otherwise, however, prosecutors lack options if asked to pursue the perpetrators of a terrorist attack carried out by noncitizens against noncitizens in a foreign country.[22] Federal prosecutors probably could not, for example, prosecute a Saudi citizen for attacking Saudi soldiers or civilians in Saudi Arabia.

The more difficult questions, of course, arise when prosecutors cannot link a prospective defendant to any violent act. Particularly in the context of terrorism, there are persons whom the government may wish to incarcerate because they *might* engage in violent acts in the future, but who have not yet engaged in conduct constituting an attempt. If the criminal justice system provides too little capacity to address that scenario, the case for reliance on military detention or an alternative preventive detention regime would become stronger.[23] A close review of existing authorities suggests, however, that the preventive scope of federal criminal law in fact is quite expansive, perhaps surprisingly so.

The "Al Capone" Strategy

As an initial matter, prosecutors at times will have the option of charging a terrorism suspect for violating loosely related or even entirely unrelated laws, much as prosecutors once took down Al Capone on charges of tax evasion. This strategy eliminates the need to link the suspect to any particular act of violence or to establish liability based on future dangerousness. Unfortunately, however, prosecutors cannot count on having the Al Capone option every time that they confront a potential terrorist.

The option of charging a defendant with a collateral or unrelated offense arises in one of two ways. First, it can arise by chance, as when the investigation of a terrorism suspect happens to unearth evidence of credit card or immigration fraud—or, perhaps more likely, when an investigation of nonterrorism offenses becomes complicated by information indicating a person's potential involvement in terrorism. Second, the government can give terrorism suspects the choice of cooperating with investigators or facing prosecution for collateral offenses, so long as the government is willing to make its investigation overt. False or misleading statements made to government investigators are felonies,[24] for example, as are efforts to mislead grand juries.[25] Combined with the sentencing enhancements available for terrorism-related offenses, such investigative charges can be effective in providing options for incarcerating persons suspected of terrorism who are not forthcoming about their activities.[26]

MEMBERS AND SUPPORTERS OF DESIGNATED GROUPS

The government will not always have collateral charging options available to it in connection with potential terrorists. When the suspect does not appear to have committed an unrelated offense and when the suspect either has not misled investigators or has not been put in a position to do so, prosecutors must instead intervene—if at all—on the basis of charges relating more directly to terrorism.

The government's capacity to prosecute preventively in that setting is most visible when the suspect appears to be acting in coordination with others. Consider first the scenario in which the government can prove that a suspect is a member of a designated foreign terrorist organization (in other words, a foreign entity that has been formally identified by the secretary of state to be involved in terrorism). In that situation, the government often—though not always—has the option of prosecuting the person for his or her membership status alone, without needing to link the defendant to any particular plot.

To achieve that end, prosecutors have a strong tool in the aforementioned 1996 statute that makes it a felony to provide material support or resources to any designated foreign terrorist organization (DFTO).[27] The material support statute offers broad power in two respects. First, it has a very permissive standard of *mens rea,* or state of mind. The government has no obligation to show that the defendant knew or intended that the support would be used for any particular purpose, let alone to facilitate a crime. Rather, it is enough that the defendant knew the identity of the true recipient of the support and either knew that the group had been designated a terrorist organization or, more likely, that the group engaged in terrorism. Second, the statute defines the range of conduct constituting forbidden "material support or resources" quite broadly:

> The term "material support or resources" means any property, tangible or intangible, or service, including currency or monetary instruments or financial securities, financial services, lodging, training, expert advice or assistance, safehouses, false documentation or identification, communications equipment, facilities, weapons, lethal substances, explosives, *personnel (1 or more individuals who may be or include oneself),* and transportation, except medicine or religious materials [emphasis added].[28]

The features of this definition combine to make it especially useful as a preventive mechanism. Most directly, as the italicized portion of the definition illustrates, a person cannot become "personnel" for a terrorist organization without violating the statute, irrespective of whether the government can link the defendant to any particular plot. In that sense, the provision functions as a prohibition on membership, facilitating prevention by predicating liability on associational status alone.[29] Moreover, even when prosecutors cannot prove membership in that sense, the broad range of conduct otherwise forbidden under the material support law frequently will provide grounds for prosecuting persons otherwise associated with such groups—again without reference to whether the government can link the individual to any particular violent plot.[30] Terrorism suspects alleged to have provided al Qaeda with logistical support, such as by transferring money or obtaining false identification, can be prosecuted in this way, as can those who provide personal services, such as serving as a bodyguard for bin Laden.

Some forms of support may also trigger criminal liability under the International Emergency Economic Powers Act (IEEPA), which empowers the president, upon declaration of a national emergency, to issue orders prohibiting transactions with specific persons or entities.[31] Violations of such orders are felonies punishable by up to ten years' imprisonment.[32]

There are, however, limitations on prosecution of the members and supporters of terrorist groups. First, neither the material support law nor IEEPA is of any use with respect to persons who are linked to groups that have not received a formal designation by the executive branch or who are not linked to any particular organization at all. That presents a problem with respect to persons who are associated with the jihad movement generally but who cannot clearly be linked to a particular, designated organization within that movement. This situation can arise, for example, when a suspect attends a training camp whose sponsorship may be unclear.[33]

Second, prosecutors cannot reach some suspects under these authorities, despite clear connection to a designated group, because of timing difficulties. Al Qaeda, for example, went undesignated as a foreign terrorist organization for purposes of the material support law until October 8, 1999.[34] That fact would preclude a material support charge for a person who admits to having provided support to or being a member of al Qaeda while attending a training camp in Afghanistan during the summer of 1999 or earlier. Nor would IEEPA provide an alternative ground for prosecution in that circumstance, since the president did not prohibit transactions with al Qaeda pursuant to that authority until September 23, 2001.[35] In the future, those limitations will gradually fade in significance, but given the large number of individuals thought to have been involved in al Qaeda in the 1990s, they will continue to have some bite in some cases. By the same token, of course, members and supporters of any new terrorist organizations that emerge will not be subject at least initially to prosecution under the support statutes in light of this inherent ex post facto limitation.

A third limitation on support liability is jurisdictional. From 1996 through 2004, the material support law provided liability only for conduct occurring "within the United States or subject to the jurisdiction of the United States." Depending on how broadly courts might prove willing to construe the concept of "subject to the jurisdiction of the United States," it might preclude relying on the material support law for members and supporters of al Qaeda even *after* the group's designation in October 1999, at least insofar as such persons were noncitizens outside U.S. territory. *If so, the material support law would not apply to the vast majority of al Qaeda members who fell into U.S. custody in Afghanistan and elsewhere in the months and years after September 11*—making it useless, for example, as a tool in dealing with the detainees held at Guantánamo Bay, Cuba. Congress dropped the jurisdictional limitation in late 2004, so this problem too will become less significant over time. For now, however, it remains quite relevant. IEEPA, for its part, still requires that the person or property in question be "subject to the jurisdiction of the United States."[36]

Finally, both the material support law and IEEPA have been subject to constitutional challenges. On the one hand, courts have not been receptive to claims that the material support prohibition violates First Amendment freedoms of expression and association.[37] Some courts have, however, accepted the argument that at least some components of its definition of material support for terrorism are unconstitutionally vague.[38] Congress attempted to address such concerns in 2004 by amending the definition of certain terms,[39] but the U.S. Court of Appeals for the Ninth Circuit recently concluded that Congress had succeeded only to a limited extent.[40] As a result, it is not clear at this time that prosecutors can rely on the terms "training," "service," or "expert advice or assistance" relating to "other specialized knowledge" when contemplating a material support indictment, and similar objections could arise in connection with IEEPA's analogous provisions. That said, those rulings have not been extended beyond the Ninth Circuit, and even there the critical "personnel" aspect of the material support definition remains viable— meaning that it remains possible throughout the country to prosecute for active membership in a designated foreign terrorist organization.

CONSPIRATORS

When material support and IEEPA charges cannot be brought for lack of evidence linking the suspect to a designated foreign terrorist organization, prosecutors can fall back on conspiracy liability. Conspiracy, along with the crime of attempt, is among the most venerable forms of inchoate criminal liability in U.S. law. Its capacity for prevention lies in the fact that it permits prosecution well before a harmful act is committed or even attempted. Prosecutors can bring charges against an alleged conspirator as soon as he or she forms an agreement to commit some particular offense—or, under some statutes, as soon as the person enters into such an agreement and also commits an overt act in furtherance of it.[41] Precisely how soon liability attaches in this model, however, is not widely appreciated. The potential conspirators need not agree to the details of the contemplated criminal act—the date, the location, or the means of accomplishing the act. They must agree only to commit a particular *type* of offense to put themselves at risk of prosecution.[42]

Conspiracy liability in this sense provides prosecutors with several advantages. The potential to intervene at an early stage along the continuum between inclination and action makes conspiracy a potentially powerful tool for preventive intervention. The existence of a conspiracy also provides prosecutors with an opportunity to exploit a key exception to the normal ban on hearsay evidence, an exception that allows prosecutors to introduce hearsay statements by co-conspirators. Prosecutors need not actually even charge a conspiracy in order to invoke that rule.[43] And though the general-purpose federal conspiracy statute provides for only a five-year maximum sentence,[44] the conspiracy statutes most likely to apply in a terrorism scenario entail much weightier sentences.[45]

On the other hand, the very reason that conspiracy liability can be useful in preventing criminal acts—that it allows prosecutors to charge plotters before they have proceeded far in their planning—can give rise to problems of persuasion at trial. The earlier the intervention, the less evidence there will be concerning defendants' commitment to carrying out their agreement. Consecutive mistrials in the ongoing prosecution of the so-called Liberty City Seven illustrate the problem. In that case, a group of men in the Miami area allegedly plotted to bomb the Sears Tower and other locations on behalf of al Qaeda; as a result, they were prosecuted under a mix of material support and conspiracy charges. According to FBI deputy director John Pistole, their plans were "more aspirational than operational," a characterization borne out in both the indictment and the evidence presented at trial.[46] Although the government presented a considerable amount of audio and video evidence—including recordings of a ceremony in which the defendants pledged loyalty to al Qaeda—it could not show that the defendants possessed any weapons or explosives or had done much beyond talk. That opened the door for the defense to claim that the men had not truly intended to harm anyone but instead had been attempting to con a supposed al Qaeda representative out of money. Two consecutive trials ended in a hung jury, with one defendant acquitted along the way, before the government finally garnered a conviction in the third trial.[47] The government might have avoided the difficulty by delaying its intervention in the alleged plot; waiting might have revealed that the defendants indeed were not serious about the plot or provided more persuasive evidence of their commitment.

Considerations of proof thus act as an important practical limitation on the broad preventive reach of conspiracy liability. But the government can sometimes overcome that limitation and thus realize conspiracy liability's full preventive potential. Witness the successful prosecution of Jose Padilla. The military held Padilla for years on the ground that he was an al Qaeda agent sent back to the United States to carry out violent attacks (he was accused of involvement in a "dirty bomb" plot, among others). With Supreme Court review of the merits of his detention pending, the government ultimately transferred Padilla to civilian custody to face criminal prosecution. Notably, however, prosecutors did not allege any facts relating to his plans in returning to the United States or any other post-September 11 conduct. They did not claim that he had become an al Qaeda member, let alone that he had agreed to carry out any particular type of violent act. The government instead focused entirely on his earlier conduct as a recruit for the "violent jihad" movement writ large. Prosecutors alleged that Padilla thereby had joined an ongoing conspiracy to commit otherwise unspecified murders and other violent acts. The defense sought a bill of particulars detailing the nature and scope of the conspiracy; the government's response confirms the broad conception of conspiracy liability at issue in the case:

> The defendants herein were part of a larger radical Islamic fundamentalist movement that waged "violent jihad" by opposing governments, institutions, and individuals that did not share their view of Islam or their goal of reestablishing a Caliphate. As it pertains to this case, these defendants supported violence, including murder, maiming and kidnappings, committed by mujahideen groups operating in various jihad theaters around the world. Specifically, the violent Islamist groups in

Egypt, Algeria, Tunisia, Libya, Somalia, Afghanistan, Tajikistan, Chechnya, Bosnia, and Lebanon.

In some of these theaters, such as Afghanistan, Bosnia and Chechnya, and Tajikistan, their violence was directed mainly towards existing central government regimes they believed were oppressing Muslims and resisting the establishment of strict Islamic states. Therefore, they engaged in armed confrontations, including murders, maiming, and kidnappings, against Serbian and Croat forces in Bosnia, Russian forces in Chechnya and Tajikistan, and opposing Muslim forces in Afghanistan. . . . In other theaters such as Egypt, Algeria, Libya, Somalia, and Tunisia, they supported the violent Islamist groups and factions committing acts of murder, maiming, and kidnapping against leaders, members, and supporters of what they viewed as apostate regimes, including other Muslims.[48]

In short, the conspiracy at issue in Padilla's prosecution was the jihad movement itself. Ultimately the jury convicted Padilla of participating in that conspiracy on the basis of evidence that he traveled to Afghanistan to receive military-style training at a jihadist camp with the intent to serve the movement in ways to be determined at some later date. The *Padilla* case thus suggests that federal criminal law permits prosecution not just of formal membership in a particular designated foreign terrorist organization but also of informal "membership" in the jihad movement itself, irrespective of whether the defendant can be linked to any particular organization or plot. And in that respect, the Padilla prosecution provides a striking example of the preventive capacity of existing criminal law. Indeed, the Padilla prosecution raises the question of what limits, if any, cabin the scope of conspiracy liability.

It is not entirely clear what to make of this precedent. The charging strategy that the government employed against Padilla may not prove to be generalizable. Jurors in other cases may prove less receptive to the notion of equating unfocused enlistment in the jihad movement with conspiracy to murder, for example, and the strategy might not succeed if used in a case unrelated to the jihad movement. But given that conspiracy is not a concept specific to terrorism, there nonetheless is some reason to be concerned that the envelope-pushing interpretation employed in the *Padilla* case might spill over into other areas of law where the government's interest in prevention is less pressing.

In any event, even if the Padilla strategy proves to have some staying power as a tool for preventive incarceration, conspiracy liability is of no use in the scenario in which a terrorism suspect appears to be acting entirely on his own—as a so-called "lone wolf."

Lone Wolves and Suspects with Uncertain Affiliations

One does not have to become a member of a terrorist organization to commit an act of political violence. The government is and should be especially concerned with anyone who has obtained military-style training from a terrorist organization, for example, whether as a member of that group or not. Indeed, the defendant who appears to have attended a terrorist-operated training camp constitutes an important category for purposes of the military detention debate. According to one summary of the proceedings of the military's Combatant Status Review Tribunals (CSRTs) at Guantánamo, for example, at least 317 detainees "took military or terrorist training in Afghanistan."[49] The government quite reasonably views persons who have received such training as potentially dangerous, irrespective of whether it can link them to plans for any particular act of violence.

The material support law is not suited to the task of prosecution in this scenario, since it forbids the *provision* rather than the *receipt* of training. In 2004, therefore, Congress enacted a new statute specifically addressing that situation. That law made it a crime to "knowingly receive military-type training from or on behalf of" any designated foreign terrorist organization.[50] As with the material support law, the new training law requires no particular showing of intent on the part of the defendant, just knowledge of the identity and nature of the organization in question.[51] It thus constitutes an ideal tool for preventive prosecution with respect to an especially important category of terrorism suspects—or it might be at some point in the future. For the time being, ex post facto considerations ensure that this statute does not apply to those whose training occurred prior to December 17, 2004—which is to say virtually the entire population in U.S. custody. Moreover, even going forward, the statute will apply only when the government can attribute the training to a particular group that has been designated a terrorist organization by the secretary of state. These hurdles may explain why prosecutors have charged only one defendant under the training statute since its enactment.[52]

That brings the discussion to the most challenging scenario from the point of view of substantive criminal law: the person whom the government cannot link to a designated foreign terrorist organization or to any particular co-conspirators and cannot show to have attempted any particular violent act but who nonetheless poses a credible threat of committing a terrorist act in the future (perhaps because of the person's stated or apparent intentions, the person's receipt of training, or both). How, if at all, can prosecutors intervene in such a situation, assuming that the decision is made to incapacitate rather than surveil the person?

Conventional inchoate liability theories do not extend to this scenario. The situation described above sounds most akin to an attempt scenario, albeit one that has not progressed to the point that attempt liability would actually attach. In the wake of September 11, however, prosecutors actually developed an inchoate crime theory that *does* encompass this situation. Their solution lies in the 1994 material support statute that preceded enactment of the 1996 act discussed above.[53] The 1994 material support statute is both narrower and broader than the 1996 one. It is broader in that it is not limited to support provided to designated foreign terrorist organizations—it applies *without respect to the identity of the recipient of the support.* It is narrower, however, in that it *does* require proof that the defendant intended or at least knew that the support would be used by the recipient to carry out or facilitate any of several dozen criminal acts identified as predicates in the statute. In short, the 1994 law makes it a crime to provide support for the commission of certain *crimes* rather than to certain *organizations.*

Notably, the predicate crimes supporting liability under the 1994 law include numerous conspiracy provisions. Thus, even if a defendant is not actually a party to a conspiracy, he or she still may be liable under the statute if he or she provided aid to others knowing or intending that they would engage in the conspiracy. That may seem like a narrow scenario, one that adds relatively little prosecutorial power to what conspiracy liability already provides. In practical terms, however, the 1994 law may prove important insofar as it enables prosecutors to offer jurors a plausible alternative in circumstances in which they have difficulty establishing the existence of the conspiracy itself—as in the "lone wolf" scenario described earlier.[54]

The prosecution of Hamid Hayat presents a striking example of how prosecutors can employ the 1994 law in this fashion. In 2002 a government informant began recording conversations with Hayat, including discussions of his going to Pakistan to obtain training to become a *mujahid.* Though plainly sympathetic with the notion, Hayat was noncommittal about actually following through on such plans. Nonetheless, he traveled to Pakistan in 2003, ostensibly for an arranged marriage. The government suspected, however, that he was there at least in part to receive training, and upon his return the FBI took him into custody. A lengthy interrogation session eventually produced a confession that he had attended a jihad training camp of some kind, as well as the following exchange regarding his plans now that he had returned to the United States:

FBI: So jihad means that you fight and you assault something?

Hayat: Uh-huh.

FBI: Give me an example of a target. A building?

Hayat: I'll say no buildings. I'll say people.

FBI: OK, people. Yeah. Fair enough. People in buildings. . . . I'm trying to get details about plans over here.

Hayat: They didn't give us no plans.

FBI: Did they give you money?

Hayat: No money.

FBI: Guns?

Hayat: No.

FBI: Targets in the U.S.?

Hayat: You mean like buildings?

FBI: Yeah, buildings. . . . Sacramento or San Francisco?

Hayat: I'll say Los Angeles or San Francisco.

FBI: Financial, commercial?

Hayat: I'll say finance and things like that.

FBI: Hospitals?

Hayat: Maybe, I'm sure. Stores.

FBI: What kind of stores?

Hayat: Food stores.[55]

That confession, combined with recorded conversations and other indications that Hayat held extremist views, constituted the bulk of the evidence against him. Because prosecutors had no evidence regarding the identity of the organization from whom Hayat had received training, he could not be charged under the 1996 material support law, IEEPA, or the training statute. In theory they might have prosecuted him using a broad conspiracy charge comparable to that employed in the *Padilla* case, but serious problems might have arisen given their lack of evidence regarding the identity and aims of other persons with whom Hayat supposedly was working. Instead, prosecutors charged

Hayat under the 1994 material support law, along with other charges involving false statements to investigators. Specifically, the indictment charged that Hayat had provided material support "knowing and intending that the material support and resources were to be used in preparation for, and in carrying out, a violation of Title 18, United States Code, Section 2332b (Acts of Terrorism Transcending National Boundaries)."[56] That is to say, they charged him with making himself available as "personnel" in anticipation of carrying out his own future acts of violence in the United States, the details of which were as yet quite indefinite. The charge thus avoided the difficulty of establishing the elements of a conspiracy while still enabling prosecutorial intervention at a stage that was far earlier than would be possible with, say, an attempt allegation. In that sense the *Hayat* case stands alongside the *Padilla* case as a high-water mark in post–September 11 efforts to date to expand the preventive capacity of substantive criminal law relating to terrorism.

Is the 1994 law thus a catch-all prevention statute, capable of reaching the most nebulous of plots even in the absence of a link to a designated foreign terrorist organization? It is tempting to conclude that it is, given the outcome in the Hayat prosecution. However, there are at least three limitations to bear in mind. First, as with the broad approach to conspiracy liability illustrated by the Padilla prosecution, the broad approach to liability under the 1994 law illustrated by the Hayat prosecution may or may not prove to be generalizable beyond the particular circumstances in that case. That is to say, another jury grappling with the same case or a future jury dealing with another case might require greater specificity before reaching a guilty verdict. Second, it is important to note that even in the *Hayat* case prosecutors did have to establish intent on the defendant's part to support an unlawful or violent act, however unclear the details of that act might be. Hayat's confession, whatever else might be said about it, provided an evidentiary basis for the jury to find that he had such intent. Had he admitted only that he attended a training camp, without more, it is doubtful that he would have been convicted. Third, the 1994 law, like its later counterpart, once was subject to a significant jurisdictional prerequisite. Until Congress passed the Patriot Act in late 2001, liability under this statute attached only with respect to conduct that occurred "within the United States." For an important cohort of potential defendants—including those who provided support to the jihad movement outside the United States prior to late 2001—prosecutors therefore cannot rely on the 1994 law no matter how broadly the courts interpret it. In other words, like other criminal statutes, it is a more powerful prospective than retrospective tool.

Federal Criminal Law, Military Detention, and Military Commissions in Comparative Perspective

The substantive detention criteria of federal criminal law relating to terrorism are quite broad but subject to at least a handful of significant limitations. That raises the question of how those criteria compare with the alternatives provided by both the definition of "enemy combatant" employed at Guantá-namo to determine who is subject to military detention and the range of charges available to prosecutors before military commissions. Again setting aside questions of procedure, the substantive scope of federal criminal law compares reasonably well to both.

The United States has invoked the law of armed conflict to support two separate detention frameworks in the post–September 11 period. For the vast majority of military detainees, it has relied on the principle that captured combatants may be detained for the duration of hostilities. And it also has invoked the authority to prosecute a small subset of those individuals for war crimes before military commissions. Invocation of both models has proven exceedingly controversial, with a range of critics—including judges, in some instances—concluding that the government in at least some circumstances has exceeded whatever authority it may have to invoke these frameworks. The merits of those criticisms are beyond the scope of this chapter. My goal in referencing the military models is merely to provide a point of comparison, with the military alternatives depicted in the best possible light in order to present the sharpest potential contrast with the scope of federal criminal law. Accordingly, let us assume for the sake of argument that the government has correctly stated the scope of its military detention authority.[57]

The Military Detention Comparison

Consider first the range of persons deemed eligible for military detention for the duration of hostilities, separate and apart from any notion of criminal prosecution. In *Hamdi* v. *Rumsfeld,* the Supreme Court expressly approved application of the principle of detention for the duration of hostilities at least with respect to Taliban fighters detained while bearing arms in Afghanistan during Operation Enduring Freedom. The government, of course, understands its detention authority to extend beyond that limited circumstance. Thus, according to the rules applied at Guantánamo during Combatant Status Review Tribunals, the government may detain for the duration of hostilities the following class of persons:

An "enemy combatant" for purposes of this order shall mean an individual who was part of or supporting Taliban or al Qaeda forces, or associated forces that are engaged in hostilities against the United States or its coalition partners. This includes any person who has committed a belligerent act or has directly supported hostilities in aid of enemy armed forces.[58]

Close review of this definition, which the Obama administration has adjusted in litigation only slightly, reveals three distinct grounds for detention. First, there are *fighters.* That is, irrespective of membership, a person may be detained if he or she personally participates in violent acts in connection with hostilities. Second, there is *membership.* Members of al Qaeda or the Taliban may be detained, irrespective of their individual conduct. In addition, members of other, unspecified forces also may be detained insofar as their organizations are engaged in hostilities either with the United States or its coalition partners.[59] Third, there are *supporters.* The definition incorporates not just the members of the groups referenced above, but also those who support those groups.

Federal criminal law includes substantive detention criteria that closely track those categories, particularly regarding persons linked to al Qaeda or the Taliban. It compares less well in that military detention grounds extend to organizations that have not been assigned a formal designation, at least with respect to members and supporters of such groups who have not actually engaged in hostilities themselves.

Consider first the category of *fighters.* Federal criminal law covers much, but not quite all, of this ground for detention. Any person who uses, attempts to use, or conspires to use lethal force against U.S. personnel overseas may be prosecuted.[60] In a traditional armed conflict, of course, such liability would be offset by the right of privileged belligerents to use lethal force without being subject to domestic criminal prosecution. In an insurgency scenario such as those currently under way in Afghanistan and Iraq, however, it is probable, if not entirely certain, that the members of hostile forces will not qualify for the privilege.[61]

Insofar as a defendant allegedly fought against U.S. allies rather than U.S. personnel, however, it is less clear that any criminal charges would apply. As noted above, federal criminal law prohibits war crimes by U.S. nationals and military members, and it prohibits the overseas murder of certain internationally protected persons who are not U.S. citizens, such as foreign diplomats.[62] But in general, it does not prohibit the use of lethal force against other noncitizens overseas unless that use of force in some manner stems from plotting undertaken by the defendant or the defendant's co-conspirators in the United States.[63]

The second category of persons subject to military detention under the government's current understanding of that authority includes those who are *members* of al Qaeda, the Taliban, and other hostile forces, without respect to whether a member personally has engaged in hostilities. Again, federal criminal law covers much if not all of this ground. Through the personnel provision of the material support statute, the government may prosecute individuals simply for being members of al Qaeda, though for noncitizens outside the United States that authority may come into play only after 2004, depending on whether the facts in a particular case would render the person "subject to the jurisdiction of the United States" at the relevant time. The material support law does not extend to the Taliban at all, as the Taliban has not been designated as a foreign terrorist organization under that statutory framework. IEEPA sanctions, by contrast, do apply to the Taliban, but as explained above, that statute also entails jurisdictional limitations that preclude its use against noncitizens whose conduct occurred entirely overseas.

That leaves the question of whether members of other entities engaged in hostilities against the United States could be prosecuted on the basis of membership alone in federal court.[64] At least some such entities might not be subject to the formal designations that are prerequisites to material support and IEEPA liability, taking those options off the table. That would leave prosecutors to rely instead on conspiracy charges and charges under the 1994 law, subject again to potential problems of extraterritorial jurisdiction.

Finally, there is the matter of *supporters* of the entities encompassed by the government's enemy combatant definition who are not actually members of the group (or at least cannot be shown to be such) and who have not engaged in fighting themselves. Notoriously, a government attorney once argued that the definition of "enemy combatant" would encompass not just those who *knowingly* provide support to al Qaeda but even a "little old lady in Switzerland who writes checks to what she thinks is a charity that helps orphans in Afghanistan but [that] really is a front to finance Al-Qaeda activities."[65] In that view, there simply is no *mens rea* requirement for support in the military detention context, though the Obama administration's refinement of the definition does require that the support be substantial. The material support law, on the other hand, at least requires proof that the defendant knew the true identity of the recipient of support as well as the fact that the entity was a designated terrorist organization or the fact that the entity engaged in terrorism.

Criminal prohibitions on support in this limited respect are narrower than the government's asserted authority to detain militarily on support grounds. But setting aside the innocent donor scenario, the criminal prohibition against support covers the most important scenarios encompassed by the "enemy combatant" definition—support rendered to al Qaeda and the Taliban—though it does not necessarily extend to other groups that may engage in hostilities against the United States or its allies. If such groups already have been formally designated, then the overlap is complete. At least some such groups, however, likely will not have been designated at the time support was given to them by the person that the government wishes to prosecute.

The Military Commission Comparison

Detention for the duration of hostilities is not the only form of military detention authority that the government has invoked with respect to terrorism since September 11. It also has invoked a separate strand of detention power under the laws of armed conflict insofar as it seeks to prosecute a subset of detainees for war crimes before military commissions. On close inspection, federal criminal law relating to terrorism compares well with the charges available in the military commission system at the time of this writing.

According to the Military Commissions Act of 2006 (MCA), commissions may try unlawful enemy combatants for a range of widely recognized war crimes, including murder of protected persons, attacking civilians or civilian objects, and denial of quarter.[66] Those offenses overlap with federal criminal law insofar as U.S. nationals and internationally protected persons are involved; however, insofar as they include attacks by noncitizens on noncitizens in overseas locations, the MCA appears to reach beyond federal criminal law. (Recall that the federal War Crimes Act applies only to U.S. nationals and members of the U.S. military.)

The MCA also lists a handful of offenses comparable to the "preventive" prosecution statutes discussed above, though whether those offenses can be prosecuted by military commission remains a point of sharp legal controversy. In particular, the MCA provides liability for both conspiracy and the provision of material support, and those charges played an important role in some of the early commission proceedings, including the prosecutions of Salim Hamdan and David Hicks. It initially appears to provide the government with charging options that it might not have in federal criminal court, given that the civilian material support law did not apply to overseas conduct of noncitizens until late 2004. Ultimately, however, the government may not be able to resort to such charges in the military commission system at all. Critics allege that neither conspiracy nor material support constituted war crimes prior to enactment of the MCA and that to prosecute them as war crimes in connection with conduct that predated the MCA would violate the norm against ex post facto prosecution.[67] It remains to be determined whether such challenges will succeed, but the important point for now is that no such concerns plague conspiracy and material support liability in the federal criminal justice system. Federal criminal law, in that sense, may ultimately outstrip the scope of the substantive offenses prosecutable by military commission.

Summary

The foregoing survey suggests that the federal criminal justice system entails broad grounds for prosecution in terrorism-related cases, including prevention-oriented scenarios. A combination of laws, including conspiracy statutes and multiple material support provisions, gives prosecutors a number of options for preventive intervention. These charging options cover most of the situations that would support military detention under the government's current understanding of its authority, as well as many (though not all) charges that might be brought before a military commission. That said, the scope of federal criminal law relating to terrorism does have its limits:

—It provides relatively little coverage for violence directed by noncitizens against noncitizens overseas.

—It does not reach the members and supporters of nondesignated groups who are not personally linked to violence or other unlawful activity, at least not without resort to a broad conception of conspiracy.

—Most significant, ex post facto considerations may preclude application of the two material support laws to noncitizen al Qaeda members and supporters who operated outside the United States prior to 2001 (for the 1994 material support law) or 2004 (for the 1996 material support law).

At the same time, some of the features that render the scope of federal criminal law so broad in other respects—particularly the version of conspiracy liability employed successfully in the Padilla prosecution—give rise to concerns that federal criminal law may become *too* expansive in response to the pressure to prevent terrorism, or at least that expansive liability theories that may be justified in the context of terrorism prevention might spread to other areas of the law in which the justification is less clear.

This assessment suggests that critics of the federal criminal justice system overstate the case insofar as they describe federal criminal law as primarily retrospective in nature and not well-tailored to the imperatives of terrorism prevention. On the other hand, the limitations identified above do help explain why the government may have believed that it lacked adequate charging options for some individuals whose relevant conduct occurred prior to the September 11 attacks.

Procedural Safeguards in Terrorism-Related Prosecutions

Substantive grounds for detention are only one factor in the calculus that defines the capacity of a detention system. Another major consideration is the framework of procedural safeguards by which a system determines whether the detention grounds have been satisfied in a given instance. To observe that federal criminal law provides broad grounds for prosecution in terrorism-related cases thus does not provide a complete picture of how federal criminal prosecution might compare with military detention or with proposed alternatives.

According to conventional wisdom, the procedural safeguards in the federal criminal justice system are considerably stricter than those employed in the military systems noted above, and at least somewhat stricter than whatever rules might be employed in an alternative preventive detention regime. Critics of enhanced reliance on federal criminal law view that as a compelling reason to think twice before placing greater weight on the prosecutorial option. From that point of view, the robust procedural safeguards of federal criminal prosecution create an undue risk that the government will be unable to incapacitate suspects in circumstances in which it should be able to do so. Proponents of a prosecutorial model disagree, arguing that critics' procedural concerns are unwarranted.

In the discussion that follows, I survey some of the main procedural questions that critics of enhanced reliance on the criminal justice system have highlighted. I do not propose to rehearse the debate in full detail. A short survey of the key disputes suffices to show that at least some of the purported procedural obstacles to prosecution are not quite as insuperable as some critics have suggested. On the other hand, the survey also shows that procedural rules do limit the criminal justice system in ways that do not apply in alternative detention systems, particularly the military detention system. That does not invalidate the argument that the government should rely more heavily or even exclusively on criminal prosecution. It does, however, enable us to identify the particular procedural safeguards that are most consequential in distinguishing the criminal justice system from existing and proposed alternatives.

The survey below focuses on issues discussed in a comprehensive and influential white paper that former federal prosecutors Richard Zabel and James

Benjamin wrote in 2008 on behalf of Human Rights First.[68] The paper is both fair-minded and well-researched. In it, the authors provide a survey of the procedural questions that critics have suggested might preclude use of the criminal justice system in connection with the prosecution of suspected terrorists. Zabel and Benjamin conclude that by and large those obstacles are overstated, but they are careful to flag a handful of issues that are not so easily dismissed, and they also are careful to note that military detention and military prosecution remain appropriate for at least some individuals captured in connection with combat operations. I relay their key conclusions in the pages below, distinguishing those issues for which critics' concerns appear overstated and those for which their concerns are warranted. I also elaborate on points that warrant further discussion.

Comparatively Innocuous Procedural Safeguards

Zabel and Benjamin lay to rest many procedural concerns with relative ease. The first question that they address, for example, is whether federal courts would have difficulty asserting jurisdiction over suspects who came into U.S. custody through unorthodox means, such as capture overseas by U.S. or allied military forces or security services, followed by rendition rather than extradition to the United States.[69] Citing the *Ker-Frisbie* doctrine, they conclude that an objection to jurisdiction based on the irregular circumstances of capture most likely would not succeed, even in the event that the defendant alleges abusive treatment during an earlier stage of detention.[70] That appears to be correct, indicating that questions of jurisdiction ought not to play a significant role in the debate.

Likewise, the authors present a strong—though not necessarily indisputable—argument that *Miranda* concerns are overstated. The concern on that score is that the privilege against self-incrimination precludes the use of inculpatory statements that defendants might make to soldiers and other government agents who capture or interrogate them overseas.[71] Zabel and Benjamin contend that "it is likely that the courts would recognize an exception to *Miranda* under the 'public safety' exception first articulated in *New York v. Quarles*,[72] or, more generally, based on the argument that civilian law-enforcement principles such as *Miranda* simply do not apply in battlefield conditions."[73] Thus, they note, in *United States v. Khalil* the Second Circuit Court relied on *Quarles* to sustain the admissibility of incriminating statements made by a terrorism defendant whom police had interrogated, without *Miranda* warnings, concerning bombs found at the scene of his arrest.[74] Zabel and Benjamin dispatch other potential procedural problems, such as concerns related to the right to a speedy trial, in similar fashion.[75] But not every procedural question raised by proposals to rely more extensively on criminal prosecution in terrorism-related cases can be dismissed so readily.

Comparatively Significant Procedural Safeguards

At least three sets of procedural safeguards associated with criminal prosecution combine to produce a gap between the reach of the criminal justice system and that of some existing and proposed alternatives to it. First, the rules associated with a criminal defendant's ability to access classified information can, in limited circumstances, disrupt the government's capacity to prosecute. That risk is largely mitigated by statute, but it has not been entirely eliminated and poses a particular problem insofar as it arises in connection with the government's disclosure obligations. (This problem, along with proposals for its further mitigation, is discussed in depth in chapter 5.) Second, it is likely that a substantial proportion of the intelligence that the government has derived (and will continue to derive) from the interrogation of captured individuals cannot be used in a criminal prosecution, even if it is assumed, for the sake of argument, that the interrogation was not abusive. Third, the requirement of proof beyond a reasonable doubt by definition ensures that criminal prosecution will not be an option in a situation in which the government has some lesser degree of proof linking a suspect to terrorism.

None of this is to say that it is desirable or appropriate to maintain or establish a system that differs on those three dimensions. Rather, the point is simply to demonstrate that the claim that alternative mechanisms—certainly including the current approach to military detention and potentially including proposed national security courts—have broader reach than does the criminal justice system depends in significant part on those particular procedural distinctions. And a critical point is that these criminal justice safeguards are hardwired to a considerable extent, as they derive from constitutional sources.

The Disclosure Dilemma

Consider first the battery of issues associated with the government's interest in preserving the secrecy of classified information, an interest that often is in tension with a defendant's interest in a fair trial and, at times, with a prosecutor's interest in being able to access and use all possible inculpatory information. Zabel and Benjamin conclude that current statutes—particularly the Foreign Intelligence Surveillance Act (FISA) and the Classified Information Procedures Act (CIPA)—largely suffice to reconcile those competing interests as a general proposition, subject to a few potentially significant caveats.[76]

With respect to FISA, the key question is the government's ability to employ in a federal prosecution the results of surveillance undertaken to collect intelligence (pursuant to a FISA warrant) as opposed to surveillance conducted under the authority of the ordinary criminal investigation warrant application process. Zabel and Benjamin note that post–September 11 developments, including the USA Patriot Act and a related ruling by the Foreign Intelligence Surveillance Court of Review, aim to ensure the government's freedom to employ the fruits of FISA surveillance in criminal cases even when its primary purpose at the time that it conducted such surveillance was criminal prosecution, so long as foreign intelligence collection was a *significant* purpose of that surveillance.[77] They also note, however, that one district court recently held that this standard violates the Fourth Amendment, reasoning that a Title III warrant is required as a constitutional matter in any circumstance in which the government's primary purpose is criminal prosecution.[78] That opinion may yet be overturned on appeal, but in the event that it proves to have staying power, it may reduce the range of circumstances in which the government can use intelligence in support of criminal prosecution.

The other statute emphasized by Zabel and Benjamin is CIPA, which creates a framework in which judges grapple with the tension between the government's interest in maintaining the secrecy of classified information and a defendant's constitutional right to make use of classified information already in his or her possession or to obtain such information from the government.[79] Zabel and Benjamin argue that judges have had considerable success employing CIPA in prosecutions involving sensitive national security information. They do note, however, that the CIPA system faces special hurdles when defendants insist on representing themselves, as CIPA depends in part on the government's ability to share classified information with a security-cleared attorney acting on behalf of the defendant—but not with the defendant himself.[80]

Zabel and Benjamin's discussion of CIPA leads directly into a discussion of the questions that arise in connection with a criminal defendant's disclosure rights in national security cases under two important Supreme Court cases. *Brady* v. *Maryland* established that criminal defendants have a constitutional right to the timely disclosure of exculpatory information,[81] and *Giglio* v. *United States* held that that rule extends to information that the defendant could use to impeach the government's witnesses.[82] In criminal cases implicating national security, the question arises of just how broadly those disclosure obligations run throughout the government. Plainly they apply to the information in possession of prosecutors and criminal investigators involved in preparing a case. But do they also apply to the intelligence agencies—for example, the CIA, the Defense Intelligence Agency, and the National Security Agency?[83]

The Supreme Court held in *Kyles* v. *Whitley* "that the individual prosecutor has a duty to learn of any favorable evidence known to the others acting on the government's behalf in the case, including the police."[84] That implies *some* limit to the search-and-disclose obligation, but does little to flesh out the precise nature of that limit. Lower courts have gone into more detail, however, employing a "close alignment" test in which the obligation extends to the "prosecution team" and, according to some courts, to other agencies insofar as they actually participated in the preparation of the prosecution's case.[85] Indeed, during the Padilla prosecution,[86] the court directed disclosure not just from the prosecution team but also from "any other agencies 'that have cooperated intimately from the outset of [the] investigation' and the files of any other agencies where the prosecutor gains access to [evidence] in preparing his case for trial."[87]

Given the uncertain scope of the *Brady* and *Giglio* obligations in this context, it is difficult to say with confidence whether other courts would reach a similar conclusion when faced with the issue.[88] Some might direct more limited discovery, while others might direct something more expansive. Wherever they draw the line, however, future terrorism prosecutions can be expected to give rise to similar issues routinely—especially if the government relies on criminal prosecution more extensively. That, in turn, raises an important but often-overlooked question: is there a risk that growing awareness of potential disclosure obligations will cause some in the intelligence community to grow more reluctant to share intelligence with federal criminal investigators and prosecutors?

CIPA, to be sure, provides a mechanism for mediating the impact of disclosure obligations on the government's legitimate interests in secrecy. The statute ensures that judges will exhaust all opportunities to reconcile the government's interest with the defendant's rights, including the creation of sanitized substitutes and stipulations, before compelling the government to choose between disclosing the information or else facing penalties that might include dismissal of the indictment. However, CIPA notwithstanding, it remains possible that the government will in some cases be forced to make just that choice. And the prospect of that result (or perhaps even just the prospect of CIPA litigation generally) might reduce the willingness of the intelligence community to cooperate with prosecutors on the front end of a criminal investigation, thus expanding the gap between the full range of information that the government might possess supporting the incapacitation of a terrorism suspect and the subset of that information available for use in court.[89] Certainly, it is possible that the problem will not materialize; indeed, one might argue that it also is possible that the intelligence community actually will grow more willing to share information with prosecutors as they come to trust CIPA. The important point, however, is that the possibility of decreased cooperation cannot be dismissed out of hand.[90]

THE CONFRONTATION DILEMMA

A second cluster of procedural issues that may generate substantial hurdles in connection with terrorism prosecutions involves admissibility under the Federal Rules of Evidence and the Confrontation Clause. On this issue, Zabel and Benjamin note that critics can point to few, if any, examples of actual terrorism prosecutions derailed by adverse evidentiary rulings.[91] That may well be true, but the important question is whether cases exist that could not be brought in the first place in light of the likelihood of such rulings. Prosecutorial discretion takes place in the shadow of procedural and evidentiary rules, after all, and thus it is possible that some cases were not pursued because of foreseeable problems with the admissibility of evidence.

In any event, Zabel and Benjamin identify three categories of potential problems under the general heading of admissibility, concluding that none should prove especially troublesome in the final analysis. Those categories include: "(a) authentication and chain of custody requirements; (b) the difficulties of putting on witnesses from all over the world, some of whom may be serving [on] active duty in the armed forces during a trial; and (c) the hearsay rule."[92] With respect to authentication, Zabel and Benjamin correctly point out that the Federal Rules of Evidence are more flexible than often is assumed, with the ultimate question being whether the proponent of the evidence has provided the judge with "sufficient" evidence to establish that the item is what the proponent claims it to be.[93] Strict chains of custody are of course helpful in satisfying this standard, but they are not actually required. And for what it is worth, courts in terrorism cases have been willing to permit chain-of-custody witnesses to testify without revealing their true identities.[94] Similarly, Zabel and Benjamin conclude that technology, including two-way videoconferencing, can overcome the problem of witnesses being unavailable because they are engaged in military operations overseas or otherwise cannot or should not be compelled to travel to the United States.[95]

This leaves the question of hearsay statements—that is, statements that were made out of court and that are offered to prove the truth of the matter asserted. The government may wish to introduce out-of-court statements in a terrorism prosecution for either of two reasons. First, it may wish to use them for the sake of convenience when the declarant is engaged in combat or other government operations overseas at the time of trial. Second, it may wish to introduce them out of necessity in circumstances in which the statement was made by a detainee during custodial interrogation or by a source who cooperated with the government. In the latter scenarios, the declarant may no longer be in U.S. custody, may be unwilling to repeat the statement if given the opportunity to testify, or may no longer be available to authorities at all. Depending on the circumstances of the interrogation, the government might also prefer to present an out-of-court statement in order to limit the defendant's ability to impeach his own testimony in cross-examination directed at the circumstances of his interrogation. Particularly in light of concerns about abuse of prisoners, the question of whether and when courts should admit out-of-court statements in terrorism cases takes on special significance and gives rise to controversy.

Are such statements admissible? As a default matter, the Federal Rules of Evidence requires exclusion of out-of-court statements when offered for their truth.[96] Yet the default rule is riddled with exceptions, leading Zabel and Benjamin to conclude that it would not constitute a significant obstacle to the admission of such evidence. They note in particular that it does not apply to declarations against interest, that is, out-of-court statements that may put the speaker at greater legal risk;[97] statements by co-conspirators made in the course of and in furtherance of the conspiracy;[98] and admissions by party-opponents (to wit, the defendants themselves).[99] In short, the authors conclude, concerns about hearsay are largely unwarranted.[100]

That assessment is probably correct insofar as a defendant's *own* statements are concerned; the rules, after all, define a defendant's own statements to be "non-hearsay" exempt from the default rule.[101] But the picture is more complicated with respect to statements made by *others,* particularly when such statements are made in the course of custodial interrogations. Such statements by definition do not come within the scope of the exception covering the defendant's statements. They also do not constitute co-conspirator statements, because the statement does not further the conspiracy and because the timing requirement cannot be met once a conspirator has been taken into custody. In a few instances such statements *might* qualify as statements against interest. But judges generally will parse narratives that inculpate another person so as to ensure that this exception admits only those portions of a narrative that inculpate the *declarant,* not a third party. And judges will do so bearing in mind the possibility that the declarant may in fact be attempting to curry favor or otherwise improve his own lot by casting blame on another.[102] The hearsay rule thus may indeed be an obstacle to the admission of much intelligence gleaned from interrogation—even noncoercive, nonabusive interrogation.

Even if prosecutors can overcome the hearsay rule by means of one exception or another, it does not follow that a court will admit the statement in question. The Sixth Amendment's Confrontation Clause, which guarantees a defendant the right to confront witnesses against him, constitutes a separate and potentially insurmountable obstacle even when a hearsay exception applies.[103] The Confrontation Clause forbids admission of any out-of-court statement if the declarant was not subject to cross-examination at the time of the statement and cannot be cross-examined with reference to it now and if the statement is "testimonial" in nature, meaning that the declarant reasonably could foresee its use by the government as evidence in a criminal case.[104] Most if not all interrogation scenarios result in the production of testimonial statements, and so the critical question is whether the government can produce the declarant for cross-examination at trial. That may be possible in many instances, but presumably it will not be possible in some nontrivial number of cases. Moreover, unlike with the hearsay rule, exceptions to the Confrontation Clause are quite limited. In its most recent opinion on the subject, the Supreme Court identified exceptions only for the "dying declaration" scenario and the forfeiture-by-wrongdoing scenario, in which the defendant intentionally procured the declarant's unavailability.[105] Neither scenario will likely arise with any special frequency in connection with efforts to admit the results of interrogation during criminal prosecutions related to terrorism. For good or ill then, the Confrontation Clause ensures that there will be some cases in which the government cannot translate presumably reliable intelligence into admissible evidence.[106]

The Burden of Proof

A final procedural distinction worth emphasizing is the requirement of proof beyond a reasonable doubt in criminal cases, which is a constitutional requirement of the criminal justice system, not subject to legislative amendment.[107] By definition, it excludes conviction in circumstances in which the government can muster only proof by a preponderance of the evidence or even proof by clear and convincing evidence. The military commission system employs the same standard,[108] meaning that there is no gap between the two systems along this dimension. But military detention, at least as employed in connection with enemy combatants held at Guantánamo, requires only proof sufficient to satisfy the preponderance standard—even when courts engage in habeas corpus review of the factual predicate for such detentions.[109] Moreover, most schemes for administrative detention or a national security court seem to envision detention based on a showing of less than proof beyond a reasonable doubt. From that perspective, the military detention system entails a broader capacity for detention than does the criminal prosecution alternative.[110]

Implications and Recommendations

The foregoing survey suggests that many common assumptions in the current detention policy debate are mistaken. The problems posed by criminal procedure rules are less severe than critics often suppose; however, those procedures do not offer quite as much flexibility as their proponents claim, particularly given the potential impact of disclosure obligations, evidentiary rules, and the burden of proof. We can say much the same concerning substantive grounds to detain. Contrary to conventional wisdom, the substantive grounds to prosecute currently provided by federal criminal law are quite expansive and prevention oriented. It is simply a mistake to conceive of federal criminal prosecution as limited to the post hoc prosecution of persons who already have committed harmful acts. Particularly as a result of broad interpretations of the concepts of conspiracy and material support, a range of prevention-oriented charging options are available to federal prosecutors in terrorism-related cases. Those grounds come close to approximating the detention criteria currently employed in the military system, while being both broader and narrower than the grounds currently available for war crimes trials before military commissions. Or at least they come close now; prior to 2004, the two material support statutes were much narrower in terms of their extraterritorial jurisdiction. In any event, there continue to be reasons to believe that existing criminal laws are both too narrow and too broad—insufficiently tailored, in short—in certain respects.

Regardless of whether criminal prosecutors will be asked to carry more of the responsibility for incapacitating terrorists in the future, Congress should do what it can to improve the tailoring of the criminal justice system in light of the concerns noted above.[111] In particular, Congress should adopt the following package of reforms, which offsets expansion of substantive criminal liability in some areas by imposing restrictions in others and which also addresses those procedural concerns that can be adjusted and that do not raise difficult questions regarding the fundamental fairness of the criminal law model.

The first key reform is to expand the prohibition on the receipt of military-style training. As explained above, current law prohibits the receipt of military-style training from any designated foreign terrorist organization. This statute is useful, but it is too narrow. It will often prove impossible for prosecutors to establish the precise sponsorship of a training camp. In other instances, training will have come from militant groups that have not yet been formally designated as terrorist groups. Congress should expand this prohibition by eliminating the designation requirement. In its place, the law should prohibit the receipt of weapons or explosives training from any nongovernment entity outside the United States, subject to an affirmative defense that the defendant intended to use the skills thus acquired solely for purposes that would be lawful if conducted in the United States (such as hunting, in the case of firearms, or mining, in the case of explosives). If such a law were on the books at the time, it would have provided a well-tailored charge in both the *Padilla* and *Hayat* cases.

Second, Congress should expand the War Crimes Act to include attacks on civilians committed by noncitizens during armed conflict. Currently, federal prosecutors could not act with respect to a non–U.S. national alleged to have committed certain war crimes against non–U.S. nationals overseas, including attacks intentionally targeting civilians or civilian objects. Yet as things stand now, such actions *would* be covered by the War Crimes Act if committed by a U.S. national or a member of the U.S. armed forces. While closing that gap might raise difficult questions with respect to the extraterritorial jurisdiction of federal criminal law,[112] it would enable federal prosecutors to target terrorists who have not yet moved to attack Americans but present a high risk of doing so and already have attacked civilians of other nationalities.

Third, Congress should calibrate the maximum sentence for providing material support to a designated foreign terrorist organization with reference to the defendant's *mens rea*. This proposal constitutes both a retraction and an expansion of the existing material support law. Arguably, the current maximum sentence for a material support violation—fifteen years—is too severe for a defendant who the government cannot prove acted with ill intent. Yet it is arguably too lenient when the government can prove a murderous motive. Recalibrating the maximum sentence would enhance punishment for the worst offenders while blunting constitutional objections in other cases, objections that stem from a potential mismatch between the severity of punishment and the actual significance of a defendant's conduct.

Fourth, Congress should add a certification requirement to the 1994 material support law to ensure that its broad scope does not spill over into areas unrelated to terrorism. This survey illustrates just how broad the preventive scope of certain federal criminal laws has become, particularly with respect to material support liability under the 1994 law and conspiracy liability in general. That expansion may well be warranted in circumstances involving political violence, but neither the 1994 material support law nor some conspiracy statutes are currently limited to the context of terrorism.[113] Therefore, at least in theory, the robust approaches to inchoate criminal liability seen in *Padilla* and *Hayat* could be applied to less exotic circumstances, such as narcotics rings, street gangs, or other forms of organized crime. Such migration may or may not make good policy sense, but in any event it is a possibility that legislators ought to consider. Unless and until they affirmatively decide to permit such migration, Congress should act to prevent it by adding a certification provision to the 1994 law comparable to that found in its 1996 counterpart: the law should require a senior Justice Department official to state in writing that the alleged conduct was intended to intimidate or coerce a government or civilian population. Congress might even consider making that requirement an actual element of the offense. Either approach would reduce, if not eliminate, the risk of prosecutors' deploying this statute in circumstances unrelated to terrorism, thus cabining to terrorism cases the impact of the broad, prevention-oriented approach illustrated by prosecutions such as in the *Hayat* case.

Fifth, Congress should study and hold hearings on the scope of conspiracy liability. The 1994 material support law is not the only form of criminal liability that has proven in recent years to be much broader and more prevention-oriented than commonly assumed; the same is true of conspiracy liability, as illustrated by the *Padilla* prosecution. It is not entirely clear, however, how best to respond to that observation. The unusual aspect of the conspiracy theory employed in *Padilla* was its lack of focus: prosecutors identified the entire global jihad movement—not just al Qaeda or some specific group of individuals—as a single violent crime conspiracy. That raises a series of difficult questions. Is it in fact a problem to frame conspiracies that broadly? If so, does that approach actually add such value in the terrorism context that it ought to be preserved, at least in that setting? And if so, are there good reasons not to extend it to other criminal contexts? If not, is it possible to craft legislation that would confine this approach to the terrorism setting? None of the answers to those questions are clear. They therefore warrant serious consideration by Congress.

Sixth, Congress should define the scope of the government's search-and-disclose obligation in cases involving classified information. The procedural dilemmas noted above would be less acute if Congress clarified the scope of the government's obligation to search for and disclose exculpatory and impeachment information that might be in the hands of some within the intelligence community. To be sure, such legislation would not necessarily be the final word on this issue. If Congress were to define the scope of the obligation as extending only to a single prosecutor's desk, for example, there is little doubt that courts would reject the proposed limitation as unconstitutional. In the far murkier circumstances associated with the files of agencies other than prosecutors and criminal investigators, however, courts might well conform to a fair-minded legislative effort to codify and elaborate the meaning of the "closely aligned" test and the "prosecution team" concept. That, in turn, might help reduce the risk that the intelligence community might resist cooperating with criminal investigators and prosecutors on the margins.

Finally, Congress should amend CIPA to address the situation in which the defendant insists on self-representation. Zabel and Benjamin point out that CIPA does not expressly address the awkward situations that can arise when a defendant seeks to represent himself in a case involving classified information disputes.[114] They note that this issue arose in the Zacarias Moussaoui trial and that Judge Leonie Brinkema resolved it by providing Moussaoui's standby counsel with access to the materials in question but did not allow Moussaoui himself access.[115] It remains to be determined whether that solution will pass constitutional muster—the issue is among many currently on appeal as a result of that prosecution—but assuming that it does, Congress should consider amending CIPA to account for this situation in a systematic way.

I have suggested in this chapter that some critics of the criminal justice system's capacity to neutralize terrorism suspects have overstated their case with respect to both the substantive detention grounds and the procedural safeguards of that system. I also have suggested, however, that some proponents of the criminal prosecution solution fail to give adequate weight to the limitations that the system entails.

My analysis, standing alone, cannot answer the question of whether the United States can live with a system that relies primarily on criminal prosecution or whether it should instead either maintain the status quo or develop an alternative detention mechanism.[116] As Matthew Waxman argues in chapter 2, determining the best path forward requires in the first instance a thorough grasp of the strategic goals that the U.S. government seeks to achieve through detention. Ultimately, it is a question of policy that must be made under conditions of great uncertainty with respect to both the positive and the negative consequences that may follow from a particular choice. At the very least, however, that question should be informed by a thorough grasp of the substantive and procedural limitations of the criminal justice system both as it currently stands and as it might be amended.

What's more, since virtually everyone agrees that the criminal justice system should be used when it can be used effectively, Congress can and should take the modest steps suggested above to optimize its capacity to respond to the problem of terrorism. Criminal prosecution is certain to remain a pillar of counterterrorism policy, whatever choice may ultimately be made regarding the use of alternative detention systems. It may as well be as strong a pillar as the country can build.

Notes

1. See Richard B. Zabel and James J. Benjamin Jr., *In Pursuit of Justice: Prosecuting Terrorism Cases in the Federal Courts* (New York: Human Rights First, May 2008) (www.humanrightsfirst.info/pdf/080521-USLS-pursuit-justice.pdf).

2. See, generally, Robert Chesney and Jack Goldsmith, "Terrorism and the Convergence of Criminal and Military Detention Models," *Stanford Law Review* 60 (2008), p. 1079.

3. See Peter Finn, "Guantánamo Closure Called Obama Priority," *Washington Post,* November 12, 2008, discussing the incoming administration's interest in shuttering Guantánamo, and Steven Lee Myers, "Bush Decides to Keep Guantánamo Open," *New York Times,* October 20, 2008, discussing the same. The Obama administration will almost certainly continue to employ some form of military detention at least with respect to persons captured by the United States in connection with ongoing combat operations. Cf. Zabel and Benjamin, *supra,* note 1, at 2, observing that "as part of ongoing military operations, soldiers and sailors will capture and detain enemy fighters, without punishing them, in order to disable them from fighting against the United States. This is both lawful and fundamental to the effective prosecution of war, and it does not generally implicate the criminal justice system."

4. See William Glaberson, "Post-Guantánamo: A New Detention Law?" *New York Times,* November 14, 2008, surveying the debate.

5. See, for example, Human Rights First, *How to Close Guantánamo: Blueprint for the Next Administration* (Washington: Human Rights First, August 2008) (www.humanrightsfirst.org/pdf/080818-USLS-gitmo-blueprint.pdf), arguing that federal criminal prosecution provides an adequate basis for incapacitating terrorism suspects and recommending on that basis that military detainees at Guantánamo either be prosecuted in federal court, transferred to other countries, or simply released; Sarah E. Mendelson, *Closing Guantánamo: From Bumper Sticker to Blueprint* (Washington: Center for Strategic and International Studies, July 15, 2008) (http://www.csis.org/media/csis/pubs/080715_draft_csis_wg_gtmo.pdf); Steven I. Vladeck, *A Critique of "National*

Security Courts" (Washington: Constitution Project, June 2008) (www.constitution project.org/pdf/Critique_of_the_National_Security_Courts1.pdf), p. 2, disputing the view that Article III courts are not adequate venues for prosecution; Stephen J. Schulhofer, "Prosecuting Suspected Terrorists: The Role of the Civilian Courts," *Advance: The Journal of the ACS Issue Groups* (2008), pp. 63–64, asserting that "terrorism suspects can and should be indicted and tried for their alleged crimes in the ordinary civilian court system" (www.acslaw.org/files/Prosecuting-Suspected-Terrorists.pdf). The most thorough analysis of the substantive and procedural aspects of the federal criminal justice system as it relates to terrorism is *In Pursuit of Justice,* the report that Zabel and Benjamin produced for Human Rights First; see *supra,* note 1. Zabel and Benjamin conclude that the "system is reasonably well-equipped to handle most international terrorism cases" (ibid., at 2). Zabel and Benjamin are careful to note, however, that the military detention of persons captured in "ongoing military operations . . . is both lawful and fundamental to the effective prosecution of war"(ibid.). The report thus is best understood as rebutting the claim that a "national security court" should "displace the criminal justice system" but not as a challenge to the use of military detention in at least some circumstances (ibid.).

6. See, for example, Andrew McCarthy and Alykhan Velshi, "We Need a National Security Court," 2006, submission for AEI book on outsourcing U.S. law (www.defend democracy.org/images/stories/national%20security%20court.pdf), arguing that rules of process disfavor reliance on criminal prosecution of terrorists; Benjamin Wittes, *Law and the Long War* (New York: Penguin Press, 2008), describing an array of procedural obstacles that can arise in connection with criminal prosecution of terrorism suspects who may be too dangerous to release; Michael B. Mukasey, "Jose Padilla Makes Bad Law," *Wall Street Journal,* August 22, 2007, questioning the utility of criminal prosecution as a mechanism to incapacitate terrorists; Jack Goldsmith and Neal Katyal, "The Terrorists' Court," *New York Times,* July 11, 2007, arguing that "[c]riminal prosecution[s] should still take place where they can" but that "they are not always feasible"; Amos N. Guiora, "Military Commissions and National Security Courts after Guantánamo," *Northwestern University Law Review* 103 (2008), pp. 203–04, stating that "because they lack specialization in the intelligence arena, Article III courts are improper venues for trying suspected terrorists"; Glenn M. Sulmasy, "The Legal Landscape After *Hamdan*: The Creation of Homeland Security Courts," *New England Journal of International and Comparative Law* 13 (2006), p. 1; A. John Radsan, "A Better Model for Interrogating High-Level Terrorists," *Temple Law Review* 79 (2006), pp. 1227, 1276–82.

7. See, for example, William Glaberson, "Bin Laden Driver Sentenced to Short Term," *New York Times,* August 7, 2008, describing the debate regarding the implications of the split sentence and verdict for the fairness of the system.

8. See *Boumediene v. Bush,* 579 F. Supp.2d 191 (D.D.C. 2008), determining that the government lacked sufficient evidence to detain all but one of six detainees captured originally in Bosnia.

9. I have argued elsewhere that the poor fit between the assumptions underlying the law of armed conflict and the particular characteristics of al Qaeda have given rise to an ad hoc convergence process in which the procedural aspects of military detention (and possibly also the substantive aspects) have gravitated toward those normally associated with the criminal prosecution model, while the criminal prosecution model as applied to terrorism has experienced similar pressure to gravitate toward the features of the traditional military detention model. See Chesney and Goldsmith, *supra*, note 2. The latest developments in connection with habeas review of military detention decisions tend to confirm that descriptive account.

10. Detention capacity is not the only variable that may be used to compare existing and proposed systems, but it is a central one. Examples of other relevant considerations include the opportunities that each system presents for gathering intelligence and also each system's perceived domestic and international legitimacy, factors that affect their long-term sustainability and the extent to which other states will cooperate with them. Ultimately, of course, the question of which considerations matter depends on the strategic goals to be achieved by counterterrorism policy.

11. See, for example, Carol S. Steiker, "Foreword: The Limits of the Preventive State," *Journal of Criminal Law and Criminology* 88 (1998), pp. 771–76. The theoretical benefit of the preventive turn in criminal law is straightforward: far better, from the point of view of the victim and of society, that harms are prevented altogether rather than just punished after the fact. On the other hand, the very nature of preventive intervention involves uncertainty as to whether a harmful act actually would have occurred; therefore it cannot be known whether any given instance of preventive prosecution in fact realizes a harm-prevention benefit. That is the dilemma of the preventive state, and it is inherent in all forms of inchoate criminal liability. This dilemma is not new. The criminal law has long provided inchoate criminal liability through concepts such as attempt, conspiracy, and solicitation. But as the bounds of those concepts are pushed, and as new inchoate crime concepts are introduced, the dilemma sharpens.

12. See 18 U.S.C. § 2339A and 18 U.S.C. § 2339B.

13. 18 U.S.C. § 2339D.

14. For a more in-depth review of additional criminal statutes not discussed in detail below, see Zabel and Benjamin, *supra*, at 43–51, discussing, inter alia, seditious conspiracy and treason prosecutions.

15. Marc Sageman, *Understanding Terror Networks* (University of Pennsylvania Press, 2004).

16. 18 U.S.C. § 2332b(a).

17. For a list of dozens of such statutes, see Robert M. Chesney, "Beyond Conspiracy? Anticipatory Prosecution and the Challenge of Unaffiliated Terrorism," *Southern California Law Review* 80 (2007), pp. 425, 495–98. For discussion of terrorism defendants prosecuted under these provisions, see Zabel and Benjamin, *supra*, at 39–42, discussing §§ 2332, 2332a, and 2332b prosecutions.

18. 18 U.S.C. § 2332(d).

19. 18 U.S.C. § 2332a. The reference to "WMD" in the language of the statute is misleading to laypeople. The statute defines weapons of mass destruction to include "destructive device" as defined in 18 U.S.C § 921, which includes bombs, grenades, rockets, missiles, mines, and any projectile-firing weapon with a bore greater than one-half inch. See 18 U.S.C. § 921(a)(4). It also is worth noting that a number of federal crimes can be tried on an extraterritorial basis when they occur within the U.S. government's "special aircraft jurisdiction" or "special maritime and territorial jurisdiction."

20. 18 U.S.C. § 2441.

21. 18 U.S.C. § 1116.

22. The Torture Act (18 U.S.C. § 2340A) provides a limited exception. It provides universal jurisdiction to prosecute those who commit or attempt torture, regardless of the citizenship involved, so long as the person can be found in the United States.

23. Ex post facto considerations would preclude a solution in which the government simply enacts new, more capacious criminal laws, though it certainly might want to enact such laws in that situation in order to make it possible over time to move away from noncriminal measures.

24. See 18 U.S.C. § 1001(a), prohibiting efforts to conceal material facts.

25. See, for example, 18 U.S.C. § 1623, prohibiting false statements to a grand jury, and 18 U.S.C. § 1503, criminalizing efforts to influence grand jury proceedings through corruption, threats, or intimidation.

26. Cf. *United States* v. *Benkahla,* 530 F.3d 300 (4th Cir. June 23, 2008), affirming the conviction of a terrorism suspect for making false statements to FBI investigators and to two grand juries and for obstruction of justice and affirming application of the terrorism-sentencing enhancement.

27. 18 U.S.C. § 2339B.

28. 18 U.S.C. § 2339A(b), incorporated by reference in 18 U.S.C. § 2339B(g)(4).

29. The Supreme Court in 1953 approved the criminalization of associational status, subject to a constitutional requirement that the government prove that the defendant intended to further the unlawful ends of an organization and that the defendant's membership was active rather than merely nominal. See *Scales* v. *United States,* 367 U.S. 203, 226-27 (1961).

30. Insofar as groups such as al Qaeda eschew formal membership structures, this capacity proves all the more important.

31. See 50 U.S.C. § 1702.

32. 50 U.S.C. § 1705. But see *Al-Haramain Islamic Foundation, Inc.* v. *Bush,* 507 F3d 1190. 1206 (D. Or. November 6, 2008), holding that the government denied due process to an entity subject to an IEEPA blocking order by failing to provide adequate notice before the designation and that the phrase "material support" as used in an executive order implementing IEEPA authority after the 9/11 attacks is unconstitutionally vague.

33. For a discussion of the organizational complexities of the global jihad movement, see Chesney, *supra,* note 17, at 437–46.

34. See Secretary of State, "Foreign Terrorist Organizations" (Office of the Coordinator for Counterterrorism, 1999) (www.state.gov/s/ct/rls/rpt/fto/2682.htm).

35. See George W. Bush, "Blocking Property and Prohibiting Transactions with Persons Who Commit, Threaten to Commit, or Support Terrorism," Executive Order 13224, September 23, 2001 (http://fas.org/irp/offdocs/eo/eo-13224.htm).

36. 50 U.S.C. § 1702(a).

37. See, for example, *United States* v. *Hammoud,* 381 F.3d 316 (4th Cir. 2004), rejecting such arguments.

38. See, for example, *Humanitarian Law Project* v. *Mukasey,* 509 F.3d 1122 (9th Cir. 2007), petition for rehearing *en banc* pending (2008).

39. 18 U.S.C. § 2339A(b)(2, 3).

40. See Humanitarian Law Project, *supra,* rejecting challenge to the terms "personnel" and "expert advice or assistance" (as it refers to "scientific" and "technical" knowledge) but accepting challenge to terms "training," "service," and "expert advice or assistance" (as it refers to "other specialized knowledge").

41. For a general overview of conspiracy law, see Neal K. Katyal, "Conspiracy Theory," *Yale Law Journal* 112 (2003), p. 1307.

42. See Chesney, *supra,* note 17, at 449–56.

43. See Federal Rules of Evidence 801(d)(2)(E). Statements that would qualify under this rule almost certainly would overcome Confrontation Clause objections to admissibility on the ground that they are not "testimonial."

44. See 18 U.S.C. § 371.

45. See, for example, 18 U.S.C. § 956(a)(2)(A), imposing maximum sentence of life for conspiracies to murder or kidnap individuals outside the United States; 18 U.S.C. § 2332b(c)(1)(F), punishing conspiracies to commit violence transcending national boundaries with the same maximum sentence as would apply had the act been completed.

46. Alberto Gonzales and John Pistole, "Terrorist Arrests," press conference, U.S. Department of Justice, Washington, D.C., June 23, 2006 (www.washingtonpost.com/wp-dyn/content/article/2006/06/23/AR2006062300942.html).

47. See Julienne Gage, "2nd Mistrial in 'Liberty City 7' Case," *Washington Post,* April 17, 2008; Curt Anderson, "5 Miami Men Convicted of Sears Tower Attack Plot," *Associated Press,* May 12, 2009.

48. Russell R. Killinger to Kenneth Swartz and Jeanne Baker, July 7, 2006, "Defendant Hassoun's Motion for Clarification of Court's Ruling as to What Government Must Particularize Regarding the 'Manner and Means' of the Conspiracy," *United States* v. *Hassoun,* 04-cr-60001 (S.D. Fla. July 25, 2006).

49. See Wittes, *supra,*note 6, at 81.

50. See 18 U.S.C. § 2339D. The "term 'military-type training' includes training in means or methods that can cause death or serious bodily injury, destroy or damage

property, or disrupt services to critical infrastructure, or training on the use, storage, production, or assembly of any explosive, firearm or other weapon, including any weapon of mass destruction" 18 U.S.C. § 2339D(c)(1). Given the detail of this definition, it is unlikely that the "training" term in § 2339D will be struck down on grounds of vagueness, as has occurred with the "training" term employed with respect to § 2339B.

51. See 18 U.S.C. § 2339D(a).

52. See *United States v. Maldonado,* No. 07-cr-124 (S.D. Tex.), alleging receipt of training from al Qaeda while in Mogadishu, Somalia. Maldonado pled guilty to the § 2339D charge in 2007, sparing the government the need to prove that he knew at the time that he was receiving training from al Qaeda.

53. 18 U.S.C. § 2339A.

54. There are obstacles with § 2339A to bear in mind. First, because § 2339A employs the same definition of "material support or resources" as does § 2339B, prosecutions under § 2339A may be vulnerable to vagueness challenges with respect to definitional terms such as "service." Second, prior to an amendment in late 2001, § 2339A applied only to material support that is provided *inside* the United States, meaning that the statute may have little or no application to those who attended foreign training camps or otherwise became involved in terrorist plots prior to 9/11.

55. Mark Arax, "The Agent Who Might Have Saved Hamid Hayat," *Los Angeles Times Magazine,* May 28, 2006; Rone Tempest, "In Lodi Terror Case, Intent Was the Clincher," *Los Angeles Times,* May 1, 2006.

56. First Superseding Indictment, *United States v. Hamid Hayat,* No. 05-cr-240 (E.D. Cal. 2005).

57. Cf. *Al-Marri v. Pucciarelli,* 534 F.3d 213 (4th Cir. 2008) (*en banc*), confirming authority to detain a suspected al Qaeda agent captured in the United States but offering a variety of accounts for the scope of that authority.

58. Gordon England, "Combatant Status Review Tribunal Process," *Implementation of Combatant Status Review Tribunal Procedures for Enemy Combatants Detained at Guantánamo Bay Naval Base, Cuba* (Washington: Department of Defense, July 29, 2004) (www.defenselink.mil/news/Jul2004/d20040730comb.pdf).

59. The question of whether persons may be detained on the basis of affiliation with groups other than al Qaeda or the Taliban as such is at issue in *Parhat v. Gates,* currently pending in the D.C. Circuit Court of Appeals.

60. See 18 U.S.C. § 2332. If the defendant uses explosives in the act, he also faces prosecution under 18 U.S.C. § 2332a. Charges in that scenario may also lie under §2339A, insofar as the fighter's role is more in the nature of support.

61. Cf. *United States v. Lindh,* 212 F.Supp.2d 541, 552-58 (E.D. Va. 2002), rejecting the claim of combatant's privilege by a Taliban member.

62. See 18 U.S.C. § 1116, prohibiting such murders.

63. Cf. 18 U.S.C. § 956(a), prohibiting conspiracies in the United States to engage in violence overseas.

64. On this point, it should be noted that it is not clear that courts will permit the government to employ an interpretation of the scope of military detention that extends to groups lacking a sufficient nexus to al Qaeda or the Taliban. In *Parhat v. Gates,* for example, it appears that the D.C. Circuit Court of Appeals, exercising its CSRT review authority pursuant to the Military Commissions Act of 2006, may have called into question whether membership in the East Turkestan Islamic Movement (a Chinese Uighur organization with links to the global jihad movement) sufficed to justify detention. See *Parhat v. Gates,* No. 06-1397 (D.C. Cir. June 20, 2008), requiring the government to release or transfer Parhat or else hold a new CSRT consistent with the court's classified conclusions.

65. *In re Guantánamo Detainee Cases,* 355 F.Supp.2d 443, 475 (D.D.C. 2005), rev'd sub nom. *Boumediene v. Bush,* 476 F.3d 981 (2007), rev'd, 128 S. Ct. 2229 (June 12, 2008).

66. See 10 U.S.C. § 950v(b). Cf. Rome Statute of the International Criminal Court, Art. 8(2)(a)(i), willful killing of protected persons, Art. 8(2)(b)(i, ii), attacks on civilians and civilian objects, Art. 8(2)(b)(vi), denial of quarter.

67. Cf. *United States* v. *Hamdan,* On Reconsideration Ruling on Motion to Dismiss for Lack of Jurisdiction 8-9 (Mil. Com. December 19, 2007), rejecting ex post facto claim on the ground that the detainee was not protected by Constitution's ex post facto clause, available at p. 1290 of the document collection posted at www.defenselink.mil/news/Dec2007/Hamdan%20VOL%20I%20December%205%20and%206%202007%20Session.pdf. See also ibid. (July 2008), affirming holding as to ex post facto clause in the aftermath of the Supreme Court's *Boumediene* decision.

68. See Zabel and Benjamin, *supra,* note 1.

69. See ibid. at 61–64.

70. See ibid. at 61.

71. See ibid. at 101–05.

72. 467 U.S. 649 (1984).

73. Zabel and Benjamin, *supra,* note 1, at 103.

74. See ibid. at 103–04 (citing 214 F.3d 111 (2d Cir. 2000)). Zabel and Benjamin also note that a similar question was presented in connection with the prosecution of John Walker Lindh (who had been interrogated in Afghanistan without being informed of his rights under *Miranda* for two days) but that Lindh pled guilty before the court ruled on the admissibility of those statements. See ibid. at 104-05.

75. See ibid. at 111–13. But see Gregory S. McNeal, "Beyond Guantánamo: Obstacles and Options," *Northwestern University Law Review* 103 (2008), pp. 45–46, discussing speedy trial concerns.

76. See Zabel and Benjamin, *supra,* note 1, at 77–90.

77. See ibid. at 81.

78. See ibid., citing *Mayfield* v. *United States,* 504 F. Supp.2d 1023, 1042-43 (D. Or. 2007).

79. See Public Law No. 96-456, 94 Stat. 2025, 2025-31 (1980), codified at18 U.S.C. app. 3.

80. See Zabel and Benjamin, *supra,* note 1, at 89. See also Schulhofer, *supra,* note 5, at 64–67.

81. 373 U.S. 83 (1963).

82. 405 U.S. 150 (1972).

83. See, generally, Jonathan M. Fredman, "Intelligence Agencies, Law Enforcement, and the Prosecution Team," *Yale Law and Policy Review* 331 (1998), p. 529, surveying the issue.

84. 514 U.S. 419, 437 (1995).

85. See Zabel and Benjamin, *supra,* note 1, at 96–98, citing *United States* v. *Brooks,* 966 F.2d 1500, 1503 (D.C. Cir. 1992), adopting a "closely aligned" standard; *United States* v. *Pelullo,* 399 F.3d 197, 217-18 (3d Cir. 2005), articulating a "prosecution team" test, requiring disclosure with respect to the prosecution team and in connection with other agencies that "have cooperated intimately from the outset" of the criminal investigation or from which prosecutors had acquired evidence to be used in the case.

86. Ibid. at 98.

87. See ibid., citing *United States* v. *Padilla,* No. 04-cr-60001 (S.D. Fla. May 19, 2006) (Dkt. No. 346). It may be worth noting that the federal district judges conducting habeas review of military detention decisions have recently begun to grapple with the same issue. At the time of this writing, only one judge had issued a ruling on the subject, concluding that the government has an obligation to disclose exculpatory information that the Justice Department encounters in the course of preparing the government's factual returns or in preparing for the habeas hearing itself. See *Boumediene* v. *Bush,* No. 04-1166 (D.D.C. August 27, 2008), case management order, at 1.E (https://ecf.dcd.uscourts.gov/cgi-bin/show_public_doc?2004cv1166-142). That ruling may well generate an appeal, inconsistent decisions by other judges facing the same issue, reconsideration by the judge in that particular case, or all of the above. Cf. Lyle Denniston, "Update: *Bismullah* Effect Spreading?" SCOTUSBlog, August 29, 2008 (www.scotusblog.com/wp/update-bismullah-effect-spreading/), observing that the judge who made the ruling may yet reconsider it in light of a contemporaneous motion by detainees in that case.

88. See Fredman, *supra,* note 83.

89. That gap will exist in any event due to the fact that some intelligence information cannot be employed in court because of promises made to the sources of the information (such as a foreign intelligence service) or because of the impact of the Federal Rules of Evidence or the Confrontation Clause. See *infra.*

90. Zabel and Benjamin do not directly address the problem of resistance from the intelligence community, though they do note that prosecutors in the *Moussaoui* litigation were obliged to notify the court after Moussaoui's conviction and sentencing that they had learned, belatedly, that the CIA had made recordings of the interrogation of key witnesses and that those recordings had been destroyed. See Zabel and Benjamin, *supra,* note 1, at 10. They also note that "in practice, it is not always easy to conduct a thorough *Brady* search in a large-scale investigation in which agencies such

as the CIA or the Defense Department may have worked closely with prosecutors. Although these agencies have reportedly become more responsive to the needs of the justice system over time, their sometimes complicated recordkeeping systems and far-flung operations can present obstacles to an efficient *Brady* review."

91. See ibid. at 107.

92. Ibid.

93. See ibid at 107–08. See also Federal Rules of Evidence 901(a).

94. Zabel and Benjamin, *supra,* note 1, at 108, citing developments in the Padilla prosecution.

95. See ibid. at 108–09. Zabel and Benjamin note that a number of circuits have upheld such procedures against challenge under the Confrontation Clause, but that one—the Eighth Circuit in *United States v. Bordeaux,* 400 F.3d 548, 552-55 (2005)—has taken the contrary view. See ibid. at 109.

96. See Federal Rules of Evidence 802.

97. See Federal Rules of Evidence 804(b)(3).

98. See Federal Rules of Evidence 801(d)(2)(E).

99. See Federal Rules of Evidence 801(d)(2)(A).

100. See Zabel and Benjamin, *supra,* note 1, at 109–10.

101. See Federal Rules of Evidence 801(d)(2)(A).

102. See *Williamson* v. *United States,* 512 U.S. 594 (1994).

103. Cf. Schulhofer, *supra,* note 5, at 69: "No matter how exceptional the circumstances, it seems doubtful that constitutionally acceptable procedures could be devised for presenting classified evidence at a criminal trial without fully disclosing it to the defendant."

104. See *Crawford* v. *Washington,* 541 U.S. 36 (2004); *Davis* v. *Washington,* 547 U.S. 813 (2006).

105. See *Giles* v. *California,* 128 S. Ct. 2678 (2008). The Court held that exceptions exist only insofar as they would have been recognized at the time of the founding in the late 1780s. In theory, then, the Court eventually may recognize additional exceptions, though there is no particular reason to believe that any such exception would prove especially relevant in the context of statements made to interrogators.

106. This question likely will be resolved differently in the context of habeas corpus review of military detention decisions. Neither the Federal Rules of Evidence nor the Confrontation Clause necessarily are applicable in that context, and the only judge to rule on the topic as of the time of this writing has concluded that "[h]earsay evidence that is relevant and material to the lawfulness of petitioner's detention may be admissible. The opposing party will have an opportunity to challenge the credibility and weight accorded any hearsay evidence." See *Boumediene* case management order, *supra,* note 87, at II.D.

107. See *In re* Winship, 397 U.S. 358 (1970), holding that application of the beyond-a-reasonable-doubt standard is required as a matter of due process.

108. See 10 U.S.C. § 949l(c)(1), added by Military Commissions Act of 2006.

109. See, for example, *In re* Guantánamo Bay Detainee Litigation, Misc. No. 08-442, 4 (D.D.C. November 6, 2008), case management order, stating that "the government bears the burden of proving by a preponderance of the evidence that the petitioner's detention is lawful."

110. Which is not to say that the government will prevail easily in justifying its use of the military detention power during habeas review. In the very first ruling on the merits in a Guantánamo habeas proceeding, Judge Leon determined that the government had failed to meet the preponderance standard (despite permissive evidentiary procedures enabling the government to make use of hearsay and to limit disclosure to cleared counsel and not the petitioners themselves) with respect to five of six petitioners. See *Boumediene* v. *Bush*, 579 F.Supp.2d 191 (D.D.C. 2008).

111. Of course, some of the limitations discussed above already have been addressed through changes such as the removal of jurisdictional limitations on § 2339A in 2001 and § 2339B in 2004, and in light of ex post facto considerations, there simply is not anything that can be done to close the gaps that remain with respect to conduct that predates those changes. Not all limitations are subject to that qualification, however.

112. The same can be said for amending § 2339D in the manner suggested above. In that regard, it is worth noting that §§ 2339A, 2339B, and 2339D all currently apply extraterritorially without respect to the citizenship of the defendant. Section 2339B(d)(1)(C) provides, for example, that jurisdiction exists whenever "an offender is brought into or found in the United States, even if the required conduct for the offense occurs outside the United States." See also 18 U.S.C. § 2339D(b)(3), stating the same.

113. One of the most frequently charged conspiracy statutes is 18 U.S.C. § 956(a), which makes it a felony to conspire, while within the United States, to travel abroad to commit murder or other violent crimes. The statute was the basis for the core conspiracy charge in *Padilla*, for example, but by its terms could apply just as well to nonpolitical violence.

114. See Zabel and Benjamin, *supra,* note 1, at 89.

115. See ibid.

116. Many other considerations bear on the question, such as postconviction release. Although some of the violent crime statutes discussed above provide for life sentences or even the death penalty, the more exotic, prevention-oriented statutes such as § 2339B and IEEPA most certainly do not. Material support defendants, for example, typically receive ten-year sentences, while IEEPA defendants receive eight-year sentences. See Robert M. Chesney, "Federal Prosecution of Terrorism-Related Offenses: Conviction and Sentencing Data in Light of the 'Soft-Sentence' and 'Data-Reliability' Critiques," *Lewis and Clark Law Review* 11 (2007), pp. 851, 879–88. Even Jose Padilla, convicted of a violent crime conspiracy, received only seventeen years and four months. And though it is tempting to treat Padilla's sentence as exceptional because the judge clearly acted, in part, out of concern for his experience in being held

as a military detainee for several years, that may actually be a scenario that recurs often in the most important cases. In any event, the important point is that a criminal conviction does not produce a sentence designed to be coextensive with the period during which the defendant may remain dangerous in the future, even if such considerations do enter into the sentencing analysis to some degree. As a result, a criminal sentence may run much shorter—or much longer—than it would if prevention of harm were the only consideration. Accordingly, evaluations of the adequacy of criminal prosecution should address not just the substantive and procedural rules relating to the baseline determination of guilt, but also the magnitude of the sentences likely to be produced.

ROBERT S. LITT *and* WELLS C. BENNETT

5

Better Rules for Terrorism Trials

Nearly eight years after the attacks of September 11, 2001, the government's legal, practical, and moral authority to detain suspected terrorists without trial remains a subject of fierce debate. Nonetheless, there is general agreement among those who support preventive detention as well as those who oppose it that the government can and should prosecute some individuals for terrorism-related criminal activity. Potential defendants could theoretically include the planners of or participants in actual terrorist attacks; U.S. citizens or legal residents who knowingly provide financial or other support to organizations such as Hamas, al Qaeda, or the Tamil Tigers; even homegrown sympathizers or "wannabe" terrorists whose grandiose plots may or may not prove to be unrealistic.

Prosecutors have, in fact, brought many such cases in federal court. Many of them have resulted in convictions; some have not. Yet in the years since September 11, no consensus has formed about the best way to try persons accused of terrorism-related crimes.[1] Rather, a tripartite debate rages:

—The Bush administration and others who generally view terrorism as a military problem doubted the efficacy of criminal trial. They favored instead trial by military commission whenever possible, arguing that traditional criminal trials in federal court are hamstrung by rules of procedure that make them not merely ineffective in securing convictions but affirmatively dangerous to national security.[2] They correctly pointed out that military commissions are not a jury-rigged invention of the post–September 11 world but are a well-established method of trying war criminals.[3] The Obama administration, after freezing the commissions at the outset of its term of office, now wishes to revive them in a somewhat revised form.

—Civil libertarians contend that the traditional laws of war cannot be transferred without change to a potentially endless war on terror; that the current system of military tribunals lacks credibility and is legally flawed; and that the alleged inadequacies and dangers of criminal trials have been vastly overstated.[4] They argue that therefore all terrorism trials should take place in federal courts under traditional rules.

—Finally, a third group argues that the United States needs a special tribunal of some sort—a so-called "national security court"—that operates under special rules designed to overcome the problems attendant to trials in federal court.[5]

The dispute about the optimal forum in which to try terrorists is, in reality, a dispute about what rules should apply in those trials. Do the existing rules of procedure and evidence in federal criminal cases pose unacceptable and unnecessary hurdles to the successful prosecution of terrorists? To the extent that they do, are less strict rules—for some or all terrorism trials—compatible with the Constitution and good policy? This chapter suggests answers to those questions, while addressing only in passing whether those trials should take place in federal court, a court martial, a military commission, or some new national security court. The need for a coherent set of rules—regardless of the forum in which those rules apply—is underscored by recent events. The Obama administration has now declared that it will retain the military commissions established by its predecessor, with added procedural safeguards.[6] Given the questions that have been raised over the last seven years about the legality and fairness of military commissions, the viability of their new iteration will depend greatly, if not entirely, upon what their precise procedures are, the extent to which they depart from the familiar rules of procedure for criminal cases, and the administration's ability to justify those departures.

We conclude that for the most part, there is no reason to depart dramatically from existing federal court rules and procedures. Although trying alleged terrorists places burdens on the prosecution, defense counsel, the intelligence community, and the courts, the available evidence does not establish the need for dramatic changes. We do suggest some minor modifications that could be made, consistent with the Constitution and overall fairness, to deal with particular concerns.

In one respect, however, the current situation calls for more substantial changes, both to limit the risk of improper disclosure of information that could damage U.S. national security and to make the criminal justice system operate more smoothly and fairly in counterterrorism cases. The Constitution, federal law, and the rules of criminal procedure all require the disclosure of much evidence to the accused in a criminal case and require that the accused be allowed to call witnesses in his defense and confront his accusers. When the evidence is classified or the witnesses themselves are terrorists, current procedures can create a Hobson's choice between potential danger to national security from the disclosure of classified evidence or access to detained individuals, on the one hand, and restrictions on a defendant's right to defend himself, on the other.

Congress could significantly ameliorate, if not entirely eliminate, those problems by authorizing the creation of a national security bar—a permanent corps of security-cleared lawyers who would be available to represent defendants in terrorism-related cases—and changing the rules for handling classified evidence when a defendant is represented by a member of the new bar. Many former government lawyers or others already have security clearances and have shown that they can be trusted to protect government secrets just as much as prosecutors can. Members of a national security bar would have full access to all classified information that is otherwise subject to disclosure—access as unencumbered as if no national security issues were involved in the case at all. They would participate in all court proceedings about classified information—proceedings that now are often held on an ex parte basis. To the extent that other detained terrorists are potential witnesses, cleared counsel could participate in depositions of those witnesses. But they would be barred from disclosing classified information to their client or to any co-counsel who is not also a member of the proposed national security bar.

Critically, however, the choice of whether to be represented by a member of the national security bar or by other counsel would be up to the defendant, not the government or the court. The defendant, after a hearing in open court, could choose between having counsel with full access to information but restricted communication with the defendant and having counsel with full communication with the defendant but restricted access to information. By allowing for the participation of counsel with a security clearance, creation of a national security bar should minimize the risk of improper disclosure; by placing the choice in the hands of the defendant, it should minimize the burden on constitutional rights.

This proposal is not a panacea. It does not deal fully, for example, with the problem of the defendant who represents himself and then seeks access to classified information. Nor does it ensure that legally acceptable alternatives will always be available to prevent the need to disclose classified evidence—

such as the testimony of a detainee who is being held for intelligence interrogation—although it should minimize the number of such situations. Creation of a national security bar to represent alleged terrorists, combined with the flexible use of deposition testimony and substitutes for classified information—all accomplished through the participation of cleared counsel—can ameliorate but will not entirely eliminate the conflict between a defendant's rights and the imperatives of national security.

Still, establishing a national security bar and modifying the rules for handling classified information should enable the justice system to conduct trials that look as much as possible like normal criminal trials, while handling classified information more deftly than it now does. Current procedures can result in both unfairness to defendants and undue burdens on prosecutions. There is, unfortunately, no cost-free method of resolving the problems created by criminal trial of alleged terrorists. Benefits in speed, ease of conviction, and protection of information are accompanied by costs in accuracy, fairness, and public perceptions, and vice versa. What follows is our assessment of the right way to strike the balance between these countervailing interests, with particular emphasis on how a national security bar might alleviate current problems.

Three Basic Premises

We begin by discussing three important underpinnings of our analysis: the likely continued existence of a system of detention of terrorists without trial, the unavailability to the public of complete information about the problems with criminal terrorism trials, and a general preference for existing trial procedures unless they are shown to be inadequate.

A Continued Detention System

The first of our three premises is that some system of noncriminal detention will continue to exist. We recognize that this is a controversial position. Our belief that preventive detention will continue reflects a judgment about political realities, rather than the underlying legal, moral, and policy issues. President Obama ordered Guantánamo's closure as one of his first official acts, but in establishing a task force to review "lawful options available to the Federal Government with respect to the apprehension, detention, trial, transfer, release, or other disposition" of terrorists, he made clear that the possibility of detention without criminal trial has not been ruled out.[7] And in subsequent court filings, the new administration reiterated its predecessor's assertion of broad authority to detain captured terrorists.[8]

Certainly, military law has historically permitted the detention of enemy combatants until the end of hostilities.[9] Authors like Benjamin Wittes have argued that there are at least some current detainees who would be threats to U.S. national security if released but whom the government may not be able to try in court; they also argue that it is likely that U.S. forces will apprehend in the future other captives for whom detention may be a more practical option than trial.[10] We doubt that the government will want to deprive itself of that option.[11]

That assumption has implications for our analysis, because the need for looser criminal trial rules is inversely related to the scope of the government's authority to detain terrorists outside the criminal process. To the extent that security risks or procedural impediments make it difficult or impossible to try terrorists, the risks to national security can be lessened by expanding the government's authority to detain. On the other hand, if detention is prohibited or severely limited, the resulting security gap will lead to pressure for more flexible trial procedures. If there is a class of persons who are both dangerous and not triable under existing law—a proposition that some have disputed[12]—and the government's choice is limited to trying them using procedures that diverge from the norms in criminal courts or releasing them, we expect that the government will follow the former path. The assumption that some detention authority will continue to exist thus informs our judgment about the need to change the rules for criminal trials.

Reliance on Public Information

The dispute over whether there exists a class of persons who should be detained without trial reflects a second, methodological, constraint on our analysis: it is based entirely on publicly available sources. That imposes an important limitation, one that although seemingly obvious often goes unacknowledged. Much of the information most relevant to the effectiveness of current federal criminal trial procedures remains secret. The government may decline to bring some terrorism cases to trial in light of procedural or national security constraints that have nothing to do with the merits of the cases.[13] Likewise, federal courts and military commissions must delete classified information from their decisions. Without access to the information that may have dissuaded the government from bringing particular indictments or to the classified materials that drove the courts' decisions, it can be hard to know whether a particular rule was obeyed, whether it needs adjusting, or whether it can be adjusted while maintaining the country's fundamental values.

The debate over federal courts' handling of classified information illustrates this shortcoming and its import. Two exhaustively researched studies have reviewed public materials and rejected the oft-made argument that terrorism cases cannot be successfully tried in federal court because trial procedures do not ensure sufficient protection of national security interests.[14] According to the studies, of the two most widely cited security breaches in terrorism trials, one never happened and the other did not result from the inadequacy of existing rules but from the prosecution's failure properly to invoke those rules.[15] Both studies go on to catalog criminal terrorism cases that have been conducted without compromising sensitive information.[16] They consequently dismiss critics' security concerns, arguing that federal judges do an excellent job of protecting U.S. secrets while ensuring a fair process for the accused.

But evaluating trial procedures by examining only actual prosecutions is like evaluating the dangers that salmon face when swimming upstream by looking only at those fish that reach their goal. Just as that approach to piscine ecology misses the impact of bears, fatigue, and fishermen, analyzing the effectiveness of criminal prosecutions by assessing only those cases that have been brought fails to account for cases that may not have been brought because of hidden but insurmountable problems. In the case of criminal trials, for example, there is a huge group of potential cases that has very publicly *not* been brought as criminal prosecutions: the overwhelming majority of the nearly 800 detainees who have passed through the detention facility at Guantánamo Bay, Cuba. How many of those detainees could have been charged successfully? More specifically, how many of those whose incapacitation represented an urgent national security priority could have been tried? How many other suspects were never even taken into custody because prosecutors believed existing rules would preclude a trial? Without such data, any evaluation that we undertake will necessarily be incomplete. If we knew more about this undisclosed information, both our perspective and our proposals might be different.

Nevertheless, we are constrained by the known facts, rather than possible but unknown ones. While we recognize the gaps in the information available to us, we believe that for both policy reasons and political reasons, decisions about the rules governing terrorism trials should be based on evidence and not speculation or hypotheticals. The conceded lack of complete information, however, necessarily renders our conclusions tentative and subject to revision.

Adherence to Normal Criminal Procedures

Our third premise is that the framework for trying terrorists should deviate from the rules ordinarily applied in federal criminal trials only when necessary.

Those rules have evolved over many centuries to achieve an appropriate balance between punishment of the guilty and protection of the innocent. In establishing rules for the trial of terrorists, the possibility of error cannot be discounted. Certainly the U.S. experience with the Guantánamo detainees suggests that the heat of battle, the fog of intelligence, and the venality or ignorance of third parties can lead to unfounded charges of terrorist activity.[17] Loosening the rules would surely make conviction of terrorists easier, but accuracy of conviction is no less important than ease of conviction, even in the context of terrorism.[18]

Moreover, the existing rules for federal criminal trials provide courts a great deal of flexibility, and various statutory innovations have been developed to deal with novel problems as they arise. Finally, while we cannot identify and analyze with certainty cases in which the government may have felt that it could not make use of the criminal justice system, the fact remains that it has repeatedly prosecuted terrorists and those associated with terrorists with considerable success.[19] The burden should be on those who seek to modify those procedures.

There also are pragmatic reasons to start with the procedures already applied in federal courts. They are established and familiar, for one thing. As the erratic experience of setting up military commissions has shown, it is likely to be easier to strike an appropriate balance by embroidering around the edges of existing procedures than by weaving new ones. Moreover, the international stature of the United States—and hence, ultimately, its national security—will continue to suffer to the extent that people around the world perceive its government as treating Muslim terrorists different from the way it treats other terrorists—whether U.S. citizens or non-Muslim aliens.

In addition to the various specific concerns raised about trials in federal courts, critics make two general theoretical arguments for starting anew, either with military commissions or with a national security court. One is that because "We are at war," treating terrorism as a law enforcement problem is inadequate to protect the nation. Military commissions can try enemy combatants for violations of the laws of war, and the procedures in those tribunals need not comply with ordinary evidentiary or even constitutional rules, so long as procedural deviations are properly authorized and comport with the law of war's minimal standards.[20] Procedural modifications to federal court trials, on the other hand, must be consistent with the Constitution. Thus, it is argued, military proceedings or a national security court will permit the flexibility needed to try terrorists.

There is considerable force to that argument but, in the end, it is not persuasive. One can acknowledge that the nation's fight against Islamic terrorists must have a significant military component without accepting that it must have *only* a military component or that the component devoted to adjudicating criminal activity must reside in the military. The claim that criminal trials are inadequate to protect the nation's security is speculative. It rests largely on the fact that the September 11 attacks occurred despite earlier indictments and trials of Islamic terrorists. However, since that time—years during which the great majority of terrorism prosecutions continued to occur in federal court—there have been no terrorist attacks. Of course, the absence of terrorist attacks since September 11 does not establish that the prosecution of terrorists in criminal court and the vigorous military and intelligence response to terrorism have adequate deterrent and protective effect. But it does suggest that the contrary argument—that they are not adequate—is in no way proven and is a shaky basis for fundamental changes to the nation's legal structures.

Similarly, it is now a commonplace that the "war" against Islamic terrorists is in many respects different from other armed conflicts. There is no defined "battlefield" and no readily identifiable way of determining when the conflict will end. Indeed, the Bush administration relied on the novel nature of its "war on terror" to deny persons seized and detained in Afghanistan and elsewhere the protections of the Geneva Conventions. And while that approach has since been repudiated by the Obama administration, the decisions of the Supreme Court in cases such as *Boumediene*[21] suggest that the laws of war as previously understood cannot be mechanically translated to the new armed conflict. Military commanders in the field should retain full authority to try war criminals seized on the field of battle; but in our view, when terrorists have been captured away from the field of battle or transported and detained, the exigencies of war do not furnish a persuasive justification for trying them before a military commission.[22]

The other theoretical argument advanced against trying terrorists in federal court is the fear of "spillover." Judges faced with the inevitable clash of procedure and security in a terrorism case may be tempted—consciously or not—to bend the rules to favor the government. Michael Mukasey, at the time a judge and later attorney general of the United States, predicted that "if conventional legal standards are adapted to deal with a terrorist threat, whether by relaxed standards for conviction, searches, the admissibility of evidence or otherwise, these adaptations will infect and change the standards in ordinary cases with ordinary defendants in ordinary courts of law."[23] The

desire to immunize the criminal justice system against the infection potentially caused by the virus of terrorism trials is frequently advanced as a reason
to establish a separate national security court.[24]

That argument, too, is not without force. History does teach that tools created to advance limited prosecutorial goals tend to expand throughout the justice system, like ink on a blotter. For example, the RICO statute[25] was initially
enacted to combat traditional criminal organizations such as the mafia, but
now it is routinely used in run-of-the-mill fraud or corruption cases. Similarly, the statutory power of federal law enforcement agencies to subpoena
records without judicial authority has spread from the national security context to a variety of ordinary criminal investigations.

At the end of the day, however, that concern does not justify jettisoning the
existing trial system. For one thing, there has been little indication to date that
pro-government distortions of the law in terrorism cases are "infecting" ordinary criminal trials. Quite the contrary, the principal concern expressed about
criminal trials has been that they afford terrorists too many rights, and there
is some irony in the fact that some of those who worry about spillover of
pro-government rulings are the same ones who strongly claim that criminal
trial rules are too favorable toward terrorism defendants.[26]

More important is that even if a military commission system remains, as
now appears likely, or a national security court is created, some terrorism
cases will continue to be tried in the federal courts. Under current law, military commissions cannot try U.S. citizens, and no one really has suggested that
they, or a national security court, be allowed to do so.[27] Nor has there been any
effort to try aliens seized in the United States before existing military commissions. In addition, some other nations have declared military commissions to be illegitimate and may not extradite people to face trial before
them.[28] The result is that some people will have to face trial in traditional
federal court proceedings irrespective of whether the United States experiments with other options. The problem of spillover therefore is going to exist
under any circumstances, and having one system for trying terrorists is probably better than having two.

Concerns about Trying Terrorists

It does not follow, however, that the United States should continue to follow
the existing rules merely because they are the existing rules. If federal trial procedures seriously inhibit or preclude prosecution of terrorists, new ones
should be considered, so long as they are consistent with fundamental fairness

and the Constitution. The concerns that have been expressed about trying suspected terrorists under normal rules can be roughly classified in three groups:

—fears that terrorist trials would result in the release of information that would compromise national security

—complaints about the burdens imposed by evidentiary and procedural rules

—worries about the costs and burdens that terrorism trials place on the courts.

The weightiest set of concerns is the first category. Broadly understood, the fear is that the panoply of constitutional and statutory rights afforded criminal defendants would necessarily result in *the disclosure of classified or other information that would endanger national security.* The Constitution guarantees a defendant tried in federal court a variety of rights, including the rights to counsel, to confront the witnesses against him, to subpoena witnesses on his own behalf, and to a public trial. It also requires the government to disclose exculpatory evidence to the defendant.[29] And the Federal Rules of Criminal Procedure require advance disclosure of much evidence, including statements of witnesses.[30]

These requirements present unavoidable challenges in a terrorism case. First, defendants in cases involving classified information—whether espionage cases or terrorism cases—often make wide-ranging demands for discovery of classified information.[31] Or, as Zacarias Moussaoui did, they may demand that persons whom the government has detained and is interrogating for intelligence purposes be produced as witnesses on their behalf.[32] They may claim that they are entitled to extensive disclosure of statements of witnesses or potential witnesses. Release of intelligence information to a terrorism defendant may create the risk that the information will be disclosed; even information that is not classified may be sensitive and of value to enemies. Release of such information may also discourage the cooperation of foreign intelligence services that are sympathetic to U.S. antiterrorism efforts yet unwilling to have their assistance revealed.[33] Moreover, the witnesses whose testimony a defendant seeks may have been subject to interrogation techniques that the government does not want to reveal, although that concern has been reduced by the extensive disclosure of information about CIA coercive interrogation techniques in the months following the inauguration of the Obama administration.

On the other hand, the government itself may face the need to use classified information in prosecuting a defendant. For example, critical evidence against a defendant may come from intercepted communications, yet the government may not wish to reveal that it has the ability to intercept those communications. In such situations, the government has a major problem: a bedrock principle of constitutional law prohibits the use of secret evidence against a defendant. The government, therefore, would be faced with a Hobson's choice: forgo use of potentially critical evidence against a defendant or risk its disclosure to enemies.[34]

The second category of concerns is that *the federal evidentiary rules are too strict* and that they would foreclose terrorism prosecutions or make them exceedingly difficult. Commonly cited examples include the following:

—When a crime is committed in the United States, police are able to secure the crime scene and observe a careful chain of custody rules as they gather evidence. But evidence of terrorist operations often is seized overseas, sometimes in the course of military operations, during which ensuring a clear chain of custody would be impracticable.[35]

—Similarly, terrorists often are apprehended abroad under circumstances in which it is not possible to give them effective *Miranda* warnings.[36] How does one provide counsel before interrogating a captive seized in North Waziristan?[37] In addition, U.S. military or intelligence officers cannot be expected to obtain warrants before seizing evidence abroad.

—Restrictions on the use of hearsay evidence imposed by the Federal Rules of Evidence and the Constitution would greatly diminish prosecutors' capabilities, as terrorism cases may need to rely on information provided by witnesses who cannot be hauled from the battlefield or who are not amenable to process.[38]

All of these rules, according to critics, make trial of terrorists in federal court especially difficult.

Third, opponents of federal court trials claim that *federal courts simply cannot handle terrorism trials*. Unruly defendants can transform the normally staid trial environment into chaos. The problem is especially acute when defendants exercise their constitutional right to represent themselves. An uncontrolled atmosphere inures to the benefit of terrorists, who can exploit a highly visible forum for attacking the United States and its policies and recruiting sympathizers.[39] The most frequently cited example here is the case of Zacarias Moussaoui, which was characterized by courtroom outbursts and a barrage of intemperate motions.[40] Some fear also that terrorists would use the forum of a trial to convey coded messages to their allies.[41]

A related worry is that public trials create an unacceptable risk to the physical security of judges, court personnel, and jurors. One federal judge has warned that "witnesses and jurors may be subjected to threats of violence or become the targets of attack. The willingness of terrorist organizations to retaliate against civilian participants in a terrorist trial cannot be over-looked."[42] Jurors in such cases may be intimidated from reaching a fair verdict.

What Should the Rules Be?

As Robert Chesney argues in chapter 4, many of the objections to current trial rules are overstated or rest on misapprehension of the applicable rules. Other objections—those relating to a defendant's access to classified infor-mation, the prerequisites for introducing a defendant's own statements against him, and the possible use of out-of-court statements by third parties—are more substantial. Fortunately, Congress could address some of those with relatively simple changes to current trial procedure. The most important among them include creating a national security bar and revising the proce-dures for dealing with classified information to account for the advantages of a reliable and experienced bar of security-cleared defense attorneys.

The Non-Problems

A number of the objections to the normal rules of criminal procedure disap-pear on closer inspection. For example, there is no ironclad rule requiring that a chain of custody be established before a document or other physical object is introduced into evidence. The Federal Rules of Evidence require only that before evidence can be introduced, the government must provide enough evidence "to support a finding that the [evidence] is what [the government] claims."[43] That is hardly an onerous burden, and the government can meet it in many different ways. The government has been able, for example, to use documents seized from al Qaeda training camps and turned over to law enforcement.[44] And in cases involving corruption in the Iraq Oil-for-Food program, the government successfully authenticated and introduced docu-ments seized from Iraqi ministries.[45]

More important is that it is difficult to imagine a fair trial system that allows the introduction of evidence on a lesser standard—that is to say, when there is *not* enough evidence to conclude that the evidence is what the gov-ernment claims. What probative value could a piece of evidence have if a juror cannot say what it is?[46] Indeed, the rules for the military commissions that were set up because of the supposed deficiencies in the criminal trial process included an authentication standard essentially identical to that pro-vided by the Federal Rules of Evidence.[47]

Similarly, federal courts have a wide range of tools to deal with dangerous or obstreperous defendants, including shackling them or removing them from the courtroom,[48] empaneling anonymous juries to prevent intimidation of jurors,[49] and imposing so-called Special Administrative Measures that limit an incarcerated defendant's ability to communicate with others.[50] The government's witness security program likewise can help guarantee the safety of individuals who testify for the prosecution.[51]

The problem of disruptive behavior can be most acute in the case of the pro se defendant, as the case of Zacarias Moussaoui showed. Here too, however, courts have experience in dealing with defendants who wish to make their trial a public or political platform or who are unable to control their behavior. As with any other constitutional right, the right to represent oneself can be forfeited by conduct.[52] A pro se defendant, just as much as a lawyer, must obey court rules and respect decorum. And just as the court can deny admission to or sanction a lawyer who ignores those rules, it can revoke the right of an incorrigible defendant to represent himself. Moreover, while Moussaoui's trial may have been a "circus,"[53] it is hard to see that his antics did any lasting damage to national security, to the criminal trial system, or indeed to anyone except Moussaoui himself.

While it is, of course, theoretically possible that a defendant could use the public forum afforded by a trial to communicate with co-conspirators, the extent of the genuine danger presented by such communications and the defendant's ability to make them without being detected are uncertain at best.[54] Moreover, as the experience with Combatant Status Review Tribunals and military commissions in Guantánamo has demonstrated, any forum in which a suspected terrorist can be tried offers the opportunity for disruption or public statements. And while providing special protective measures is costly and undoubtedly burdens the court system, the United States as a nation is willing to accept substantial additional costs, for example, in nonterrorism cases in which the death penalty is sought. Surely it should be willing to bear them when national security is at stake.

Finally, the Fourth Amendment's limitations on searches and seizures are unlikely to impose any significant restrictions on the use of evidence against terrorism defendants. The Supreme Court held in a 1990 case that the Fourth Amendment has "no application" to searches of aliens conducted outside of the United States, so that no alien would be able to complain of the seizure abroad of evidence used against him.[55] Following that decision, at least one court has held that warrants are not required for searches conducted abroad by U.S. officials—even in the rare cases in which they are directed at U.S. persons—and that such searches are limited only by a flexible "reasonableness" requirement that is likely to be met in most terrorism cases.[56] Therefore, even apart from the current Supreme Court's increasing hostility toward the exclusion of evidence as a remedy for illegal searches and seizures, the Fourth Amendment is unlikely to present any obstacles to prosecution of terrorists.

The Real Problem—and a Partial Solution

To understand the problems presented by the use of classified information in criminal cases, it is helpful to outline briefly how federal courts currently deal with such evidence. The principal tool is the Classified Information Procedures Act (CIPA).[57] When a defendant seeks access to classified material, the court must first determine whether that information is properly subject to disclosure under the applicable rules. If so, and if the government does not wish to disclose the classified information, it may ask the court to substitute either "a statement admitting relevant facts that the specific classified information would tend to prove" or "a summary of the specific classified information"; the court may permit the use of a substitution only if it would "provide the defendant with substantially the same ability to make his defense as would disclosure of the specific classified information." If the court finds that no substitution would be adequate and the government still refuses to disclose the classified information, the court may strike testimony, find relevant facts adverse to the government, or dismiss the charges in whole or in part. Hearings under CIPA may be held without the presence of defense counsel.

Congress passed CIPA itself without terrorism trials in mind. The law was developed largely to deal with cases in which a defendant with prior access to classified information sought to frustrate prosecution by threatening to disclose the information in the course of his trial—the so-called "graymail" problem. More recently, the government has used the law affirmatively to permit it to use evidence derived from classified information—normally in the form of an unclassified substitution approved under CIPA—as part of its own case against the defendant. The core point of CIPA is statutory recognition of a few key principles: that a court cannot compel the government to disclose classified information; that if classified information is otherwise disclosable under the rules, the government must either disclose it or provide sufficient information to put the defendant in essentially the same position that he would have been in had he had access to the classified information; and that if it cannot do either of those things, it cannot proceed with its case against him.

CIPA is generally considered to have worked well in preventing the unauthorized disclosure of classified information,[58] but it has been attacked as insufficiently protective of a defendant's rights. And while CIPA manages and alleviates the government's Hobson's choice between its ability to prosecute a case and its ability to keep its secrets, eliminating the problem altogether is probably impossible, since the conflict reflects the core requirements of the Fifth and Sixth Amendments. But it is possible to address the problems that CIPA poses for the defense with salutary consequences for the functioning of the judicial system as a whole.

First, because the government is entitled under CIPA to make submissions to the court ex parte—that is, without sharing them with the defendant or his counsel—the court often is forced to make judgments on whether a substitute is adequate to enable the defendant to put on his defense without input from those who are most familiar with what that defense is. Second, because the defendant usually will not have the security clearances necessary to review classified information, information often is shared with the defense counsel that the lawyer cannot discuss with his or her client, arguably infringing the defendant's right to counsel.[59] Indeed, sometimes even the substitution that the government prepares is classified and may not be shared by counsel with the defendant.[60] In cases that rely heavily on classified information, as many terrorism-related cases do, the strictures of CIPA therefore often lead to burdens on the prosecution, the defense, or both and to decisionmaking by the courts without the benefit of the best argumentation possible.

A National Security Bar

Current CIPA procedures do not guarantee in terrorism cases either that a defendant will receive a trial that is both fair and perceived as fair or that federal judges will base their decisions on the strongest possible presentations; moreover, CIPA's mechanism for protecting classified information is cumbersome and time consuming. The core of our proposal is that Congress should establish a national security bar, consisting of lawyers with the highest level of security clearance, who would agree to be available to represent defendants in terrorism-related cases.

The idea that counsel in a case involving classified information should have a security clearance is not new, of course. But creating a national security bar would offer many advantages over the existing system, in which defense lawyers often must seek security clearances on an ad hoc basis.[61] Establishing a national security bar would eliminate the lengthy delays and disputes over individual clearances, which have frustrated speedy resolution of many terrorism cases. Under the current approach, the court, the defense, and the prosecution must all await the conclusion of a defense lawyer's clearance investigation, the outcome of which is not assured. Creating a national security bar will solve the delay problem—and assure the defendant that he will not have to find a new lawyer in the event that his chosen lawyer's clearance application proves unsuccessful. Members of a national security bar would also acquire expertise in dealing with CIPA and the other difficult issues raised by terrorism cases, eliminating the need to "reinvent the wheel" in each trial and ensuring speedier and more consistent outcomes.

Finally, the existence of a permanent national security bar should make the procedural changes to CIPA proposed here more palatable. The intelligence community, justifiably concerned with the protection of sources, methods, and information, regularly resists disclosure of classified information in criminal cases, even to cleared counsel. If, however, the intelligence community knows that the defense counsel is someone who has been cleared in advance and found reliable, rather than someone selected initially by the defendant and then cleared, it may be more willing to accept the following proposed modifications to existing CIPA procedures.

First, no discoverable information at all would be withheld from counsel who is a member of the national security bar, nor would any ex parte submissions to the court be permitted. All normal discovery rules would apply, and anything that the government is otherwise obligated to produce under the law would be provided to such counsel, regardless of its classification level. Unclassified material, of course, can be provided to any counsel. In other words, having a national security bar would enable terrorism trials to look a great deal more like regular trials.

Second, as under existing law, counsel would be barred from discussing classified information with his or her client—or with uncleared counsel. But the defendant would have the right to decide whether to accept this restriction on his right to counsel. At the outset of any case, the defendant would be offered a choice: he could accept counsel from the national security bar—either as sole counsel or as co-counsel—with the concomitant limitation on that counsel's ability to discuss classified information with him, or he could reject such counsel, with the understanding that decisions regarding disclosure of classified information would then be made without the participation of the defense.

Third, no information that is not provided to the defendant personally would be used against him. If the facts are to be determined by the judge rather than a jury—for example, if the defendant waives the right to a jury trial, or if classified information is relevant in connection with a sentencing hearing—a second judge or a magistrate should make the relevant determinations under

CIPA to avoid "tainting" the trier of fact with inadmissible information.[62] Of course, CIPA's requirement that resulting substitutions provide the defendant a full opportunity to make his defense would continue to apply.

This approach should greatly ameliorate the burdens that the CIPA process currently places on defense counsel. Permitting cleared counsel access to all discoverable information, regardless of classification, would ensure that a court's decisions under CIPA are made on the basis of the fullest information. It is no disrespect to the court or the prosecutors to suggest that an assessment of whether a substitution leaves the defendant in the same position as the original information is more likely to be accurate if defense counsel participates than if defense counsel does not participate.[63]

Nevertheless, from the defendant's point of view, this procedure is still imperfect. It is undeniably true that the participation of the defendant himself is often critical to formulating a defense.[64] Yet CIPA's restrictions on the disclosure of classified information to the defendant have repeatedly been upheld as constitutional,[65] and in other contexts, courts have approved the disclosure of information to defense counsel that cannot be shared with the defendant personally.[66] The new procedures would give the defendant the ability to make a voluntary choice between full communication with less informed counsel or more limited communication with fully informed counsel. In our opinion, the defendant would be better off if his counsel has full information and can participate fully in the CIPA process, but the choice should be the defendant's, not the court's or the government's.[67]

Critically, although this system would result in the disclosure of much more classified information to defense counsel, it should not increase the risk of improper dissemination of that information. A large number of defense attorneys have served in sensitive positions in the government without violating its trust. Many lawyers in private practice already have clearances at the top level in connection with matters that they are working on, whether criminal cases or business transactions involving companies that do classified work, and they manage to keep government secrets secure. There is no reason to believe that those lawyers are less trustworthy—or less careful—than prosecutors are.[68] By creating a national security bar, in other words, Congress can at once speed up and facilitate complicated adjudications, give fuller disclosure of key information to defense counsel, keep government secrets safe, and improve the quality of information and argument presented to U.S. courts.

When a defendant chooses to exercise his right to represent himself, of course, the situation becomes more complicated. Such a defendant may be willing to accept a member of the national security bar as "standby" counsel to handle classified matters, and that choice should be accepted by the courts.[69] But exclusion of an uncleared pro se defendant from the CIPA process does not violate the Constitution. By choosing to act as his own lawyer, a defendant loses many benefits of being represented by counsel: he cannot interview potential witnesses; his access to evidence is more limited; he may lose the ability to consult freely with experts; he cannot have confidential conversations about his defense. Before permitting a defendant to represent himself, a court must assure itself that he is knowingly and voluntarily forgoing those benefits.[70] In a terrorism case, access to classified information is simply one more right the defendant would have to waive—bearing in mind that the end result of the CIPA process must still leave him in a position to make his defense.

The most complicated issues regarding classified and other sensitive information will arise in the context of defense attempts to obtain testimony from witnesses that the government wishes to keep away from court. That problem is especially acute when the witnesses themselves are terrorism detainees—as the witnesses in the *Moussaoui* case were. The Constitution guarantees a defendant the right to secure the attendance of witnesses to testify on his behalf, so long as their testimony is material and favorable, and they are subject to subpoena if they are within the control of the government.[71] While CIPA itself does not directly address this issue, the court in the *Moussaoui* case—where the issue arose acutely—drew on CIPA to require substitutions that would put the defendant in the same position as he would have been in had the testimony of those witnesses been available.[72] In other cases, however, it may not be possible to craft substitutions that are as effective for the defense as actual testimony would be.

In some cases, the problem can be dealt with by pretrial deposition of the witness, via video hookup if necessary.[73] During the deposition, the parties may be separated, with the witness testifying from an undisclosed location and the defendant, counsel, and the district court participating from the courtroom.[74] Delays and pauses also could be employed as needed to make sure the government had the opportunity to keep highly classified material out of court. And the defendant could be limited to listening to the witness and speaking to his or her counsel, to minimize the possibility of improper communication.[75]

Moreover, if the government anticipates that a detainee will, intentionally or unintentionally, reveal sensitive information in the course of his testimony, the CIPA process may provide protection.[76] If a witness possesses information that affects national security, the government can classify the information and, to the extent that the witness's deposition testimony touches on the classified information, it will be governed by CIPA.[77] Cleared counsel could take the deposition without the defendant being present and could then work with the court to craft an unclassified substitute.[78] Here again, participation by a member of a dedicated national security bar could provide assurance to the government that disclosure will not unduly risk national security.

If all circumstances unite to create a kind of perfect storm, not even a national security bar will do much to help. For example, in the case of a defendant who insists upon representing himself and rejects standby counsel from the national security bar, courts will have to use creative solutions on a case-by-case basis to ensure that the defendant is not deprived of the right to call witnesses on his own behalf. Possible solutions include depositions upon written questions or video depositions supervised by the court in which there is a delay after each question and answer to permit editing and objections. Creation of substitutes for a witness's testimony by the government and the court without the participation of the defendant or standby counsel should be used only as a last resort. Such procedures will not completely eliminate the risk that a detainee witness might be able to communicate valuable information to a defendant; however, communication between individuals who already are in government custody may not present a significant risk to U.S. interests. Moreover, prosecutors often will be able to reduce even that residual risk by designing indictments so as to make detainee testimony immaterial or by working with the court and the defense to develop a legally adequate substitute for classified detainee statements. In short, even the worst case should be manageable.

Residual Problems

The creation of a national security bar will not by itself solve all of the major difficulties with trying terrorists. There are other issues that make terrorism trials difficult, and while having a cadre of cleared counsel involved in every stage of the proceedings may make dealing with them easier in individual cases, it will not correct the underlying problems. Some of those problems may be addressable through policy changes or subtle doctrinal shifts by the courts. Others are probably intractable and simply reflect limitations on criminal prosecution as a means of disabling terrorists.

The Government's Use of Defendant Statements

In a criminal trial, statements of a defendant made in response to interrogation may not be admitted against him unless they are voluntary and unless the defendant had been advised of his *Miranda* rights. Requiring that terrorist suspects captured abroad be read their *Miranda* rights before being questioned would undoubtedly be impractical and might well interfere with obtaining needed intelligence. Nevertheless, the U.S. Court of Appeals for the Second Circuit, in a well-reasoned opinion arising out of the 1998 bombings of the U.S. embassies in Kenya and Tanzania, assumed (without deciding) that statements from a defendant taken in violation of *Miranda* could not be admitted in a trial of that defendant, even if the defendant was a nonresident alien and the interrogation occurred overseas.[79]

How exactly *Miranda* will affect terrorism cases in the long run remains unsettled. For one thing, holding that *Miranda* limits the admissibility against terrorist suspects of statements that they make under interrogation does not necessarily lead to the conclusion that if the United States managed to capture Osama bin Laden, it would have to warn him of his right to remain silent before questioning him and immediately cease questioning if he invoked that right.[80] As the Second Circuit noted, *Miranda* has a well-established "public safety" exception that permits the use against a defendant of his unwarned statements "[w]hen exigent circumstances compel an un-warned interrogation in order to protect the public."[81] A plausible application of that rule would permit interrogation of captured terrorists without a *Miranda* warning so long as the interrogation was primarily intended to gather intelligence rather than to build a criminal case against the defendant—even if the information elicited proved to be evidence against him.[82] Applying that standard should not be too difficult; courts already are experienced in distinguishing interrogation for evidentiary purposes from interrogation needed to protect public safety.[83] Still, it remains to be seen in which direction constitutional doctrine will head on this point. The results over time may have significant implications for the vitality of many terrorism prosecutions.

Still more difficult problems arise with statements elicited from a defendant by more or less coercive interrogation techniques. Statements offered against a defendant in federal court must meet the Fifth Amendment's voluntariness standard, regardless of where or by whom they were elicited.[84] For a statement to be voluntary it must be "the product of a rational intellect and a free will."[85] Statements that are the product of torture or other techniques calculated to overbear a defendant's will are not admissible. The rules of evidence for military commissions originally promulgated by the Bush administration allowed considerably more flexibility in admitting statements obtained through some form of coercion, but President Obama has now prohibited the use of all statements obtained either by torture or by cruel, inhuman, or degrading treatment.[86] The original standard was presumed to be permissible because specific constitutional protections do not apply to military proceedings, which are subject to far looser procedural requirements.[87]

Nonetheless, some still argue that courts should allow, in a terrorism case, the introduction of statements of a defendant that do not meet traditional voluntariness standards. Simply put, the costs of permitting use of this sort of evidence are too great. One of the principal purposes of the voluntariness requirement is to ensure the reliability of a defendant's statements, and a principal objection to the use of coercive interrogation techniques has been that persons subject to such interrogation may make false statements to end the coercion.[88] In our opinion, admission of statements that are not voluntarily made is inconsistent with fundamental national values and will likely damage U.S. credibility throughout the world. As a practical matter, in any event, with the Obama administration's repudiation of coercive interrogation techniques more generally, this problem should arise with much less frequency, if at all, in the future.[89]

Without access to classified information, we cannot say whether there are persons now in custody who cannot be convicted without the use of statements that were coerced from them. The assumption, however, that the government will retain the ability to detain such persons if they are deemed a continuing danger makes the exclusion of coerced statements an acceptable risk.

The Government's Use of Statements Made by Third Persons

Another problem is that witnesses against a terrorist defendant often may be unavailable, or available only at great cost and effort. Military personnel who apprehended and interrogated a defendant may be in combat, and acquaintances who know the defendant and his activities may be unwilling to travel to the United States to testify. Much of the evidence against those currently in custody appears to have come from the interrogation of other detained terrorists, whom the government may not wish to bring to the courtroom for legitimate national security reasons. Ordinarily, statements made by third parties who are not present to testify and are not subject to cross-examination may not be admitted against a defendant in a criminal trial.

However, numerous exceptions permit the introduction of certain kinds of hearsay—including statements made in furtherance of a conspiracy, statements against the speaker's interest, records of regularly conducted activity, statements that are not offered for the truth of what was said, and statements about an event made while the event was happening.[90] Most significant, the Federal Rules of Evidence contain a "residual exception" permitting the introduction of *any* out-of-court statement if it is "evidence of a material fact," if it is "more probative . . . than any other evidence which the proponent can procure through reasonable efforts," and if introduction of the statement would be consistent with the general purpose of the rules of evidence and the interests of justice.[91] Before offering a statement under that rule, the government has to notify the defendant. Moreover, the defendant is permitted to attack the credibility of the person making the statement just as he could if the person had testified, and the government is required to produce for the defendant material that could be used for that purpose.[92]

These rules provide a great deal of leeway, permitting the introduction of many probative out-of-court statements. For example, if, in a hypothetical scenario posited to demonstrate the problems created by the hearsay rule, a friend of Osama bin Laden's mother were to testify that she told the friend about a warning of an attack that she received from her son shortly before September 11, it is not hard to imagine that testimony about the mother's statement would be admitted under one or more of the hearsay exceptions.[93] But the flexibility of the hearsay rules is limited by the Sixth Amendment to the Constitution, which affords a defendant the right "to be confronted with the witnesses against him," and the Supreme Court has defined that right to prohibit the introduction of any "testimonial" statements against a defendant unless the defendant is able to cross-examine the person making the statement. While the Court has not provided a full definition of the term "testimonial," it seems likely that it would cover most statements made in response to questioning by law enforcement or intelligence agents.[94] The Confrontation Clause would thus limit the government's ability to rely on statements made by a captured terrorist to government agents that incriminate his former confederates, no matter how reliable and probative they might be.

However, it is critical to note that the Confrontation Clause does not present an absolute bar to the use of such statements. Because it merely requires that the defendant have an opportunity to cross-examine the witness, the government always has the option of bringing the witness in question to testify at trial. In such a case, "the Confrontation Clause places no constraints at all on the use of [the witness's] prior statements."[95]

That situation is one in which Congress might consider modifying the Federal Rules of Evidence. Under present law—in one of those gossamer distinctions that the law is famous for—if a witness has given a statement inculpating the defendant but disavows it when testifying, the prior statement cannot be used as substantive evidence against the defendant; it can be used only to impeach the witness, unless the prior statement was made under oath and made during a trial, hearing, or other proceeding.[96] In other words, if a detained terrorist suspect has told interrogators that a defendant is a member of al Qaeda but later testifies and denies it, the earlier statement can be used only to prove that the witness is lying—not to prove that the defendant is (or was) actually a member of al Qaeda. And if there is no other evidence that the defendant was a member of al Qaeda, the government's proof may fail.[97] Because that limitation is imposed only by rule and not by the Constitution, however, it could be modified, and so long as the witness is subject to cross-examination and all circumstances surrounding the making of the prior statements can be brought out in court—including the relevant interrogation techniques so that the reliability of the prior statement can be adequately assessed—admission of such statements would not seem to do violence to fundamental principles of justice.

Existing procedures also can alleviate problems arising under the Confrontation Clause. Specifically, relatively liberal use of video depositions offers a way to avoid removing soldiers from the field to testify in court or to obtain the testimony of detained terrorists. The federal rules permit pretrial depositions of witnesses and the use of that deposition testimony at trial.[98] And while both the federal rules and the Confrontation Clause require that the defendant be present at such a deposition if it is to be introduced against him at trial, courts have held that the requirement can be satisfied if the defendant is linked by video to the deposition and has a private line to consult with counsel.[99] Moreover, taking testimony via deposition affords certain advantages: because the deposition itself is not a public proceeding, the tape can be edited before it is played in court to remove irrelevant political statements or disruptive comments.[100] Such depositions could be taken at U.S. consulates or military bases overseas.[101]

Depositions may not be possible in all cases, however. There may well be cases in which the government does not want to expose a witness to any kind of examination, either because interrogation is still proceeding and a deposition would disrupt it or for security reasons. Moreover, a witness who gave important statements may be in the custody of a foreign government that does not wish to permit access for a deposition, or the witness may simply be unwilling to testify. In some instances, a reasonable delay of trial might permit deposition of someone who is still undergoing valuable intelligence interrogation. But cases undoubtedly will remain in which the government is unable or reluctant to produce a witness for cross-examination, either at trial or for deposition, and under existing rules would have to forgo use of the witness's statements, however probative.

That, however, is not a novel problem. Any experienced prosecutor has confronted situations in which he or she has been unable to use important and probative evidence or has been able to do so only with significant risks. Informants may be uncooperative, unavailable to testify, or subject to substantial impeachment, which could undermine the prosecution's case. Public disclosure of evidence that might be important in convicting one defendant might frustrate another investigation. Nor is it unusual for other government agencies to have an interest in those decisions. For example, other law enforcement bodies may oppose disclosure of the identity of an informant or the State Department may believe, in a case with international ramifications, that foreign policy considerations should trump prosecution. Indeed, disagreements between the Department of Justice and the intelligence community over the extent of disclosure in espionage cases are the rule rather than the exception.

Prosecutors thus have experience in making the kind of judgments that would be required when critical evidence against a potential terrorist cannot be used because of Confrontation Clause concerns. They also have experience working closely with—if often in tension with—the intelligence community to resolve competing interests. In some instances, careful selection or drafting of charges could permit a case to move forward without the use of the challenged evidence.[102] In some instances, the government will conclude that no viable case can be brought against a suspected terrorist and will likely fall back on some sort of detention authority to prevent the release of genuinely dangerous individuals who cannot be prosecuted. And in some instances, the government will conclude that prosecuting a terrorist—exposing his crimes to the public and securing a just sentence—outweighs the costs and risks of exposing witnesses to deposition testimony.

But in our view, the theoretical concerns that have been raised about the use of hearsay testimony—concerns that, so far as appears on the public record, have not prevented successful prosecution in many cases—should not lead the government to set up a system that abandons the fundamental values embodied by the Confrontation Clause. As Justice Scalia noted:

> The [Confrontation] Clause's ultimate goal is to ensure reliability of evidence, but it is a procedural rather than a substantive guarantee. It commands, not that evidence be reliable, but that reliability be assessed in a particular manner: by testing in the crucible of cross-examination. The Clause thus reflects a judgment, not only about the desirability of reliable evidence (a point on which there could be little dissent), but about how reliability can best be determined.[103]

Some Final Thoughts

The proposals that we advocate here represent a balancing of values and a prediction about risks, based on the available information. They represent our best judgment about the most effective way to protect all of the national interests affected by the prosecution of terrorists: to secure the conviction of the guilty while enabling the acquittal of the innocent; to guard national secrets while holding trials that not only are fair but are perceived to be fair; and to protect a defendant's rights without endangering national security.

Some of our proposals may bump up against limits imposed by the Constitution. Courts may find, for example, that allowing extensive use of depositions in which the defendant participates only by video hookup or requiring defendants to choose between counsel with access to classified material and counsel with whom they can communicate fully do not comport with constitutional norms. In our opinion, however, it is worth taking the risk that those procedures might be struck down, both because we believe that they are in fact proper, and because, for the reasons discussed above, we believe that it is preferable to make every effort to try alleged terrorists in proceedings that reflect as closely as possible the proceedings in normal criminal trials.

Finally, we do not in any way minimize the costs and burdens that the procedures that we advocate will impose on the intelligence community and the criminal justice system. Trial of an accused terrorist will be an expensive, time-consuming, and labor-intensive process. It will require many difficult decisions on the part of the government and a great investment of resources by the law enforcement and intelligence communities. But the cost of such trials, while substantial, is almost a rounding error to the overall cost of U.S. efforts to combat terrorism.[104] And as many have noted, there is no greater priority for the government than to protect the nation's security. If that is the case, the government should be willing to accept those costs and burdens for the sake of ensuring that the nation is protected in a manner that is consistent with maintaining both its fundamental values and its long-term stature in the world.

Notes

1. The term "terrorism-related crime" is not self-defining. Equating it to prosecution for violations of particular statutes is both overinclusive (since it could include prosecutions of domestic terrorists that do not present the same problems as those discussed in this chapter) and underinclusive (in that, for example, prosecution of al

Qaeda members for immigration violations or false statements could present those problems). The need to define the term is most acute if terrorists are to be tried in special tribunals, to delineate the tribunal's jurisdiction.

2. See, for example, Ruth Wedgwood, "The Case for Military Tribunals," *Wall Street Journal*, December 3, 2001.

3. See Curtis Bradley and Jack Goldsmith, "The Constitutional Validity of Military Commissions," *Green Bag* 5, vol. 2 (2002), pp. 249, 250–52, recounting U.S. use of military commissions during the Revolutionary War, Civil War, and World War II; Jack Goldsmith and Cass Sunstein, "Military Tribunals and Legal Culture: What a Difference Sixty Years Makes," *Constitutional Commentary* 19, no. 1 (Spring 2002), noting widespread praise for the establishment of a military commission to try captured Nazi saboteurs.

4. See, for example, Neil Lewis, "Red Cross Criticizes Indefinite Detention in Guantánamo Bay," *New York Times*, October 10, 2003; Anthony D. Romero, "End Military Commissions," *Huffington Post*, February 12, 2008 (www.huffingtonpost.com/anthony-d-romero/end-military-commissions_b_86249.html); Richard B. Zabel and James J. Benjamin Jr., *In Pursuit of Justice: Prosecuting Terrorism Cases in the Federal Courts* (New York: Human Rights First, May 2008) (www.humanrightsfirst.info/pdf/080521-USLS-pursuit-justice.pdf); Kenneth Roth, "After Guantánamo: The Case against Preventive Detention," *Foreign Affairs* 87, no. 2 (May-June 2008), p. 2: "[S]uspects tried before military commissions can be convicted, and even executed, on the basis of statements secured by coercion. Rules protecting interrogation methods from disclosure coupled with lax hearsay rules mean that these men could be sentenced to death based on second- or third-hand affidavits summarizing statements obtained through abuse, without any meaningful opportunity to challenge the evidence."

5. See, for example, Andrew C. McCarthy and Alykhan Velshi, "We Need a National Security Court," working paper, American Enterprise Institute, 2006 (www.defenddemocracy.org/images/stories/national%20security%20court.pdf); Harvey Rishikof, "A Federal Terrorism Court," working paper, Progressive Policy Institute, 2007. Many proposals for a national security court encompass trial as well as preventive detention, an issue that is beyond the scope of this chapter.

6. See Statement of President Barack Obama on Military Commissions, May 15, 2009 (www.whitehouse.gov/the_press_office/Statement-of-President-Barack-Obama-on-Military-Commissions/).

7. See Executive Order 13492, "Review and Disposition of Individuals Detained at the Guantánamo Bay Naval Base and Closure of Detention Facilities," January 20, 2009. See also Executive Order 13493, "Review of Detention Policy Options," January 22, 2009, § 1(e).

8. Memorandum, "In Re: Guantanamo Bay Detainee Litigation: Respondents' Memorandum Regarding the Government's Detention Authority Relative to Detainees Held at Guantanamo Bay," no. 05-0763 (JDB) (D.D.C., January 29, 2009), p. 3: "The President has the authority to detain persons that the President determines planned,

authorized, committed, or aided the terrorist attacks that occurred on September 11, 2001, and persons who harbored those responsible for those attacks. The President also has the authority to detain persons who were part of, or substantially supported, Taliban or al-Qaida forces or associated forces that are engaged in hostilities against the United States or its coalition partners, including any person who has committed a belligerent act, or has directly supported hostilities, in aid of such enemy forces."

9. Benjamin Wittes, *Law and the Long War: The Future of Justice in the Age of Terror* (New York: Penguin Press, 2008), p. 151: "The power to lock up the enemy is a matter of black-letter law written on pure white paper with indelible ink"; *Hamdan v. Rumsfeld*, 548 U.S. 557, 635 (2006); *Hamdi v. Rumsfeld*, 542 U.S. 507, 518 (2004).

10. Wittes, *Law and the Long War*, p. 158. It has been reported that some of those released from Guantánamo in fact returned to terrorism. See Robert F. Worth, "Freed by the U.S., Saudi Becomes al Qaeda Chief," *New York Times*, January 23, 2009; Rajiv Chandrasekaran, "From Captive to Suicide Bomber," *Washington Post*, February 22, 2009.

11. It is possible that the courts may determine that detention is prohibited by the Constitution. As discussed below, we believe such a holding would increase the pressure to enact more flexible procedures to try terrorists.

12. See, generally, Roth, "After Guantánamo," note 4 above.

13. For example, critical information about a terrorist may have been obtained from a foreign intelligence service that does not want its cooperation revealed.

14. Zabel and Benjamin, *In Pursuit of Justice*, note 4 above; Serrin Turner and Stephen J. Schulhofer, *The Secrecy Problem in Terrorism Trials*, Liberty and National Security Project, Brennan Center for Justice, New York University School of Law, 2005.

15. Columnist Charles Krauthammer claimed that the defendants in the Embassy Bombings case learned through government disclosures that U.S. intelligence services had been tapping Osama bin Laden's satellite phone. As a consequence, Krauthammer wrote, bin Laden stopped using the phone and the United States was deprived of vital intelligence about al Qaeda's activities during the months leading up to 9/11. Charles Krauthammer, "In Defense of Secret Tribunals," *Time*, November 26, 2001. Andrew McCarthy, lead prosecutor on the Blind Sheik case, has recounted that he was required to turn over to the defendants a list of unindicted co-conspirators—al Qaeda targets who were not yet suspects but who were being tracked by the intelligence community. According to McCarthy, "[w]ithin a short time of its being sent, the [list] had found its way to bin Laden in Sudan. It had been fetched for him by al-Qaeda operative Ali Mohammed who, upon obtaining it from one of his associates, forwarded it to al-Qaeda operative Wadith El Hage in Kenya for subsequent transmission to bin Laden" (McCarthy and Velshi, "We Need a National Security Court," p. 11, n. 19). According to Turner and Schulhofer, however, Krauthammer was mistaken: bin Laden had stopped using his satellite phone long before the trial, apparently in reaction to press reports regarding the U.S. intelligence community's monitoring efforts; in any event, prosecutors and defense counsel from the Embassy Bombings case agree that no sensitive

information was disclosed during the trial. Turner and Schulhofer, *Secrecy Problem in Terrorism Trials*, p. 9. In the Blind Sheik trial, McCarthy and his colleagues never sought a protective order that would have prohibited counsel from sharing the unindicted co-conspirators list with the defendants. Zabel and Benjamin, *In Pursuit of Justice*, p. 88.

16. Zabel and Benjamin, *In Pursuit of Justice*, pp. 87–89; Turner and Schulhofer, *Secrecy Problem in Terrorism Trials*, pp. 22–25.

17. Wittes, *Law and the Long War*, pp. 74–75, citing press reports and academic studies casting doubt on the guilt of many detainees held at Guantánamo Bay.

18. It has been argued that the threat that terrorism presents to national security is sufficient to justify altering the traditional criminal law balance between conviction of the guilty and protection of the innocent. See, for example, McCarthy and Velshi, "We Need a National Security Court," pp. 7–8. While the gravity of the threat may justify a detention regime with lower standards, it is an insufficient basis for modifying the system of trying people for crimes that could potentially result in life imprisonment or the death sentence.

19. According to one tally, between September 12, 2001, and September 11, 2008, federal prosecutions led to the conviction of more than 400 terrorists, many on charges that were not related to terrorism. Karen Joy Greenberg, "Terrorist Trial Report Card: September 11, 2008," Center on Law and Security, New York University School of Law, 2008, p. 2. Prominent cases in which convictions have been secured over the years after trial or by guilty plea include those of Ramzi Ahmed Yousef, the Blind Sheik, the perpetrators of the Embassy Bombings, Zacarias Moussaoui, Richard Reid, Jose Padilla, and John Walker Lindh.

20. See *Ex Parte Quirin*, 317 U.S. 1, 44 (1942), finding that Fifth and Sixth Amendment protections did not apply in a commission convened to try offenses against the law of war. See also *Hamdan*, 548 U.S. at 621–635, finding that military commissions were improperly authorized and violated Geneva Conventions. Two justifications have been advanced in support of the constitutionality of lower standards for trying accused terrorists before military tribunals or a national security court. The first is that military proceedings do not need to conform to the requirements of the Constitution. See *Quirin*, 317 U.S. at 44; *In Re Yamashita*, 327 U.S. 1, 23 (1945), rejecting, among other things, Fifth Amendment challenges to military commission procedures; cf. *Davis v. United States*, 512 U.S. 452, 457 n. 1 (1994), noting but not deciding the question of whether the Self-Incrimination Clause applies in military court. The second is that "alien enemy combatants . . . have no rights under the U.S. Constitution." McCarthy and Velshi, "We Need a National Security Court," pp. 17, 30–31, n. 55; *Johnson v. Eisentrager*, 339 U.S. 763, 782–85 (1950). Neither proposition has been tested as applied to terrorists after 9/11.

21. *Boumediene* v. *Bush*, 128 S.Ct. 2229 (2008), holding that writ of habeas corpus is available to Guantánamo detainees, despite prior cases barring writ for military detainees.

22. Cf. *Al Maqaleh* v. *Gates,* no. 06-1669 (D.D.C. April 2, 2009), holding that writ of habeas corpus is available to detainees captured outside the active theater of combat and moved there for detention.

23. Michael Mukasey, "Jose Padilla Makes Bad Law," *Wall Street Journal,* August 22, 2007. See also John Farmer, "The Wrong Weapon against Terrorism," *International Herald Tribune,* January 13, 2008, criticizing the Padilla prosecution and observing that "when terrorism cases are treated as ordinary criminal prosecutions, the principles of law that they come to embody will guide law-enforcement conduct and be cited by the government not just in terrorism cases but in other contexts"; *Al-Marri* v. *Pucciarelli,* 534 F.3d 213, 310 (4th Cir. 2008) (Wilkinson, J., concurring in part and dissenting in part): "In adopting corrective measures to deal with the unique problems presented by terrorism prosecutions, courts may dilute the core protections of the criminal justice system in other cases. . . . The government will seek to take advantage of 'terrorist precedents' in other cases."

24. See, for example, McCarthy and Velshi, "We Need a National Security Court," p. 13: "Principles and precedents we create in terrorism cases generally get applied across the board. This, ineluctably, effects a diminution in the rights and remedies of the vast majority of defendants—for the most part, American citizens who in our system are liberally afforded those benefits precisely because we presume them innocent. It sounds ennobling to say we treat terrorists just like we treat everyone else, but if we really are doing that, everyone else is necessarily being treated worse."

25. 18 U.S.C. § 1961, et seq.

26. Compare McCarthy and Velshi, "We Need a National Security Court," p. 13, quoted note 4 above, with McCarthy and Velshi, "We Need a National Security Court," pp. 9–11, arguing that federal discovery requirements reveal intelligence information to accused terrorists.

27. *Military Commissions Act,* Public Law 109-366, 120 Stat. 2600 (2006), § 948b (a), establishing procedures for trial of alien enemy combatants. See also McCarthy and Velshi, "We Need a National Security Court," p. 36, proposing a "national security court" with jurisdiction over the detention and trial of "alien combatants captured during the war on terror." In *Quirin,* 317 U.S. 1, the Supreme Court approved the use of a military tribunal to try a group of German saboteurs seized in the United States, one of whom was an American citizen. However, even the Bush administration Department of Justice was uncertain that that aspect of *Quirin* would be followed today. See Patrick F. Philbin, Memorandum to the Counsel to the President, "Legality of the Use of Military Commissions to Try Terrorists," November 6, 2001, pp. 14–6.

28. See Neal Katyal, "Now Can We Try Using Courts-Martial for Enemy Detainees?" *Slate,* July 11, 2006: "England refuses to recognize the commission system, with its attorney general calling them completely 'unacceptable' because they fail to offer 'sufficient guarantees of a fair trial in accordance with international standards.'"

29. See U.S. Const., Amends. V-VI; *Brady* v. *Maryland,* 373 U.S. 83 (1963).

30. Federal Rules of Criminal Procedure 16 and 26.2.

31. McCarthy and Velshi, "We Need a National Security Court," pp. 9–11.

32. Robert Chesney and Jack Goldsmith, "Terrorism and the Convergence of Military and Criminal Detention Models," *Stanford Law Review* 60, no. 4 (February 2008), p. 1107.

33. McCarthy and Velshi, "We Need a National Security Court," p. 11.

34. Chesney and Goldsmith, "Terrorism and the Convergence of Military and Criminal Detention Models," pp. 1107–08.

35. See, for example, John B. Bellinger, "Remarks on the Military Commissions Act," *Harvard International Law Journal Online* 48, no. 1 (January 2007), p. 5; Senate Committee on the Judiciary, *Hamdan v. Rumsfeld: Establishing a Constitutional Process,* "Testimony of Mr. Steve Bradbury, Acting Assistant Attorney General, Office of Legal Counsel, Department of Justice," 109th Cong., 2nd sess., 2006, p. 4.

36. *Miranda v. Arizona,* 384 U.S. 486 (1966).

37. See, for example, Wedgwood, "The Case for Military Tribunals"; Senate Committee, *Hamdan v. Rumsfeld,* p. 4.

38. Wedgwood, "The Case for Military Tribunals," note 2 above; Senate Committee, *Hamdan v. Rumsfeld,* pp. 4–5.

39. *Al-Marri,* 534 F.3d at 310: "[W]hile a showcase of American values, an open and public criminal trial may also serve as a platform for suspected terrorists. Terror suspects may use the bully pulpit of a criminal trial in an attempt to recruit others to their cause."

40. Wittes, *Law and the Long War,* p. 172: "Moussaoui . . . was a nutcase who tried to represent himself, filed crazed pleadings, and made ludicrous courtroom speeches in which he repeatedly compromised any potential defense by admitting to key elements of the charges against him—for example, that he was a member of al-Qaeda, pledged to attack America. For months, he refused to cooperate with his court-appointed lawyers, and when the judge took away his ability to act as his own counsel, he pleaded guilty—thereby relieving the government of the burden of proving a tricky case."

41. *Al-Marri,* 534 F.3d at 307: "Likewise, terror suspects may take advantage of the opportunity to interact with others during trial to pass critical intelligence to their allies." See also *In Re Terrorist Bombings of U.S. Embassies in East Africa,* 552 F.3d 93, 149 (2d Cir. 2008), in which the district court refused to disclose a letter written by the defendant to the public, because the district court "didn't know whether there are codes in this letter" and did not want "to become the medium by which the defendants seek a larger audience [*internal citations omitted*]."

42. *Al-Marri,* 534 F.3d at 309 (Wilkinson, J., concurring in part and dissenting in part).

43. Federal Rule of Evidence 901(a).

44. Zabel and Benjamin, *In Pursuit of Justice,* p. 108, describing the introduction against Jose Padilla of a mujahidin form bearing his fingerprints. See also *United States v. al Moayad,* 545 F.3d 149, 172-73 (2d Cir. 2008), upholding authentication of the

mujahidin form based on testimony of an FBI agent in Pakistan who received material seized during post–9/11 raids of an al Qaeda facility in Afghanistan and transmitted it to FBI headquarters.

45. One of the authors represented a cooperating defendant in these cases.

46. This point needs to be distinguished from the possibility that the evidence needed to authenticate a document or other piece of evidence might be classified, which is simply an aspect of the overall problems attendant to the use of classified information at trial.

47. Under the Military Commission Rules of Evidence, evidence can be admitted if "the military judge determines that there is sufficient basis to find that the evidence is what it is claimed to be." Military Commission Rule of Evidence 901(a).

48. See, for example, *In Re Terrorist Bombings,* 552 F.3d at 149-50, approving the shackling of a defendant after the defendant had charged the bench during a pretrial hearing and after codefendants had stabbed a prison guard during pretrial detention; *United States* v. *McKissick,* 204 F.3d 1282, 1299 (10th Cir. 2000), approving the requirement that a defendant wear a stun belt under his clothes during trial after U.S. marshals informed the court that the defendant's fellow gang members might attempt to interrupt proceedings; *Illinois* v. *Allen,* 397 U.S. 337, 344 (1970), authorizing district courts to remove obstreperous defendants until they agree to comport themselves; *United States* v. *Williams,* 431 F.3d 1115, 1119-20 (8th Cir. 2005), approving the removal of an obstreperous pro se defendant who continued to harass and interrupt the trial judge after repeated warnings.

49. See *United States* v. *Wong,* 40 F.3d 1347, 1376 (2d Cir. 1994), permitting an anonymous jury procedure when justified by threat to jurors and when the district court takes precautions to ensure that the defendant's rights are protected. Anonymous juries were empaneled in both the Embassy Bombings and World Trade Center bombing cases. Benjamin Weiser, "First Day of Jury Selection in U.S. Embassy Bombings," *New York Times,* January 3, 2001; Benjamin Weiser, "Bomb Trial Judge Tries to Put Jury at Ease," *New York Times,* August 10, 1997.

50. 28 C.F.R. § 501.3; *United States* v. *Ali,* 396 F.Supp. 703, 708-10 (E.D.Va. 2005), approving pretrial measures which prevented the defendant from communicating with individuals outside prison other than his attorneys or with other inmates; *United States* v. *El Hage,* 213 F.3d 74, 81-82 (2d Cir. 2000).

51. 18 U.S.C. § 3521.

52. *Faretta* v. *California,* 422 U.S. 806, 834 n.46 (1975); *United States* v. *Moussaoui,* Crim. no. 01-455-A (E.D. Va. Nov. 13, 2003).

53. Wittes, *Law and the Long War,* p. 172.

54. In *United States* v. *Sattar,* 395 F. Supp. 2d 79 (S.D.N.Y. 2005), a lawyer and a paralegal for Sheik Abdel Omar Rahman violated Special Administrative Measures (SAMs) by conveying messages between their client and members of a terrorist organization, indicating Rahman's support for the group's resumption of violence. It appears from the court's opinion that the government became aware relatively early of the

potential violation of the SAMs, as many of the conversations were monitored, so that if they presented any genuine and immediate danger the government could have intervened.

55. *United States* v. *Verdugo-Urquidez,* 494 U.S. 259 (1990).

56. *In re Terrorist Bombings,* 552 F.3d at 171.

57. 18 U.S.C. App. III. In addition to CIPA, courts have other tools available to protect classified or sensitive information from improper disclosure. For example, undercover intelligence agents can testify anonymously or under an assumed name. Courtrooms can be closed to the public, on a limited basis, when especially sensitive information is being discussed. See, for example, *United States* v. *Marzook,* 412 F. Supp. 2d 913, 919, 923-24 (N.D. Ill. 2006), permitting Israeli intelligence officers to testify in a closed courtroom under assumed names. As noted above, Special Administrative Measures can be used to control, at least partially, a defendant's ability to communicate with outside individuals.

58. According to former CIA general counsel Jeffrey Smith, "CIPA is awkward and cumbersome, but it works." Turner and Schulhofer, *Secrecy Problem in Terrorism Trials,* p. 25. See also Association of the Bar of the City of New York, Committee on Federal Courts, *Indefinite Detention of 'Enemy Combatants': Balancing Due Process and National Security in the War on Terror,* February 6, 2004, reviewing CIPA's performance and finding "no indication that [CIPA], reasonably interpreted by federal judges, is inadequate to the task of protecting national security interests while affording defendants a fair trial." We are not aware of any case in which the CIPA process has resulted in the improper disclosure of classified information. But see Harvey Rishikof, "Is It Time for a Federal Terrorist Court? Terrorist Prosecutions: Problems, Paradigms, and Paradoxes," *Suffolk Journal of Trial and Appellate Advocacy* 8 no. 1 (2003), p. 12, claiming that under CIPA classified material will invariably seep into the public domain.

59. Compare *Geders* v. *United States,* 425 U.S. 80 (1976), invalidating a court order that prevented counsel from communicating with the defendant during overnight recess in trial proceedings, with *United States* v. *bin Laden,* no. 98-cr-1023, 2001 WL 66393, n. 5 (S.D.N.Y. Jan. 25, 2001), rejecting the defendant's claim that his Sixth Amendment rights had been violated because only defense counsel could review classified materials.

60. One of the authors has been involved in a nonterrorism criminal case in which the government provided classified information allegedly relevant to sentencing to the judge on an ex parte basis, over defense objections, and in which the court approved classified substitutions (rather than unclassified ones) that counsel could not share with the defendant. See also *Marzook,* 435 F. Supp. 2d at 746-47, portions of suppression hearing conducted ex parte pursuant to CIPA.

61. Before the September 11 attacks, the National Commission on Terrorism had concluded that "where national security requires the use of secret evidence in administrative immigration cases, procedures for cleared counsel . . . should be used." National Commission on Terrorism, 2002, p. 32 (www.gpo.gov/nct). Turner and

Schulhofer have specifically called upon Congress to create a cleared counsel bar, within either a federal public defender's office or that of a legal aid society, through which lawyers can seek top secret clearances in advance of their appointment or retention in terrorism cases. Turner and Schulhofer, *Secrecy Problem in Terrorism Trials,* p. 27.

62. The desirability of having judges acquire expertise in dealing with issues relating to classified information is one of the stronger arguments in favor of a specialized national security court.

63. In any criminal case, the prosecution reviews its own files and makes its own determination, without judicial supervision, of what material is subject to disclosure. Practical considerations support this practice; it simply is not possible for a judge to review the government's entire file in every case. The government's practices in making disclosures to the defense have recently been sharply criticized. See Eric H. Holder, "Attorney General Announces Increased Training, Review of Process for Providing Materials to Defense in Criminal Cases," press statement, Department of Justice, April 14, 2009 (www.usdoj.gov/opa/pr/2009/April/09-opa-338.html). And there is no similar practical justification for excluding defense counsel when the government, having reviewed its files, goes to the court under CIPA.

64. See *United States* v. *Cobb,* 905 F.2d 784, 792 (4th Cir.1990): "To remove from [the defendant] the ability to discuss with his attorney any aspect of his ongoing testimony [would] effectively eviscerate his ability to discuss and plan trial strategy."

65. See, for example, *United States* v. *Abu Ali,* 528 F.3d 210, 248-55 (4th Cir. 2008); *bin Laden,* 2001 WL 66393 at n. 5.

66. See, for example, *United States* v. *Herrero,* 893 F.2d 1512, 1526-27 (7th Cir. 1990), stating that defense counsel could not disclose the identity of a confidential informant to the defendant; *Morgan* v. *Bennett,* 204 F.3d 360, 367 (2d Cir. 2000), barring defense counsel from revealing the identity of a cooperating witness.

67. It has been suggested that if the defendant makes a sufficient showing of need, counsel should be permitted to share classified information with the defendant, and that Special Administrative Measures should be relied on to ensure that the information is not further disseminated. Turner and Schulhofer, *Secrecy Problem in Terrorism Trials,* pp. 27–28. That is not an acceptable solution: foreign governments may well be reluctant to share information if a court might subsequently order it disclosed to a defendant, nor does the proposal take account of the possibility that a defendant might be acquitted and released.

68. As discussed above, Lynne Stewart, a lawyer for the Blind Sheik, was convicted of having improper communications with her client. She did not disclose classified information, however, but rather transmitted statements between him and terrorist organizations. *United States* v. *Sattar,* 395 F. Supp. 2d 79 (S.D.N.Y. 2005).

69. *Faretta,* 422 U.S. at 834 n.46, recognizing the authority to appoint standby counsel, even over the defendant's objection. Generally speaking, a defendant is not entitled to "hybrid representation," combining self-representation with representation by counsel. *Cross* v. *United States,* 893 F.2d 1287, 1291-92 (11th Cir. 1990). But

while hybrid representation is not required by the Constitution, neither is it forbidden, and the interests of justice would be well served by permitting it in this context, so long as standby counsel plays no role in the actual trial.

70. *Faretta,* 422 U.S. at 835.

71. U.S. Const., Amend. IV. See also, for example, *United States* v. *Moussaoui,* 382 F.3d 453, 463 (4th Cir. 2004); *United States* v. *Resurreccion,* 978 F.2d 759, 762 (1st Cir. 1992).

72. *Moussaoui,* 382 F.3d at 477-82. Congress could and should adopt proposals making CIPA expressly applicable to witness testimony. See, for example, *Terrorism Prevention Act of 2006,* S 3848, 109th Cong., 2nd sess., *Congressional Record* 108 (September 6, 2006): S9045-9046, § 3(d), extending CIPA to nondocumentary evidence.

73. Federal Rule of Criminal Procedure 15.

74. This was, in essence, what the district court proposed in Moussaoui's case, after ruling that several detainees possessed information material to his defense but that the government had not proposed legally adequate, unclassified summaries for the detainees' statements. See *United States* v. *Moussaoui,* 2003 WL 21263699, no. CR 01-455-A, at n. 3-6 (E.D. Va. Mar. 10, 2001); *United States* v. *Moussaoui,* 382 F.3d at 458.

75. See *United States* v. *Mueller,* 74 F.3d 1152, 1156-57 (2d Cir. 1996), approving taking a deposition from a witness residing in England, when the defense counsel attended the deposition and cross-examined the witness and the defendant could listen to the witness and speak to the defense counsel by telephone.

76. A deposition transcript can be edited to remove such testimony and prevent its further dissemination.

77. Federal law provides for the classification of information when, among other things, the classifying authority determines that the unauthorized disclosure of the information reasonably could be expected to result in identifiable damage to national security. Executive Order 13292 , "Further Amendment to Executive Order 12958, as Amended, Classified National Security Information," 68 *Fed. Reg.* 15, 315 (Mar. 25, 2003), § 1.1 (1)-(4). The government has taken the position that information can be classified if it meets this standard, even if it was not derived from the government.

78. The most sensitive area will likely relate to interrogation techniques used on the witness. But CIPA has been successfully used to craft substitutions even in the case of allegedly coercive interrogations. *United States* v. *Marzook,* no. 03 Cr. 978 at 4-5 (N.D. Ill. 2006), approving substitutions regarding interrogation of the defendant by Israeli agents.

79. *In re Terrorist Bombings,* 552 F.3d at 199-205 (2d Cir. 2008). The court upheld the defendants' convictions on the grounds that abbreviated *Miranda* warnings sufficed under the circumstances and that the defendants had thereafter agreed to answer questions voluntarily.

80. See Wedgwood, "The Case for Military Tribunals." Cf. *Miranda,* 384 U.S. at 473-74, requiring cessation of interrogation upon invocation of the right to silence.

81. *In re Terrorist Bombings,* 552 F.3d at 203 n. 19; see *New York* v. *Quarles,* 467 U.S. 649 (1984); *United States* v. *Khalil,* 214 F.3d 111, 121-22 (2d Cir. 2000), finding

Miranda inapplicable to unwarned questioning of a suspect in whose apartment a bomb was found to determine whether other bombs existed. In addition, *Miranda* has no application to interrogations conducted by foreign law enforcement or intelligence agencies, even if U.S. agents participate to some extent. *Abu Ali,* 528 F.3d at 227-30, finding *Miranda* inapplicable when U.S. agents suggested questions to Saudi interrogators but Saudis controlled and conducted the interrogation.

82. In the Embassy Bombings case, the interrogations were conducted not by intelligence agents but by law enforcement officers and were focused on the past bombing. *In re Terrorist Bombings,* 552 F.3d at 181-86.

83. See, for example, *United States* v. *Everman,* 282 F.3d 570, 572 (8th Cir. 2008), refusing to suppress inculpatory statements when police officers did not provide *Miranda* warning before asking a suspect whether he had any weapons nearby; *United States* v. *Dodge,* 852 F.Supp. 139, 142-43 (D.Conn. 1994), applying the public safety exception when police had asked a defendant about the location of a pipe bomb and the defendant had told them that it was in his bag; *United States* v. *Newton,* 181 F.Supp. 2d 157, 178 (E.D.N.Y. 2002), applying public safety exceptions to statements made by a defendant regarding the location of a hidden firearm.

84. *Dickerson* v. *United States,* 530 U.S. 428, 444 (2000).

85. *Mincey* v. *Arizona,* 437 U.S. 385, 399 (1978); *United States* v. *Charles,* 476 F.3d 492, 497-98 (7th Cir. 2007).

86. The original rules for military commissions contained no restrictions on the admissibility of a defendant's statements, other than that they had to have "probative value to a reasonable person." Military Commission Order No. 1 § 6(D)(1) (March 21, 2002). With the passage of the Military Commissions Act of 2006, Congress forbade admission of all statements obtained by "torture" but permitted admission of statements resulting from "cruel, inhuman, or degrading treatment" if they were made prior to December 30, 2005, if "the totality of the circumstances renders the statement reliable and possessing sufficient probative value" and if "the interests of justice would best be served by admission of the statement into evidence." 10 U.S.C. § 948r. By order dated May 13, 2009, the Obama administration amended the military commission rules to prohibit the admission of any statement obtained by "cruel, inhuman, or degrading treatment," whenever the statement was obtained. See Jeh C. Johnson, Memorandum to the Secretary of Defense, "Changes to the Manual for Military Commissions," May 13, 2009, p. 2.

87. See note 21, *supra.* It is not clear, however, that genuinely coerced statements could be used as evidence even in a military tribunal. In *Hamdan,* 548 U.S. at 631-35, the Court held that military commissions must meet the requirement of Common Article 3 of the Geneva Conventions that they afford "all the judicial guarantees which are recognized as indispensable by civilized peoples" and that this provision should be interpreted in light of Article 75 of Protocol 1 to the Conventions. Article 75, in turn, provides among other things that "no one shall be compelled to testify against himself or to confess guilt." "Protocol Additional to the Geneva Conventions of 12 August

1949, and relating to the Protection of Victims of International Armed Conflicts," June 8, 1977, *United States Treaties and Other International Agreements*. With the passage of the Military Commissions Act, Congress overruled that aspect of *Hamdan*. Among other things, the statute deemed that revamped commissions satisfied Common Article 3, and it prohibited commission defendants from relying upon the Geneva Conventions as a source of rights. See *Military Commissions Act*, §§ 948b(f), (g). At least one appellate court has approved that aspect of the statute. See, for example, *Noriega* v. *Pastrana*, no. 08-11021, 2009 WL 929960 (11th Cir., Apr. 8, 2009).

88. In *Dickerson* v. *United States,* 530 U.S. at 433, the Supreme Court stated:

> The roots of [the voluntariness] test developed in the common law, as the courts of England and then the United States recognized that coerced confessions are inherently untrustworthy. See, e.g., *King* v. *Rudd,* 1 Leach 115, 117-118, 122-123, 168 Eng. Rep. 160, 161, 164 (K. B. 1783) (Lord Mansfield, C. J.) (stating that the English courts excluded confessions obtained by threats and promises); *King* v. *Warickshall,* 1 Leach 262, 263-264, 168 Eng. Rep. 234, 235 (K. B. 1783) ("A free and voluntary confession is deserving of the highest credit, because it is presumed to flow from the strongest sense of guilt . . . but a confession forced from the mind by the flattery of hope, or by the torture of fear, comes in so questionable a shape . . . that no credit ought to be given to it; and therefore it is rejected"); *King* v. *Parratt,* 4 Car. & P. 570, 172 Eng. Rep. 829 (N. P. 1831); *Queen* v. *Garner,* 1 Den. 329, 169 Eng. Rep. 267 (Ct. Crim. App. 1848); *Queen* v. *Baldry,* 2 Den. 430, 169 Eng. Rep. 568 (Ct. Crim. App. 1852); *Hopt* v. *Territory of Utah,* 110 U. S. 574 (1884); *Pierce* v. *United States,* 160 U. S. 355, 357 (1896).

See also Peter Margulies and Laura Corbin, "Reliability and the Interests of Justice: Interpreting the Military Commissions Act of 2006 to Deter Coercive Interrogations," *Roger Williams University Law Review* 12, no. 2 (Spring 2007), p. 762: "Coercion cases have recognized two underlying rationales for the prohibition [against admitting coerced confessions]: the actual unreliability of the confession and the possibility that the confession is unreliable because of undue government pressure." The reliability of information obtained through enhanced interrogation techniques remains the subject of debate. See Greg Miller, "Panetta Tells Senate Panel He'll Examine the Effectiveness of Coercive Interrogation," *Los Angeles Times,* February 7, 2009.

89. The stricter standards will not completely hamstring interrogators. The constitutional standard of voluntariness permits some degree of pressure or trickery by interrogators, so long as the defendant's will was not overborne. See *Frazier* v. *Cupp,* 394 U.S. 731, 739 (1969), finding that police misrepresentation of codefendants' statements during interrogation of a defendant, standing alone, does not render confession involuntary; see also, for example, *United States* v. *Miller,* 984 F.2d 1028, 1031 (9th Cir. 1993), finding that psychological pressure does not automatically render a confession involuntary.

90. Federal Rules of Evidence 801, 803, and 804.

91. Federal Rule of Evidence 807.

92. Ibid.; Federal Rule of Evidence 806; *Giglio* v. *United States,* 405 U.S. 150 (1972).

93. See Wedgwood, "The Case for Military Tribunals": "Osama bin Laden telephoned his mother in Syria shortly before September 11 to warn her that a major event was imminent, and that he would be out of touch for some time. If the mother confided to a close friend about her son's warning, still one could not call the friend to give testimony [if bin Laden were prosecuted in federal court], for technically it would be hearsay."

94. *Crawford* v. *Washington,* 541 U.S. 36 (2004). An argument can be made that statements made in response to interrogation for intelligence purposes, unlike statements made to police questions in the course of a law enforcement investigation, should not be subject to this prohibition. In a later case—*Davis* v. *Washington,* 547 U.S. 813, 822 (2006)—the Court held that statements made to a police 911 operator were not "testimonial," articulating the distinction as follows:

> Statements are nontestimonial when made in the course of police interrogation under circumstances objectively indicating that the primary purpose of the interrogation is to enable police assistance to meet an ongoing emergency. They are testimonial when the circumstances objectively indicate that there is no such ongoing emergency, and that the primary purpose of the interrogation is to establish or prove past events potentially relevant to later criminal prosecution.

Statements made in the course of intelligence interrogations are arguably intended to meet an ongoing emergency rather than to prove past events. But in many respects they look more like the kind of interrogation in a police station that is subject to the Confrontation Clause than they look like a 911 call, and so we assume that use of these statements would be barred. See *Davis,* 824 n.2, specifically declining to consider whether and when statements made to non–law enforcement personnel are "testimonial" for confrontation purposes.

95. *Crawford* v. *Washington,* 541 U.S. at 59 n. 9.

96. Federal Rule of Evidence 801(d)(1)(A).

97. Compare *United States* v. *Tafallo-Cardenas,* 897 F.2d 976, 979-981 (9th Cir. 1990), prohibiting admission of witness's prior, unsworn statement to FBI agents as evidence that the defendant had instructed the witness to transport drugs, while noting that statement could be used to attack witness's credibility; and *United States* v. *Livingston,* 661 F.2d 239, 243-44 (D.C. Cir. 1981), holding that a sworn statement taken by a postal worker at the witness's home was not made during a "proceeding" and could not be admitted as evidence that the defendant had robbed a post office; with *United States* v. *Murphy,* 696 F.2d 282, 283-84 (4th Cir. 1982), when a witness testified that he could not recall whether the defendant took part in a bank robbery and the witness's inconsistent grand jury testimony was admitted as evidence that the defendant did in fact take part in the robbery.

98. Federal Rule of Criminal Procedure 15.

99. See, for example, *Abu Ali,* 528 F.3d at 239-42; *United States* v. *Medjuck,* 156 F.3d 916, 920-21 (9th Cir. 1998); *United States* v. *McKeeve,* 131 F.3d 1 (1st Cir. 1997).

100. In addition, Rule 15 provides that a defendant who persists in disruptive conduct can be excluded from a deposition. Federal Rule of Criminal Procedure 15(c)(1)(B).

101. In some instances, terrorists may be detained by the United States in countries that prohibit or limit the taking of testimony, and arrangements may have to be negotiated to permit this.

102. In chapter 4 of this volume, Robert Chesney discusses the wide range of statutes under which potential terrorists can be prosecuted.

103. *Crawford* v. *Washington,* 541 U.S. at 61.

104. No single number authoritatively describes the monetary cost of the U.S. counterterrorism effort. With that said, the publicly available information leaves no doubt that the cost of criminal trials will not even distantly approach the expenditures for military and intelligence activities in the global war on terror. See Amy Belasco, *The Cost of Iraq, Afghanistan, and Other Global War on Terror Operations since 9/11,* CRS Report RL3310 (October 15, 2008), summary page, estimating that $864 billion had been spent on the wars in Afghanistan and Iraq and on enhanced global security activities since 9/11 and projecting expenditures of up to $1.7 trillion by 2018.

DAVID A. MARTIN

6

Refining Immigration Law's Role in Counterterrorism

The federal government relied heavily on immigration laws in its immediate response to the September 11 terrorist attacks, which were carried out by aliens who were present in the United States on short-term visas. Hundreds of foreigners, swiftly deemed of "special interest," were taken into custody on immigration charges, often of the most routine variety. Their removal proceedings were closed to the public under a blanket order issued by the attorney general. Many noncitizens were subjected to exceedingly strict application of the inadmissibility and deportability grounds of the immigration statute, as well as a hardening of the criteria for release pending their hearings. Even those who conceded deportability and could have been sent readily to their countries of nationality often found themselves lingering in a kind of preventive detention, because they were forced to remain incarcerated on the basis of the removal order, frequently for months, pending their clearance by the FBI for release. Months later, thousands of other persons already in the United States were called in for special immigration status review, close questioning, and fingerprinting if they came from a specified list of predominantly Arab or Muslim countries, under a system called the National Security Entry-Exit Registration System (NSEERS). A significant percentage of them were detained and processed for removal. Admission procedures for all future travelers were tightened, including by expanding requirements for consular interviews and by doing often time-consuming background checks against disparate databases.

All substantive work on this chapter was completed before the author became principal deputy general counsel at the Department of Homeland Security in January 2009. The views expressed here are the personal views of the author and do not necessarily represent the position of the U.S. government or of the Department of Homeland Security.

The immigration laws were pressed into service because they were available and flexible, affording discretion that could be directed at targets deemed immediate and urgent. The advantages of the laws quickly commended themselves to the key decisionmakers in the executive branch. The disadvantages of that approach, however, became widely apparent only over time. Many of the steps taken, both in isolation and particularly in cumulative effect, hampered useful trade and travel, impaired scientific and scholarly exchange, imposed competitive disadvantages on many U.S. businesses, and clouded the traditional American attitude of openness and welcome, which has been valuable to diplomacy, business, and the successful integration of immigrant populations.

U.S. immigration laws remain available and flexible, and they still afford discretion that will likely catch the eye of any administration responding to a future terrorist crisis. It is therefore worth thinking now about how best to balance counterterrorism against the other interests that U.S. immigration law must serve. In the years that followed September 11, the Departments of State and Homeland Security have worked to repair some of the damage caused by the initial deployment of immigration authorities, but U.S. law needs more work to optimize a vital balance—one that gives adequate space to American values and economic interests while still holding fast to important security gains. Some progress can be achieved simply by making wiser use of the discretion bestowed by the immigration laws. But other improvements are best secured by reworking the existing legal architecture, some of it through statute and other parts through administrative regulations. In this chapter, I suggest the following specific legal changes:

—First, although the general effort to "push out the borders" by doing more screening of visitors overseas before they arrive in the United States has been valuable, Congress should change the laws to authorize flexibility and a more selective, risk-based approach to extensive screening. In particular, it should rescind the requirement that no visa can be issued without a face-to-face consular interview.

—Second, capturing biometric information on arriving and departing foreigners is highly valuable, but Congress should rescind the unrealistically costly mandate for fingerprinting *all* departing noncitizens at land borders. It should, however, look for ways to strengthen the statutory authority for including all relevant criminal information, including that held by the FBI, in the Automated Biometric Identification System (IDENT) database, which is the key to biometric checks in the immigration arena.

—Third, the alien registration law is a powerful tool that can be quickly deployed in a crisis, and to that end Congress probably needs to retain the current flexible statutory authority to impose new specialized registration requirements. The negative lessons of the alien registration program initiated after September 11, however, should greatly constrain future imposition of such a requirement on resident populations.

—Fourth, the terrorism-based grounds of inadmissibility and deportability are written with remarkable breadth. Congress should either narrow them, particularly as applied to refugees, asylum seekers, and deportation cases, or it should strengthen and streamline waiver procedures and make adequate resources available for prompt waiver decisions.

—Fifth, immigration detention should be used only for its classic functions: to guard against flight risk and to restrain dangerous individuals pending their removal hearings and then only as needed to secure removal. Decisions to detain should be subject to safeguards ensuring reasonable and timely review. Both before and after the issuance of a removal order, immigration authority should not be used as a de facto preventive detention power.

—Sixth, Congress should improve the mechanisms for use of classified evidence in immigration proceedings, ensuring that they can be relied on in a limited class of appropriate cases. But Congress should also strengthen the safeguards available to some classes of individuals subjected to such procedures.

Clarifying U.S. Objectives

In a speech that he gave to a conference of mayors six weeks after the September 11 attacks, Attorney General John Ashcroft offered insight into the government's heavy early reliance on immigration laws:

> Robert Kennedy's Justice Department, it is said, would arrest mobsters for "spitting on the sidewalk" if it would help in the battle against organized crime. It has been and will be the policy of this Department of Justice to use the same aggressive arrest and detention tactics in the war on terror.
>
> Let the terrorists among us be warned: If you overstay your visa—even by one day—we will arrest you. If you violate a local law, you will be put in jail and kept in custody as long as possible. We will use every available statute. . . . Our single objective is to prevent terrorist attacks by taking suspected terrorists off the street.[1]

If that were really the country's single objective, the immigration laws would afford a nearly foolproof method for negating the actions of foreign terrorists. The government could use those laws to forbid entry at U.S. borders to *anyone* not holding U.S. nationality. Moreover, nothing in the Constitution as it has been consistently interpreted since the 1890s[2] would prevent Congress from amending current law to require the departure of all foreign nationals now present, even if they hold green cards and have lived here since infancy. The constitutional dimensions of legislative and executive discretion are remarkably sweeping.

But, of course, such a closure policy would come at colossal cost—certainly to the resident aliens cruelly uprooted and to the core identity of the United States as a nation of immigrants, but also to the country's economy, which is inextricably reliant on foreign commerce and the personal travel associated with it. In the 21st century, no nation can prosper or achieve even modest economic success without ready contact with the rest of the world. Moreover, as is increasingly recognized, the global battle against terrorism cannot be won just by detaining, killing, or repelling terrorists. The United States must prevail in a battle of ideas, in a contest for the support and even the affection of the world's population. The nation's immigration heritage has served it well over the decades in that effort—as has its now-tarnished reputation for protecting human rights. That advantage has come in part through the ready availability of student and exchange visitor programs for foreign citizens who are likely to become leaders in their own countries, for example, and also through the long-term residence of significant diaspora populations that maintain links with family and friends in their countries of origin. Further, the historic U.S. strength in integrating immigrants and encouraging newcomers to identify with the national project has made it harder for foreign-based terrorism to take root in U.S. ethnic communities. Immigrants who identify with the host society are far more likely not only to paint a favorable picture of America for friends back home but also to alert law enforcement to indications of terrorist planning within their communities and to cooperate further with efforts to disrupt or prosecute.[3]

Hence, the design of the best immigration laws cannot pretend to serve any single objective in the struggle against terrorism. Certainly the immigration machinery's potential to keep dangerous persons from U.S. territory must be used systematically and professionally. That remains a highly significant policy goal. But measures to achieve that end must be balanced against—or often simply shaped in a way that minimizes harm to—other vital objectives. These include

—sustaining the wide range of contacts with other cultures and populations (through both temporary and permanent migration) that enrich U.S.

cultural and social life, nurture friendly ties with other countries, and support a vibrant economy

—sustaining and bolstering the integration of the permanent immigrant population

—avoiding procedures that themselves alienate applicants for benefits or discourage legal migration because they are overly complex or intrusive, take inexplicably long to produce a decision, or regularly result in outcomes seen as unfair, arbitrary, or discriminatory.

Since at least 2004, the existence of competing and offsetting goals has gained increasing recognition. Facilitation of lawful immigration is now frequently mentioned in the same breath as prevention of migration of dangerous persons—captured in the oft-repeated mantra of "secure borders, open doors."[4] Many of the steps taken under the immigration laws immediately after September 11, 2001, outlined above, have been abandoned or eased. The intrusive NSEERS call-in registration, which was criticized as a kind of ethnic profiling that damaged relations with immigrant communities, ended about a year after it was launched.[5] The presumption that immigration court hearings will be open to the public has been restored, subject to closure on a case-by-case basis. Artificially delayed deportations that resulted in de facto preventive detention have ended, following a strongly critical report on the practice by the inspector general of the Department of Justice.[6] Long delays in processing have been ameliorated as funding has increased, databases have been better integrated, and the intelligence agencies became better staffed and organized.

Though progress has been uneven and problems linger in each of those areas, government policy has definitely moved toward a more nuanced understanding of the ways in which immigration enforcement must be balanced with facilitation in order to maximize successes in the struggle against terrorism. Nonetheless, further refinement in both practice and legal framework would be valuable. With the complex objectives listed above in mind, I examine several key legal and policy areas.

Whom to Exclude or Deport?

Preventing the entry into or the sustained presence within the United States of dangerous persons requires two separate judgments by immigration agencies: First, how can they marshal the facts that enable them to identify those who are involved in terrorism? Second, what type of involvement in or connection with terrorism should lead to negative immigration decisions?

Developing the Facts

The U.S. admissions system historically has deployed a double layer of screening: scrutiny by a consular officer overseas of a person's eligibility for admission before a visa is issued and a second and potentially equally demanding review by an immigration inspector at the port of entry, even if the person holds a duly issued visa. One of the major responses to September 11 has been to "push out the borders"—that is, to try to maximize successful and rigorous screening well before a person embarks on a trip or shows up at the port of entry. That means designing systems to support more effective consular work or, for persons allowed to travel without a visa, to maximize the data available to U.S. officials well before the individual arrives on U.S. soil—ideally, before he or she even boards the plane.

FACE-TO-FACE INTERVIEWS

Some of the September 11 hijackers had obtained temporary visas, known as nonimmigrant visas, for travel to the United States without undergoing a face-to-face interview before a U.S. consular officer. In response, in May 2003, the State Department issued a new policy requiring a personal interview for nearly all categories of applicants for nonimmigrant or immigrant visas. Congress tightened that requirement and wrote it into the statute in the 2004 Intelligence Reform Act.[7] Support for the change derived in part from the belief that interviews conducted by skilled officers would be more likely than paper reviews to identify terrorists or at least detect danger signs. The State Department has enhanced consular training in analytic interview techniques and has cooperated with the intelligence community to develop non-obvious lines of questioning that might help flag potentially dangerous individuals.

While a presumption in favor of personal interviews makes sense, the rigid statutory mandate to conduct them in every case does not. The chances of detecting a resolute terrorist simply through a sequence of consular questions remain slim despite the enhanced training, particularly because the officer may devote only between four and six minutes to a typical case. That timing benchmark, which includes the time spent checking databases, is a consequence of the sheer volume of nonimmigrant applications. The "white-noise effect" that results from having to interview everyone reduces the odds of detecting high-risk travelers.[8] Congress should, therefore, ease the statutory interview requirement to permit the State Department to apply more selective standards, to be set administratively on the basis of systematic risk analysis. Devoting more time to those cases that present significant risk factors should improve security. At the same time, eliminating a rigid requirement for consular interviews each time a foreigner needs a visa—a requirement that often requires a costly trip within the traveler's own country to reach the consulate—would ease a burden that serves to discourage travel and encourages businesses to locate elsewhere.

IMPROVED ACCESS TO DATABASES AND INTELLIGENCE INFORMATION

More important to successful screening than face-to-face interviews is enhancing the timely availability to consular officers and immigration inspectors at the border of the best intelligence possible. That is, policymakers should not expect consular officers and immigration inspectors to play more than an occasional and adventitious role in actually detecting or unearthing terrorist plots through their questioning of applicants. What they should expect, however, is that those officers will have the best possible intelligence and law enforcement information about the people before them. The significance of immigration control measures as a counterterrorism tool lies overwhelmingly in offering an opportunity for *using* intelligence to minimize the risk of violent acts on U.S. soil, not for obtaining such intelligence. The intelligence and law enforcement communities will be the primary actors in gathering that information.

Linking databases and providing user-friendly and comprehensive systems to frontline decisionmakers has been a significant focus of both statutory changes and administrative adjustments since September 11—a daunting task because the databases had developed in a haphazard and disconnected fashion. Disparate agencies used different and inconsistent systems and, before September 2001, jealously guarded their own information, only grudgingly yielding morsels to immigration officials. Reforms have made considerable headway over the last six years in improving the situation, driven in part by congressional mandates for consolidation and interoperability but also by administrative innovation in centralizing key processes and efficiently allocating the time of skilled analysts through an automated targeting system.[9]

One of the main remaining challenges is to improve the timeliness of final resolution whenever the initial database query produces a "hit," indicating, at least preliminarily, that negative information exists in one of the relevant databases about someone attempting to come to or remain in the United States. When that occurs, all further processing of the requested immigration benefit (typically visa issuance, extension of a period of admission, or adjustment of status to permanent residence for someone already present in the

United States) ordinarily ceases. The matter is then referred to the appropriate intelligence or law enforcement agency to determine whether the negative information actually relates to that particular individual and whether it is sufficiently clear and serious to warrant denial of the benefit. The identity confirmation step can be speedy if the information is coded to biometrics rather than biographical information, but Congress also requires a check of FBI records that are kept by name and date of birth in connection with most benefit decisions. The first step in those cases is to decide whether the negative information relates to the applicant in question or to another person with a similar name and date of birth. Many cases present difficult judgment calls, requiring labor-intensive review by analysts. That kind of delay, which has sometimes extended as long as four years, frustrates and alienates the applicant and often a host of U.S. citizens and residents expecting or relying on the person's approval—such as would-be employers, family members, or prospective academic or scientific colleagues. Since 2004, processing delays, overwhelmingly the product of delays in security screening, have triggered thousands of federal lawsuits seeking orders commanding the Bureau of Citizenship and Immigration Services (USCIS) of the Department of Homeland Security (DHS) to proceed promptly to a final decision. The litigation itself is a costly waste of resources, and the delays threaten to discourage legal and desirable migration while conveying a negative image of a fearful, uncertain, indecisive United States.

Here too, the legal framework could be eased to permit approval of some benefits even before the completion of the inherently imprecise name-check process. Some improvements already have taken place, without statutory change. In April 2008, DHS and the FBI reached an agreement on process changes that made remarkable headway against the name-check backlog in just the first six months of operation, and it may serve eventually to remove this corrosive delay problem from applicants' list of grievances.[10] One crucial step was the provision of substantial new staff for the FBI's analyst ranks, but in an important change, USCIS also determined that it could issue some benefits even before receiving the final name-check results from the FBI. This advance approval applies only to certain categories of persons who already are present in the United States (and therefore equally capable of committing dangerous acts whether or not the benefit is delayed), who have passed all biometric screening without any indication of threat, whose FBI name check has been pending for 180 days, and for whom the benefit can easily be withdrawn if negative information comes to light.[11] The last criterion precludes the application of this streamlining measure to naturalization proceedings.

Detecting Fraud and Collecting Biometric Identifying Information

If a terrorist can successfully use another person's identity, then he or she can obviously defeat even the best systems for prompt checking of available intelligence and law enforcement information. Skilled questioning by an inspector or consular officer, as discussed above, can help spot inconsistencies or oddities that will trigger closer scrutiny of identity fraud. Beyond that, the increasing use of biometric identifiers, as required in many pieces of immigration-related legislation since September 11, helps guard against such fraud, as does increasing international standardization of identity documents with counterfeit-resistant features and embedded machine-readable biometric data.

One element of the U.S. Visitor and Immigrant Status Indicator Technology (US-VISIT) screening system—planned to become eventually a comprehensive DHS system monitoring aliens' entry and exit—provides an important protection against a specific kind of fraud. Under the earliest system component widely deployed (beginning in 2004), aliens arriving at a port of entry have had to submit to facial photographing and the electronic capture of two fingerprints (of the right and left index fingers), conducted right at the primary inspection booth—a procedure that added about 15 seconds to each inspection. At about that time, consular officers began to capture the same two fingerprints (photos having long been required) at the time of visa issuance. The system thus permits prompt comparison of the two sets of fingerprints, to ensure that the person applying for admission is the same person cleared to receive a visa.[12]

The database that provides the foundation for US-VISIT, known as IDENT, also affords swift access to key watchlist information on possible terrorists and increasingly to the FBI's comprehensive fingerprint system, known as the Integrated Automated Fingerprint Identification System (IAFIS). Continued improvement in the interoperability of the various systems, as mandated in various statutes, is critical to maximizing the efficient use of both immigration and law enforcement resources in finding and either prosecuting or removing dangerous individuals, and arrangements need to be concluded for more efficient sharing of some FBI data with IDENT. The decision of former DHS secretary Michael Chertoff in 2005 to alter US-VISIT so that the fingerprint readers will capture all ten fingerprints, rather than just the index fingers, also represents a significant security gain. That change will increase the chances of detecting terrorists by comparing the full fingerprint set against latent prints lifted from terrorist sites—including prints collected by the Department of Defense. Though challenges remain, US-VISIT has generally proven itself to be a gratifyingly successful technological venture.[13]

The Visa Waiver Program

Some critics have urged an end to the statutorily authorized visa waiver program—which allows short-term visa-free travel (lasting no more than ninety days) to citizens of selected countries—seeing it as an especially vulnerable entry point for dangerous individuals. As of December 31, 2008, thirty-five countries were on the visa waiver list, most of them European democracies that accord a reciprocal privilege to U.S. citizens. But critics point out that some noted terrorists, including Richard Reid (the "shoe bomber") and Zacarias Moussaoui (the "twentieth hijacker"), were nationals of visa waiver countries. They allege that a border inspector's quick query of the databases in the primary inspection line at an airport affords an insufficient opportunity to detect dangerous travelers. Pressure for a speedy decision is even higher at the border or at ports of entry than at consulates, and even if a given person is referred for secondary inspection, he or she is already on U.S. soil and therefore must be either detained or released on bond here if a protracted inquiry ensues.

Although those concerns have some merit, Congress should definitely continue the visa waiver program. It epitomizes the trade-offs needed to serve the multiple objectives entailed in the use of an immigration system as a counterterrorism tool. Requiring all nationals from the thirty-five high-volume countries involved to obtain visas, even for short trips, would deter some travel, sow ill will, probably reduce U.S. travel opportunities, and create a monumental additional workload on an already taxed consular corps. Nonetheless, Congress needs to take advantage of innovations that can reduce the vulnerabilities inherent in the visa waiver system. Statutory changes have already gone some distance in that direction. Visa waiver travelers must now have machine-readable passports, thus facilitating accurate and speedy database checks by airport inspectors.[14] Under a separate initiative, airlines are now required to send data on all passengers to U.S. border authorities well before a plane arrives from an overseas location. This Advance Passenger Information System (APIS) affords Customs and Border Protection (CBP) officers additional time before landing for checking passenger names against databases in order to identify those whom CBP should either reject or at least subject to more intensive review at the border.[15] Furthermore, in order to join the visa waiver program, countries must agree to cooperate fully in sharing terrorist-related intelligence and also in following other security-enhancing practices.

A new law passed in 2007 adopts a practice like one pioneered by Australia, which is designed to provide still more extensive advance information on visa waiver passengers. It makes use of an automated electronic system for travel authorization, hence its shorthand moniker, ESTA. Under ESTA, a prospective traveler from a visa waiver country must apply, ordinarily through the Internet many days or weeks before the flight, for travel authorization, providing at that time specified biographical information that allows DHS to check for "law enforcement or security risk." If none is found, the person will receive a code indicating eligibility for travel to the United States without a visa. Eventually, airlines will be able—and required—to check the code through an automated system before permitting the individual to board the aircraft for the United States. All such persons will still be subject to inspection and a new database check at the port of entry.[16]

Specifying Disqualifying Links to Terrorism

Exactly how to deploy the immigration laws with respect to applicants for admission believed to be linked to terrorism depends on exactly what sort of link authorities can demonstrate and with what degree of certainty. If they have enough evidence for a criminal conviction of the person for terrorist activity and he is applying, for example, under a false identity that he believes has not been discovered, then the authorities are probably best advised to use his application as a kind of sting. They can treat his trip as a lucky opportunity to take him into criminal custody upon arrival for trial. A similar approach makes sense with dangerous persons for whom the evidence is insufficient for criminal trial, but who would meet the presumably less demanding standards for preventive detention of active terrorists—provided, of course, that Congress chooses to adopt such a detention regime (see chapters 2 and 3). Excluding such individuals from admission denies the United States the benefit of their capture. It might keep them away from their targets on U.S. soil, but it would leave them at large in some other country, where they could continue to plan or help carry out terrorist activity directed at U.S. interests at home or abroad or at allied nations and their populations.

But in all likelihood, such cases will present themselves only rarely. The most significant use of immigration law as a counterterrorism tool will occur when there is some evidence to indicate that an individual is dangerous but the evidence is not of sufficient quantity or quality to ensure the person's conviction on a charge of terrorism. The best that the United States can do, given lesser quality information on a given suspect, may be to keep him or her off the streets of the country by means of exclusion or, if the person is already present, by means of removal. But that objective presents a thorny set of questions of its own: What sorts of links merit such treatment? And what sorts of evidence, reflecting what degree of certainty, ought to be required to exclude or deport a suspect?

The answer, for reasons developed below, should vary with the individual's stake in the process. Lesser indications of terrorist involvement should be enough to justify denial of an ordinary visa. By contrast, deporting a legally admitted alien should require stronger indications of knowing or intentional connection to terrorist groups—particularly if that person holds lawful permanent resident status. And the law should also require stronger showings in connection with the denial of an application for political asylum or refugee status.

STATUTORY EVOLUTION

Congress has greatly expanded the sweep of the immigration law provisions that address links to terrorism since the comprehensive redesign of the grounds for exclusion and deportation of aliens enacted in 1990. One important theme of that revision, which was undertaken as the cold war was ending, was to forswear an era of "ideological exclusion" or "guilt by association" believed to mark the former anti-Communist exclusion and deportation provisions. Those laws, which prohibited entry not only to members of communist organizations but also to those who wrote about or taught "the economic, international and governmental doctrines of world communism" had provoked ongoing controversy and a string of judicial challenges.[17]

The 1990 grounds for inadmissibility and deportability, which are only roughly comparable to the old, addressed terrorism, rather than Communist membership or writings, and focused on involvement in dangerous activities, not allegedly dangerous thinking.[18] The basic provision enacted that year rendered excludable any alien who "has engaged in a terrorist activity" or who "a consular officer or [immigration officer] knows, or has reasonable ground to believe, is likely to engage after entry in any terrorist activity."[19] Later clauses in that section spelled out what Congress meant by "terrorist activity" and "to engage in terrorist activity." The definitions included the provision of material support to *individuals* involved in terrorism, but only if the provider of support knows or reasonably should know that the aid would assist another "in conducting a terrorist activity"—that is, in carrying out the acts of violence that the statute identified as terrorism.[20]

In 1996, Congress added the provision of material support to terrorist *organizations* as a ground for exclusion, but it provided a detailed procedure, under section 219 of the Immigration and Nationality Act (INA), calling for the secretary of state to designate terrorist organizations as such and to publish the list before support for them could become grounds for exclusion.[21] The secretary had to compile an administrative record that would permit judicial review of its listing, albeit under deferential standards of review. At least in principle, that process helped clarify the situation for persons contemplating gifts to organizations operating in areas beset by armed conflict or terrorist resistance. It more effectively put potential donors on notice of which contributions would jeopardize their immigration status—or indeed render them liable to fines or imprisonment under a new provision of the criminal code, which criminalized the provision of support to the formally listed organizations, even when given by U.S. citizens.[22] But the list of designated foreign terrorist organizations never included more than thirty groups before September 11, 2001. Experience in implementing the provisions apparently led some in the Justice Department to worry that guilty parties would escape sanctions when their support went to an unlisted organization, because the statute made it much too easy for them to cast doubt on whether they knew or reasonably should have known about an organization's activities or how their gift would be used.

In the USA Patriot Act, passed in 2001 one month after the September 11 attacks, Congress greatly expanded the terrorism-related grounds for exclusion and deportation, casting an extremely wide net ensnaring all sorts of connections to terrorism. The statute added a second and far more streamlined process for the secretary of state to use in designating additional organizations as terrorist organizations. Organizations designated under that process became known as tier II organizations. The old process survived as tier I. (As of January 2009 there were forty-four tier I and fifty-nine tier II organizations.[23]) Then the act added a tier III of striking breadth, defining "terrorist organization" to include any "group of two or more individuals, whether organized or not, which engages in the activities described in subclause (I), (II), or (III) of clause (iv)."[24] Those three subclauses cover committing or (with certain limitations) inciting a terrorist act, preparing or planning a terrorist act, and gathering information on potential targets. Tiers II and III apply primarily to aliens, because material support to such organizations renders an alien inadmissible or, if already admitted, deportable, whereas the law applying criminal penalties to donations still does not automatically cover support to organizations unless they are listed through the tier I process. Congress did permit aliens an escape clause for providing unwitting support to tier III organizations, but, evidently to minimize manipulative use of such a claim, it shifted the burden of proof regarding knowledge from the government to the individual. The escape clause applied only when "the actor can demonstrate that he did not know, and should not reasonably have known, that the act would further the organization's terrorist activity." By 2005, Congress thought even that provision too lax and so made the individual's burden of proof still more demanding. Under current law, the donor to an organization that is proven— even long after the date of the support—to be a tier III organization must make a showing of insufficient knowledge or notice "by clear and convincing evidence" in order to escape negative immigration consequences.[25]

Congress in 2005 also expanded the application of the now-sprawling terrorism-related grounds along another dimension. Theretofore, only a subset of the more serious links to actual terrorist activities that might justify denial of a visa or refusal of admission at the border—essentially only past or ongoing engagement in terrorist activity—were designated as grounds for deportation of someone who had initially been lawfully admitted.[26] The 2005 amendments removed that constraint, essentially making the entire list of links to terrorism, including mere membership or negligent donation to a tier III organization, grounds for deportation. As now written, that deportability ground allows deportation when an immigration officer has "reason to believe" that the person is likely to engage in terrorist activity in the future— a standard that probably equates to probable cause.

Overall Evaluation

The message of Congress's successive amendments from 1996 through 2005 seemed to be to cast as wide a net as possible in order to make sure that no real terrorist could use soft language or clever legal arguments to escape exclusion or deportation. The drafters either did not worry that the broad language might snare many innocents for whom some unwitting tie to terrorism might be shown many months or years later or saw the problem as one to be dealt with through sound use of prosecutorial discretion. One difficulty with the latter expectation, however, has always been the highly diffuse nature of charging decisions within INS and DHS—perhaps even more so now that charging authority has been distributed among the three bureaus and numerous field offices of DHS. Another problem resides in the internal incentives that affect many officers after September 11. They do not want to be pilloried if they grant an individual a benefit—or if they decline to charge an individual—and the person turns out to be a terrorist. The safest course for the officer is always to file a charge if it seems to fit at all. Thus, the disproportion written into the statute resists administrative amelioration.

Perhaps one could still defend such remarkable statutory breadth as reflecting an implicit cost-benefit analysis. Congress put its thumb heavily on the side of the scales favoring U.S. safety and security. In that view, at any hint of a connection to terrorism, the nation should decline to run the risk of admitting a person into or allowing a person to stay in the United States. But that kind of crude, across-the-board weighing makes for bad policy. It takes no account of the highly disparate individual stakes that are presented in different sorts of immigration adjudications, particularly the distinctions between those applying overseas for a first-time admission versus a long-term lawful permanent resident facing deportation for sending a donation incautiously to an ostensibly charitable group that proves to have links to a terrorist organization.

That lack of perspective and sense of proportion finally drew sustained attention over the past few years in the context of the application of the "material support" grounds to the overseas refugee resettlement program and to domestic asylum adjudications. The Justice Department and DHS took the inflexible position that the terrorist exclusion provisions admit of no exceptions for persons who provide material support at gunpoint or under other forms of duress or in circumstances where U.S. foreign policy actually *favors* the supported organization that has been engaged in armed resistance against an abusive government.

That interpretation brought an abrupt halt to some refugee resettlement initiatives that the administration otherwise saw as highly desirable to revive a resettlement program that had been especially hard hit by the security retrenchments following the September 11 attacks.[27] (Refugee admissions fell below 29,000 annually for two years, from an average level of more than 75,000 per year in the preceding five years.[28]) Specific groups of Burmese refugees in Thailand were far into the consideration process when it was pointed out that the material support exclusion applied to them because of their association with armed rebel groups fighting the pariah Burmese military regime, which the United States government has denounced and placed under sanctions. Later it became apparent that even Hmong refugees who had aided the United States and its allies during the Vietnam War also were barred from admission under that interpretation.

In the context of asylum seekers, tales emerged of persons clearly in grave danger of persecution from paramilitary groups in Colombia who were disqualified from asylum status because they had yielded to violent extortion by the very groups whose persecution had prompted their flight. That is, they provided "material support" to terrorist organizations simply by ransoming a kidnapped child. The obvious fact that such persons clearly would not repeat such support if given refuge in the United States made no difference. Nor did the fact that denying them asylum probably violated U.S. obligations under the refugee treaties cause a rethinking of the interpretation.

The administration finally began addressing those particular policy embarrassments through the use of a waiver provision that permits the relevant cabinet secretaries to exempt certain groups or individuals from the material support exclusion. But it took several years to reach internal agreement within the government concerning how to activate the waiver mechanism, and its actual use is still proceeding very slowly.[29]

The United States needs a better way to calibrate the application of the terrorism-related grounds for exclusion or deportation to take into account the interests on the opposite side of the scales. The country cannot adopt for the long run a stance that across the board relentlessly favors security in immigration decisions. It needs to establish more precisely the types of links to terrorism that would disqualify a migrant, refugee, or asylum seeker, with attention to the stakes involved for the individual. Otherwise, the process unnecessarily undercuts several of the countervailing objectives listed earlier in this chapter—particularly in reaching outcomes that are seen as deeply unfair or arbitrary or that detract from the historic role of the United States as a refuge from persecution. From that broad observation flow several specific suggestions about how to differentiate among cases.

DISTINGUISH BETWEEN EXCLUSION AND DEPORTATION

Congress erred badly in 2005 by applying the same sweeping terrorism-link standards that apply to decisions on admission or exclusion to decisions on deportation. A person applying for the first time for a nonimmigrant visa or for admission to the United States has only limited stakes in the adjudication of his or her case. To place a heavy benefit of the doubt on the side of exclusion if there are any significant signs of links to terrorism may be wholly justifiable. Critics may still charge that doing so amounts to finding "guilt by association,"[30] but the practice does not deserve the opprobrium associated with that epithet. What is being decided is not guilt (followed by criminal punishment) but merely a prudential judgment that leads to a disappointed expectation, not deprivation of benefits already being enjoyed. Moreover, because terrorist networks are by their very nature clandestine, officials ordinarily have little to rely on in judging whether an applicant presents a risk of terrorism other than evidence of past associations, activities, and statements. To be sure, the chance—indeed, the likelihood—remains of barring innocent persons in the process. But the relative consequences of false positives versus false negatives justify such an approach in most visa and initial admission decisions.

That is not to say, however, that the United States needs the full prolixity of the current terrorism-related ground for inadmissibility to provide that cushion of safety. Congress could achieve the same result with a leaner provision mandating the denial of a visa or admission to the country when there is "reason to believe" that the person has committed or is likely to commit terrorist acts—that is, using only the core portions of the relatively spare 1990 version of the exclusion ground. Congress should revisit the current statute and search for ways to render the terrorist exclusion standards more precise and intelligible.

But even with the relatively low-stakes nonimmigrant visas, the U.S. government needs to apply greater care and rigor in its decisionmaking, policed by a reasonable supervisory review structure. Perceptible stakes still exist for the individual—as well as for a host of U.S. citizen friends, family members, or business associates. The clumsily handled case of Tariq Ramadan, a Muslim scholar who was blocked from taking a faculty position at the University of Notre Dame but whose visa denials the government had based on shifting rationales, stoked legitimate disaffection in academic and other circles.[31]

In the deportation setting, by contrast, the stakes can be enormously high, particularly when the government seeks to deport a lawful permanent resident. Congress should repeal the 2005 amendment and restore a system that makes only a subset of more dangerous links to terrorism—actual engagement in terrorist activity—grounds for deportation of a person who has been lawfully admitted. Indeed, it might be good to take as well a fresh look in order to indicate with more specificity the kinds of links that should result in loss of lawful admission. In particular, in the deportation setting the law should demand more of the government to prove the individual's knowledge and intent in connection with any assistance or support later shown to have gone to terrorist activity or organizations.

The truth is that despite the 2005 changes, terrorism-based deportations—in apparent contrast to visa refusals—remain quite rare. While the government has doubtless targeted persons with terrorist affiliations for removal, if those people were initially admitted as nonimmigrants, it is usually possible to secure their removal on more conventional grounds, such as overstay or violation of status. Such conventional charges present government attorneys far fewer problems of proof and case management than charges rooted in terrorist activity. And I am unaware of the lodging in recent years of any terrorism-based removal charges against lawful permanent residents. Hence a sweeping *deportability* ground based on terrorist affiliation is clearly not indispensable to effect the removal of apparently dangerous nonimmigrants. Sweeping deportability provisions have significant bite only with regard to green-card holders—that is, in exactly the situation in which a more focused and precise approach is called for, given the demands of justice for those who initially made their homes here with the full approval of the U.S. government.

The "Good Guys" Claim, Duress, and de Minimis Support

The application of the material support provision in the refugee and asylum settings, including some litigation over the latter, has revealed further issues regarding the legal specification of disqualifying links to terrorism.

In *Matter of S-K-*, the government argued that a Burmese asylum seeker was excluded from protection, no matter what her risk of persecution, because she had given money to the Chin National Front, a Burmese resistance organization engaged in armed conflict with the Burmese government.[32] Her action apparently fit within the sweep of the material support provision, though she countered with numerous indications that the U.S. government considered the Burmese regime a "group of thugs" that had thwarted the assumption of office by Aung San Suu Kyi and her party, the National League of Democracy, which won parliamentary elections in Burma in 1990. In essence, she argued that the immigration judge or the Board of Immigration Appeals (BIA) should adjudge the regime illegitimate, such that armed resistance would be considered a just cause. The Chin National Front could then be deemed the "good guys" and hence not terrorist in nature.

The overall system for applying the terrorism-related grounds for removal needs the capacity to judge the illegitimacy of regimes and the justice of the cause of some armed groups that fall within the sweeping language of the tier III definition or whose actions fit the broad statutory definition of terrorism. Nelson Mandela would probably have run afoul of this provision, as might those who rose up against the Hungarian Communist regime in 1956. The statute itself, however, leaves no room for this kind of "just war" determination—and so is significantly out of keeping with the way in which most people respond to the efforts of various resistance movements.

Nonetheless, the Board of Immigration Appeals was correct to refuse to permit immigration judges to make such judgments of legitimacy, regarding either governments or resistance movements. There is simply too much room for widely disparate views among adjudicators about the merits of regimes and their opponents—a phenomenon that became glaringly apparent in the 1980s and 1990s, in cases involving both the extradition and deportation of members of the Irish Republican Army.[33]

How then should such decisions be made? Though any decisionmaking system on such sensitive issues entails real disadvantages, the right place for "just war" judgments is probably the State Department, in consultation with the Department of Homeland Security. The current provision, which allows unreviewable waivers for certain groups and organizations at the discretion of appropriate cabinet members, provides a reasonable mechanism for implementing this needed accommodation.[34] Since 2006, department secretaries have designated approximately a dozen groups for exemption. Congress also appropriately reinforced this mechanism in December 2007 by enshrining some exemptions in statute and expanding the reach of the discretionary waiver provision.[35] Ultimately the asylum seeker in *S-K-* received asylum, after a group waiver for the Chin National Front permitted the immigration judge to reach the merits of her persecution claim.[36]

The Departments of Justice and Homeland Security have also chosen to use the unreviewable waiver process as a way of dealing with claims that an individual provided support to a terrorist group under duress and so should not be held responsible for the act.[37] That is a more questionable approach, although it is better than simply ignoring claims that support was provided only as a result of coercion. The waiver process, reasonably adapted to the groupwide decisions needed when confronting a "good guys" claim, does not fit as well with the inherently individual issues presented by a duress claim. Though the duress waiver process currently in place does contemplate individualized review by DHS adjudicating officers, at present that is usually just a paper review based on a record compiled elsewhere, ordinarily in immigration court. Congress should consider whether immigration judges could handle this highly case-specific issue in the course of adjudicating asylum claims. The evidence presented in court in the process of proving a risk of persecution will necessarily overlap with evidence relevant to deciding whether the individual acted under duress in giving support to a terrorist organization— ransom to free a kidnapped relative, "revolutionary taxes," or food demanded at gunpoint. Such an assignment of decisional authority would also give the responsibility to an official who can readily cross-examine the witnesses on the duress question, instead of relying on adjudication by officers who, months later, see only a cold record. Immigration judge decisions that apply an overly generous conception of duress or that ignore evidence of genuine, ongoing dangerousness of an individual—which would disqualify the refugee claimant under the refugee treaty[38]—would remain subject to government appeal to the BIA. If necessary, BIA decisions could also be referred for a final ruling by the attorney general personally, under long-established provisions for administrative review.

Finally, the government has held to a reading of the material support provision that admits of no exceptions for trivial assistance, apparently once arguing that even the provision of a glass of water to a terrorist would constitute material support.[39] It is hardly obvious that such a reading of current law is correct; the adjective "material" in "material support" strongly suggests some threshold of substantiality, though the law is vague about how to determine that threshold. In any case, in order to avoid manifestly arbitrary results, the system, either by interpretive change or statutory amendment, should allow adjudicators to find a person admissible despite de minimis amounts of assistance. The final decision, however, should of course turn on what other evidence might exist regarding the person's terrorist connections or the person's knowledge or intent at the time of the contribution. I do not argue that adjudicators (in refugee cases as well as ordinary visa cases) must ignore minor amounts of assistance. I argue only that such an act should not be automatically disqualifying.

Detention

The government looked to immigration law in the immediate aftermath of the September 11 attacks in large part because it could justify detention of certain foreign nationals even in the absence of proof sufficient to support criminal charges against them. Hence it helped take persons viewed as possible terrorists "off the street"—an objective that Attorney General John Ashcroft regarded as the Justice Department's single most important aim in October 2001. Many aliens deemed suspicious had violated their admission status and thus were subject to immediate removal charges and detention pursuant to those charges. For others, the government could muster plausible charges based on bitingly close scrutiny of all past immigration filings by the alien, unearthing misstatements, falsehoods, or highly technical deficiencies that ordinarily are ignored.

As an emergency improvisation in the face of a grave crisis, such an approach was perhaps understandable. But as long-term legal architecture, it is inadvisable. And it led to pathologies in application. As the Justice Department inspector general determined, following a lengthy inquiry into the matter that focused on detainees in the New York City area, immigration law was misused when the Justice Department ordered blanket detention without bond for more than 700 "special interest" detainees whom it had picked up in connection with the September 11 investigations. The report also found misuse when detention of many individuals continued for as long as a year, awaiting FBI clearance of their deportation, even after entry of a final, executable removal order—perhaps one eagerly sought by the person who knew that he was present illegally and preferred prompt deportation to lengthy detention. A later phase of the inspector general's investigation also uncovered serious episodes of physical mistreatment of the immigration detainees during that period.[40]

Detention Following a Removal Order

Post-order detention should adhere to the rules derived from *Zadvydas* v. *Davis,* a Supreme Court decision issued shortly before September 11, which limited the duration of immigration detention. The Court held squarely that indefinite detention after a removal order has been entered is invalid under the current immigration statutes, while signaling along the way that such a practice would also raise serious constitutional problems, at least as applied to previously admitted aliens.[41] After a removal order is final, the government should move as quickly as possible to deport the individual. If it cannot effectuate a removal order for reasons other than the individual's noncooperation—for example, because of the home country's refusal to provide travel documents or because the individual is stateless and no country will take him—then the detainee is entitled to supervised release within a guideline period, which *Zadvydas* sets presumptively at six months.

If prompt removal appears seriously to threaten some other government interest—for example, if the government believes the suspect to be an active terrorist—the answer is not to create a longer-term detention authority out of existing powers that were never meant to serve that purpose. Any longer-term detention should take place only on criminal charges or under whatever separate mechanism Congress adopts for that purpose. If preventive detention is to be used, based on a rough analogy to the incarceration of prisoners of war to prevent their return to hostilities, it should take place under a regime specifically created by Congress for that purpose, with democratically debated limits and safeguards, rather than through stretches and distortions of immigration law.

The difficult and freighted topic of preventive detention receives close scrutiny elsewhere in this volume. It is sufficient to note here that the *Zadvydas* decision does not close the door to a properly designed regime of this sort. Writing just eleven weeks before the September 11 attacks, the Court presciently stated that it was not addressing "terrorism or other special circumstances where special arguments might be made for forms of preventive detention."[42] Whatever the Court might do to apply that notion in a case that squarely presents the terrorism issue—as *Zadvydas* itself did not—the justices hardly meant their dictum as a recommendation for preventive detention on the basis of immigration charges and delayed removal. Congress would do better to use this potential opening in case law to address preventive detention under its own separate legal architecture.

Detention Pending Immigration Hearings

In the pre-hearing setting, use of immigration detention should return to the purposes it has classically served. The traditional grounds for detaining rather than releasing an individual while a hearing is pending have been flight risk and dangerousness, judged case by case—not because an individual appears on a broader "special interest" list compiled elsewhere.[43] Evidence of terrorist affiliation or activity is of course relevant in both instances, and the system should permit reliance on such evidence in deciding to deny bond. The system should also permit the government, subject to safeguards discussed below, to use classified information in making the initial detention decision and in defending its no-bond or high-bond determinations before immigration judges or federal habeas courts. The government has long argued that current statutes permit such use, but the statutory foundation is at best unclear.[44] Congress should amend the provisions to extinguish all doubt about the propriety of considering classified information in connection with pre-hearing detention decisions.

One other technical but important pre-hearing detention issue deserves attention, perhaps to be followed by statutory or at least regulatory fixes. Before September 11, regulations required an alien arrested without warrant to be taken before an examining officer within twenty-four hours for a decision on whether to file formal charges or to release him pending further proceedings. In emergency rulemaking completed on September 17, 2001, the Justice Department amended that provision to allow forty-eight hours for those determinations, with an exception allowing an unspecified additional "reasonable period of time" in the event of "an emergency or other extraordinary circumstance."[45] The highly critical report written by the DOJ inspector general on September 11 detainees, discussed above, found that this escape clause had fostered sloppy practices that contributed to lengthy detention without the filing of charges.[46] The liberty interests at stake in these judgments are substantial, and prompt presentation to an examining officer is a modest but crucial step to help avoid the dangers associated with warrantless arrests followed by incommunicado detention. Congress should amend the statute to provide a firm charging deadline in such cases.

It is also noteworthy that the September 2001 regulatory change softening the deadline for confirmation of charges against detainees contributed to a rather striking reaction by Congress later that month when it considered early drafts of the USA Patriot Act. The executive branch initially proposed a provision that would have given the attorney general broad and largely unreviewable authority to certify specific aliens as likely terrorists, who would then be subject to a strict regime of mandatory detention. Made wary of indefinite detention by the earlier regulation, congressional leaders insisted on adding safeguards to what became a new section of the Immigration and Nationality Act (INA).[47] They inserted a requirement that such certifications be done personally by the attorney general or the deputy attorney general and not be further delegated. Even with the power thus confined—and acting while the rubble of the twin towers still smoldered—Congress also mandated that any detainee under that provision had to be released unless charged within seven days under the immigration laws or the criminal code. If, at the end of immigration court proceedings, removal of the person could not be secured, Congress allowed for ongoing detention (in an apparent effort to override the statutory holding of *Zadvydas* for this limited category of individuals), but here too it imposed restrictions. It required the attorney general to review the case every six months, and it made prolonged detention explicitly subject to habeas corpus review in the federal courts. The care Congress applied to cabining this detention power, even in the alarmed atmosphere that prevailed in October 2001, underscores the need for well-designed legal limits.[48]

Procedures

Immigration procedures also require attention in creating an improved legal architecture for the struggle against terrorism.

Closed Hearings

The chief immigration judge, acting on September 21, 2001, on orders from the Justice Department, directed that the immigration court hearings of some 700 "special interest" detainees be closed to the public. That directive was at least in tension with preexisting regulations that established a baseline expectation of open hearings while permitting closure only based on criteria that seemed to demand case-by-case application.[49] The department defended the new policy, arguing that it would prevent terrorist organizations from knowing the pattern of arrests and the kinds of information that the government had uncovered. Nonetheless, the blanket closure drew sharp condemnation, as well as notable court challenges, filed by individual alien respondents and by media organizations and members of Congress. The Sixth Circuit found the practice invalid, in an opinion filled with somber warnings, including this: "Democracies die behind closed doors."[50] The Third Circuit, however, upheld the closure order as a permissible response to the emergency situation created by the September 11 attacks.[51] Before the Supreme Court took up a certiorari petition in the latter case, the Justice Department signaled that the affected hearings had virtually all been completed and that it did not contemplate adding other cases to the "special interest" list. Against that backdrop, the Court declined review.

It is hard to see, based on the public record, what concrete gains were achieved by the blanket closure, while its disadvantages were fairly evident. It compounded suspicions about the fairness of the removal proceedings themselves, and it fueled charges that the government was improperly targeting defendants on the basis of their ethnicity or religion. The department's apparent disinclination to replicate such a practice in the future is thus highly justified. Limited case-by-case closure, coupled as necessary with appropriate protective orders forbidding participants to reveal information, should be both sufficient to meet legitimate government needs and far less likely to sow doubts about the justice of the procedures.

Secret Evidence

The government's information about the risk of terrorist acts from persons applying for admission to or already present in the United States often comes from intelligence sources. But use of such confidential information against an individual can raise exceedingly difficult issues. From the point of view of a high-level government manager, the chance to shield crucial operational information from close scrutiny by the individuals targeted or by courts has sometimes made room for hard-to-monitor abuses or shoddy practices on the part of certain officers, who have relied too much on rumor or accusation planted, for example, by personal enemies or estranged spouses. From the targeted individual's point of view, contending with such shadowy information can appear Kafkaesque. Notified in summary fashion, if notified at all, that he is being denied a benefit or subjected to deportation because of information indicating terrorist connections, he is left almost wholly at sea in trying to develop an explanation or a defense. If he is innocent, he probably has no idea what past conduct or association triggered the alleged problem, and so does not know where to begin to prepare a response. More detail would help him to figure out what he needs to counter. But it is precisely such detail that would endanger intelligence sources or methods, if it turns out that the target subject really is a dangerous person who can pass on the details to confederates. That is, the government sometimes cannot reveal accurate information having a legitimate or critical bearing on a case without endangering a valuable source who has forwarded the information at great peril or who can supply future information only if he or she is not compromised. In short, very weighty interests can be found on both sides of the debate over the use of secret information.

THE SPECTRUM

The current U.S. system allows the use of confidential information at various stages of the immigration and removal process, but through different mechanisms and with different levels of protection for the subject alien. Judicial and political controversies over the years have led to modest improvements in practice, but closer scrutiny of the legal framework with an eye toward aligning the safeguards more closely with the individual stakes at issue would be worthwhile. I begin with a summary of the spectrum of procedures for the use of confidential information under current law.

First, consular officers consistently have had the power to use classified information in making a determination concerning visa applications. Visa records, by law, are confidential, and visa refusals are shielded from nearly all forms of administrative and judicial review.[52] The more compelling issue of the last two decades has been to make sure that intelligence information is readily accessible to the deciding officer and to the immigration inspectors at U.S. ports of entry. Improved watchlists and better database integration and access have made significant headway toward that objective.[53]

Second, in the early 1950s, the Supreme Court found no due process problems with the use of confidential information as the basis for ex parte decisions by the attorney general's delegates to exclude aliens applying for admission—even when the excluded alien was the war bride of a U.S. soldier or a twenty-five-year lawful resident returning after an unexpectedly lengthy stay abroad.[54] The Court, in fact, approved the procedure without even insisting on judicial examination, *in camera,* of the negative information. Political efforts, however, eventually led to the discrediting of the government's case regarding the war bride and to her eventual admission and also to the eventual release on parole of the twenty-five-year resident. In neither case was there any evident harm to the republic.[55]

Nonetheless, the secret procedure endured, having been codified by Congress in the Immigration and Nationality Act, and it has found sporadic use in succeeding decades.[56] Beginning in the 1980s, however, reviewing courts began to insist more regularly on receiving an unclassified summary of the negative information, coupled with *in camera* review by the judge of the information itself. Changing course from earlier practices, the Justice Department acceded to that information sharing—thereby usually gaining judicial approval of the exclusion order.[57]

Third, a generally similar process applies to consideration of applications for what is called "relief from removal" filed by persons who are in deportation proceedings. Such applications come from persons who concede formal deportability—based, for example, on overstaying admission on a student or tourist visa—but seek the right to remain anyway by invoking provisions in the laws that trump those that authorize their removal. The primary relief provisions are those providing for political asylum, permanent admission based on marriage to a U.S. citizen (adjustment of status for an "immediate relative"), or discretionary forgiveness (called cancellation of removal) for aliens present more than ten years whose removal would cause exceptional hardship. U.S. law explicitly allows the immigration judge to rely on classified information, unshared with the individual, in deciding on such applications, and dictum in an early Supreme Court case indicated that there would be no due process problems with the practice.[58] The government's ability to shield information relevant to relief, even if it could not shield information used to establish baseline deportability itself, is more significant than might initially appear. The vast majority of removal proceedings involve no contest over deportability but focus instead on relief claims. Today, immigration judges and reviewing courts ordinarily require *in camera* submission of the classified information to permit the court's informed review, but the individual usually will see no more than a scrubbed, unclassified summary.

A series of such relief cases in the 1990s triggered wide public controversy.[59] Several skeptical judges found deficiencies in the use of secret evidence to deny relief, and in a few cases the Justice Department ultimately decided not to contest the reversal, apparently following a more intensive internal review of the secret evidence (which had ordinarily been supplied by the FBI) in light of judicial resistance. The resulting embarrassment led to the development of new internal procedures, overseen by the deputy attorney general, for more rigorous scrutiny of such information before INS could invoke the confidential procedures.[60]

Fourth, using classified information to decide applications for relief, for which the alien bears the burden of proof, has traditionally been distinguished from the government's use of classified information in proving baseline deportability—especially against aliens whom the government lawfully admitted—for which the government bears the burden. In the latter setting, as distinguished from exclusion at a port of entry, the constitutional protection of due process clearly applies. And it applies with sufficient strength to cast significant doubt on the use of secret evidence to the individual's disadvantage.[61] Moreover, as a practical matter, classified information is likely to be relevant to baseline deportability only in the case of a green-card holder, who by definition was lawfully admitted for *permanent* residence.

In 1996, aware of the heightened due process protection in such cases, Congress created a special tribunal known as the Alien Terrorist Removal Court (ATRC).[62] The court's procedures allow the government to use secret evidence to establish deportability, even against lawful permanent residents, but they create an extensive array of safeguards. The members of the ATRC are appointed by the chief justice for five-year terms from among sitting federal judges with life tenure. Hence even the initial decision on the merits, as well as all rulings on motions or procedures along the way, are to be made by independent federal judges, not administrative officials. The judge oversees the preparation of an unclassified summary of the confidential information.

In addition, the statute provides for appointed counsel at government expense for ATRC proceedings, something not required in any other sort of immigration case. In most cases likely to reach the tribunal, it also ensures that counsel will be drawn from the ranks of specialists with high-level security clearances. Such lawyers can review all the classified information and offer arguments or engage in cross-examination of government witnesses in closed proceedings, although they cannot share that information with their client. The ATRC has never been used, testifying to the rarity of circumstances in which the government needs to use classified information in establishing baseline deportability. But the court's basic procedural design, with specially designated Article III judges and the use of specially cleared counsel as defense lawyers, has served as the sometimes unacknowledged model for a host of post–September 11 proposals to establish specialized procedures to address terrorism-related litigation.[63]

EVALUATION

The current legal framework obviously permits the use of classified information in immigration procedures administered by different government players, with a varied array of safeguards. Since the 1950s, two significant checks and balances have been expanded, albeit unevenly. Congress should make both more systematic and place them on a more explicit legal footing.

First is the increased use of internal administrative review before the government relies on secret information—best exemplified by the special scrutiny implemented by the deputy attorney general's office after litigation setbacks in the late 1990s. It would be worthwhile to enshrine that procedure in binding legal requirements. Regulation is probably more appropriate than statute as the vehicle, to ensure the flexibility to adjust the process as the government gains experience in using the system and continues to refine its intelligence processes.

The second change consists of an increasing role for federal courts, primarily through the courts' own insistence on greater sharing of confidential executive branch information *in camera* when the courts are reviewing administrative decisions. That method, of course, is not likely to be as effective in testing the accuracy of such information as would a full adversarial process driven by the respondent or his counsel, and judges' expertise in evaluating the bases for classifying the information will be limited. But even if less reliable than standard courtroom processes, this kind of judicial review remains a genuine check, administered in a forum wholly independent of the enforcement agencies and capable at least of detecting outliers representing gross errors or abuse of the process. Of real operational significance, even when judges ordinarily uphold the administrative decision (as one would expect), is the simple fact that judicial review can occur. The genuine prospect that the judge may look in detail at the underlying information and its sources helps to promote rigor and discipline in the internal agency monitoring processes.

This second evolutionary change—a greater reviewing role for the courts—may therefore be most significant, in practice, for its impact in strengthening the first, the internal government review mechanisms employed before the government uses secret evidence in an actual case. Congress could amend the statutes to provide an explicit but carefully channeled foundation for these features of modern practice, as they have evolved. The statute could specify that courts reviewing removal orders or benefit denials will have full access *in camera* to the underlying information and, if necessary on a proper finding of exceptional need, to related information in the possession of the government. The statute should also emphasize that courts are ultimately to employ a standard of review that is highly deferential to the intelligence experts and responsible officials. The point is not to substitute a judge's judgment for that of the department responsible for protecting security, but instead to catch outliers and, in the process, create a healthy dynamic that will induce greater rigor on the part of the administrators in evaluating secret evidence before deploying it against an individual.[64]

POSSIBLE FURTHER CHANGES TO THE LEGAL FRAMEWORK

As is evident, the statutory scheme for use of secret evidence, though it developed disjointedly rather than through one insightful exercise in statutory design, generally provides an increasing array of procedural safeguards as the individual stakes increase. Visa applicants overseas have the fewest protections, whereas a lawful permanent resident facing a deportation order based on secret evidence can claim all the protections afforded by the ATRC. In general such a spectrum is sensible and appropriate. The main question is whether Congress and the executive branch have placed the boundaries between the layers of protection in the appropriate places—that is, whether some situations should invoke more safeguards than they do now or, indeed, whether some should invoke fewer.

The ATRC goes about as far as possible in providing substitute safeguards meant to avoid injustice while still withholding secret information from the individual. If secret evidence is to be used at all to secure deportation of a lawful permanent resident, those safeguards should be regarded as essential. It is still worth considering whether someone who was given full U.S. approval for permanent residence and hence came to rely on treating the United States as his or her home should be subject to deportation at all, unless the government is willing to place all its evidence on the public record and subject it to full adversarial testing.[65]

Whatever the decision on that question, Congress should consider amending the Immigration and Nationality Act to require the use of ATRC procedures in a wider array of circumstances than its current narrow jurisdiction allows. For example, Congress could use it for circumstances in which the de facto stakes for the individual are far higher than the current formal categories recognize. For example, an applicant for adjustment of status who has married an American wife and has made a home with her—and assuming that no question exists about the genuineness of the marriage—may be, in formal terms, merely an applicant for relief from removal. But in reality he has far more riding on the decision than someone who merely wishes to extend his stay as a tourist or student—and indeed more than someone whose adjustment claim is based only on a U.S. employment offer. Similarly, the stakes in an asylum claim can be far higher than in an ordinary removal case because an erroneous denial may subject the person to persecution or torture. Here too it might make sense to consider using some variant of ATRC-style procedures before asylum or related protections are denied solely on the basis of classified information.

One objection to that proposal could arise from the potential expense and complexity of ATRC procedures compared with those of the pared-down process that is the norm in immigration court. At present, however, secret evidence cases of any of the types discussed here are rare and would involve only modest incremental costs. Moreover, when secret evidence cases arise, they typically trigger major public controversies over the fairness and accuracy of the ultimate decisions. Adding a few cases to the ATRC's currently empty docket could be seen as an investment in improving the deportation system's reputation and protecting the legitimacy of its outcomes. Alternatively, Congress could deploy variations on the ATRC structure to reduce the cost. For example, it could empower immigration judges, rather than life-tenured federal judges, to conduct proceedings in certain subsets of secret evidence cases—but proceedings that employ elements of the basic ATRC framework, including the use of counsel with high security clearances, at government expense if necessary.

Under the current system, the fewest safeguards apply to visa applicants still overseas; hence the chance of error to the disadvantage of a perfectly innocent applicant is increased. No doubt real injustices happen sometimes when the government uses untested secret evidence in such cases. Nonetheless, given the volume of visa cases and the relatively low stakes usually at issue, arguments for change here are not highly persuasive. There might be a case, however, for some sort of closer scrutiny, particularly via internal State Department review, for carefully defined classes of visa applicants for whom the stakes are generically higher, such as those seeking permanent immigration based on family ties.

Alien Registration

In 2002 the Justice Department launched the National Security Entry-Exit Registration System, providing for a specific form of detailed questioning of selected persons coming to or already in the United States.[66] As applied at the border, the system potentially covered persons from all nationalities, to be selected on the basis of individual criteria suggesting risk. But the system apparently also called for applying NSEERS to nearly all males ages sixteen to forty-five arriving from a wide range of countries in the Middle East. The department required persons covered by NSEERS to report to the INS again thirty days after the initial intensive interview and then annually thereafter. When those individuals were ready to depart the country, they were required to exit through one of a handful of designated airports where they would be subjected to detailed exit interviews.

Had the government confined NSEERS to the questioning of new entrants at ports of entry, it might have triggered only mild controversy. What made it highly contentious, however, was a second phase that added a mandate for a special call-in registration for specified adult male aliens already present, though not those holding green cards. That phase resulted in additional and detailed INS questioning and fingerprinting of more than 80,000 persons from twenty-five listed countries—all of them predominantly Arab or Muslim nations, save North Korea. The process also resulted in the arrest of about 13,000 people who were discovered to lack valid status. Because the call-in procedure was based explicitly on nationality, age, and gender alone, it drew extensive criticism—denounced as, at a minimum, an overly intrusive law enforcement technique and at worst a form of racial or ethnic profiling.[67] Studies have concluded that the 2002 call-ins seriously angered foreign countries whose nationals were subjected to NSEERS and risked alienating resident populations whose cooperation remains crucial in the ongoing effort to detect and defeat terrorist operations in the United States.[68] There is no indication that it generated enough worthwhile information to justify that significant cost.[69]

The call-in was ordered under the alien registration provisions of the Immigration and Nationality Act, which permit the attorney general—and now the secretary of homeland security—to prescribe special registration procedures for particular groups, over and above the normal and routine alien registration normally done when an alien first enters the country.[70] Though the government discontinued the NSEERS call-in program in December 2003 and greatly simplified and later eliminated the annual reporting requirements for those already tagged by the system (while retaining the exit procedures), some critics have called for repeal or modification of the INA sections permitting that form of special registration.[71]

Repeal would be an overreaction. The government needs the authority, on exceptional occasions, to require extra inquiry of specified nonresident alien populations in response to international crises. It has used enhanced registration in earlier emergencies, including the confrontation with the newly installed revolutionary regime in Iran after U.S. diplomats were taken hostage in 1979–80.[72] Nonetheless, the negative reaction to NSEERS, coupled with its apparently thin yield of useful information, should chasten its future use. Clearly, the government should use this special registration power sparingly and always tailor it to minimize any perception that entire ethnic communities have come under suspicion.

Conclusion

The United States has come a long way since the clumsy and often gratuitously harsh deployment of immigration controls in the days shortly after the September 11 attacks. The government now has, at least in preliminary form, an important array of new tools that permit officials to identify more accurately persons applying for admission or actually arriving on U.S. soil and to match those persons with any negative information available to the government. The government is sharing intelligence more readily; its communications systems have made strides toward achieving interoperability; and frontline decisionmakers have readier access to the information they need. Much remains to be done to refine those changes and minimize their intrusion on legitimate privacy interests and civil liberties. Legal reform can help in that process. But the overarching need is to make sure that the system operates with a steady awareness that mere crackdown is deeply counterproductive. To foster success in the struggle against terrorism, the system cannot just exclude and arrest people on the belief that they might be dangerous. The United States must retain—or recapture—the openness and welcome to foreigners that traditionally characterized this country and contributed mightily to its economic success and its cultural richness. That sense of balance and perspective not only manifests fidelity to the best of America's core identity, but also represents an indispensable element of any sound counterterrorism strategy.

Notes

1. John Ashcroft, "Prepared Remarks for the U.S. Mayors Conference," speech, U.S. Mayors Conference, Washington, October 25, 2001 (www.usdoj.gov/archive/ag/speeches/2001/agcrisisremarks10_25.htm).

2. See, for example, *Fong Yue Ting* v. *United States,* 149 US 698 (1893); *Nishimura Ekiu* v. *United States,* 142 US 651 (1892).

3. See Edward Alden, *The Closing of the American Border: Terrorism, Immigration, and Security since 9/11* (New York: HarperCollins, 2008), pp. 8–24; Robert Leiken, "Europe's Immigration Problem, and Ours," *Mediterranean Quarterly* 15 (2004), p. 203.

4. See "Rice-Chertoff Joint Conference on Secure Borders and Open Doors," *Interpreter Releases* 83 (2003), p. 161.

5. Thomas Alexander Aleinikoff, David A. Martin, and Hiroshi Motomura, *Immigration and Citizenship: Process and Policy,* 5th ed. (Eagan, Minn.: Thomson West, 2003), pp. 1247–49; "DHS Amends, but Does Not Abolish, Special Registration Requirements," *Interpreter Releases* 80 (2003), p. 1633.

6. Office of the Inspector General, *The September 11 Detainees: A Review of the Treatment of Aliens Held on Immigration Charges in Connection with the Investigation of the September 11 Attacks* (U.S. Department of Justice, 2003) (www.usdoj.gov/oig/special/0306/press.pdf), hereafter cited as OIG Review.

7. Immigration and Nationality Act (INA), § 222(h), 8 U.S.C. § 1202(h), as added by the 2004 Intelligence Reform and Terrorism Prevention Act, § 5301, Public Law No. 108-458, 118 Stat. 3735. Exceptions are permitted for persons under fourteen or over seventy-nine years of age, certain diplomats, and a limited range of applicants for renewed visas in the same category after an earlier grant through a face-to-face interview.

8. Stephen Yale-Loehr, Demetrios G. Papademetriou, and Betsy Cooper, *Secure Borders, Open Doors: Visa Procedures in the Post-September 11 Era* (Washington: Migration Policy Institute, 2005), p. 37 (www.migrationpolicy.org/pubs/visa_report.pdf).

9. See Thomas R. Eldridge and others, *9/11 and Terrorist Travel: Staff Report of the National Commission on Terrorist Attacks upon the United States* (National Commission on Terrorist Attacks upon the United States, August 21, 2004), pp. 68–69; Yale-Loehr, Papademetriou, and Cooper, *supra,* at 90–9; Alden, *supra,* at 38, 240–52.

10. See U.S. Citizenship and Immigration Services, "USCIS and FBI Release Joint Plan to Eliminate Backlog of FBI Name Checks," news release, April 2, 2008.

11. "USCIS Revises Field Guidance on Background Checks for Certain Applications," *Interpreter Releases* 85 (2008), p. 417.

12. See T. Alexander Aleinikoff, David A. Martin, Hiroshi Motomura, and Maryellen Fullerton, *Immigration and Citizenship: Process and Policy,* 6th ed. (Eagan, Minn.: Thomson West, 2008), pp. 674–75, hereafter cited as AMMF.

13. See Alden, *supra,* at 254; Rey Koslowski, *Real Challenges for Virtual Borders: The Implementation of US-VISIT* (Washington: Migration Policy Institute, 2005) (www.migrationpolicy.org/pubs/Koslowski_Report.pdf); Office of Inspector General, *US-VISIT System Security Management Needs Strengthening,* OIG-06-16 (Department of Homeland Security, December 2005), pp. 3–8.

14. INA § 217(a)(3), 8 U.S.C. § 1187(a)(3) (2007).

15. See INA § 217(a)(10), 8 U.S.C. § 1187(a)(10) (2007); AMMF, *supra,* at 671.

16. INA § 217(a)(11), (h)(3),), 8 U.S.C. § 1187(a)(11), (h)(3).

17. See Peter H. Schuck, "*Kleindienst* v. *Mandel*: Plenary Power v. the Professors," in *Immigration Stories,* edited by David A. Martin and Peter H. Schuck (New York: Foundation Press, 2005), pp. 169–96.

18. See AMMF, *supra,* 565.

19. 8 U.S.C. § 1182(a)(3)(B) (1998).

20. Ibid. at § 1182(a)(3)(B)(iii). The definition of terrorism appeared in § 1182(a)(3)(B)(ii) and was fairly broad, but less so than the current version. It included *inter alia,* hijacking, kidnapping, and assassination, plus the use of any "explosive or firearm (other than for mere personal monetary gain)" with intent to endanger individuals or cause substantial property damage.

21. 8 U.S.C. § 1189 (2008).

22. 18 U.S.C. §§ 2339A and 2339B (2008).

23. See Department of State, Terrorist Designation Lists (www.state.gov/s/ct/list/).

24. INA § 212(a)(3)(B)(vi), 8 U.S.C. § 1182(a)(3)(B)(vi).

25. INA § 212(a)(3)(B)(iv)(VI)(dd), 8 U.S.C. § 1182(a)(3)(B)(iv)(VI)(dd).

26. INA § 237(a)(4), 8 U.S.C. 1227(a)(4) (2004 version) listed as a ground of deportability only being party to ongoing acts defined as "engaging in terrorist activity," thus leaving out such things as mere membership in a terrorist organization or endorsement of a terrorist act. The post-2005 version decrees deportability for anyone who meets the description of any part of the terrorism-related ground for inadmissibility, INA § 212(a)(3)(B), 8 U.S.C. § 1182(a)(3)(B) (2008).

27. See AMMF, *supra,* 567–82; Rachel Swarns, "Provision of Antiterror Law Delays Entry of Refugees," *New York Times,* March 8, 2006, p. A20.

28. David A. Martin, *The United States Refugee Admissions Program: Reforms for a New Era of Refugee Resettlement* (Washington: Migration Policy Institute, 2005), p. 17.

29. INA § 212(d)(3)(B), 8 U.S.C. § 1182(d)(3)(B). The waiver was activated through *Federal Register* notices that exempted specific groups from application of the material support provision and set up a procedure for DHS to decide on individual waivers in cases in which an individual claims to have acted under duress. See AMMF, *supra,* 580–82; 72 *Federal Register* 9954, 26138 (2007).

30. See, for example, David Cole, "Enemy Aliens," *Stanford Law Review* 54 (2002), pp. 953, 966–70; *American-Arab Anti-Discrimination Committee* v. *Reno,* 70 F.3d 1045, 1063 (9th Cir. 1995), vacated, 525 U.S. 471 (1999).

31. See *American Academy of Religion* v. *Chertoff,* 463 F.Supp.2d 400 (S.D.N.Y. 2006); Tariq Ramadan, "Why I'm Banned in the USA," *Washington Post,* October 1, 2006, p. B1.

32. 23 I&N Dec. 936 (BIA 2006).

33. See In the Matter of Pearson, EOIR Case No. A: 72-472-870 (U.S.I.C. Mar. 27, 1997); *McMullen* v. *INS,* 788 F.2d 591 (9th Cir. 1986).

34. INA § 212(d)(3)(B), 8 U.S.C. § 1182(d)(3)(B).

35. Consolidated Appropriations Act, 2008, Public Law No.110-161, Div. J, § 691, 121 Stat 1844, 2364-66 (December 26, 2007).

36. See Matter of S-K-, 24 I&N Dec. 289 (AG 2007); Matter of S-K-, 24 I&N Dec. 475 (BIA 2008). The Attorney General made it clear that the legal doctrine announced in the original BIA ruling in *S-K-* would remain controlling.

37. 72 *Federal Register* 9954, 26138 (2007).

38. The principal refugee treaty realistically excludes from *nonrefoulement* protection persons whom there are "reasonable grounds for regarding as a danger to the security" of the haven country. Convention relating to the Status of Refugees, Art. 33(2), done 28 July 1951, 189 U.N.T.S. 137. It is not reasonable to treat coerced donations to a terrorist organization as an indication of danger to the security of the United States once the person is given refuge here.

39. See *Singh-Kaur* v. *Ashcroft,* 285 F.3d 293, 299 (3d Cir. 2004), and ibid. at 304–05 (Fisher, J., dissenting).

40. See OIG Review, *supra*; Office of the Inspector General, *Supplemental Report on September 11 Detainees' Allegations of Abuse at the Metropolitan Detention in Brooklyn, NY* (U.S. Department of Justice, 2003) (www.usdoj.gov/oig/special/0312/final.pdf).

41. 533 U.S. 678 (2001). Later the Court held that the same limits apply as a matter of statutory construction to all persons, whether or not they had previously been admitted, but in a decision that rested entirely on statutory construction without indications that such limits are constitutionally required. *Clark* v. *Martinez,* 543 U.S. 371 (2005).

42. 533 U.S. at 696.

43. See Matter of Drysdale, 20 I&N Dec. 815 (BIA 1994); Matter of Patel, 15 I&N Dec. 666 (1976). For the future, the objectives apparently sought through the "special interest" list should be addressed, if at all, through a more tightly drawn statute for preventive detention of persons shown to present a specified level of threat of future terrorist activity.

44. INA § 240(b)(4)(B), 8 U.S.C. 1229a(b)(4)(B), gives aliens the right to examine evidence used against them, with this exception: "but these rights shall not entitle the alien to examine such national security information as the Government may proffer in opposition to . . . an application by the alien for discretionary relief under this Act." The Department of Justice has regularly argued that prehearing release on bond is a form of discretionary relief within the meaning of that provision. One court accepted that argument under an earlier version of the statute, but the issue cannot be regarded as settled. United States ex rel. *Barbour* v. *District Director,* 491 F.2d 573 (5th Cir. 1974), cert. denied, 419 U.S. 873 (1974).

45. 8 C.F.R. § 287.3(d), as amended by 66 Fed.Reg. 48335 (2001).

46. OIG Review, *supra,* 27–36.

47. INA § 236A, 8 U.S.C. § 1226a, added by the USA Patriot Act, § 412(a), Public Law No. 107-56, 115 Stat. 350 (2001).

48. See David A. Martin, "Preventive Detention: Immigration Law Lessons for the Enemy Combatant Debate," *Georgetown Immigration Law Journal* 18 (2004), pp.305, 314–15, based on testimony given before the 9/11 Commission.

49. 8 C.F.R. § 3.27 (2001).

50. *Detroit Free Press* v. *Ashcroft,* 303 F.3d 681, 683 (6th Cir. 2002).

51. *North Jersey Media Group* v. *Ashcroft,* 308 F.3d 198 (3d Cir. 2002), cert. denied, 538 U.S. 1056 (2003).

52. INA § 222(f), 8 U.S.C. § 1202(f), providing for confidentiality of visa records; AMMF, *supra*, 651–56, discussing the tight limits on administrative and judicial review.

53. See Yale-Loehr, Papademetriou, and Cooper, *supra*, at 90–97.

54. United States ex rel. *Knauff* v. *Shaughnessy,* 338 U.S. 537 (1950), the case of the war bride; *Shaughnessy* v. *United States* ex rel. Mezei, 345 U.S. 206 (1953), the case of the twenty-five-year resident.

55. Charles Weisselberg, "The Exclusion and Detention of Aliens: Lessons from the Lives of Ellen Knauff and Ignatz Mezei," *University of Pennsylvania Law Review* 143 (1995), p. 933.

56. INA § 235(c), 8 U.S.C. § 1225(c).

57. See, for example, *Azzouka* v. *Sava,* 777 F.2d 68 (2d Cir. 1985), cert. denied, 479 U.S. 830 (1986); *El-Werfalli* v. *Smith,* 547 F.Supp. 152 (S.D.N.Y. 1982); *Avila* v. *Rivkind,* 724 F.Supp. 945 (S.D.Fla. 1989).

58. INA §240(b)(4)(B), 8 U.S.C. § 1229a(b)(4)(B); *Jay* v. *Boyd,* 351 U.S. 345, 357 n. 21 (1956). Because this comment was dictum, other courts have found that more substantial procedural protections may be required, and the issue cannot be regarded as settled.

59. See AMMF, *supra,* at 1050–59.

60. These developments are summarized in David A. Martin, "Offshore Detainees and the Role of Courts after *Rasul* v. *Bush:* The Underappreciated Virtues of Deferential Review," *Boston College Third World Law Journal* 25 (2005), pp. 125, 157–59.

61. See *Kwong Hai Chew* v. *Colding,* 344 U.S. 590 (1953); *Landon* v. *Plasencia,* 459 U.S. 21 (1982).

62. INA §§ 501-507, 8 U.S.C. §§1531-1537, added by the Anti-terrorism and Effective Death Penalty Act of 1996, § 401(a), Public Law No. 104-132, 110 Stat. 1259.

63. See, for example, Peter H. Schuck, "Terrorism Cases Demand New Hybrid Courts," *Los Angeles Times,* July 9, 2004, p. B14.

64. I have explored that dynamic in some detail in Martin, "Offshore Detainees," *supra,* at 146–60.

65. Treating this question at some length in an earlier essay, I concluded that lawful permanent residents should not be subject to deportation on the basis of secret evidence. David A. Martin, "Graduated Application of Constitutional Protections for Aliens: the Real Meaning of *Zadvydas* v. *Davis,*" *Supreme Court Review* 2001 (2002), p. 47. That essay also explores the appropriate level of safeguards applicable to the use of secret evidence in cases affecting other categories of aliens.

66. 8 CFR § 264.1(f), as amended by 67 *Federal Register* 52585 (August 12, 2002).

67. See Alden, *supra,* at 106–16, 223.

68. See Muzaffar A. Chishti et al., *America's Challenge: Domestic Security, Civil Liberties, and National Unity after September 11* (Washington: Migration Policy Institute, 2003), pp. 42–45 (www.migrationpolicy.org/pubs/Americas_Challenges.pdf); *9/11 and Terrorist Travel, supra,* at 159–60.

69. See ibid. at 159–61; Alden, *supra,* at 248, 294–95.

70. INA § 263, 8 U.S.C. § 1303.

71. For example, "AILA Urges Repeal of Special Registration," AILA InfoNet Doc. No. 03010940 (posted January 9, 2003) (www.aila.org/content/default.aspx?bc=6714%7C6729%7C6752%7C8091); Mary M. Sevandal, "Special Registration: Discrimination in the Name of National Security," *Journal of Gender, Race, and Justice* 8 (2005), p. 735.

72. See *Narenji* v. *Civiletti,* 617 F.2d 745 (D.C.Cir. 1979), cert. denied, 446 U.S. 957 (1980).

DAVID S. KRIS

7

Modernizing the Foreign Intelligence Surveillance Act: Progress to Date and Work Still to Come

In December 2005, the *New York Times* reported[1] and President George W. Bush confirmed[2] that the National Security Agency (NSA) had been conducting electronic surveillance of international communications to or from the United States without obeying the Foreign Intelligence Surveillance Act of 1978 (FISA).[3] Disclosure of the NSA surveillance program, sometimes referred to as the Terrorist Surveillance Program (TSP) or the President's Program, ignited a wildfire of political and legal controversy, with most of the debate centered on the president's constitutional power, as chief executive and commander in chief, to disregard FISA and conduct electronic surveillance without following the law's detailed procedures.

My purpose in these pages is not to rehash that controversy but to look forward. Seen from a different perspective, the NSA surveillance program was less a stand-alone collection program than the opening gambit in a seven-year effort to "modernize" FISA—an effort that concluded, at least temporarily, in July 2008, with the FISA Amendments Act (FAA).[4] In essence, modernizing FISA means amending the statute to permit explicitly what the NSA undertook beginning in the fall of 2001, and perhaps more. It is at least in part a response to technological and other changes that have stressed the underlying assumptions of a law written thirty years ago. And the task of modernization may not be complete.

This chapter represents the author's personal views, not those of any current or former employer or affiliates. The substantive work on the chapter was completed before the author returned to the Justice Department in 2009. The original version of this chapter was cleared for publication by the Department of Justice under 28 C.F.R. § 17.18 in November 2007, and the current version was later cleared.

Indeed, as I explain in this chapter, the current regime itself may some day require an update, for at least three distinct reasons. First, the FISA Amendments Act is complex. Complexity of that sort in a statute that often must be applied under pressure poses risks for both security and liberty, because it can cause both under- and overcollection of intelligence. For the long run, Congress may want to overhaul the U.S. national security collection statutes and criminal investigative statutes. Specifically, Congress may want to consolidate and simplify those laws and iron out the conflicts between them.[5]

Second, if current trends continue, the country's laws may need to rely even less on geography in determining when to require investigators to obtain a warrant. One of the hallmarks of modern technology is mobility. Cell phones, BlackBerries, and other technologies that operate throughout the world can make it difficult and sometimes impossible for intelligence officials to know where a surveillance target is located. The more often that is true, the less logical it will be to rely on geography to determine what process must be used before switching on surveillance. If the government cannot determine a person's location, after all, it cannot properly apply statutes that depend on that location. Current law, even under the FISA Amendments Act, depends on the geographical difference between targets in the United States and those outside.

Third, the overwhelming increase in the volume and use of digital information left by individuals in the hands of third parties may in the future compel more attention to standards governing retention and dissemination of information. The next generation of surveillance statutes will need to reflect the fact that countless digital footprints left by individuals in the course of modern life—particularly in combination with one another—may contain revealing information. Many of the hardest decisions will lie in balancing privacy interests against investigative needs.

I do not present in this chapter a specific legislative roadmap. The FAA did the heavy lifting on that score, at least for the short term, and my ignorance of how the new law is actually being applied requires me to be both more abstract and less prescriptive than that. Instead, my purpose is to argue that the FAA was not necessarily the end of the modernization of FISA and also to illustrate in broad strokes the hard legislative work that may come next— whether in five to ten years or further into the future. To that end, this chapter proceeds in three parts. First, it reviews the essential substantive and procedural requirements of traditional FISA—the version of the statute in effect before the FAA and its temporary predecessor statute—and discusses the main arguments for and against modernization of the statute. It then describes and analyzes the FAA and compares it to traditional FISA, highlighting how the statute has changed. Finally, it turns to the future, anticipating possible problems with the postmodernization version of FISA and exploring what may be the next wave of developments in surveillance law. Predictions are always risky, and so my conclusions are of necessity especially tentative on that score. My primary goal throughout is to identify issues rather than to resolve them. I hope to begin the discussion, not end it.

The Problem of Premodern (Traditional) FISA

Traditional FISA is a very complex statute, but for present purposes it has three essential substantive elements.[6] First there is the bedrock requirement that the government must show and a judge of the special Foreign Intelligence Surveillance Court (FISC) must find probable cause that the "target" of the surveillance—the entity from or about whom the government seeks information—is either a "foreign power" or an "agent of a foreign power."[7] Those terms are defined in detail in the statute,[8] but it is enough for now to acknowledge that they mean more or less what an outside observer would think that they mean. For example, a "foreign power" includes not only a foreign government, but also an international terrorist group, like al Qaeda; an agent of a foreign power includes someone who works on behalf of a foreign power in certain specified ways, like Osama bin Laden.[9]

Second, there must be probable cause that the target of the surveillance—the foreign power or agent of a foreign power—is using or about to use the "facility" at which the surveillance will be directed.[10] FISA does not define the term "facility," but legislative history makes clear that it is the electronic analogue to "location" in an ordinary physical search. For example, traditional examples of "facilities" include a ten-digit telephone number or a standard name@domain e-mail address.[11]

Third, traditional FISA dictates the use of specific "minimization procedures" that require the government, in implementing surveillance, to balance its foreign intelligence needs against Americans' privacy interests. In particular, minimization procedures must be "reasonably designed in light of the purpose and technique of the particular surveillance, to minimize the acquisition and retention, and prohibit the dissemination, of nonpublicly available information concerning unconsenting United States persons consistent with the need of the United States to obtain, produce, and disseminate foreign intelligence information."[12] Specific minimization procedures can differ from case to case depending on the facts and circumstances, and they are in part classified to avoid suggesting countermeasures to U.S. adversaries.[13]

Procedurally, traditional FISA generally requires the approval (and signatures) of two senior government officials—for example, the attorney general and the director of the FBI—and a judge of the FISC of claims that the statutory requirements have been met for each target and facility being surveilled.[14] By and large, the government has to get their written approval before surveillance of any target or facility may begin, although exceptions to the general rules exist for, among other things, emergencies.[15]

Details aside, the key point is that traditional FISA electronic surveillance is very different from ordinary foreign intelligence surveillance—that is, surveillance not regulated by the statute. Such surveillance is not new; indeed, Congress wrote FISA to exclude much of the foreign intelligence collection conducted abroad. With respect to that sort of activity, the director of national intelligence sets general collection requirements—for example, "determine the order of battle of the army of the (fictitious) government of Zendar"—and the intelligence community collects against those requirements without case-by-case approval from the attorney general or any judge. The collectors follow an executive order and their own internal minimization and related procedures,[16] but they undeniably enjoy more flexibility than they do under FISA.

Indeed, the government has stated that, in the post–September 11 era, traditional FISA requirements unduly restrict its "speed and agility."[17] As noted above, each traditional FISA application requires the signature of at least two senior national security officials.[18] A former director of national intelligence (DNI) complained that it takes "200 man hours" to prepare an application "for one [telephone] number."[19] Today, the government files well over 2,000 FISA applications a year—more than ten times the number of applications that it filed when the law was first enacted and more than twice as many as it did before September 11, 2001.[20] Therefore, in defending the NSA surveillance program, the Bush administration explained that the "President authorized the TSP because it offers . . . speed and agility. . . . Among the advantages offered by the TSP compared to FISA is *who* makes the probable cause determination and how many layers of review will occur *before* surveillance begins [italics in original]."[21]

This is the essence of what was—and remains—at stake in the debate over FISA's modernization: whether and to what extent the government should be subject to FISA's individualized warrant requirement in conducting its foreign intelligence surveillance rather than to internal executive branch regulation guided by the Fourth Amendment. The fundamental challenge was—and remains—defining the types of surveillance that demand a premium on speed and agility and the types that demand a premium on protection of civil liberties, and determining in each case precisely how to strike the balance between those competing purposes. The choices concern not only the substantive standards for surveillance, but also the question of who applies those standards, in what manner, and at what time.

The Arguments for FISA's Modernization

Three main arguments were presented for modernizing FISA, only the first of which the Bush administration advanced publicly with any force. The first argument was that FISA needed an overhaul because, in the years since 1978, the statute's regulatory reach had been artificially expanded by the transition from satellite to fiber optic cable for carriage of transoceanic communications. Satellites use radio waves to carry international calls, and FISA has never regulated surveillance of international radio communications to or from the United States (unless the surveillance targets a particular, known U.S. person who is located in the United States).[22] But traditional FISA *did* regulate surveillance of international wire or cable communications, to or from the United States, when it was conducted in the United States, even if the target was a non-U.S. person. Therefore, the government claimed, surveillance of international communications that were formerly conducted outside of FISA became subject to the statute because of changing technology. As it turns out, a review of telecommunications history shows that claim to be exaggerated: the transition from satellite to cable was neither as dramatic nor as unanticipated as the government argued.

Many senior government officials advanced the historical argument in favor of modernizing FISA. For example, in 2006 General Michael Hayden, director of the CIA (and former director of the NSA), testified before Congress that for

> reasons that seemed sound at the time, the current statute makes a distinction between collection "on a wire" and collection out of the air. When the law was passed, almost all local calls were on a wire and almost all long haul communications were in the air. In an age of cell phones and fiber optic cables, that has been reversed . . . with powerful and unintended consequences for how NSA can lawfully acquire a signal.[23]

Similarly, Hayden's successor at the NSA, General Keith Alexander, wrote to Congress that "[w]hen FISA was enacted in 1978, almost all transoceanic communications into and out of the United States were carried by satellite" and therefore were "intentionally omitted from the scope of FISA."[24] General

Alexander went on to explain that it was the subsequent and unanticipated migration from satellite to fiber optic cable for overseas calling "rather than a considered judgment by Congress [that] has resulted in the considerable expansion" of FISA's regulatory reach.[25] Echoing those sentiments nine months later, Kenneth Wainstein, the Justice Department's assistant attorney general for national security, testified that in 1978 "almost all transoceanic communications into and out of the United States were carried by satellite, which qualified as 'radio' (vs. 'wire') communications."[26] Finally, in 2007 Admiral Mike McConnell, director of national intelligence, testified that when FISA "was passed in 1978, almost all local calls were on a wire and almost all long-haul communications were in the air, known as 'wireless' communications."[27] Today, he asserted, "the situation is completely reversed; most long-haul communications are on a wire and local calls are in the air."[28]

The historical record does not bear out those statements in the strong form that they were articulated.[29] In and around 1978, transoceanic communications were transmitted in relatively large quantities by *both* satellites (radio) and coaxial cables (wire); both kinds of systems were expected to continue in service for many years; and the use of fiber optics was already anticipated for undersea cables.[30]

The first transatlantic communications cable was laid in 1858,[31] approximately midway between the invention of the telegraph (1839) and of the telephone (1876).[32] Although the first cable failed very quickly, a new and more durable cable was laid in 1866.[33] That and other telegraph cables lacked the bandwidth to carry voice communications, however, and the first transatlantic telephone call was therefore made by conventional radio signal in 1915, the same year that transcontinental telephone service became available by wire within the United States.[34] Commercial transatlantic telephone service, still using radio, was initially offered between the United States and the United Kingdom in 1927 (one call at a time, and apparently at a rate of $75 for the first three minutes).[35] In the 1930s, coaxial cable came into use for telephone calls within the United States,[36] and microwave radio transmitters were first used domestically in the following decade.[37]

The first relatively high-capacity transatlantic cable became operational in 1956 and remained in service until 1979, the year after FISA was enacted. A similar cable was laid across the Pacific Ocean, from California to Hawaii, the following year.[38] Over the next several years, additional coaxial cables were laid across both oceans, with larger capacities and longer life spans.[39]

Satellite communications developed later, and while they had taken over a significant part of the transoceanic communications burden by the 1970s, they never wholly displaced wire communications. The first commercial communications satellite, Telstar I, was launched in 1961, and more durable satellites followed in 1963 and subsequent years.[40] By 1974, Intelsat could boast that its satellites carried "5,000 international telephone circuits," including both transatlantic and transpacific channels.[41] By 1975, there were three Intelsat IV satellites in orbit carrying transatlantic calls (and two carrying transpacific calls), each with a capacity of approximately 4,000 circuits.[42] The satellites could transmit overseas calls using microwave signals (and could also broadcast television signals).[43] By 1976, AT&T was preparing to launch three new communications satellites, explaining that "[s]atellites, along with undersea cables, have been used to provide overseas telephone service for the last 11 years" but that the three new ones "will be our first use of satellite channels for domestic telephone calls."[44] Indeed, satellites were first used by AT&T for domestic communications later that year, having been "integrated with the microwave radio and coaxial cable circuits that make up the bulk of [AT&T's] interstate telecommunications network."[45] The company also noted in its 1976 report that improvements to its microwave capacities were "under development" and "could more than double the capacity of our existing microwave routes without large capital investment."[46] During the course of the 1970s, satellites carried a significant—and increasing—percentage of transoceanic calls.[47] But even well after FISA's enactment, at the end of the 1970s—when, one source reports, "more than two-thirds of all international telephony was routed through satellite channels"[48]— millions and millions of calls still crossed the oceans on underwater cables.

Moreover, even as satellite use was increasing, fiber optic cable was already on the horizon.[49] Based on test deployments in Atlanta, Georgia, AT&T predicted in its 1975 report that fiber optics could be in use "perhaps in the early 1980s."[50] The following year, the company announced that results of testing "exceeded our expectations and pointed to an early application of this new communications technology."[51] By the 1978 report, fiber optic cable had come "through a year-long service test in Chicago with flying colors" and was to be installed "in the Atlanta metropolitan area linking two central offices and a long distance switching center."[52] The company also announced in that report that fiber optics were "expected to be used for local lines, long distance routes, and undersea cable."[53]

In short, at the time that Congress was considering and enacting FISA, from 1974 to 1978, it does not appear to be the case that "almost all" overseas calls were carried on satellites; the actual portion was probably somewhere between one-half and two-thirds.[54] But while history reveals the government's exaggerations, that does not mean that its position has been altogether false. The migration from satellite to fiber optics for carriage of transoceanic communications did reduce the value of FISA's exemption for international radio communications[55] and did affect the NSA's ability to conduct surveillance, even if the effect was not as extreme as the government has claimed.

There was, however, a second, related point that was not as well understood. Congress wrote FISA to permit warrantless surveillance not only of international radio communications, but also of international wire or cable communications, as long as the wire surveillance was conducted *outside* the United States—for example, in the Atlantic Ocean. Today, it appears, the government wants or needs to conduct that surveillance *inside* the United States, probably because it needs the assistance of the telecommunications providers and their equipment. Bringing the surveillance into this country, however, also brought it under traditional FISA provisions. One of the key issues in the debate about FISA's modernization, therefore, was whether the change in the location of the surveillance continued to justify the statute's application.

FISA's legislative history makes clear that its accommodation of certain NSA warrantless wiretapping was no accident. Over the years leading to FISA's enactment in 1978, three basic versions of the statute emerged.[56] The first would have expanded the criminal wiretapping law, known as Title III, to national security surveillance.[57] Under that approach, FISA essentially would have regulated the interception of all wire and oral communications (and later, electronic communications) in the United States.[58] That version gained little legislative traction, however, apparently because the government could not tolerate it. As one member of Congress explained,

> [I]n April 1974, when we held hearings on several bills, including a proposal to require a court order prior to any interception of oral or wire communications in foreign intelligence cases . . . Assistant Attorney General Henry Petersen, speaking for the administration, stated to the subcommittee, 'Let me be very brief. We oppose these bills. That is it.' During the subsequent 2-year period, Mr. Petersen and his successors, as well as intervening Attorneys General, consistently opposed the concept of legislation imposing judicial restraints on foreign intelligence wiretapping."[59]

The second basic version of the bill, which was supported by the executive branch, would have confined FISA essentially to what are now the last three subsections of the definition of "electronic communication"—those concerning domestic wire communications (both ends in the United States) and wire communications between the United States and another country (one end in the United States) if acquired inside the United States; domestic radio communications; and techniques, such as bugging by microphone, conducted in the United States.[60] Attorney General Edward Levi testified in favor of a bill of that type in March 1976.[61] He explained that "the definition of electronic surveillance . . . restricts the scope of the bill to interceptions within the United States" and that it would cover "the use of electronic surveillance to intercept any communication between persons in the United States" but that "government operations to collect foreign intelligence by intercepting international communications . . . [are] not addressed in this bill."[62] In response to questions, Levi observed that the bill would not apply to "a radio communication of an international kind which is picked up in some kind of a sweeping operation or some other kind of operation"[63] or to "the transatlantic kinds of sweeping overhearing."[64] In short, as he made clear,[65] "Congress knows that there is an important area here which is not covered by this legislation."[66]

In subsequent appearances before Congress, Levi repeated his points about the limits of FISA, referring explicitly to NSA surveillance. For example, he explained that while "one doesn't generally discuss them in public . . . we do know that there is a kind of sweeping operation by the NSA which is dealing with international communications not covered here. And that is uncovered in this bill."[67] Indeed, Levi summarized testimony given in a closed hearing by the director of the NSA, General Lew Allen, about "an awesome technology—a huge vacuum cleaner of communications—that had the potential for abuses."[68] The attorney general and other government officials told Congress repeatedly and explicitly that the second version of FISA contained large exceptions designed primarily to accommodate the NSA's signals intelligence activities.

In an apparent effort to assuage concerns arising from FISA's limits, the third and final basic version of FISA was introduced in 1977. It retained the three-part definition of "electronic surveillance" from the prior version but added a fourth part. The new language extended FISA to surveillance of any "particular, known, United States person who is in the United States," whether the surveillance involved domestic or international communications, whether those communications were acquired from a wire or radio wave, and whether the surveillance occurred inside or outside the United States.[69] Attorney General Griffin Bell, who had succeeded Levi, explained that the new language "closes a gap that was present in last year's bill by which Americans in the United States could be targeted for electronic surveillance of their international communications. In this bill, such targeting will require a prior judicial warrant."[70]

That alone is powerful evidence that some of the limits of FISA were understood by that time. Although he characterized the new language as a gap-filler, Bell made clear that it applied only to surveillance "intentionally" targeting particular, "known" U.S. persons in the United States, giving examples of cases that would remain outside the scope of the bill.[71] In short, even the third and final basic version of FISA contained exceptions designed to accommodate the NSA. The statute would not regulate wire surveillance of international communications conducted outside the United States or radio surveillance of international communications in any location, even if the communications in question were to, from, or about U.S. persons in the United States—as long as the surveillance did not target any particular, known U.S person in the United States. And Congress was told expressly that watch list surveillance using subject-matter keywords, such as "terrorism," would not be deemed to target any particular, known U.S. person, even if it inevitably acquired vast numbers of communications made by U.S. persons.[72]

To put it simply, FISA left the government free to monitor a great deal of international communications, including communications to or from Americans, without seeking warrants—provided that it intercepted microwave satellite signals or tapped wires or cables using facilities located offshore or on foreign soil.

At some point after FISA's enactment, however, the government apparently developed a desire or a need to conduct surveillance of international communications on wires *inside* the United States. The reasons cannot be fully discussed here, but they may have included technological or other operational issues associated with the use, location, or accessibility of fiber optic cables[73] and the convenience (or perhaps necessity) of working with the assistance of telecommunications providers in the United States, particularly as the volume and nature of international communications expanded. General Hayden testified that the "explosion of modern communications in terms of its volume, variety and velocity threatened to overwhelm" the NSA beginning in the 1990s.[74]

The publicly available record suggests that the NSA's technological problems in this area may have been recognized as early as 1987, a year before the first transatlantic fiber optic cable went into service.[75] In 1990 the Office of Intelligence Policy and Review (OIPR) of the Department of Justice (DOJ) wrote a memo to the Office of the Deputy Attorney General explaining that it had been "working with the National Security Agency for the past three years to develop possible amendments to the Foreign Intelligence Surveillance Act to meet a need created by technological advances."[76] Those advances appear to have affected the "NSA's collection of international and foreign communications"[77] in particular, creating a "practical imperative" for legislation.[78] The 1990 memo cited draft legislation on which DOJ and the NSA were "close to agreement" and that would have "provide[d] for Attorney General certification, rather than court order" for surveillance.[79] However, the 1990 memo also identified several "policy and tactical issues" counseling against seeking new legislation.[80] Those issues appear to have overcome the practical imperative in 1990, resulting in no amendments to FISA.

More recently, however, the government's need to conduct surveillance inside the United States, with the assistance of providers, has been clearly articulated. In March 2008, at a meeting sponsored by the American Bar Association, Ken Wainstein, the assistant attorney general for the Justice Department's National Security Division, explained:

> [W]e rely on the communications providers to do our intelligence surveillances. We can't do [the surveillances] without them because . . . we . . . don't own the communications systems. We need to rely on their assistance. And there's cooperation and there's cooperation. . . . Yes, we can compel the phone companies, or compel the communications providers to do a surveillance, and even if they . . . resist a directive . . . we can go to the FISA Court to get our orders enforced. Problem is, throughout that time, we're dark on whatever surveillance it is that we want to go up on.[81]

The change in wire surveillance operations requiring use of facilities in the United States rather than abroad appears to be a significant part of the government's motive for seeking FISA's modernization.

Third and final among the reasons to modernize FISA was the problem of e-mail. The e-mail argument was the easiest to understand and also the most compelling: with respect to e-mail, advancing technology had clearly expanded traditional FISA's reach. The difficulty lay—and still lies—in finding an appropriate solution to the problem.

As noted above, traditional FISA never regulated surveillance of wire or radio communications transmitted between two parties abroad. For example, if a U.S. citizen traveled to Paris and telephoned another U.S. citizen in London, the U.S. government was always able (as a legal matter) to monitor the call without a warrant under FISA. And that was the case regardless of where the government did its monitoring—in other words, even if the call was routed through the United States and wiretapped here.[82] Over time, however, changing technology brought foreign-to-foreign e-mail within traditional FISA's scope. That is, the government could not conduct warrantless surveillance in the United States of stored e-mail messages exchanged between two parties located abroad.[83] That problem arose because many Internet service providers store e-mail messages on servers inside the United States. If a person in Paris checks his e-mail account from a cybercafé, he may be connecting to a server located in the United States. Under traditional FISA, if the U.S. government acquired his e-mail from storage on that server, it generally required a warrant. Indeed, the statute applied even if all of the e-mail messages in question had been exchanged between the person in Paris and another person in London and even if both persons were non-U.S. persons.[84]

Nearly everyone who understood this problem agreed that it required a legislative solution. There is no reason to distinguish between foreign-to-foreign e-mail messages acquired from servers located in the United States (at least if acquired in near real time) and foreign-to-foreign telephone calls acquired from switches located in the United States. Since the latter were exempt from FISA, the former also should have been exempt.

As it turns out, however, an operational difficulty hindered efforts to fashion a narrowly tailored solution to this recognized anomaly. Changes in telecommunications technology and increased globalization have made it difficult for the government to determine—consistently, reliably, and quickly—the location of parties to an electronic communication, at least when those parties do not want to be found.[85] In particular, the problem is that people can now read and write e-mail from anywhere—whether from a home in New York City or a cybercafé in Paris.[86] As a result, when the government copies an e-mail message from an ISP server, it may not know where the recipient of the message is located. Indeed, depending on how frequently the recipient checks his e-mail, the government may read the message *before* he does. The NSA's technological abilities are legendary, but (as far as the public record reveals) it cannot predict the future, and it therefore cannot determine, in every case, where the recipient of an e-mail message *will be* if and when he eventually logs in to read his e-mail.[87]

As a result of that geographical uncertainty, it was—and remains—very difficult to amend FISA in a way that exempts *only* foreign-to-foreign e-mail messages but *not* e-mail messages to or from persons located in the United States. An exemption limited to foreign-to-foreign e-mail does not help if the government cannot verify the "to foreign" part of the e-mail; on the other hand, an exemption that does not require such verification could include international (one end in the United States) or even purely domestic e-mail.[88]

Even if the government could verify location reliably, consistently, and quickly, some persons abroad may exchange e-mail not only with people in other foreign locations, but also with people in the United States. Surveillance of such a person's e-mail account will acquire both types of messages. A FISA exemption limited to foreign-to-foreign communications therefore effectively leaves in place the requirement for a warrant for every (or almost every) overseas target using an ISP in the United States, not only because the government may not be able to quickly segregate the foreign-to-foreign messages, but also because it cannot afford to ignore the messages sent to or from the United States. If the government must seek a FISA order for a target's e-mail communications when one end is in the United States, an exemption for foreign-to-foreign communications has little practical value.

Technical and legal details aside, the core of the problem is that non-U.S. persons located abroad can now communicate inside U.S. cyberspace. That presents a strange constitutional combination of seemingly unprotected persons (non-U.S. persons with no ties to the United States except an e-mail account with a U.S. ISP) using highly protected facilities (the U.S. servers of the U.S. ISP) to correspond with one another. That combination tends to frustrate both the U.S. intelligence community, which feels the need to search aggressively within those facilities in an effort to root out the terrorists, and civil libertarians, who fear that such rooting around inevitably compromises the privacy interests of innocent Americans who are by far the majority of users of those facilities. It also may help explain the puzzlement that each side of the current policy debate apparently felt and still may feel about the other's position.

The FISA Amendments Act of 2008

The FISA Amendments Act, which replaced a temporary predecessor statute—the Protect America Act—is a very complex statute, but its essential provisions can be summarized easily. The FAA allows the government, "[n]otwithstanding any other provision of law," to engage in the "targeting of persons reasonably believed to be located outside the United States to acquire foreign intelligence information."[89] For targets who are non-U.S. persons, there is no probable cause requirement; the only thing that matters is the government's reasonable belief about the target's location. The targeting must be "to acquire foreign intelligence information,"[90] which includes information necessary to protect against the full range of foreign threats to national security, and information with respect to a foreign power that is necessary to the national defense or foreign affairs.[91] The targeting is not limited to any particular facility or place,[92] which means that the government can direct surveillance or other acquisition methods at various facilities without obtaining a separate authorization for each one.

The acquisition authority granted by the FAA is subject to several essential requirements and limitations:

—First, the acquisition "may be conducted only in accordance with" what are referred to in the statute as "targeting procedures,"[93] which must be "reasonably designed" to "ensure that any acquisition . . . is limited to targeting persons reasonably believed to be located outside the United States" and to "prevent the intentional acquisition" of communications "known, at the time of the acquisition," to be purely domestic.[94] Domestic communications remain subject to surveillance under traditional FISA provisions.[95]

—Second, the acquisition "may be conducted only in accordance with" some version of traditional "minimization procedures,"[96] which must be "consistent with" FISA's definition of that term for electronic surveillance or physical searches.[97]

—Third, a senior Justice Department official and the director of national intelligence must certify in advance (or if necessary, a week after acquisition begins)[98] that the targeting and minimization procedures satisfy the statutory requirements, that a "significant purpose" of the acquisition is to obtain foreign intelligence information, and that the acquisition involves the assistance of an electronic communications service provider.[99]

—Fourth, when the targeted person is a United States person—a U.S. citizen or green card holder, for example—more restrictive measures apply, depending primarily on whether the acquisition occurs inside or outside the United States.[100]

Under the FAA, the FISA Court reviews the targeting and minimization procedures to ensure that they satisfy the statutory requirements and the Fourth Amendment[101] and orders modifications if necessary; the court reviews the certification only as a matter of form, to ensure that it "contains all the required elements."[102] The court issues its order to the government only—there is no provision in the law for a secondary order to the telecommunications provider. Instead, the government itself issues a "directive" to providers requiring their assistance.[103] Providers may challenge such directives in the FISC,[104] and the government may seek FISC orders compelling compliance from a recalcitrant provider.[105] Thereafter, noncompliant providers may be punished for contempt of court.[106] The law contains reporting and oversight procedures, including review by inspectors general of the government's compliance with the targeting and minimization procedures and of the number of targets originally believed to be abroad but later determined to have been located in the United States.[107]

Comparing the FAA to traditional FISA is an interesting exercise. The new statute ushered in significant changes with respect to the limits on FISA's scope, contracting it in some respects and enlarging it in others.[108] Moreover, a comparison reveals important differences in the law's coverage with respect to the three main groups of communications subject to acquisition: domestic communications, communications in which one end is in the United States, and foreign-to-foreign communications.

Traditional FISA established four significant limits on the statute's regulatory scope with respect to surveillance. First, the statute did not apply when all parties to a wire or radio communication were located abroad, even if they were U.S. persons and even if the surveillance was conducted inside the United States. Such foreign-to-foreign wire and radio communications were simply outside the statute's scope. Under the FAA, that has changed, because surveillance targeting a U.S. person located abroad will generally be subject to provisions requiring a judicial finding of probable cause that the target is an agent of a foreign power.[109] This will be the case even if the U.S. person abroad is communicating with another person located abroad. In that respect, it would be fair to say that the new law has expanded FISA.[110]

The opposite is true, however, with respect to stored e-mail. As explained earlier, although traditional FISA has never regulated surveillance of foreign-to-foreign wire or radio communications, it *did* regulate surveillance of foreign-to-foreign e-mail if the e-mail was acquired from storage inside the United States, and that was the case even if all parties to the e-mail were non-U.S. persons. The FAA corrected that anomaly, with the result that foreign-to-foreign e-mail exchanged between foreigners no longer requires a FISA warrant, even if acquired from storage in the United States.[111] In that respect—concerning foreign-to-foreign e-mail exchanged between foreigners—the FAA contracts FISA's coverage.

The second major limit in traditional FISA is that it does not apply when the surveillance target is located abroad and the surveillance occurs abroad. Again, the FAA both expands and contracts FISA in this area. It expands FISA because a provision[112] of the new statute requires a judicial finding of probable cause for such surveillance targeting U.S. persons located abroad. But it contracts FISA because a different provision[113] eliminates the need for a traditional FISA order even if the surveillance (or other acquisition activity) targeting a non-U.S. person located abroad occurs inside the United States.

The third major limit is that traditional FISA does not apply to wire surveillance when the target is a non-U.S. person and the surveillance occurs abroad. As discussed above, the main effect of the FAA is to enlarge that exception to cover situations in which the surveillance occurs inside the United States, as long as the foreign target is reasonably believed to be located abroad. In that respect, it can be said that the FAA contracts FISA's regulatory reach.

Fourth and finally, traditional FISA does not apply to radio surveillance not targeting a U.S. person located in the United States when any party to the radio communication is outside the United States. That exception is essentially unchanged under the FAA.

A similar comparison can be made by dividing the world of electronic communications into three groups and analyzing each group under traditional FISA and the FAA. The three groups are

—U.S.-to-U.S. communications, also known as domestic communications
—foreign-to/from-U.S. communications, also known as one-end-U.S. communications
—foreign-to-foreign communications.

Purely domestic communications, in which both parties are located in the United States, include, for example, a telephone call or e-mail from Washington to New York. By and large, FISA has always regulated surveillance of domestic communications; certainly that was the case in 1978. The FAA provides expressly that its exemption from traditional FISA warrant requirements does not apply to intentional acquisition of known domestic communications, at least when the target is a non-U.S. person.[114] Accidental acquisition is possible, and the statute leaves room for fact-intensive questions about whether and when the government "knows" that a communication is domestic.[115] But in theory, at least, the government cannot use the FAA to target domestic communications for warrantless interception, even if exchanged between and among visiting foreigners in the United States.

The second group is for communications in which one party is located in the United States but one is not. That includes, for example, a telephone call or e-mail from New York to London or from London to New York. Here, FISA has always been a mixed bag. As described above, in 1978 Congress deliberately allowed the NSA to conduct warrantless surveillance of international calls as long as it was not targeting individual Americans located in the United States. Vacuum-cleaner surveillance of communications to or from the United States, which did not target anyone in particular, thus was permitted if the NSA took certain operational steps—namely, applying the vacuum cleaner either to a radio communication or to a wire or cable located outside the United States. And that was the rule even if the surveillance acquired calls to, from, or about U.S. persons located in the United States.

The key with respect to surveillance of these one-end-U.S. communications was that no "particular, known" American in the United States could be targeted.[116] For example, to paraphrase one witness who testified in the congressional hearings leading to FISA, the NSA could not run its vacuum cleaner over a transatlantic telephone cable with filters set to record all calls mentioning "David Kris." That kind of surveillance clearly would be designed to obtain information from or about a particular, known American located in the United States and would therefore be subject to FISA. On the other hand, however, the NSA could set its filters to record all calls mentioning the word "terrorism"—because that does not target anyone in particular—and could keep those calls even if some of them were made by David Kris or other U.S. persons living in the United States.[117]

Under the FAA, the government will have both more and less authority in this area. It will still need a warrant to target any particular, known American in the United States.[118] But it will no longer need a traditional FISA warrant to target a non-U.S. person located abroad, even if the surveillance occurs on wires or cables inside the United States. In that sense, the FAA represents a contraction of FISA.[119] On the other hand, the government will need a judicial finding of probable cause to target a U.S. person located abroad, whether the surveillance occurs inside the United States[120] or abroad.[121] That is an expansion of FISA, at least with respect to surveillance conducted abroad.

The third and final group in the taxonomy is for foreign-to-foreign communications, in which all parties are located abroad. That includes, for example, a telephone call or e-mail from London to Paris. As noted earlier, traditional FISA never regulated surveillance of a wire or radio communication between two foreign locations, even if made by two Americans and even if acquired inside the United States, as can happen because of the way the world's telephone lines are laid out. But, as also noted earlier, it did regulate surveillance of an e-mail exchanged between persons in two foreign locations if the e-mail was acquired from storage inside the United States, even if both the sender and recipient of the e-mail were foreigners. Under the new statute, if the target is a non-U.S. person located abroad, FISA does not require a warrant;[122] if the target is an American, it requires a judicial finding of probable cause.[123]

The Future of FISA's Modernization

The FISA statute needed to be modernized. Despite the government's some-what exaggerated claims about the history of the migration from satellite to fiber optic cable for transmission of international communications, it is clear that by 2008 FISA regulated more than it had in 1978.[124] As a practical matter, if not a legal one, the statute had expanded; its expansion had created operational difficulties for the U.S. intelligence community; and a majority of Congress ultimately concluded that those difficulties deserved redress in the FAA.

However, the FAA probably represents only an interim solution to the problem of FISA's modernization. That is true for at least three reasons. First, it is very complicated. Second, it continues to rely on location as a trigger for legal requirements. Third, its regulatory approach may not put enough emphasis on the government's retention and dissemination of information, at least for the long run. Each of those points bears emphasizing.

The FAA is a very complex statute. As amended, FISA now admits of at least five different categories of full-content acquisition:

—traditional electronic surveillance
—traditional physical searches
—surveillance or searches targeting non-U.S. persons reasonably believed to be abroad
—surveillance or searches targeting U.S. persons reasonably believed to be abroad when information acquisition occurs in the United States
—surveillance or searches targeting U.S. persons reasonably believed to be abroad when information acquisition occurs outside the United States.

FISA has always been an arcane and difficult law, but the FAA's intricacy risks confusing the government officials who must apply it, often under substantial time pressure. That can lead to errors of both major types: improperly acquiring communications in a fashion that undermines liberty and privacy and improperly refraining from acquiring communications in a fashion that undermines security. I do not say that such errors are inevitable; I mean only to say that they are possible and that avoiding them may require effort and training.[125]

For the long run, at least, it is possible to imagine a simpler world in which national security investigations are governed by only two major collection statutes. The first statute would apply more or less as broadly as a grand jury subpoena, perhaps also including surveillance currently conducted by using pen registers and trap-and-trace devices.[126] That could replace the various national security letter statutes,[127] the FISA pen/trap provisions,[128] the mail cover regulations,[129] and perhaps the section of the Patriot Act that permits acquisition of business records.[130] All of those laws allow government investigators to acquire certain information, but they do not authorize full-blown searches or wiretapping. For example, a grand jury may issue subpoenas to virtually anyone requiring them to produce documents or other information relevant to the question of "whether or not a crime has been committed" based "merely on suspicion that the law is being violated, or even just because it wants assurance that it is not."[131] Similarly, national security letters are, in effect, subpoenas issued by the FBI or other intelligence agencies that direct certain kinds of businesses (such as banks) to provide certain kinds of records (such as financial records) to the government.[132] A section of the Patriot Act authorizes the government to ask the FISA Court for an order directing any recipient to produce any "tangible thing" in furtherance of an investigation.[133] A "mail cover" is a request made to the U.S. Postal Service to record information on the outside of any envelope or other mail sent to or from a person (it cannot be used to read a letter or other material inside an envelope).[134] Finally, pen registers and trap-and-trace devices allow the government to learn with whom a given person is communicating, though not the contents of the communication; for example, these devices record the numbers dialed on a telephone but not what is said during the call. It is possible to imagine one consolidated statute to replace some or all of these provisions, setting up a simpler, clearer system for regulating investigative techniques other than wiretapping and searches in a national security investigation.

The second major statute would govern any acquisition of information for which a warrant would be required if undertaken for law enforcement purposes in the United States. If the government has to go before a judge and demonstrate probable cause in a criminal investigation, it would have to do so in a national security investigation. For example, the government would use the second statute to enter and search a home or office, to conduct a wiretap, or to place a hidden microphone. Again, this proposal would simplify current law—for example, it would treat physical searches and wiretapping similarly, eliminating any need for separate definitions of those terms in national security law.[135] This approach is clearly workable, as it has governed collection of information on Americans located abroad under a presidential order since 1981 and is now incorporated into the FISA Amendments Act.[136]

Under the second statute, approval would be required from the FISA Court in some instances; in others, approval would be required only from someone within the executive branch. The law could mirror the FAA—for example, by requiring court approval when the collection technique targets a particular, known U.S. person in any location, any person reasonably believed to be in the United States, or any communication known at the time of acquisition to be purely domestic.[137] Unlike the FAA, however, the law would consolidate all of the various authorities into one place, with a core of common requirements and additional requirements added to that core depending on the facts.

Apart from its simplicity, such an approach would also have the virtue of incorporating law enforcement standards. That would yield at least two benefits. First, it would foster public trust (and public debate). For better or worse, the American people understand and trust law enforcement surveillance standards better than they understand and trust intelligence surveillance standards. They would be more comfortable with the use of law enforcement standards for a baseline and more able to understand and debate any exceptions to those standards deemed necessary for intelligence collection.

Second, this approach would also help the executive branch because it would foster cooperation and cross-pollination between law enforcement and intelligence officials, an especially important benefit after the demise of the FISA wall, which kept intelligence and law enforcement officials at arm's length, and the creation of the Justice Department's National Security Division, which combined intelligence and law enforcement personnel with the mission of protecting national security.[138] At present, the law governing national security investigations, which includes FISA, national security letter statutes, and the aforementioned section of the Patriot Act, differs from the law governing ordinary criminal investigations, such as the wiretapping law known as Title III,[139] and the rules governing the use of grand jury subpoenas and administrative subpoenas. Experts in one area are not always expert in the other, making it harder for law enforcement and intelligence professionals to work together. A combined regulatory approach could reduce that problem: law enforcement surveillance experts who work on intelligence matters would face a much gentler learning curve if FISA were based on the criminal wiretapping laws. In short, it is easier for everyone, in and out of government, to master one statutory collection regime rather than two.

To be sure, the criminal wiretapping laws are hardly a model of simplicity. In fact, in the long run, they may benefit from a review themselves. Title III, enacted in 1968 and amended substantially by the Electronic Communications Privacy Act (ECPA) in 1986, is at least a little out-of-date too. There have been many proposals to amend these laws, some of them quite intelligent.[140] It is important for the law to keep pace with technological change, and there are a number of relatively modest updates that could bring the laws more into line with current uses of the Internet and computer systems. Alternatively, again for the long run, a more radical overhaul may be appropriate, eliminating current distinctions between wire, oral, electronic, short-term stored, long-term stored, and other forms of communications in favor of a more general approach. It is possible to imagine a surveillance statute that, in the first instance, protects all information (including but not limited to communications) that can reasonably be expected to remain private, whether or not an intermediary is involved, in the storage or transmission of the information.[141] In effect, that would treat all (or some designated subset of) communications as if they were made directly between the communicating parties, without an intermediary. It also would eliminate many of the distinctions in the Stored Communications Act—for example, the distinction between providers of electronic communication services and remote computing services—that stem from the Internet of the 1980s and at least arguably no longer make sense.[142] In any event, the important point is that the law enforcement and intelligence collection statutes could proceed from a single, simple foundation, even if they ultimately diverge to some degree.

A second potential problem with the FAA is that it continues to rely on the location of the surveillance target. For now, that may be the best that the government can do. For the long run, however, depending on how events unfold in the world of communications, more radical change may be needed. If the government genuinely cannot determine a person's location, it makes no sense to use geography as a trigger for FISA's warrant requirements. In those circumstances, a geographical approach will always be too broad or too narrow—treating all communicating parties, or none, as if they were in the United States.

Moreover, even if the intelligence community could make reliable judgments concerning target locations, distinctions based on a person's location may no longer serve U.S. policy goals. It may be that Americans now expect protection from surveillance by their own government not only when at home but also when abroad, as reflected in the FAA.[143] If so, perhaps nationality should be the key factor, so that U.S. persons are protected in all locations and non-U.S. persons are protected in none. The problem with that approach, however, is that uncertainty may also plague determinations of nationality.[144] In 1978 a person's location gave rise to reasonable presumptions about his status as a United States person.[145] Today, even if location can be ascertained, the rise of global travel and web-based communications makes such a presumption far less defensible. For example, investigation may identify xyz@isp.com as the e-mail address of a possible terrorist, without revealing the nationality of the person or persons who use that address.

Geographic distinctions concerning acquisition of information, as well as targets of acquisition, may also be open to question in the future, especially with the move from circuit-switched to packet-switched communications networks. A circuit-switched communication involves a dedicated point-to-point connection that allows the entire communication to be acquired at one place or another between those points. In such a situation, the acquisition generally occurs where the wire is tapped. But a packet-switched network breaks communications into packets that are transmitted on multiple paths from origin to destination. When e-mail is acquired from storage, as discussed above, the point of acquisition is easily known, but if current or future technology permits acquisition of packets in multiple locations, the point of acquisition may be harder to determine.

Third, any future surveillance regime must take into account radical changes in the volume and use of information. As a result of advancing technology, more and more human activities—from supermarket purchases to payment of highway tolls—leave permanent digital footprints. This trend promises to continue, and therefore the coming years will probably see an ever-expanding universe of communications and other information, which government (and the private sector) will want to acquire. It seems almost inevitable that the government will, in the future, have access to more information.[146]

At the same time, more and more of that information is being maintained in the so-called computing cloud, where end users access software-based services from, and often store data on, remote servers or other remotely located computers. For example, Google provides Google Apps, which includes not only e-mail but also calendar, word processing, and other services that are accessible through a web browser.[147] Windows Live offers similar services, including online file storage, photo sharing, calendar, and e-mail functions.[148]

The proliferation of cloud computing services, online backup-storage companies, and photo-sharing sites as well as social networks[149] means that more and more personal data will be held by third parties beyond the physical control of end users. That creates opportunities for surreptitious surveillance under FISA and has significant implications for privacy in general. In one way, it makes the government's job easier, because such information is far more readily accessible—there is no need to sneak into a user's house to scan his hard drive if it is backed up daily to a web site.

Over the longer run, however, although the radical increase in the volume and accessibility of data threatens privacy, it does not necessarily enhance security. The risk is that the government may be overwhelmed or may face what William James called a blooming, buzzing confusion[150]—in more technical terms, a profusion of homogenized information packets, devoid of reliable geographical order, subject to growing divergence between physical location and communications location, and distorted by the use of various forms of virtual space, leaving nationality (and other attributes) of communicants largely indeterminate. In the future, if not today, the government may have access to more information about *what* is happening but less ability to determine *who* is making it happen and *where* that person can be found.[151]

In this world of larger haystacks,[152] the government will need to focus more regulatory efforts, and oversight, on retention and use (dissemination) of information, rather than on collection alone. To be sure, current law includes minimization procedures that govern not only acquisition but also retention and dissemination of information,[153] but those protections probably could be strengthened. Better training, data tagging, identity protection, access control, incorruptible audit trails, and standards and procedures for correcting errors in the database will be required. The alternative means less privacy and less security than the United States currently enjoys.

Notes

1. James Risen and Eric Lichtblau, "Bush Lets U.S. Spy on Callers without Courts," *New York Times,* December 16, 2005.

2. The president stated, "I authorized the National Security Agency, consistent with U.S. law and the Constitution, to intercept the international communications of people with known links to al Qaeda and related terrorist organizations. Before we intercept these communications, the government must have information that establishes a clear link to these terrorist networks." George W. Bush, "Weekly Radio Address," December 17, 2005 (www.whitehouse.gov/news/releases/2005/12/20051217. html). For an explanation of why the president's program violated FISA, see David Kris and Douglas Wilson, "The President's Statutory and Constitutional Authority to Conduct Foreign Intelligence Surveillance and Searches—The NSA Surveillance Program," in *National Security Investigations and Prosecutions* (Eagen, Minn.: West, 2007), hereinafter referred to as NSIP.

3. 50 U.S.C. §§ 1801 et seq. In *ACLU v. NSA,* 493 F.3d 644, 650 (6th Cir. 2007), the lead opinion described "three publicly acknowledged facts about the [NSA surveillance program] – (1) it eavesdrops, (2) without warrants, (3) on international telephone and e-mail communications in which at least one of the parties is a suspected al Qaeda affiliate." The opinion explained that the "plaintiffs have not shown, and cannot show, that the NSA's surveillance activities include the sort of conduct that would satisfy FISA's definition of 'electronic surveillance,' and the present record does not demonstrate that the NSA's conduct falls within FISA's definitions." Ibid. at 682.

It is reasonably clear, however, that the NSA surveillance program did involve "electronic surveillance" as defined by FISA, because the government claimed that orders of the Foreign Intelligence Surveillance Court, issued in January 2007, authorized all surveillance previously conducted as part of the NSA program and the FISC's relevant jurisdiction is limited to "electronic surveillance" as defined by FISA. See NSIP, chapters 7 and 15.

4. Public Law No. 110-261, 122 Stat. 2436 (2008). The forthcoming edition of NSIP will contain a detailed discussion of the FAA.

5. The desire to improve collection statutes must be balanced against the need for stability. The problem of "change fatigue" in the operational community can be real, and there are situations in which the perfect is the enemy of the good. I also emphasize my own lack of awareness of how the FISA Amendments Act is actually working in practice and the correspondingly tentative nature of this discussion.

6. For a more complete discussion of the required elements of a traditional FISA application for electronic surveillance, see NSIP, chapter 6. Traditional FISA remains in effect, even after enactment of the FISA Amendments Act, and is still available for use when the FAA does not apply (for example, for surveillance targeting persons known to be inside the United States). Accordingly, this chapter generally refers to traditional FISA in the present tense.

7. See 50 U.S.C. § 1805(a)(3)(A).

8. See 50 U.S.C. § 1801(a)-(b).

9. For a discussion of the terms "target," "foreign power," and "agent of a foreign power," see NSIP, chapter 8.

10. 50 U.S.C. § 1805(a)(3)(B).

11. For a discussion of the term "facility," see NSIP, chapters 6 and 15.

12. 50 U.S.C. § 1801(h).

13. For a more complete discussion of "minimization" under FISA, see NSIP, chapter 9.

14. 50 U.S.C. §§ 1805-1806. For a discussion of the requirements of a FISA application and order, see NSIP, chapter 6.

15. See NSIP, chapter 6. There are four exceptions to this general requirement, as explained in NSIP, chapter 12. One exception is for emergency surveillance. See 50 U.S.C. § 1805(f).

16. See, for example, Executive Order 12333; DOD 5240-1R; USSID-18. For a discussion of these and related standards, see NSIP, chapter 2.

17. See, for example, CNN, "Administration Defends NSA Eavesdropping to Congress," December 23, 2005 (www.cnn.com/2005/POLITICS/12/23/justice.nsa/index.html).

18. See NSIP, chapter 6.

19. See Chris Roberts, "Transcript: Debate on the Foreign Intelligence Surveillance Act," *El Paso Times*, August 22, 2007 (www.elpasotimes.com/news/ci_6685679), hereinafter *El Paso* transcript.

20. In 1979, the first year after FISA's enactment, the government filed 199 applications; in 2001, it filed 932 applications; in 2007, it filed 2,371 applications; and in 2008, the last year for which data are available, it filed 2,082 applications. See NSIP, chapter 13.

21. Responses to Joint Questions from House Judiciary Committee Minority Members, Response to Question 32, released March 24, 2006, hereinafter HJC Minority QFRs 3-24-06. The government's explanation continues:

> Under the TSP, professional intelligence officers, who are experts on al Qaeda and its tactics (including its use of communications systems), with appropriate and rigorous oversight, make the decisions about which international communications should be intercepted. By contrast, because FISA requires the attorney general to "reasonably determine" that "the factual basis for issuance of" a FISA order exists at the time he approves an emergency authorization, *see* 50 U.S.C. ß 1805(f)(2), as a practical matter, it is necessary for NSA intelligence officers, NSA lawyers, Justice Department lawyers, and the Attorney General to review a matter before even emergency surveillance would begin.

HJC Minority QFRs 3-24-06, Response to Question 32 (second alteration in original). In sum, the government reports, the "relevant distinction between the two methods—and the critical advantage offered by the TSP compared to FISA—is the greater speed and agility it offers." HJC Minority QFRs 3-24-06, Response to Question 34.

22. See NSIP, chapter 7. Unless otherwise indicated in context, this chapter uses the following terms with the following meanings:

—"Transoceanic" refers to a communication transmitted between locations separated by an ocean—for example, a telephone call from New York to London. A similar term is "intercontinental."

—"International" refers to a communication transmitted between the United States and a foreign country—for example, a telephone call from New York to London or from Mexico City to New York. A similar term is "one-end-U.S."

—"Foreign-to-foreign" refers to a communication transmitted between locations outside the United States—for example, a telephone call from Paris to London.

—"Domestic" refers to a communication transmitted between locations inside the United States—for example, a telephone call from Washington, D.C. to New York.

—"American" when used to refer to a person means a "United States person" as defined by FISA, which includes an American citizen and a lawful permanent resident alien. 50 U.S.C. § 1801(i).

—"Wire surveillance" refers to electronic surveillance of a "wire communication" as defined by FISA, which includes acquisition of the contents of a communication "while it is being carried by a wire, cable, or other like connection." 50 U.S.C. 1801(*l*).

—"Radio surveillance" refers to electronic surveillance of a radio communication, which includes acquisition of the contents of a communication while it is being carried by a radio wave, as discussed in NSIP, chapter 7.

23. U.S. Senate, Committee on the Judiciary, "Testimony of General Michael V. Hayden, Director of Central Intelligence," 109th Cong., 2nd sess., July 26, 2006 (http://judiciary.senate.gov/testimony.cfm?id=698&wit_id=5604), hereinafter Hayden Testimony 7-26-06.

24. Lieutenant General Keith B. Alexander to Senator Arlen Specter, December 19, 2006, answer to Question 2a for Senator Specter (www.fas.org/irp/congress/2006_hr/alexander-qfr.pdf), hereinafter Alexander QFRs 12-19-06.

25. Alexander QFRs 12-19-06.

26. U.S. House of Representatives, Permanent Select Committee on Intelligence, "Statement of Kenneth L. Wainstein, Assistant Attorney General, National Security Division, Department of Justice," 110th Cong., 1st sess., September 6, 2007, p. 4 (www.usdoj.gov/nsd/docs/2007/wainstein-statement-9-6-07.pdf), hereinafter Wainstein Testimony 9-6-07. See also U.S. House of Representatives, Permanent Select Committee on Intelligence, "Statement of Kenneth L. Wainstein, Assistant Attorney General, National Security Division, Department of Justice,"110th Cong., 1st sess., September 20, 2007, p. 4 (www.usdoj.gov/nsd/docs/2007/wainstein-HPSCI-statement-9-20-07.pdf), hereinafter Wainstein Testimony 9-20-07.

27. U.S. Senate, Select Committee on Intelligence, "Statement of Director of National Intelligence Michael McConnell," 110th Cong., 1st sess., May 1, 2007, p. 3 (http://intelligence.senate.gov/070501/mcconnell.pdf), hereinafter McConnell Testimony 5-1-07.

28. McConnell Testimony 5-1-07 at 4.

29. Not everyone accepted the government's claim at the time it was made. For example, Kate Martin and Lisa Graves, the director and deputy director of the Center for National Security Studies, wrote to Congress on May 1, 2007, that "even a general examination of telecommunications history . . . reveals that the scenario they posit is not accurate. While satellites were increasingly used in the 1970s . . . American telephone companies were continuing to rely on transoceanic cables for international calls, with newer transatlantic cables sunk even the year after FISA passed." Kate Martin and Lisa Graves, "Constitutional Failings of the Foreign Intelligence Surveillance Modernization Act," U.S. Senate, Select Committee on Intelligence, May 1, 2007, 10 (http://intelligence.senate.gov/070501/martingraves.pdf), hereinafter Martin-Graves Statement 5-1-07.

30. For background on the international telecommunications industry in the late 1970s and early 1980s, see, for example, *ITT* v. *FCC*, 725 F.2d 732, 736-737 (D.C. Cir. 1984). For background on the Federal Communication Commission's (FCC's) licensing power for overseas communications, see *FCC* v. *RCA*, 346 U.S. 86 (1953). For an explanation of how international communications were transmitted from the United States via satellite earth stations and cable head ends located in gateway cities, see *Western Union* v. *FCC*, 568 F.2d 1012, 1014-1015 (2d Cir. 1977).

31. Amos Joel, "Retrospective: Telecommunications and the IEEE Communications Society," *IEEE Communications Magazine,* 50th anniversary commemorative issue (May 2002), p. 6, hereinafter "Retrospective."

32. "Retrospective" at 6–7.

33. "Retrospective" at 6.

34. Bell Telephone, "100 Years of Service" (www.porticus.org/bell/att/1975/1975_his.htm), hereinafter "100 Years of Service"; see also "Milestones in AT&T History" (www.corp.att.com/history/milestones.html), hereinafter "Milestones"; "Retrospective" at 8-10.

35. "Milestones."

36. "100 Years of Service."

37. "Retrospective" at 10. See "100 Years of Service"; see Federal Communications Commission, International Bureau, *Trends in the International Telecommunications Industry* (September 2005), p. 2, hereinafter FCC Trends Report 2005; cf. FCC Trends Report 2005 at 9.

38. IEEE, "1952–1964," in *History of the Technology* (www.ieee.org/web/aboutus/history_center/conferences/comsoc/chapter2.html). Other transpacific cables included the COMPAC and ANZCAN cables. See, for example, *In re* Inquiry into the Policies to be Followed in the Authorization of Common Carrier Facilities to Meet Pacific Telecommunications Needs During the Period 1981-1995, 94 F.C.C.2d 867 (1983).

39. "Retrospective" at 10. For a chart of the various TAT cables, including some of the more modern fiber optic cables, see Jim Lande and Linda Blake, "Trends in the U.S. International Telecommunications Industry," Industry Analysis Division, Common Carrier Bureau (Federal Communications Commission, June 1997), p. 25, table 11, hereinafter FCC Trends Report 1997.

40. "Retrospective" at 12.

41. Intelsat, "Our History: The 1970s, A Decade of Expansion"(www.intelsat.com/about-us/history/intelsat-1970s.asp).

42. Delbert Smith, *Communication via Satellite: A Vision in Retrospect* (Leiden, Netherlands: BRILL, 1976), p. 154; D. I. Dalgleish, *Introduction to Satellite Communications* (London: Institution of Electrical Engineers, 1989), p. 14; cf. Image of the Day Gallery, "In a Sound Chamber," NASA (www.nasa.gov/multimedia/imagegallery/image_feature_527.html). Intelsat IV had a "capacity of about 6,000 circuits." Boeing, "Fifth Generation Commercial Communications Satellite," Intelsat IV (www.boeing.com/defense-space/space/bss/factsheets/376/intelsat_iv/intelsat_iv.html). For details on the launch dates and deployment of the Intelsat IV and other Intelsat satellites, see *In re* Communications Satellite Corporation, 56 F.C.C.2d 1101 (1975); see also, for example, *In re* Comsat, 32 F.C.C.2d 537 (1971), authorizing Comsat to launch Intelsat IV (F-3) on or about September 17, 1971.

43. "Retrospective" at 12.

44. AT&T, 1975 Annual Report to Shareholders (www.porticus.org/bell/att/1975/att_1975.htm), hereinafter AT&T 1975 Report, at 10.

45. AT&T, 1976 Annual Report to Shareholders (www.porticus.org/bell/att/1976/att_1976.htm), hereinafter AT&T 1976 Report, at 11.

46. AT&T 1976 report at 12.

47. In November 1971, AT&T was providing 703 cable, 631 satellite, and 13 high-frequency radio telephone circuits between the United States and Europe and was anticipating rough parity between cable and satellite circuits through 1980. *In re* AT&T, ITT, RCA, and Western Union, 35 F.C.C.2d 801 (1972). In 1974 the FCC allowed AT&T to "maintain, until mid-1976, a 1-to-1 satellite-to-cable circuit ratio to countries accessing only one Atlantic satellite or a 2-to-1 satellite-to-cable ratio to countries accessing both Atlantic satellites." *In re* AT&T, 52 F.C.C.2d 128 (1975), describing the 1974 decision.

48. "Satellite Communication," *Encyclopedia Britannica* (2007) (www.britannica.com/eb/article-224536).

49. AT&T 1975 Report at 10.

50. AT&T 1975 Report at 21.

51. AT&T 1976 Report at 12.

52. AT&T, 1978 Annual Report to Shareholders (www.porticus.org/bell/att/1978/att_1978.htm) at 7.

53. Ibid. By 1980, the FCC was already reviewing plans for undersea fiber optic cables. *In re* Inquiry into the Policies to be Followed in the Authorization of Common Carrier Facilities to Meet North Atlantic Telecommunications Needs During the 1985–1995 Period, 82 F.C.C.2d 407 (1980).

54. In 1985 AT&T appears to have proposed "to move from a 52 percent satellite/48 percent cable use ratio, which will obtain at year-end 1985 under balanced loading to a ratio of 40 percent satellite/60 percent cable by year-end 1989." *In re* Inquiry into the Policies to be Followed in the Authorization of Common Carrier Facilities to Meet North Atlantic Telecommunications Needs During the 1985–1995 Period, 100 F.C.C.2d 1405 & n.16 (1985).

55. 50 U.S.C. § 1801(f)(3).

56. Of course, many variations of the bills were introduced and considered at various times.

57. 18 U.S.C. § 2510 et seq. For a discussion of the interplay between Title III and FISA, see NSIP, chapters 7, 14, and 15.

58. An example of the first model was S. 2820, the "Surveillance Practices and Procedures Act of 1973," which was sponsored by Senator Gaylord Nelson as "a direct response to abuses." U.S. House of Representatives, U.S. Senate, Committee on the Judiciary and Committee on Foreign Relations, Subcommittee on Administrative Practice and Procedure, Subcommittee on Constitutional Rights, Subcommittee on Surveillance, *Joint Hearings on Warrantless Wiretapping and Electronic Surveillance–1974*, 93rd Cong., 2nd sess., April 3, 1974, p. 256, hereinafter FISA Hearings 4-3-74. Under this bill, FISA would have mirrored Title III in scope. See FISA Hearings 4-3-74 at 274: "Essentially, the procedures parallel those contained in existing law for wiretaps for domestic crimes."

59. U.S. House of Representatives, Committee on the Judiciary, Subcommittee on Courts, Civil Liberties, and the Administration of Justice, "Statement of Representative

Kastenmeier," *Hearings on Foreign Intelligence Surveillance Act,* 95th Cong., 2nd sess., June 22, 1978, hereinafter FISA Hearings 6-22-78; see U.S. Senate, Committee on the Judiciary, Subcommittee on Criminal Laws and Procedures, *Hearing on Foreign Intelligence Surveillance Act of 1976,* 94th Cong., 2nd sess., March 29, 1976, 233-265, hereinafter FISA Hearings 3-29-76.

60. See FISA Hearings 3-29-76 at 1. For a detailed discussion of current 50 U.S.C. § 1801(f), see NSIP, chapter 7.

61. For the language of the bill supported by the Ford administration, see FISA Hearings 3-29-76 at 122-123; U.S. Senate, Select Committee on Intelligence, Subcommittee on Intelligence and the Rights of Americans, *Electronic Surveillance within the United States for Foreign Intelligence Purposes,* 94th Cong., 2nd sess., June 29, 1976, 180-181, hereinafter FISA Hearings 6-29-76.

62. FISA Hearings 3-29-76 at 11, 20.

63. FISA Hearings 3-29-76 at 15.

64. FISA Hearings 3-29-76 at 17.

65. There was some initial ambiguity about whether the bill would apply to international calls "from a citizen in this country, to an agent in a foreign country, a long distance call of that type," because Levi initially affirmed unequivocally that such a call would be within the scope of the statute. FISA Hearings 3-29-76 at 15. In response to later questions, however, he indicated (accurately) that the statute would apply to such communications only when they "involve a wire," as opposed to a radio wave, FISA Hearings 3-29-76 at 15, and only when "the tap is placed within the United States," FISA Hearings 3-29-76 at 20.

66. FISA Hearings 3-29-76 at 25.

67. U.S. House of Representatives, Committee on the Judiciary, Subcommittee on Courts, Civil Liberties, and the Administration of Justice, *Foreign Intelligence Surveillance Act,* 94th Cong., 2nd sess., April 12, 1976, 98-99, hereinafter FISA Hearings 4-12-76.

68. Levi's full summary of Allen's testimony was as follows:

> He described as the responsibility of the NSA the interception of international communication signals sent through the air. He said there had been a watch list [used to select signals for review], which among many other names, contained the names of U.S. citizens. Senator Tower spoke of an awesome technology—a huge vacuum cleaner of communications—that had the potential for abuses. General Allen . . . said the mission of NSA is directed to foreign intelligence obtained from foreign electrical communications and also from other foreign signals such as radar. Signals are intercepted by many techniques and processed, sorted, and analyzed by procedures which reject inappropriate or unnecessary signals. He mentioned that the interception of communications, however it may occur, is conducted in such a manner as to minimize the unwanted messages. Nevertheless, according to his statement, many unwanted communications are potentially selected for further processing. He testified that subsequent

processing, sorting, and selection for analysis are conducted in accordance with strict procedures to insure immediate and, wherever possible, automatic rejection of inappropriate messages. The analysis and reporting is accomplished only for those messages which meet specific conditions and requirements for foreign intelligence. The use of lists of words, including individual names, subjects, locations, et cetera, has long been one of the methods used to sort out information of foreign intelligence value from that which is not of interest.

FISA Hearings 6-29-76 at 28; see FISA Hearings 6-29-76 at 39-40. For public testimony by General Allen concerning the NSA's surveillance activities, see the Church Report, Hearings before the Select Committee to Study Governmental Operations with Respect to Intelligence Activities, 94 Cong., 1 sess., October 29 and November 6, 1975, vol. 5, at 1–55.

69. U.S. Senate, Committee on the Judiciary, Subcommittee on Criminal Laws and Procedures, *Foreign Intelligence Surveillance Act of 1977*, 95th Cong., 1st sess., June 13, 1977, 136-137, hereinafter FISA Hearings 6-13-77.

70. FISA Hearings 6-13-77 at 15; see also FISA Hearings 1-10-78 at 9, Statement of Attorney General Bell. As Bell later put it in testimony before the House Intelligence Committee, "a prior judicial warrant is now required for all targeting of Americans in the United States for electronic surveillance of their international communications" as well as their domestic communications. FISA Hearings 1-10-78 at 15.

71. Bell justified this limitation with three examples. First, he explained, when the government monitors radio communications, "the identity of the person involved [may be] totally unknown and largely undiscoverable" and indeed a "high priority of this [surveillance] activity is in fact to discover the identity of the communicator." FISA Hearings 6-13-77 at 6. Bell assured Congress, however, that if an intelligence agency found "that the person was a United States person, [and] . . . failed immediately to obtain a warrant—if a warrant were required for law enforcement purposes—officials of the agency would be criminally liable." FISA Hearings 6-13-77 at 6. Second, in some cases, unknown to the intelligence community, a foreign government official may be a U.S. person, and "the qualifier 'known' is required to keep such a mistake from becoming a criminal offense." FISA Hearings 6-13-77 at 6. Third and finally, Bell explained that "agencies operating totally overseas and targeted solely against foreign communications can, through the quirks of radio communications, accidentally intercept radio communications which are intended to be wholly domestic within the United States. Over time there is a statistical certainty of this occurring at uncertain and generally infrequent intervals." FISA Hearings 6-13-77 at 6.

72. See FISA Hearings 6-13-77 at 98.

73. As discussed above, the government has specifically identified the adoption of fiber optics as a technological problem for surveillance of international communications.

74. Hayden Testimony 7-26-06.

75. See FCC Trends Report 1997 at 25 (table 11). See *In re* AT&T et al., 98 F.C.C.2d 440 (1984), order authorizing TAT-8.

76. Possible FISA Amendments Memo 11-1-90 at 1. Redactions in the memorandum make it difficult to identify the precise nature of the NSA's technological problem, but it clearly had to do with FISA's definition of "electronic surveillance." Possible FISA Amendments Memo 11-1-90 at 1–2.

77. Possible FISA Amendments Memo 11-1-90 at 1.

78. Possible FISA Amendments Memo 11-1-90 at 4. The memo explained that concerns about the 1978 version of FISA were overcome by the "practical imperative of continuing to collect foreign intelligence in the face of growing resistance from the communications common carriers whose cooperation was essential." Possible FISA Amendments Memo 11-1-90 at 4. The memo reported that the "NSA views the changing technology as creating a similar practical imperative" and that "it could also be considered a legal imperative since the existing statute prohibits . . . the collection NSA is seeking." Possible FISA Amendments Memo 11-1-90 at 4.

79. Possible FISA Amendments Memo 11-1-90 at 1, 3.

80. Among those issues were the following:

—the fact that "committee jurisdiction in both the House and Senate is concurrent between the Intelligence and Judiciary Committees" and while the "problems giving rise to the possible amendments have all been discussed with the Intelligence Committees," they had not been discussed "with the Judiciary Committees"

—concerns about separation of powers and the question of whether "putting the proposed new collection under the statute, albeit on the basis of Attorney General certification, pose[s] greater separation of powers problems than attempting to exclude the collection from the statute"

—"the risk of added congressional restrictions if the statute is opened up to amendment"

—the fact that "the proposed amendment to FISA to resolve the NSA problem . . . is certain to be written in such enigmatic terms that only those who have been briefed in executive session will understand them" thus risking "speculation in the media about what is really intended and probably deep suspicion that something sinister is going on."

Possible FISA Amendments Memo 11-1-90 at 4–5.

81. An audio recording of the meeting is available at www.abanet.org/natsecurity/multimedia/FISA_reform_panel_March_3 _2 008_WS_30144.mp3.

82. For a detailed explanation of why that is so, see NSIP, chapter 7.

83. For a detailed explanation of why that is so, see NSIP, chapter 7 (at section 7:30); see also David Kris, Slate Discussion, post 3 (www.slate.com/id/2172952/entry/2172969/).

84. See 50 U.S.C. § 1801(f)(4); NSIP, chapter 7. FISA regulates surveillance of stored e-mail in the United States because of a provision of the statute originally

designed to deal with microphone bugging and closed circuit television surveillance, 50 U.S.C. ß 1801(f)(4). The drafters of that provision certainly did not anticipate its application to foreign-to-foreign e-mail messages.

85. See statement of James Baker describing the situation in which "you cannot tell in advance (if ever) where one or both of the parties to a communication are located. This is a particular issue with Internet communications, including web-based email, as well as mobile telephone technology." U.S. Senate, Committee on the Judiciary, "Statement of James Baker," 110th Cong., 1st sess., September 25, 2007 (http://judiciary. senate.gov/testimony.cfm?id=2942&wit_id=6669). The advent of web-based communications, mobile communications devices, packet-switched networks, and increased international travel have all had dramatic effects. In 1976, for example, only "about 25 percent" of U.S. telephone subscribers could make international calls without operator assistance. AT&T 1976 Report at 11. Now, essentially everyone in the United States can dial direct and many use technologies such as Voice over Internet Protocol (VoIP). For a more complete discussion of technological changes and other issues in telecommunications, see, for example, Whitfield Diffie and Susan Landau, *Privacy on the Line: The Politics of Wiretapping and Encryption* (MIT Press, 2007). Similarly, in 1975 approximately 6 million airline passengers arrived in the United States from foreign countries; in 2005, the number had grown to approximately 29 million. Bureau of Transportation Statistics, "National Transportation Statistics," U.S. Department of Transportation (www.bts.gov/publications/national_transportation_ statistics/pdf/entire.pdf).

86. The same may be true of some mobile telephones, as the NSA has explained, and of certain VoIP services, as the FCC has explained. As stated by the director of the National Security Agency, in an era of mobile phones, "telephone area codes are less reliable indicators of the physical location of their users." Alexander QFRs 12-19-06, answer to Question 20 for Senator Feingold. In its "Consumer Advisory: VoIP and 911 Service" (www.fcc.gov/cgb/consumerfacts/voip911.pdf), the FCC explains that "interconnected VoIP service allows you to make and receive calls to and from traditional phone numbers, usually using an Internet connection." While "[t]raditional phone services have generally associated a particular phone number with a fixed address," some "interconnected VoIP services enable customers to take their home or business phone almost anywhere" they can get a connection to the Internet. "Because certain interconnected VoIP services can be used from virtually any Internet connection," the FCC explains, "the location of the caller cannot automatically be determined," including by emergency 911 operators.

87. That assumes, of course, that the "sender" and "recipient" of an e-mail message are the individual human beings who read and write the messages and that they are deemed to be "located" for purposes of FISA wherever they are physically located at the time that they click their mouse or type on their keyboard to send or open an e-mail message.

88. In a meeting sponsored by the American Bar Association in March 2008, Ken Wainstein, then the assistant attorney general for the Justice Department's National Security Division, confirmed in response to questioning that FISA's application to e-mail was part of the reason that the government was seeking to modernize the statute. See Ellen Nakashima, "Wiretap Compromise in Works," *Washington Post*, March 4, 2008. Wainstein stated: "The concern is . . . especially with e-mail, at the time of interception you don't know where the recipient is going to be. So carving the world of surveillance up between foreign to foreign and everything else is good in certain areas of surveillance, but for instance in e-mail it doesn't get you where you need to be, because at the time of surveillance you're not going to know if it's foreign to foreign or foreign to domestic and that's our—that's the dilemma." An audio recording of the meeting is available at www.abanet.org/natsecurity/multimedia/FISA_reform_panel_March_3_2 008_WS_30144.mp3.

89. 50 U.S.C. § 1881a(a).

90. 50 U.S.C. § 1881a(a).

91. 50 U.S.C. §§ 1881(a), 1801(e).

92. 50 U.S.C. § 1881a(g)(4).

93. 50 U.S.C. § 1881a(c)(1)(A).

94. 50 U.S.C. § 1881a(d)(1).

95. 50 U.S.C. § 1881a(b)(4).

96. 50 U.S.C. § 1881a(c)(1)(A).

97. 50 U.S.C. § 1881a(e); see 50 U.S.C. §§ 1801(h), 1841(4). For a more complete discussion of minimization procedures, see NSIP, chapter 9.

98. 50 U.S.C. § 1881a(g)(1).

99. 50 U.S.C. § 1881a(g)(2).

100. See 50 U.S.C. §§ 1881b, 1881c. For a discussion of the term "United States person," see NSIP, chapter 8.

101. 50 U.S.C. 1881a(i).

102. 50 U.S.C. § 1881a(i)(3)(A)-(B).

103. 50 U.S.C. § 1881a(h).

104. 50 U.S.C. § 1881a(h)(4).

105. 50 U.S.C. § 1881a(h)(5).

106. 50 U.S.C. § 1881a(h)(4)(G) and (5)(D).

107. 50 U.S.C. § 1881a(*l*).

108. See NSIP, chapter 7.

109. 50 U.S.C. §§ 1881b, 1881c.

110. Section 1881b may be best seen as a limit on the contraction of FISA, as discussed in the next paragraph, but section 1881c is a genuine expansion.

111. As noted in the previous paragraph, however, if a U.S. person located abroad is the target of such e-mail surveillance, section 1881b of the new statute will apply, even if the U.S. person is communicating with a foreigner who also is located abroad.

112. 50 U.S.C. § 1881c.

113. 50 U.S.C. § 1881a.

114. 50 U.S.C. § 1881a(b)(4). As noted above, this limit does not apply to 50 U.S.C. § 1881b and 1881c.

115. That is a potentially difficult question, and the statute requires the government to establish guidelines to address such concerns. 50 U.S.C. § 1881a(g)(2)(A)(iii).

116. See 50 U.S.C. § 1801(f)(1).

117. Of course, statements in this chapter that the NSA "could" do something mean only that it could do so legally, not operationally or technically.

118. See 50 U.S.C. §§ 1801(f)(1), 1881a(a).

119. See 50 U.S.C. § 1881a(a).

120. See 50 U.S.C. § 1881b.

121. See 50 U.S.C. § 1881c.

122. 50 U.S.C. § 1881a.

123. 50 U.S.C. §§ 1881b, 1881c.

124. This discounts the short-term amendments made by the Protect America Act.

125. Again, echoing statements made in the introduction of this chapter, I emphasize my own lack of current knowledge about how the FAA is in fact being implemented and the correspondingly tentative nature of my conclusions in this area.

126. For an example of such a statute, see U.S. House of Representatives, Committee on the Judiciary, Subcommittee on the Constitution, Civil Rights and Civil Liberties, *Hearing on H.R. 3189, the National Security Letters Reform Act of 2007*, "Statement of David Kris," 110th Cong., 2nd sess., April 15, 2008 (http://judiciary.house.gov/media/pdfs/Kris080415.pdf).

127. For a discussion of national security letters, see NSIP, chapter 19.

128. For a discussion of pen/trap surveillance, see NSIP, chapter 17.

129. For a discussion of mail covers, see NSIP, chapter 20.

130. For a discussion of section 215, which allows orders for production of business records and other tangible things, see NSIP, chapter 18.

131. *United States* v. *R. Enterprises, Inc.*, 498 U.S. 292, 297 (1991) (internal quotation omitted). For a more complete discussion of grand jury subpoenas, see NSIP, chapter 21.

132. For a more complete discussion of national security letters, see NSIP, chapter 19.

133. For a more complete discussion of section 215 orders, see NSIP, chapter 18.

134. For a more complete discussion of mail covers, see NSIP, chapter 20.

135. That could replace FISA's electronic surveillance provisions, its physical search provisions, and section 2.5 of Executive Order 12333.

136. Executive Order 12333 § 2.5; 50 U.S.C. § 1881c.

137. Of course, those limits could be refined; the basic point is that a simpler approach is available.

138. For a discussion of the FISA wall and the National Security Division, see NSIP, chapter 10.

139. 18 U.S.C. § 2510 et seq.

140. See, for example, Orin Kerr, "A User's Guide to the Stored Communications Act, and a Legislator's Guide to Amending It," *George Washington Law Review* 72 (2004), p. 1208.

141. Like ECPA itself, this would be a legislative response to Supreme Court decisions suggesting that there is no reasonable expectation of privacy in information turned over to third parties. See *Smith* v. *Maryland,* 442 U.S. 735 (1979); *United States* v. *Miller,* 425 U.S. 435 (1976). For a more complete discussion of these decisions and of ECPA, see NSIP, chapter 7.

142. See 18 U.S.C. §§ 2701-2711. Rules prohibiting voluntary disclosure to government by some or all of those intermediaries would also be needed, as is the case under the Stored Communications Act today.

143. 50 U.S.C. §§ 1881b, 1881c.

144. Another problem, reflected in FISA itself, is that non-U.S. persons located in the United States are still more likely than non-U.S. persons located abroad to be in contact with U.S. persons. And, of course, there may be problems, whether legal, political, or otherwise, with legislation that draws such a sharp distinction between U.S. persons and non-U.S. persons. See NSIP, chapter 8.

145. For a discussion of this, see NSIP, chapter 9.

146. Much of this information may be outside the Fourth Amendment's reasonable expectation of privacy. That may suggest a need to exceed the Fourth Amendment by statute, as Congress has done several times.

147. See "Software-as-a-Service for Business E-mail, Information Sharing, and Security," Google (www.google.com/a/help/intl/en/index.html).

148. See "Introducing . . . the new Windows Live(tm)" (www.windowslive.com). See also "Victory for DVRs in the Cloud," Electronic Frontier Foundation (www.eff.org/deeplinks/2008/08/victory-dvrs-cloud), referring to "a wide variety of innovative business models that rely on the use of remote computing, ranging from examples like Internet-enabled self-service photo processing and printing, to cloud computing services offered by companies like Amazon, Apple and Google."

149. See, for example, Facebook (www.facebook.com).

150. William James, *The Principles of Psychology* (New York: Courier Dover Publications, 1950), p. 462.

151. On the other hand, if concepts like end-to-end trust are established on the Internet, this trend may be checked or reversed. See, for example, Scott Charney, "Establishing End to End Trust," Microsoft Corporation, Trustworthy Computing (www.microsoft.com/mscorp/twc/endtoendtrust/default.mspx).

152. I am indebted to Jim Baker for the use of the phrase "larger haystacks" and for other assistance with this chapter.

153. See NSIP, chapter 2 (discussing minimization under Executive Order 12333 and its subordinate procedures) and NSIP, chapter 9 (discussing FISA minimization).

JUSTIN FLORENCE *and* MATTHEW GERKE

8

National Security Issues in Civil Litigation: A Blueprint for Reform

The U.S. civil litigation system is designed to resolve disputes between parties fairly and to compensate people who have been wronged. When officials or agents of the federal government are sued, open courts hold the government publicly accountable to the rule of law, protecting the basis of the constitutional republic. Opinions are generally published; proceedings are open to the press and the public at large. The assumption underlying the adversarial system is that a just outcome is achieved when each party in the dispute has an equal opportunity to make its best arguments on the legal and factual issues at stake in full view of the public eye. That requires that all parties to the litigation have access to evidence and to information that may be helpful to resolving the case.

This carefully constructed system begins to break down when a lawsuit requires the disclosure of secret information that could threaten the security of the nation. Consider the following scenarios, each of which tracks an actual case filed in U.S. courts:

—A woman sues the federal government alleging that its negligence allowed a military plane to crash, killing her husband. The government responds that the accident report contains details of secret military equipment and missions that, if disclosed, would greatly benefit the nation's enemies and that therefore it cannot allow the crucial evidence to be introduced.

—A man sues government officials alleging that they kidnapped and tortured him in a secret, illegal program. The government tells the court that even considering the case would lead to the disclosure of state secrets, putting the nation's security at risk.

—The administrator of an estate sues the federal government alleging that it violated a secret contract that the deceased had with the government to serve as a spy several years back. The government responds that the court cannot enforce a secret contract, for to do so would render it nonsecret.

—Government officials publicly acknowledge that they have been conducting warrantless electronic surveillance through a new program. A group of citizens sue the government, claiming that the program violates federal laws and the Constitution and asking the federal courts to halt the program. The government responds that disclosing how the program works or who has been subject to surveillance under it would allow the nation's enemies to evade surveillance.

With little guidance from the Supreme Court and none from Congress, federal courts have struggled to reconcile the conflicting demands of public justice and national security raised in those and similar cases. If courts dismiss cases or deny parties access to important evidence at the request of the executive branch, they may fail to provide redress to parties who have been wronged and to uphold the rule of law. If courts discount the national security implications of publicly disclosing secret evidence, they may place the security of the nation as a whole at risk.

Two broad doctrines are available in civil cases that implicate the nation's security. One is a jurisdictional or justiciability rule—in other words, a rule that forbids the court from considering the case at all. A second is an evidentiary privilege, a rule that specifies how certain types of evidence may be used in a lawsuit. In recent years, prompted by the government, some courts have increasingly conflated the two different rules under the single heading of the "state secrets privilege." Under current doctrine, the government may assert the "state secrets privilege" to ask that courts dismiss a case, prevent the use of evidence in it, or both. Defined broadly in this way, as both an evidentiary privilege and a justiciability rule, the "state secrets privilege" has become the single mechanism by which courts attempt to navigate the challenge presented by civil lawsuits related to secret national security information.

Because the executive branch usually has an interest in the outcome of cases in which it asserts the state secrets privilege, it may be tempted to abuse it to avoid political embarrassment or liability. Without proper rules in place, the executive branch can, in effect, choose whether it would like to be held publicly accountable, what evidence it will allow opponents to use against it, and when it would like its actions to be free of judicial scrutiny. In the years since September 11, as cases involving security issues have become more central to the national debate, the potential for abuse has grown.

The U.S. Congress should provide federal courts with clear legislative guidance for civil cases in which they must balance the competing demands of open justice and state secrecy. Although the Supreme Court and the executive branch also could implement such reforms, both branches have declined the opportunity to do so over many years and under many leaders.[1] The Constitution gives Congress the authority to establish rules of jurisdiction, procedures, and evidence for the courts, and Congress now has legislation pending before it that would go a long way toward realizing that goal.

To protect the state secrets privilege, several specific reforms are necessary. Congress should begin by separating the two distinct approaches to civil cases involving national security issues. It should clarify that the "state secrets privilege" is a rule of evidence and not a rule of justiciability, and it should prevent courts from dismissing cases on the basis of the state secrets privilege until they have had a chance to assess the privilege claim and see other available, nonprivileged evidence that might bear on its adjudication. Congress should also provide courts with a set of tools and standards to determine which evidence should not be disclosed in civil proceedings because of the risk of harm to national security. Those tools should include procedural rules to minimize the burden on courts; precleared experts, special masters, and attorneys to assist the judge and affected parties with specialized expertise in national security issues; and procedures to create substitute evidence when doing so would not harm national security. Congress should design the procedures so that even if some evidence cannot be made available, the cases can proceed as far toward resolution on the merits as possible, without endangering national security. Alongside this reform of the privilege, Congress should put rules in place so that, even if secret evidence prevents the civil litigation system from dispensing justice in certain cases, other government institutions can fill in for the courts by providing redress to wronged parties and ensuring that the government is held accountable.

This chapter first explains how cases involving state secrets work today in the civil, criminal, and administrative contexts. It then traces the history of how U.S. courts have handled such cases, ending with an examination of some high-profile post–September 11 national security cases. The chapter next outlines more specific suggestions for reform, presenting the options available to Congress, discussing their costs and benefits, and laying out a roadmap for reform. The chapter relates that discussion to the concept of a national security court and then offers some concluding thoughts.

The State of the State Secrets Privilege Today

Before discussing how Congress should reform procedures for civil litigation involving national security concerns, we provide some background on how U.S. courts have handled this set of issues to date.

It is difficult to identify any single, typical state secrets case because the case law is confused, if not contradictory, and because current doctrine gives judges little guidance on how to handle any particular case. The Supreme Court has directly addressed the state secrets privilege only once, in 1953, and that case provides only a few broad brushstrokes to indicate how civil matters involving national security secrets should proceed.

A few procedures have generally been followed. Once a lawsuit is filed, the executive branch—whether it is a defendant in the case or a third party—may formally intervene to assert the state secrets privilege. That requires providing the court with an affidavit from the head of the agency, claiming the privilege and explaining the national security concern. After it intervenes, the government often asks the court to dismiss the case on the basis of the privilege before the defendant responds to the allegations made in the lawsuit and before any evidence is introduced in the case. The government's motion generally argues that the case cannot proceed because the government cannot confirm or deny the plaintiff's allegations given the secret nature of the subject matter. The government typically contends that because the state secrets privilege denies the defendants evidence that they need to defend themselves, allowing the case to proceed will cause unfair prejudice to the defendants.

In some cases, the court grants the motion to dismiss, and the case ends, subject to appeal, of course. Alternatively, the court can allow the case to proceed and consider the government's assertion of the state secrets privilege with respect to either particular items of evidence or larger pieces of information at issue in the case. The court can, but often does not, ask to see the evidence that the government claims is privileged. If the court does see the evidence, it does so *in camera* and *ex parte,* without the adverse party having any opportunity to make the case for why the court should not apply the privilege. The court then determines whether the privilege applies, applying any of a number of standards, and finally, if it has not already dismissed the litigation, the case proceeds without the privileged evidence.

There are several reasons to reform this approach to civil cases involving national security issues.

—First, the uncertainty and inconsistency in current doctrine prevents the government, private parties who assist the government, and individuals harmed by the government from knowing in advance what their legal rights are.

—Second, the current use of the state secrets privilege does a poor job of protecting litigants from the unfair result of being denied access to relevant evidence, thus weakening the ability of the civil litigation system to deliver justice to harmed parties.

—Third, abuse of the privilege can allow the executive branch to flaunt the rule of law and avoid accountability.

—Fourth, state secrets have been at the center of legal disputes over high-profile government policies—surveillance, rendition, interrogation—and reforming state secrets cases may be necessary for judges to resolve these substantive legal issues.

—Fifth, the current combination of heavy executive reliance on and judicial confusion over the state secrets privilege actually places national security at risk because judges lack clear standards with which to evaluate such claims. Over time, if the executive branch continues to use the state secrets privilege wantonly to shut down legal scrutiny of its most controversial programs, some federal judge may one day consider a privilege claim to be as false as the alarm raised by the boy who cried wolf and, in the absence of clear procedures to prevent it, allow genuinely important national security secrets to become public.

In contrast, the use of secret evidence in criminal cases and other types of legal proceedings currently is governed by detailed legislation. In 1980 Congress passed the Classified Information Procedures Act (CIPA) to provide rules on the introduction of classified information in federal criminal prosecutions.[2] Congress enacted CIPA largely to deal with "gray-mailing" cases—those in which a defendant in a criminal prosecution, often a government official, threatens to use classified information in his defense and, by so doing, forces the government to dismiss the case against him. CIPA aims to allow the government to prosecute a defendant, even when that prosecution might involve classified information. CIPA thus gives courts special procedures to use in protecting classified information, in allowing the adversarial process to go forward, and in giving courts an opportunity to reach a judgment.[3]

Some have suggested reforming the state secrets privilege simply by applying CIPA in civil as well as criminal cases.[4] However, differences between civil and criminal cases would make that difficult. In the criminal context, the government is the prosecutor and may always choose to protect information by dismissing the case. In the civil context, the government will often (although not always) be the defendant and so will benefit from dismissal. Thus, whereas the government has an incentive to introduce evidence that it controls to secure a conviction in a criminal case, if it is the defendant in a civil case, it has an incentive to prevent disclosure of evidence to avoid subjecting its actions to legal scrutiny. Because of that difference in contexts, it is not possible simply to apply the existing CIPA statute to civil cases.

Indeed, no comprehensive law regulates the handling of classified information in the civil context. Congress considered codifying the state secrets privilege through a proposed "military and state secrets" rule of evidence in the 1970s but ultimately opted against codifying any privileges at all.[5] Instead, through rule of evidence 501, Congress left privileges to "be governed by the principles of the common law as they may be interpreted by the courts of the

United States in the light of reason and experience."[6] Thus Congress, like the Supreme Court, has left judges with little or no guidance on how they should handle state secrets in civil trials.

The Origins of State Secrets Doctrines

The doctrinal history of state secrets in U.S. courts is thin, a fact that has contributed to the tangled state of the law today. The state secrets privilege has a more established pedigree in England as a royal prerogative—a claim by the crown to be able to hold information beyond the reach of the law.[7] The English example, however, provides little guidance in the United States, where the Constitution recognizes no executive power beyond the law.[8] The U.S. Supreme Court first recognized a state secrets evidentiary privilege in 1953.[9] Although the government frequently cites two nineteenth-century cases as a basis for keeping certain evidence and matters out of court, neither offers a clear rule or thorough reasoning.

In 1807, the United States charged Aaron Burr with treason, making war against the United States, and inciting insurrection. Burr demanded access to certain evidence—letters in the possession of President Jefferson—in order to put on his defense. Chief Justice John Marshall heard the case, and despite some wrangling over whether he should or could compel the president to make the evidence available, was spared a decision because Jefferson voluntarily turned them over.[10] The oft-cited episode provides little doctrinal clarity on a state secrets evidentiary privilege for two reasons. First, it was a criminal prosecution, not a civil case, and the two contexts are quite different. Second, in Burr's case, Marshall never actually needed to reach a decision about the relative authorities of the president and the courts. Indeed, the Burr case was not cited as a precedent for any sort of military or state secrets privilege in the courts until the aforementioned litigation in the 1950s.[11]

In an 1875 case, *Totten v. United States,* the Supreme Court considered whether a Civil War–era secret espionage contract could be enforced in court after the war. Although the issue of secrecy was never briefed or raised in the lower courts, the Supreme Court held that both parties to the contract "must have understood that the lips of the other were to be forever sealed respecting the relation of either to the matter" and that "[t]he secrecy which such contracts impose precludes any action for their enforcement. The publicity produced by an action would itself be a breach of a contract of that kind, and thus defeat a recovery."[12] The Court's short opinion in the case also included broader language, stating that "as a general principle, that public policy forbids the maintenance of any suit in a court of justice, the trial of which would inevitably lead to the disclosure of matters which the law itself regards as confidential, and respecting which it will not allow the confidence to be violated."[13] Although the Supreme Court has never entirely explained the reasoning behind that holding, at its core the rationale seems to be that a secret espionage contract is by its own terms unenforceable in court, for to have a court enforce it would be to render it nonsecret. As one lower court explained it, "one who agrees to conduct covert operations impliedly agrees not to reveal the agreement even if the agreement is breached."[14] Note that, because the Civil War had ended long before, the Court did not ground its holding in possible harm to national security but in traditional notions of confidentiality, which can be seen not only in its choice of terminology but also in the examples that it cited—the privileges between spouses and between physicians and patients.[15]

Although neither the Burr case nor *Totten* referred to a "state secrets privilege" or a "state secrets bar to justiciability," the Supreme Court cited both cases in *United States* v. *Reynolds,* the 1953 case in which it first formally announced the existence of the privilege.[16] In that case, a suit brought by the widows of civilian engineers who died in an air force plane crash, the Truman administration sought to prevent introduction of the accident report of the crash. The government argued that disclosing the accident report, even to a federal judge, would reveal the plane's top secret mission and secret equipment and so compromise secret national security information.

Noting "that this is a time of vigorous preparation for national defense" the Court upheld the use of the privilege without requiring the government to make the accident report available to the judge.[17] In so doing, the Court offered only minimal guidance for how the state secrets privilege was to work. The Court stated that the government alone could assert the state secrets privilege; that it could do so only through a formal claim lodged by the head of the department with control over the information; and that the "court itself must determine whether the circumstances are appropriate for the claim of privilege."[18] On all other aspects of how the privilege should work, the Court was silent. The Court did not clarify what constitutes a state secret, how much deference judges should give the executive branch, or the methods and procedures the court should follow to reach such determinations. It is important to note that the Court did not suggest in *Reynolds* that cases in which the state secrets privilege was invoked were not suitable for judicial resolution—just that certain evidence might not be disclosable.

The accident report at issue in *Reynolds* was declassified decades later and discovered in 2000 by a descendant of one of the victims of the crash. The report, according to the leading scholarly expert on the case, "revealed not only serious negligence by the government, but also contained nothing that could be called state secrets."[19] In other words, the government used the state secrets privilege in *Reynolds* not to protect secret national security information, but to conceal its own negligence.

Taken together, the Supreme Court's decisions have offered only limited guidance to lower courts, the executive branch, or private parties on how civil litigation involving secret or national security information should proceed. *Reynolds* says little about how courts should proceed when the executive branch has asserted a state secrets privilege in a case. *Totten* bars the justiciability of suits over secret espionage contracts that might reveal the existence of an individual's covert relationship with the government. But the Supreme Court has never clarified whether *Totten* is limited to this narrow class of secret espionage cases, and some courts have read the cases together to imply that the justiciability and evidentiary rules may be intertwined.[20]

The State Secrets Privilege since September 11

In the years since September 11, 2001, the state secrets privilege has taken on far greater prominence in public debate—and led to much greater anxiety— than in its first decades after *Reynolds*. There are a variety of possible explanations for that. First, some scholars have suggested that the Bush administration invoked the privilege more often than prior administrations—although the evidence is inconclusive.[21] Second, the Bush administration arguably invoked the privilege in a qualitatively different manner, advocating in a larger number of cases outright dismissal without considering any evidence.[22] Third, whether or not the Bush administration invoked the privilege more frequently or more forcefully, it used it to prohibit legal rulings on entire policies—in particular its rendition, interrogation, and electronic surveillance programs— that critics have suggested are illegal, unconstitutional, and widespread.[23]

It is still too early to tell how the Obama administration will handle state secrets cases. Administration officials have criticized the Bush administration's practices, and Attorney General Eric Holder, on taking office, ordered a review of all pending cases in which the Bush administration had invoked the privilege. But in one early and important appellate case—*Mohamed* v. *Jeppesen DataPlan*—the Obama Department of Justice adhered to the Bush administration position that a case against a private company allegedly involved in the CIA's rendition program must be dismissed at the outset because the very subject matter is a state secret. The new administration's action in that case suggests that it too may assert the state secrets privilege in civil litigation to protect the details of many of the Bush administration's most controversial policies and programs.

For example, the Bush administration's warrantless domestic wiretapping program, the Terrorist Surveillance Program (TSP), is the subject of ongoing civil suits. Private individuals and civil liberties organizations have brought suit against both the government and private telecommunications companies. To date, one federal district judge has held the TSP to be illegal and unconstitutional and issued an injunction blocking the program.[24] A federal appellate court, however, overturned that ruling, based in part on the state secrets privilege.[25] In particular, the court explained, "the plaintiffs do not—and because of the State Secrets Doctrine cannot—produce any evidence that any of their own communications have ever been intercepted by the NSA, under the TSP, or without warrants."[26] Because the plaintiffs could not establish that they personally had been subjected to warrantless surveillance, they lacked standing, and the court of appeals dismissed the suit. The Supreme Court declined to grant review.

In a related series of cases, private citizens have sued telecommunications companies for their alleged participation in the warrantless surveillance program. Those plaintiffs claim to have evidence that they personally were subjected to warrantless surveillance and so (unlike the plaintiffs in the direct challenge to the government) have standing. In the main class action case, *Hepting* v. *AT&T,* although the government was not a party to the case, it intervened to ask the district court to dismiss the case on the basis of the state secrets privilege.[27] The district judge rejected the government's motion, finding that the *Totten* justiciability rule did not apply because "plaintiffs made no agreement with the government and are not bound by any implied covenant of secrecy."[28] As of this writing, the case is on appeal.[29] At the same time, in the context of amendments to the Foreign Intelligence Surveillance Act, Congress has granted a form of retroactive immunity to telecommunications companies for assistance that they provided to the government, thereby attempting to preclude the pending lawsuits.[30] The constitutionality of the retroactive immunity itself faces court challenge.[31]

The government has similarly—and thus far successfully—invoked the state secrets privilege to block judicial review of alleged secret torture and rendition of detainees. In the most prominent such case, Khalid El-Masri sued CIA director George Tenet and several private companies and individuals who assisted the CIA, alleging that the defendants illegally detained, interrogated, and tortured El-Masri in an extraordinary rendition operation. In particular, El-Masri alleged that while traveling in Macedonia, he was kidnapped and then handed over to CIA agents who flew him to a secret detention facility in Afghanistan where he was held and interrogated.[32] El-Masri was subsequently released when the government realized that he was not the terrorist that they were looking for (he had a similar name). El-Masri's story was extensively discussed in the public media.

At the government's request, however, the trial court dismissed the case on the basis of the state secrets privilege, and the Fourth Circuit Court upheld the dismissal, reading *Totten* and *Reynolds* broadly to permit dismissing cases having nothing to do with covert espionage contracts. Rather, it held, "a proceeding in which the state secrets privilege is successfully interposed must be dismissed if the circumstances make clear that privileged information will be so central to the litigation that any attempt to proceed will threaten that information's disclosure."[33] Concluding that "virtually any conceivable response to El-Masri's allegations would disclose privileged information," the Court upheld the dismissal. In so doing, it recognized the harsh penalty that its decision imposed on El-Masri, who had no judicial forum for his claims no matter how meritorious they were. The Supreme Court declined to review that decision too.

However, it is not clear that the courts are prepared to step aside entirely. In *Arar* v. *Ashcroft*, a case similar to *El-Masri*, the district court dismissed the claims, "given the national-security and foreign policy considerations at stake." A Second Circuit panel affirmed the dismissal, but in August 2008, the Second Circuit took the very unusual step of granting rehearing *en banc* on its own initiative. Oral argument was presented on December 9, 2008, and as of this writing, the court had not yet handed down a decision.

None of this is to say that, in the absence of the state secrets privilege, courts would or should halt the government's major security programs. Indeed, it is difficult to predict how federal courts would come out were they to reach the merits of whether the programs are legal or whether those affected by them are entitled to compensation. The Constitution does give the president broad latitude in acting overseas and during war, and the courts often defer on contentious foreign policy issues. But because of the broad use of the state secrets privilege, courts have been unable to resolve cases and controversies, to uphold the rule of law, to provide redress to harmed individuals, and to interpret the Constitution and laws of the United States.

Recent Congressional Interest in the Privilege

In light of the high profile that the state secrets privilege has taken on in litigation over major post–September 11 policies, members of both the House and the Senate have introduced bills to reform the state secrets privilege.[34] The Senate bill (S. 2533), introduced by senators Edward Kennedy, Patrick Leahy, and Arlen Specter, passed through the Judiciary Committee in the spring of 2008 by an 11-8 vote. The House version (H.R. 5607) was introduced in March 2008 by Representative Jerrold Nadler and others and passed through the House Judiciary Subcommittee on the Constitution, Civil Rights, and Civil Liberties in September by a 6-3 vote.[35] Action on both bills was postponed in light of a veto threat from President Bush and the 2008 election. But three days after the Obama administration adopted the Bush administration's position in *Mohamed* v. *Jeppesen DataPlan*—its first state secrets case—members of both houses of Congress reintroduced their versions of the State Secrets Protection Act (now renumbered S. 417 and H.R. 984).

Both bills would fix major concerns with how the privilege operates today—clarifying the law, putting control of the privilege back into the hands of the judiciary, preventing executive abuse of the privilege, and securing justice for litigants without compromising national security. Both versions follow a good deal of the general contours of the proposal that we outline below. Where they differ significantly from the suggestions in this chapter or from each other, we note the divergence.[36]

The Bush administration's response to these congressional initiatives was emphatic. On March 31, 2008, Attorney General Michael Mukasey sent a letter to the Senate Judiciary Committee threatening a presidential veto of the legislation and concluding that "the legislation raises serious constitutional questions concerning the ability of the Executive Branch to protect national security information under the well-established standards articulated by the Supreme Court in *Reynolds* and would effect a significant departure from decades of well-settled case law, likely resulting in the disclosure of national security information." The Obama administration has yet to state an official position on the bills, although Vice President Biden supported the State Secrets Protection Act as a member of the Senate Judiciary Committee.

The Constitutionality of Congressional Reform

The Bush administration's (and the Fourth Circuit's) position has little foundation in either the text of the Constitution or the original understanding of the Founders. Although the executive certainly has *some* constitutional authority to protect national security information from harmful disclosure, that authority is not exclusive and does not trump the constitutional powers of the legislative and judicial branches.[37] The Bush administration view derives, rather, from a pair of Supreme Court cases that are not about the state secrets privilege at all. One case, *United States* v. *Nixon*, addresses the presidential communications privilege, which is closely related to, but distinct from, the state secrets privilege. Both are forms of executive privilege, and both allow the executive branch to refuse to produce relevant documents in certain circumstances. But the *Nixon* decision distinguishes the presidential communications privilege from the state secrets privilege,[38] explaining judicial deference in national security matters: "Nowhere in the Constitution . . . is there any explicit reference to a privilege of confidentiality, yet to the extent this interest relates to the effective discharge of a President's powers, it is constitutionally based. . . . He does not place his claim of privilege on the ground they are military or diplomatic secrets. As to these areas of Art. II duties the courts have traditionally shown the utmost deference to Presidential responsibilities."[39] Nowhere does the Court suggest that the president alone controls the meaning, content, and dimension of the state secrets privilege and of the justiciability of federal cases—nor that such control derives from the Constitution. To the contrary, the court "reaffirm[ed] that it is the province and duty of this Court 'to say what the law is' with respect to the claim of privilege presented in this case." Another portion of the opinion explicitly rejects the view that certain suits challenging the president could be nonjusticiable.[40]

The Bush administration relied on *Department of the Navy* v. *Egan* in addition to *Nixon* to support its claim that the president's constitutional authority over national security information is exclusive and trumps the constitutional interests of any other branches.[41] That case concerned the president's authority to determine whether individuals were entitled to security clearances to hold executive branch positions. The Supreme Court noted that the president is "Commander in Chief of the Army and Navy of the United States" and so has authority to classify and control access to information bearing on national security and to determine whether an individual is sufficiently trustworthy to occupy a position in the executive branch. However, Congress had not passed any legislation in that area, so *Navy* v. *Egan* speaks only to the president's constitutional authority in the face of congressional inaction, not to Congress's own powers. The Court specifically notes that its conclusion applies to situations in which Congress is silent: "Thus, unless Congress specifically has provided otherwise, courts traditionally have been reluctant to intrude upon the authority of the Executive in military and national security affairs."[42] As one legal scholar concludes, the case "says nothing about presidential power to act contrary to statute. Nor does it mean that Congress has no overlapping authority in the area."[43]

The executive's claim that it has a constitutional interest in how national security information is protected in judicial proceedings is reasonable and noncontroversial. The problem arises when the executive asserts—as the Bush administration did—that it has an *exclusive* constitutional interest in this issue. Indeed, the Constitution gives Congress and the federal courts explicit authority of their own in this area. For example, Article III explicitly gives the federal courts authority to hear cases and controversies arising under the Constitution and the laws of the United States.

Congress too has several constitutional powers in this area. In addition to the foreign affairs and war powers that the Constitution explicitly gives to Congress, Articles I and III authorize Congress to create jurisdiction—and regulations for procedure and evidence—for the lower federal courts.[44] As the Supreme Court has held, "Congress retains the ultimate authority to modify or set aside any judicially created rules of evidence and procedure that are not required by the Constitution."[45] Since the state secrets privilege is an evidentiary privilege not mandated by the Constitution, it is clearly within Congress's constitutional power to create rules, standards, and procedures for how it operates. To the extent that use of the state secrets privilege interferes with the judiciary's ability to resolve cases or controversies under Article III, creating that sort of legislation is especially appropriate.

Congress's power to confer jurisdiction on the federal courts is a way for Congress to effectively delegate oversight of the execution of its laws. Moreover, it is actually a method of indirect oversight of the executive branch—the jurisdictional grant can ensure that the executive "faithfully executes" the laws passed by Congress.[46] So too, Congress creates the agencies located within the executive branch and defines their authorities and powers. And, of course, the Constitution permits Congress to enact legislation that is "necessary and proper" to achieve the government's goals.

The executive's claims to control over the state secrets privilege are no stronger than those of Congress or the courts. To the extent that an act of Congress abolishes any notion of a state secrets privilege altogether or requires the disclosure to the public of evidence that was properly subject to the privilege, it could conceivably create a constitutional question about the executive's inherent and exclusive authority even in the face of clear congressional action. But the suggestions that we advance here would not come close to that line; nor, for that matter, do the bills pending in the House and Senate.

Proposal for Reform of the Privilege

Congress should enact legislation governing civil cases in which national security issues are involved and give federal courts a set of standards, guidelines, and procedures for handling them. The following suggestions for reform are guided by three overarching goals: protecting the national security of the United States, providing access to justice, and ensuring that government actions are legal and politically accountable. Sensible legislation to achieve those goals would, in turn, be guided by several principles.

First, there should be a strong state secrets privilege in order to protect important national security information in civil litigation. The openness of the U.S. judicial system—which allows civil suits to be filed by individuals and corporations, governments, and organizations, foreign and domestic—should not create a loophole through which enemies of the United States can learn its security secrets and harm the nation. Thus, any reform should be careful to prevent the disclosure of secret information.

Second, the state secrets privilege should provide the maximum level of openness and adversariality possible, consistent with the necessity of protecting sensitive national security information from disclosure. The U.S. legal system is built on a foundation of public, adversarial proceedings that provide equal justice and accountability. Dismissing cases from the very outset is a drastic remedy—it denies justice to parties who believe that they have been harmed and prohibits the judiciary from fulfilling its constitutional role in adjudicating disputes and interpreting the laws. Any reform should therefore allow cases to proceed as far as possible toward complete resolution.

Third, a reformed state secrets privilege should prevent the executive branch from abusing the privilege to conceal illegal activity. Historically, the government has almost always succeeded in its claims of privilege, often without anyone outside of the executive branch ever seeing the allegedly privileged materials.[47] The government incurs little political or litigation cost in asserting the privilege, and as a result, the government naturally tends to overuse it. Legislative reform should prevent the executive branch from using the state secrets privilege to shield its illegal actions or to avoid scrutiny of the legality of its programs.

An Evidentiary Privilege

The state secrets privilege originated as a common law evidentiary privilege, but it has metastasized in recent years into a justiciability rule that precludes judicial consideration of a wide variety of national security cases. The post–Civil War *Totten* case, which originated the justiciability rule, stands for the relatively narrow holding that cases concerning a particular subject matter—secret espionage contracts with the government—cannot be enforced in court. Yet, as explained above, some lower courts, at the government's urging, have viewed not just the *Totten* doctrine but the state secrets privilege itself as a bar to justiciability in some cases.

Congress should clarify that the *Totten* justiciability rule is distinct from the state secrets privilege and that proper application of the privilege is strictly evidentiary. That is, the privilege may be used to prevent secret information from being disclosed as evidence in litigation, but it should not be used to block a lawsuit from proceeding altogether. Litigants should be permitted to make their case with nonprivileged evidence, if they can do so. Other jurisdictional and justiciability rules—such as the political question doctrine, sovereign immunity, standing, mootness, and ripeness—may still block cases from being heard in court. But the state secrets privilege should not operate as an additional bar to judicial consideration of certain cases.

Simple reforms to current procedure can ameliorate the concerns raised by the government in support of a more expansive privilege.[48] One argument advanced for dismissing cases on the basis of the privilege is that the defendant cannot "confirm or deny the key factual premise underlying [p]laintiffs' entire case" without revealing state secrets.[49] Under current rules of civil procedure, the defendant, in answering a complaint, is required to admit or deny allegations, and those responses might disclose important secrets. The Senate version (though not the House version) of the State Secrets Protection Act solves the problem by allowing the government to plead "state secrets" in its answer to a complaint.[50] Thus, if a plaintiff alleges, say, a secret outer space weapons program, the government can respond to the allegations, point by point, by neither confirming particular alleged factual or legal claims nor denying them but by saying instead that its response to the point is protected by the state secrets privilege. That would allow cases in which the privilege has been invoked to proceed beyond the initial pleadings stage, so that plaintiffs can at least make their case with nonprivileged evidence.

The government's second argument for using the state secrets privilege as a justiciability bar is that plaintiffs may, without access to privileged materials, lack the needed evidence to establish their claims. That is, of course, true, but it provides no basis for denying a plaintiff the opportunity to use even nonprivileged evidence to make his case. The obvious course of action is not to dismiss the case from the very beginning but to allow it to move forward with the available evidence. If the plaintiff lacks the evidence to succeed, the court can dismiss for failure to state a claim, the usual procedure when the plaintiff lacks evidence to prove his case. There is no need to dismiss the case at the outset for fear that the court may have to dismiss it later on.

The government's third rationale for claiming nonjusticiability on the basis of the privilege is that evidence that must remain secret may deprive a party of a necessary defense. Rather than force a defendant to litigate with his hands tied behind his back, the government argues that such cases simply should not be heard. That understandable concern is not insurmountable, however, and it does not require that a case be dismissed before considering any evidence. As explained below, Congress can avoid injustice to a defendant who needs privileged evidence to establish a valid defense by other, less-drastic means.

Finally, some have argued that dismissing cases before discovery conserves judicial resources, eliminating the need for a judge to personally examine large amounts of evidence. Once again, however, Congress has other options. Rules allowing special masters, indexing of materials, and document sampling can ease the burden on judges faced with a large volume of potentially secret evidence.

In sum, Congress can prescribe simple paths around the reasons asserted for allowing the state secrets privilege to block consideration of a case entirely. Congress should instead provide courts with the tools necessary to allow national security–related cases to move through the litigation process toward final resolution on the merits.

Judicial Determination of Applicability of the Privilege

Congress also should give courts a greater role in determining what evidence is privileged. Under current doctrine, the executive branch may assert the privilege, but it is the court that decides whether the privilege applies.[51] Nonetheless, the Court in *Reynolds* declined to actually review the evidence in question, and its holding accordingly does not require that a judge actually look at the evidence in making the privilege determination.[52] Following the *Reynolds* decision, some courts today, when presented with a state secrets privilege claim, simply accept the claim based on a government affidavit, abdicating the judicial role to the executive branch.[53]

Several problems arise when the court refrains from actually reviewing the assertedly secret evidence. First, as the recent declassification of the documents in the *Reynolds* case demonstrates, the government can exaggerate the nature of the secrets contained in the evidence. Second, it may be that only parts of the assertedly privileged evidence actually contain secrets, and by reviewing the documents the judge can allow nonsecret portions of the evidence to be used to resolve the case. In *Reynolds,* for example, certain portions of the accident report could have been redacted and the rest made available as evidence. Third, the assertedly secret evidence may reveal criminal or otherwise illegal activities by government officials. Although evidence of illegal activity may not be grounds for disclosing secrets that could harm the nation's security, there are benefits, discussed below, to making judges aware of such information. For those reasons, the executive branch must be required to show the assertedly privileged evidence to the judge and should be penalized by conceding the relevant issue if it chooses not to allow the judge to see the evidence.

The executive branch has objected to the security risk of removing classified documents from their secure locations, transporting them to the (comparatively insecure) courthouse, and allowing judges to review them.[54] The success of federal judges in handling secret evidence in other contexts, however, should assuage that fear: there is no known instance of a federal judge improperly disclosing or failing to secure secret evidence. Nonetheless, Congress should set rules for securing classified materials pending judicial review—for example, by borrowing the procedures used in the CIPA context.[55]

When national security requires it, court proceedings to determine whether assertedly secret evidence is privileged should be closed to the public and open only to the government or persons with appropriate security clearances. Courts should also be required to file all records and opinions related to assertedly privileged evidence under seal, unless making such documents public would not harm national security. Further, all judicial decisions concerning the privilege should be subject to expedited interlocutory appeal. That means that if a careless or rogue judge makes a decision that may endanger national security, the government can quickly appeal that decision to a court of appeals or the Supreme Court.

There are high costs to inadvertently releasing state secrets, and judicial review should take into careful consideration the national security rationale for the government's invocation of the privilege. While some have proposed that judges give no consideration at all to the executive branch's security concerns, others have argued that the executive branch is entitled to the utmost deference in its analysis.[56] The House version of the State Secrets Protection Act, for example, takes the first of these extreme positions, requiring that judges make an "independent assessment" and granting no deference to the executive's determination that evidence contains a state secret.[57] The Senate version, however, sensibly avoids either extreme, specifying that the court should give "substantial" weight to the security analysis of executive branch officials, who by virtue of their position and expertise have a great understanding of security concerns.[58]

Regardless of the level of deference specified in legislation, judges are likely to continue to show great deference to executive claims of privilege. To assist the judge in reaching a proper resolution in proceedings in which the adverse party is not represented, judges should be able to call on specially cleared experts in national security to assist them in determining whether a given piece of allegedly privileged evidence would, in fact, harm national security if released. Federal judges already have legal authority to appoint independent experts to assess government secrecy claims in other contexts,[59] and, though they rarely avail themselves of that authority, experience shows that courts have used it "with great success."[60]

Although the application of the state secrets privilege to items of evidence does not easily lend itself to adversarial proceedings, it is possible to inject some modicum of adversariality into a state secrets privilege determination. The court should hold a hearing that attorneys with appropriate security clearances should be permitted to attend to advocate for their client, subject to a court order that they not reveal anything about the proceeding to the client. It may not always be possible for clients to secure attorneys with the appropriate clearances, in part because individuals who habitually represent perceived enemies of the United States could find it difficult to secure a clearance. The pending House and Senate bills both would respond to that problem by giving judges an increased role in the security clearance process—an approach that has sparked controversy. At this point, it does not seem necessary to address large problems with the security clearance process in order to fix the state secrets privilege, and legislation on the issue would probably go best in a separate bill.[61] As a simpler and more politically palatable alternative to taking on the security clearance process, Congress could allow the court to appoint a guardian *ad litem* to represent the interests of an adverse party from a list of preselected attorneys with the requisite clearances.

Congress can give the courts still other tools to assist them with the administrative burden of determining whether the privilege applies to items of evidence. To assist the judge in understanding the evidence and the probable significance of ordering its public disclosure, the government should be required to file a detailed affidavit explaining how release of the evidence might harm the national security of the United States. The government should also create an index of the documents, similar to a so-called "*Vaughn* index" that courts frequently require in Freedom of Information Act litigation.[62]

When the volume of documents is too great, the judge should review a representative sample of the documents or turn the review over to a special master with the appropriate security clearances. In sum, Congress can provide federal judges the tools that they might need to independently evaluate privilege claims in a responsible manner.

The Definition of State Secrets

Congress should give courts not only clear procedures for reviewing evidence that the government asserts is privileged but also a clear standard for determining what evidence is privileged. The *Reynolds* decision defines the state secrets privilege only vaguely, saying that it applies when "there is a reasonable danger that compulsion of the evidence will expose military matters which, in the interest of national security, should not be divulged."[63] Other courts have allowed the use of the privilege when disclosure "could be seen as a threat to the military or diplomatic interests of the nation,"[64] would be "inimical to the national security,"[65] would "jeopardize national security,"[66] or would "adversely affect national security."[67] What, exactly, constitutes a state secret has been left to the eye of the beholder.

To resolve the uncertainty, Congress should establish a clear definition for a state secret, drawn from the current standards for classifying information: information is properly classified at the lowest level, "confidential," if it "reasonably could be expected to cause damage" to "the national defense or foreign relations of the United States."[68] Both the House and the Senate versions of the bill define a state secret as information that "would be reasonably likely to cause *significant* harm." Although the inclusion of the word "significant" may appear at first to be insubstantial, it raises the specter of a court ordering the release of information properly classified at the confidential level, which is in other contexts a crime.[69] While it is understandable that Congress wants to ensure that the possible harm reaches a certain level of seriousness, the current classification standards sufficiently guard against classifying information based on potential minor or insignificant harms.

Proper classification should not be the only test, because information exists that is not formally classified that might need to be kept secret. For example, it is conceivable that information that has not yet been formally classified due to an oversight or timing may still meet the standard.[70] On the other hand, once classified information has been made public, republication cannot further harm the national security of the United States. That is a tricky point, since an unsubstantiated allegation of a secret fact is not the same as public acknowledgment; the *New York Times* may publish a story alleging the existence of classified information, but the existence of that information may not actually be public unless it is confirmed by an executive official. Still, as with Freedom of Information Act cases, information that has been improperly classified (formally classified but actually containing no legitimate state secret) should be releasable, and a judge would make that determination.[71]

This proposed definition of "state secrets" encompasses not only national defense but also foreign relations. Some observers have suggested that secrets regarding foreign relations should not be included in the state secrets privilege or that they should be included only if the government shows that the harm will be especially significant.[72] However, the classification standard makes no distinction between national defense and diplomatic relations, and the distinction could lead to a confusing effort to determine whether a particular document pertained to national defense or to international relations. In any event, the need to protect sensitive diplomatic secrets is, in many situations, just as strong as the need to protect national defense secrets.

In keeping with the idea of a privilege, this definition should be keyed to individual items of evidence. Thus, a judge may decide to deny a plaintiff access to documents or witness testimony about, say, the government's rendition policy, but he or she cannot simply dismiss all cases involving rendition. Moreover, the privilege should extend only to those portions of an item of evidence that require classification. If the secret portions of a document can be redacted, then the nonsecret portions should not be considered a state secret.[73]

This standard for defining a state secret rejects the notion that evidence that reveals criminal or illegal activity cannot, by definition, be privileged.[74] Although the government could, therefore, use the privilege to shield illegal activity, that concern should not be addressed by defining the scope of the privilege. For one thing, it may be that the illegal activity in question is minor (a government agent parked in the wrong spot) and the benefits of revealing that in public are far outweighed by the harm of disclosing the activity (the government agent was on a secret mission). Moreover, even to determine whether evidence reveals illegal or criminal activity often requires full, adversarial, judicial proceedings.

The Effect of a Finding of the Privilege

Having clarified that the state secrets privilege should apply to particular items of evidence and not whole cases and having suggested appropriate procedures and standards for determining when the privilege applies, Congress should next establish the consequence of a judicial determination that particular items of evidence are privileged. What should happen when evidence that is properly subject to the state secrets privilege is essential to the outcome of a case? If the secret evidence cannot be used, an injustice may go unremedied or an illegal government action may continue. However, if the court discloses the evidence, it would reveal state secrets and thus harm national security.

There is an easy way to mitigate the worst impact of the privilege before making such difficult choices. Often it will be possible to craft substitute evidence that will allow the adverse party the same opportunity to litigate the claim, without endangering national security. Accordingly, whenever national security considerations permit, the judge should order the government to craft substitute evidence, as it does in military courts martial and under CIPA. The substitute evidence could be in the form of an unclassified summary of the evidence, a redacted version of the document, a government admission of the facts that the privileged information tends to prove, or any similar remedy that would allow the litigation to proceed more fairly without the privileged evidence. It should be the executive branch, not the court, that creates the substitute, both for security reasons and for reasons of judicial economy. If the government refuses to provide a plausible substitute as ordered, however, then the court should find against the government on that disputed issue of fact or law.

It will not always be possible, however, to craft substitute evidence without endangering national security. Policymakers have several options for resolving the problem of essential but privileged evidence, none of which is perfect and each of which has advantages and disadvantages:

—*Victory for the plaintiff:* a privilege finding allows the government to suppress the evidence, but the government or defendant must concede any relevant issues of law or fact.

—*Absolute privilege:* a privilege finding causes the evidence to be completely suppressed, and the case proceeds as though the privileged evidence never existed.

—*Qualified privilege:* a privilege finding allows the judge to suppress the evidence only if the judge concludes that the security harm of disclosing the evidence outweighs the justice interests of the litigants.

—*Judicial consideration of the merits:* a privilege finding allows the government to prevent disclosure of the evidence to the nongovernment parties, but the judge may use the privileged evidence in reaching a judgment on the merits of the case for either party.

—*Judicial consideration only for dismissal:* a privilege finding allows the government to prevent disclosure of the evidence, but the judge may consider the privileged evidence for the limited purpose of deciding whether the interests of justice require dismissal of the case.

The first option, *victory for the plaintiff*, would require the defendant to concede any contested issue in exchange for allowing the government to keep secret the privileged evidence. That approach would likely protect security—after all, the government has the option of protecting any information that it wishes to. But by forcing a loss on the defendant, it creates a system in which plaintiffs can win national security cases without any evidence to support their claims.[75] That could create the litigation equivalent of blackmail, as plaintiffs threaten to expose government secrets unless the defendant pays them off with a damages award. Such a result is bad enough when the government itself is the defendant, and it is even more problematic when the defendant is a private party. Forcing the government to choose between national security and its litigation interests seems unjust and would likely subject the public taxpayer to excessive payouts for frivolous lawsuits.

The second option, *the absolute privilege*, would provide for simply excising any privileged evidence from the proceedings and continuing the lawsuit with publicly available information as though the privileged evidence never existed.[76] This option does a good job of protecting security and avoids the risk of litigation blackmail, which makes the first option untenable. Unfortunately, nonprivileged evidence does not always give litigants a fair opportunity to prove their cases. In particular, there are many cases in which the public evidence shows that the plaintiff should win but the privileged evidence shows the defendant (whether a government actor or a third party) to have a complete defense. For example, the telecommunications companies that assisted the government in its domestic surveillance program apparently have documents showing that their actions were authorized by the attorney general and other senior administration officials. Under the absolute privilege (and if Congress had not granted them immunity) they might not have been permitted to use those documents in their defense and might unfairly have had a judgment issued against them. Thus, this option does not always guarantee justice.

In option three, *the qualified privilege*, the finding that an item of evidence meets the standard for the state secrets privilege is not the end of the analysis but the beginning.[77] The judge then has to weigh the government's need for secrecy against the litigant's need for disclosure. If the judge finds that the government's need is weak but the litigant's need is great, the judge may order the government to disclose the secret information. That does a better job than option two of providing justice to litigants, because in some cases the secret evidence can be used. However, because secret evidence would be explicitly revealed in the process, it does a poor job of protecting security. Evidence properly subject to the state secrets privilege should not be revealed through the litigation process. No matter how great a litigant's need for the secret material, no matter how apparently unjust the litigation outcome, and no matter how seemingly trivial the government's need for secrecy might appear in comparison, judges should not be put in the position of openly and explicitly disclosing state secrets.

The fourth option allows the judge, but not the nongovernment parties, access to the privileged information in *deciding the case on the merits.*[78] The judge, having access to the classified information, can determine which party should properly win the lawsuit and rule accordingly.[79] That is the approach adopted in the House bill. Although it is in some ways appealing, it presents several problems. One problem is lack of adversariality at the merits stage. If secret evidence is the basis for judgment on the merits, a defeated plaintiff is unlikely to accept the judgment and appeal will be difficult. More troubling, it could result in a court's using the coercive powers of the state to issue a judgment against a defendant who has not seen the evidence used against him. Although that is not as serious as using secret evidence in the criminal context, it is contrary to American notions of justice. The effect of a judgment on the merits is significant; civil procedure doctrines allow a judgment to bind not only the parties to that particular case but the parties in other cases raising the same issue. Finally, while this option might seem to provide complete protection against the disclosure of state secrets, the decision could inadvertently reveal significant underlying information. For example, if a plaintiff sues the government alleging that he was subject to a secret surveillance program and the court grants an award after having examined secret information—or grants an injunction forcing the government to shut down a program—it is fairly clear that the secret information corroborates (or at least does not refute) the plaintiff's story.

Option five would allow the court to *consider privileged evidence in deciding whether to dismiss a case* if doing so was necessary to prevent a miscarriage of justice—that is, if the defendant needed the privileged evidence to establish a valid defense.[80] This option, adopted in the Senate bill, avoids the disadvantages of many of the other options. First, it avoids the type of injustice that could occur with option two, wherein a private party has evidence revealing a valid defense but cannot use it because the government asserts that it is subject to the privilege. Second, it avoids some of the problems with permitting a judgment on the merits based on privileged evidence. Dismissal of a case does not have the binding effect on the parties involved and others that a judgment on the merits does.[81] In that way, this option reflects the spirit, if not the exact letter, of an evidentiary privilege. Third, it does an excellent job of protecting national security. No privileged evidence is publicly disclosed, and the judge's decision implies less information than would a judgment on the merits, because whether privileged evidence shows a plaintiff's claims to be meritorious is never revealed.

The downside to this approach is its asymmetry: defendants can benefit from judicial consideration of privileged information but plaintiffs cannot. When considering dismissal, the judge would be required to consider all available evidence in the case, and so, in contrast to current judicial interpretations of the privilege, the plaintiff would still have a chance to make his case. But this option makes the policy choice that the security of the nation as a whole trumps the interests of justice in the particular case.

Obtaining Justice When the Privilege Applies

The reforms of the state secrets evidentiary privilege proposed here would go a long way toward allowing the courts to hold government officials accountable for illegal actions and allowing parties who have been wronged to achieve justice. But in some limited cases, in which parties lack access to the evidence that they need to make their case, the privilege will result in civil courts being unable to administer justice and enforce the rule of law.

That does not mean that there is nothing to be done when the executive branch acts illegally or that people and parties cannot be compensated for harms that they have suffered. Rather, through implementing smart and thorough reporting requirements, Congress can ensure that it and other government institutions serve the role that civil courts are unable to fulfill because of the state secrets privilege. For example, Congress should require the Justice Department to report to the congressional judiciary and intelligence committees about its uses of the privilege. The reports should provide sufficient detail on the nature of the cases to allow Congress to understand the security and policy issues at stake and should include the affidavits that the government has provided to the court, with an explanation of why the privilege applies to particular pieces of evidence.[82] This tool is especially important in light of the executive branch's ability, through its classified interpretation of federal statutes and the Constitution, to effectively create its own secret laws.[83] Congress can then use its own legislative or oversight powers to address any concerns that it has. It can also provide compensation to parties who are harmed but, because of the privilege, are unable to obtain recourse through civil litigation. A further benefit of strong reporting requirements is that Congress can stay abreast of how its state secret reforms have been implemented, putting it in a position to make amendments as needed.

In addition, Congress should create a mechanism that allows judges who, after reviewing validly privileged evidence, have concerns that government officials may be involved in criminal or otherwise illegal acts to refer their concerns to Justice Department investigators. While some have suggested that if secret evidence contains evidence of a crime, then the privilege should not apply, that suggestion is unworkable for the reasons explained above. A better alternative would be for courts to have the option to order the attorney general to hand the evidence over to the Justice Department's inspector general for investigation and possible recommendation for prosecution.[84] Although the inspector general works under the attorney general, traditionally the inspector general has a more independent role and often functions as the conscience of the Justice Department. Neither the Senate bill nor the House bill contains such a provision.

The Justiciability Question in National Security Cases

The question still remains of whether some cases are simply inappropriate for judicial resolution because of the risk of disclosure of secret evidence. Under current Supreme Court law, one group of cases—concerning secret espionage contracts—are considered nonjusticiable, in part because of concerns about disclosing secret national security information.

The Court recently considered the breadth and viability of that doctrine. In 2005, in *Tenet* v. *Doe,* it reaffirmed and applied the rule from the 1875 *Totten* case, holding that foreign citizens could not bring suit to enforce a secret espionage contract with the CIA. The *Tenet* Court explained that, even with a state secrets evidentiary privilege in place, the justiciability bar to this type of case remained. As the Court reasoned, "[t]he state secrets privilege and the more frequent use of *in camera* judicial proceedings simply cannot provide the absolute protection we found necessary in enunciating the *Totten* rule. The possibility that a suit may proceed and an espionage relationship may be revealed, if the state secrets privilege is found not to apply, is unacceptable."[85] In a concurring opinion, two justices noted that Congress could choose to "modify the federal common-law rule announced in *Totten*" if it wished to replace the justiciability rule through the more narrowly tailored use of the evidentiary privilege.[86] But the Court itself declined to do so.[87]

As those justices indicated, Congress has a variety of options for deciding which cases the courts may hear. On one hand, Congress could overrule *Totten* and stipulate that all cases are justiciable and that the state secrets evidentiary privilege is sufficient to protect secrets from disclosure. On the other hand, the Constitution gives Congress power to set the jurisdiction of the federal courts to make some types of cases or rights nonjusticiable in court. Congress could therefore expand the *Totten* justiciability doctrine to hold that a broader class of cases—not just espionage contracts—cannot be heard in court. Congress might, for example, decide that any case alleging the existence of a secret intelligence program or a secret weapon design simply cannot be heard in federal court.

In some sense, even the most stringent application of the state secrets privilege will still allow some tiny amount of information to leak out. For example, in order for the executive branch to claim the privilege, it must necessarily imply that secret documents on that topic exist.[88] The mere holding of hearings and consideration of evidence by the court likewise suggest that such evidence exists. If the court dismisses the case on the basis of its conclusion that privileged evidence establishes a valid defense, then outside observers could conclude that the secret documents are of the sort that provide a legal defense to the claim; if the court refuses to dismiss based on the privilege, then outside observers could conclude that the documents do not provide a defense. Generally, the information that leaks through the process will be innocuous and suggest little about the underlying documents. However, in some rare cases, the small amount of information that bleeds through is itself a secret, and it may be appropriate to foreclose all judicial inquiry through a justiciability rule.[89]

Nonetheless, a justiciability rule should be a tool of last resort. As one federal appellate court put it, "[d]enial of the forum provided under the Constitution for the resolution of disputes . . . is a drastic remedy."[90] Civil courts are the best institution available for upholding the rule of law and providing redress to harmed parties. Although Congress could turn itself or its committees into a quasi-court that provides compensation to harmed parties and looks for illegal actions, it does not have the mission, the resources, or the expertise to do so.[91] Moreover, the political constraints on members of Congress—in contrast to those on Article III judges with federal tenure—may render Congress unwilling to make the difficult and unpopular decisions that justice may require. Federal judges are experts at weighing evidence in a case, interpreting the meaning of laws, and adjudicating disputes, and the Constitution assigns the federal courts precisely those functions and goals.

For those reasons, Congress should leave as many cases as possible justiciable in federal courts. After clarifying that the state secrets privilege per se may not be used to dismiss cases, Congress should wait to see how the privilege is used and then decide whether to eliminate, expand, or define the *Totten* justiciability rule. Once it is clear how the evidentiary privilege will be handled, it will be easier to determine those cases in which a justiciability rule is needed to protect national security.

Conclusions

For the reasons explained above, Congress can and should act decisively to create a set of tools, standards, and procedures for federal courts to use in dealing with secret information in civil trials. Congress should pass a law clarifying that the state secrets privilege applies to items of evidence, not entire lawsuits; providing that courts, not the executive branch, should determine whether the privilege attaches to evidence, while giving substantial weight to the advice of national security experts; defining the standard for what is subject to the privilege and what is not; and addressing how cases can best proceed when the state secrets privilege does apply to relevant information in the case.

Such a set of reforms will protect national security, allow courts to administer justice, and ensure accountability to the rule of law. Congress should stay informed about how the procedures are being implemented through the use of strong reporting requirements and should make adjustments as needed. In particular, Congress may wish, over time, to reconsider which class of cases, if any, are fundamentally ill-suited to judicial resolution and so may not be brought in federal court.

The proposed reforms are designed to be implemented within the traditional system of generalist federal courts. However, given that several scholars and commentators have proposed creating a new national security court,[92] it is worth noting that the proposals could be implemented equally well by a specialized court. Were Congress to create a special federal court tasked with hearing preventive detention cases or certain criminal prosecutions, it could also have within its jurisdiction civil lawsuits implicating state and military secrets or perhaps just the task of determining whether the privilege applies. The tools and procedures discussed in this chapter—for example, the use of special masters or guardians *ad litem* with security clearances—would work especially well in a specialized court that could develop a particular expertise in the area.

In civil litigation, as with other matters over which a national security court might have jurisdiction, the creation of such a court is far less important than the specific rules, standards, and procedures that the court uses.

That is to say, whether civil cases with national security implications are heard in traditional federal courts or in a new specialized court, Congress, the executive branch, and judges will face the same trade-offs and policy decisions. Although a specialized national security court that applied the procedures and standards described above would be effective, it is a mistake to replace the adversarial system in state secrets cases with a system modeled on the Foreign Intelligence Surveillance Court, which is open to only one party.[93] While the FISC's one-sided proceedings may be sufficient for foreign intelligence wiretaps, it would not allow individual litigants to make their cases or provide a sufficient check on illegal government activity.[94]

While the policy suggestions discussed above would be appropriate in a specialized national security court, the traditional federal courts are perfectly capable of handling state secrets cases and are well-suited to implementing the recommended policies. Accordingly, whether or not Congress wishes to create a national security court in the long run, it should act now to provide guidance for civil cases involving national security secrets. Then the federal courts can perform their most important job—providing justice and ensuring accountability to the rule of law, confident that they are taking appropriate measures to protect the nation's security.

Notes

1. In fact, the Supreme Court recently declined to review two recent cases in order to reconsider the privilege: *El-Masri* v. *Tenet*, 437 F. Supp. 2d 530 (E.D. Va. 2006), *aff'd* 479 F.3d 296 (4th Cir. 2007), cert. denied, 128 S. Ct. 373 (2007); *ACLU* v. *NSA*, 493 F.3d 644 (6th Cir. 2007), cert. denied, 128 S. Ct. 1334 (2008).

2. See 18 U.S.C. app. 3 §§ 1-16 (2006).

3. In particular, CIPA creates a procedure whereby a court can hold pretrial conferences to handle discovery issues related to classified information (CIPA, section 2); it allows a court to issue protective orders to protect against the disclosure of classified information (section 3); it permits a court, after itself reviewing the relevant evidence, to allow the government to admit contested facts or provide substitute or redacted versions of classified evidence, if disclosing the evidence would "cause identifiable damage to the national security of the United States" and the replacement "will provide the defendant with substantially the same ability to make his defense as would disclosure of the specific classified information" (section 6); it provides that if the government refuses to disclose relevant classified evidence to a defendant or prevents a defendant from using classified evidence in his defense, the court must exclude the evidence, dismiss the indictment, or find against the government on the issue (section 6); it provides for interlocutory appeal of decisions related to classified information (section 7); it

requires creating secure procedures for court handling and storage of classified evidence (sections 8, 9); and it requires reports to Congress on the use of CIPA (section 13).

4. U.S. House of Representatives, Permanent Select Committee on Intelligence, *IC21: The Intelligence Community in the 21st Century* (1996) (www.fas.org/irp/congress/1996_rpt/ic21/ic21013.htm).

5. That would have been Rule 509. See, for example, Revised Draft of Proposed Rules of Evidence for the United States Courts and Magistrates, 51 F.R.D. 315, 375 (1971); U.S. House of Representatives, Committee on the Judiciary, Subcommittee on Reform of Federal Criminal Laws, *Proposed Rules of Evidence*, 93rd Congress, February and March, 1973, pp. 180–81.

6. Federal Rules of Evidence 501; see also Louis Fisher, *In the Name of National Security: Unchecked Presidential Power and the Reynolds Case* (University Press of Kansas, 2006), pp. 140–45; Robert M. Chesney, "State Secrets and the Limits of National Security Litigation," *George Washington Law Review* 75, no. 5/6 (2007), pp. 1249, 1292 n. 251.

7. William G. Weaver and Danielle Escontrias, "Origins of the State Secrets Privilege," working paper, University of El Paso, 2008, p.14 (http://papers.ssrn.com/sol3/papers.cfm?abstract_id=1079364&rec=1&srcabs=1132905).

8. Ibid. at 40.

9. See, generally, *United States* v. *Reynolds,* 345 U.S. 1 (1953).

10. See *United States* v. *Burr,* 25 F. Cas. 30 (C.C.D. Va. 1807) (No. 14,692) (Marshall, Circuit J.); *United States* v. *Burr,* 25 F. Cas. 187, 192-93 (C.C.D. Va. 1807) (No. 14,694); see also Fisher, *supra,* at 212–52; Weaver and Escontrias, *supra,* at 48; Chesney, *supra,* at 1272.

11. Weaver and Escontrias, *supra,* at 51–52.

12. *Totten* v. *United States,* 92 U.S. 105, 106 (1875).

13. Ibid. at 106.

14. *Hepting* v. *AT&T Corporation,* 439 F. Supp. 2d 974 at 991 (N.D. Cal. 2006).

15. Ibid.; see also Weaver and Escontrias, *supra,* at 56, stating that "it is unlikely that the *Totten* Court meant to announce a general power of the president to withhold documents from courts in such a short, unbriefed opinion." But see Chesney, *supra,* at 1277, saying that "the security issue played a critical but unspoken role in . . . the Supreme Court's 1875 decision in *Totten* v. *United States.*"

16. See, generally, *United States* v. *Reynolds,* 345 U.S. 1 (1953).

17. Ibid. at 10.

18. Ibid. at 7–8.

19. Fisher, *supra,* at ix, 165–69.

20. See, for example, *Al-Haramain Islamic Foundation, Inc.* v. *Bush,* 507 F.3d 1190 (9th Cir. 2007).

21. Compare Chesney, *supra,* at 1301, stating that "the available data do suggest that the privilege has continued to play an important role during the Bush administration, but it does not support the conclusion that the Bush administration chooses to resort

to the privilege with greater frequency than prior administrations or in unprecedented substantive contexts" with Robert M. Pallitto and William G. Weaver, "State Secrets and Executive Power," *Political Science Quarterly* 120 (2005), pp. 85–108, which finds increased assertion of the privilege in recent years; Amanda Frost, "The State Secrets Privilege and Separation of Powers," *Fordham Law Review* 75 (2007), pp. 1931–64; and Carrie Newton Lyons, "The State Secrets Privilege: Expanding Its Scope through Government Misuse," *Lewis and Clark Law Review* 11, no. 1 (2007), pp. 99–132. All commentators acknowledge the limitations on this sort of analysis given how many state secrets opinions may be unpublished or otherwise not publicly available.

22. But see Chesney, *supra,* note 6, at 1307.

23. See Frost, *supra,* note 21, at 1939, noting that "the Bush Administration's recent assertion of the privilege differs from past practice in that it is seeking blanket dismissal of every case challenging the constitutionality of specific, ongoing government programs."

24. *ACLU* v. *NSA,* 438 F. Supp. 2d 754, 782 (E.D. Mich. 2006).

25. *ACLU* v. *NSA,* 493 F.3d 644 (6th Cir. 2007), cert. denied February 19, 2008.

26. Ibid. at 653.

27. See Government Motion to Dismiss at 17-18 and n.8, *Hepting* v. *AT&T,* 439 F. Supp. 2d at 985 (www.eff.org/files/filenode/att/GovMotiontoDismiss.pdf); see also Government Statement of Interest, *Hepting* v. *AT&T* (www.eff.org/files/filenode/att/USA_statement_of_interest.pdf).

28. *In re* Baycol Products Litigation 495 F. Supp. 2d 977, 991-92 (D. Minn. 2007).

29. The Ninth Circuit, in April 2007, broke off one case, *Al-Haramain Islamic Foundation, Inc.* v. *Bush,* 507 F.3d 1190, 1200 (9th Cir. 2007), because the government had inadvertently sent the plaintiff a document notifying it that its communications were subject to surveillance. The Ninth Circuit reached a decision in that case, holding that even though the government had disclosed the document, it remained protected by the state secrets privilege.

30. FISA Amendments Act of 2008, H.R. 6304, § 201.

31. *In re* National Security Agency Telecommunications Records Litigation (N.D. Cal. 2009).

32. See, generally, *El-Masri* v. *U.S.* 479 F.3d 296 (4th Cir. 2007).

33. Ibid. at 308.

34. In the interest of full disclosure: we consulted with the Senate Judiciary Committee on its version of the bill.

35. See, generally, State Secrets Protection Act of 2008, S. 2533, 110th Congress; State Secrets Protection Act of 2008, H.R. 5607, 110th Congress.

36. One major difference between the bills—unrelated to the actual workings of the privilege—is that while both bills apply to pending cases, the House bill would apply retroactively to some cases that have already been concluded and resolved. Therefore, if enacted quickly, the House bill could help resolve some of the ongoing issues related to surveillance and renditions described above. But, of course, retroactive application

would strengthen opposition to the bill and make it politically more difficult to execute, while also raising questions of fairness.

37. Neil Kinkopf, "The State Secrets Problem: Can Congress Fix It?" *Temple Law Review* 80, no. 2 (Summer 2007), p. 489, contending that the proper framework is not the unitary executive theory but the *Youngstown* case.

38. Charles Alan Wright and Kenneth W. Graham Jr., *Federal Practice and Procedure,* vol. 26A § 5673 (Eagan: West, 2008), noting that "the better view is that it is limited to 'executive communications,' though that still leaves much room for argument. Some think the privilege is limited to communications between the president and his 'advisors.' Even this is not very precise."

39. *U.S. v. Nixon* 418 U.S. 683, 710 (1974).

40. Ibid. at 692–93. Elsewhere, moreover, the *Nixon* Court rejected the very premise of the Bush administration's view that it alone could control the privilege: "In the performance of assigned constitutional duties each branch of the government must initially interpret the Constitution, and the interpretation of its powers by any branch is due great respect from the others. The President's counsel, as we have noted, reads the Constitution as providing an absolute privilege of confidentiality for all Presidential communications. Many decisions of this Court, however, have unequivocally reaffirmed the holding of *Marbury* v. *Madison,* that '[it] is emphatically the province and duty of the judicial department to say what the law is.'"

41. *Department of the Navy* v. *Egan,* 484 U.S. 518, 527 (1988), stating that "authority to protect [national security] information falls on the President as head of the Executive Branch and as Commander in Chief."

42. Ibid. at 530.

43. Kinkopf, *supra,* note 37, at 498.

44. U.S. Const. art. III, § 2, cl. 2, expressly granting Congress the power to enact "Regulations" concerning the jurisdiction of Federal courts.

45. *Dickerson* v. *United States,* 530 U.S. 428, 437 (2000); see also *Sibbach* v. *Wilson & Co.,* 312 U.S. 1, 9-10 (1941), giving the opinion that "Congress has undoubted power to regulate the practice and procedure of federal courts, and may exercise that power by delegating to this or other federal courts authority to make rules not inconsistent with the statutes or Constitution of the United States."

46. See Frost, *supra,* note 21.

47. As one scholarly study observes, "in practical terms the state secrets privilege never fails; in no one case has a court ordered the disclosure of classified material to the public or to a public forum, even if the reasons for classifying the material are quite dubious." Weaver and Escontrias, *supra,* note 7 at 6.

48. The government has generally advanced three reasons why the state secrets privilege itself acts as a justiciability rule and requires dismissal of cases: "(1) the very subject matter of this case is a state secret; (2) plaintiffs cannot make a *prima facie* case for their claims without classified evidence and (3) the privilege effectively deprives

AT&T of information necessary to raise valid defenses." *Hepting* v. *AT&T Corp.* 439 F. Supp. 2d at 985.

49. *Hepting* v. *AT&T Corp.* 439 F. Supp. 2d at 985 (N.D. Cal. 2006); see also Memorandum of Points and Authorities in Support of the Motion by Intervenor United States to Dismiss or, in the Alternative, for Summary Judgment at 11-12, *El-Masri* v. *Tenet,* 437 F. Supp. 2d 530 (No. 01417), stating that "the plaintiff's claim in this case plainly seeks to place at issue alleged clandestine foreign intelligence activity that may neither be confirmed nor denied in the broader national interest."

50. See S. 2544, § 4053, procedures for answering a complaint.

51. Ibid. at 8, noting that "the court itself must determine whether the circumstances are appropriate for the claim of privilege, and yet do so without forcing a disclosure of the very thing the privilege is designed to protect"; ibid. at 10–11, stating that "judicial control over the evidence in a case cannot be abdicated to the caprice of executive officers."

52. "[W]e will not go so far as to say that the court may automatically require a complete disclosure to the judge before the claim of privilege will be accepted in any case. It may be possible to satisfy the court, from all the circumstances of the case, that there is a reasonable danger that compulsion of the evidence will expose military matters which, in the interest of national security, should not be divulged. When this is the case, the occasion for the privilege is appropriate, and the court should not jeopardize the security which the privilege is meant to protect by insisting upon an examination of the evidence, even by the judge alone, in chambers." Ibid. at 11. Some judges have balanced the needs of the litigants against the apparent need for secrecy in determining whether to review the evidence. For example, *N.S.N. International Industry* v. *E.I. Dupont de Nemours & Co.,* 140 F.R.D. 275 (S.D.N.Y. 1991), which notes that "when a litigant must lose if the claim is upheld and the government's assertions are dubious in view of the nature of the information requested and the circumstances surrounding the case, careful *in camera* examination of the material is not only appropriate but obligatory. . . . When the litigant requesting the information had made only a trivial showing of need for it and circumstances of the case point to a significant risk of serious harm if the information is disclosed, the trial judge should evaluate (and uphold) the privilege claim solely on the basis of the government's public representations, without an in camera examination of the documents."

53. See, for example, *Nejad* v. *United States,* 724 F. Supp. 753 (C.D. Cal. 1989), dismissing a case based on "the Executive's claim that disclosure of [AEGIS] technology on the public record could be harmful to the national security" without examining the relevant documents; *Northrop Corp.* v. *McDonnell Douglas Corp.,* 243 U.S. App. D.C. 19 (D.C. Cir. 1984), stating that "although an *in camera* inspection might have been appropriate, we cannot say that the trial court erred when it decided the balance tipped in favor of the government, and quashed the subpoena without conducting an *in camera* review of the documents."

54. See Committee on Communications and Media Law, *The Press and the Public's First Amendment Right of Access to Terrorism on Trial: A Position Paper* (New York: Association of the Bar of the City of New York), p. 50, noting that the executive's primary justification for holding closed trials of terrorism suspects is "protection of classified and national security information" (www.abcny.org/pdf/report/Medial%20Law%20 Comm%20Report%20doc.pdf).

55. See CIPA § 9.

56. Letter from Michael B. Mukasey, attorney general, to Patrick J. Leahy, chairman of the Senate Judiciary Committee, March 31, 2008 (http://www.usdoj.gov/archive/ ola/views-letters/110-2/03-31-08-ag-ltr-re-s2533-state-secrets.pdf).

57. H.R. 5607 § 6(c).

58. S. 2533, § 4045(e)(3).

59. See Meredith Fuchs and G. Gregg Webb, "Greasing the Wheels of Justice: Independent Experts in National Security Cases," *American Bar Association National Security Law Report* 28, no. 4 (November 2006), pp. 1, 3–5.

60. Meredith Fuchs, "Judging Secrets: The Role Courts Should Play in Preventing Unnecessary Secrecy," *Administrative Law Review* 58 (2006), pp. 131, 174; see also *Ellsberg* v. *Mitchell,* 709 F.2d 51, 64 (D.C. Cir. 1983), encouraging "procedural innovation" in addressing state secrets issues; *Al-Haramain Islamic Foundation* v. *Bush,* 451 F. Supp. 2d 1215, 1233 (D. Ore. 2006), suggesting the appointment of a national security expert as a special master to assist in assessing the effects of disclosure; Robert P. Deyling, "Judicial Deference and De Novo Review in Litigation over National Security Information under the Freedom of Information Act," *Villanova Law Review* 37 (1992), pp. 105–11, evaluating employing special masters in FOIA national security cases.

61. See Mukasey, *supra,* note 56, expressing concern about addressing security clearances in state secrets legislation; H.R. 5607, § 5(e), requiring timely security clearance processing and other measures; S. 2533 § 4052(c), similar to H.R. 5607.

62. See *Vaughn* v. *Rosen,* 484 F.2d 820 (D.C. Cir. 1973).

63. 345 U.S. 1, 10 (1953).

64. See, for example, *Halkin* v. *Helms,* 223 U.S. App. D.C. 254 (D.C. Cir. 1982).

65. See, for example, *In re* Sealed Case, 494 F.3d 139, 142 (D.C. Cir. 2007); *In re United States,* 872 F.2d 472, 474 (D.C. Cir. 1989).

66. See, for example, *Zuckerbraun* v. *General Dynamics Corporation,* 935 F.2d 544, 546-47 (2d Cir. 1991).

67. See, for example, *Ellsberg* v. *Mitchell,* 709 F.2d 51, 56 (D.C. Cir. 1983).

68. George W. Bush, "Further Amendment to Executive Order 12958, as Amended, Classified National Security Information," Executive Order 13292, March 28, 2003 (www.archives.gov/isoo/policy-documents/eo-12958-amendment.pdf).

69. Note that our proposed definition does not explicitly say that all properly classified materials should qualify for the privilege but instead defines a "state secret" in terms of current classification standards. Since the executive branch controls the definitions of

the various classification levels, it is conceivable that explicitly tying the state secrets privilege to the standard in an executive order could lead to abuse.

70. In some circumstances, the absence of classified information is itself information that should be considered a state secret. For instance, the government may want to conceal that investigations into an assassination have discovered nothing about who is responsible. In such cases—or simply to confuse foreign enemies—the government should be permitted to file a state secrets affidavit explaining to the judge that it would like to invoke the state secrets privilege, even though the government may have no responsive documents.

71. Courts generally defer to executive branch expertise in assessing whether documents are properly classified for the purposes of FOIA exemption. But see *Weatherhead* v. *United States,* No. 95-519, slip op. at 5-6 (E.D. Wash. Mar. 29, 1996), reconsideration granted in pertinent part (E.D. Wash. Sept. 9, 1996), upholding classification upon *in camera* inspection, rev'd, 157 F.3d 735 (9th Cir. 1998), vacated and case remanded for dismissal, 528 U.S. 1042 (1999).

72. See, for example, Section of Individual Rights and Responsibilities, Association of the Bar of the City of New York, "American Bar Association Resolution on the State Secrets Privilege, Revised Report 116A" (Chicago: American Bar Association, 2007) (www.fas.org/sgp/jud/statesec/aba081307.pdf).

73. According to the "mosaic theory" of evidence, many individual seemingly innocuous pieces of information, when taken together, may in some situations reveal a secret. The danger posed by a particular piece of information cannot always be evaluated without reference to other secret information, and the privilege should therefore extend to materials that, taken together, pose a risk to national security. Our proposed definition of state secrets requires that the government make the case, for each piece of evidence, that it is so inextricably linked to secret information that its revelation would harm national security.

74. See, for example, *Black* v. *Sheraton Corporation of America,* 371 F. Supp. 97, 102 (D.D.C. 1974), stating that "any evidence which concerns the government's illegal acts are not privileged."

75. In some ways, this is the model that Congress enacted for criminal trials in CIPA, in which the government sometimes must choose between dropping the indictment and sharing classified evidence with the defendant. The contexts are different, though, and what is an appropriate trade-off when the government wishes to convict a person of a crime may not be appropriate in the civil context.

76. That is the approach taken, for example, in *Monarch Assurance P.L.C.* v. *United States,* 36 Fed. Cl. 324 (1996). See also *Jabara* v. *Kelley,* 75 F.R.D. 475 (E.D. Mich., 1977), noting that "the consequences of upholding a claim of privilege based upon military or state secrets are grave since the privilege absolutely protects against disclosure."

77. That is the approach taken with other executive privileges, such as "claims of privilege that have been asserted to protect from disclosure the identity of governmental

informers, information pertaining to ongoing criminal investigations, administrative reports and opinions that reflect policy as distinguished from factual information, and matters of tactical intelligence involving current investigatory techniques." *Jabara* v. *Kelley,* 75 F.R.D. 475, 481 (E.D. Mich. 1977).

78. See, for example, *Bareford* v. *General Dynamics Corporation,* 973 F.2d 1138, noting that "if the privilege deprives the defendant of information that would otherwise give the defendant a valid defense to the claim, then the court may grant summary judgment to the defendant"; *In re* United States, 872 F.2d 472, 476 (D.C. Cir.), cert. denied sub nom. *United States* v. *Albertson,* 493 U.S. 960 (1989); *Molerio* v. *Federal Bureau of Investigation,* 749 F.2d 815, 825 (D.C. Cir. 1984).

79. In either this option or option one, the court may decide to alter the rules to influence the outcome rather than decide the outcome directly. For instance, the court may shift the burden of proof or establish a rebuttable presumption that favors the aggrieved party. See, for example, *Halkin* v. *Helms,* 223 U.S. App. D.C. 254, which notes that "the question then becomes whether the case . . . should proceed under rules that have been changed to accommodate the loss of the otherwise relevant evidence. Such changes could compensate the party 'deprived' of his evidence by, for example, altering the burden of persuasion upon particular issues, or by supplying otherwise lost proofs through the device of presumptions or presumptive inferences."

80. That is the approach taken, for example, in *Molerio* v. *FBI,* 242 U.S. App. D.C. 137, 749 F.2d 815, 825 (D.C. Cir. 1984), stating that if the state secrets privilege so hampers the defendant in establishing a valid defense that the trier of fact is likely to reach an erroneous conclusion, dismissal is appropriate.

81. There are actually two classes of dismissal, with and without prejudice. When a case is dismissed without prejudice, the plaintiff can bring the case again, should new evidence arise; cases dismissed with prejudice cannot be brought again. Clearly, dismissal makes the most sense if it is without prejudice, so that the aggrieved party can bring suit if information is declassified in the future. Unfortunately, the Senate version does not specify that any dismissal should be without prejudice.

82. The House bill may go too far on this point, requiring the executive branch to disclose items of evidence to any member of certain committees who requests to see them. That is likely to prompt strong political and constitutional objection from the executive branch and may lead to a serious burden on the executive branch—through fishing expeditions by individual members of Congress—that outweighs the oversight benefit.

83. See U.S. Senate, Committee on the Judiciary, Subcommittee on the Constitution, Civil Rights and Property Law, *Secret Law and the Threat to Democratic and Accountable Government,* 110th Cong., 2nd sess., April 30, 2008 (www.fas.org/ sgp/congress/2008/law.html); see also Justin Florence, "Secret Laws, Secret Courts, Secret Constitution," American Constitution Society Blog, May 14, 2008 (www.acs blog.org/guest-bloggers-secret-laws-secret-courts-secret-constitution.html).

84. "The Office of the Inspector General (OIG) consists of an immediate office, which is comprised of the Inspector General, the Deputy Inspector General, and the Office of the General Counsel and five major components, each of which is headed by an Assistant Inspector General. The five OIG components are: the Audit Division, which conducts, reports on and tracks the resolution of financial and performance audits of organizations, programs and functions within the Department; the Investigations Division, which investigates alleged violations of fraud, abuse and integrity laws that govern DOJ employees, operations, grantees and contractors; the Evaluation and Inspections Division, which provides the Inspector General with an alternative mechanism to traditional audit and investigative disciplines to assess Department of Justice (Department) programs and activities; the Oversight and Review Division (O&R), which investigates sensitive allegations involving Department employees, often at the request of the Attorney General, senior Department managers, or Congress; and the Management and Planning Division, which provides the Inspector General with advice on administrative and fiscal policy and assists OIG components by providing services in the areas of planning, budget, finance, quality assurance, personnel, training, procurement, automated data processing, computer network communications and general support." Office of the Inspector General, "OIG Organization," U.S. Department of Justice (www.usdoj.gov/oig/offices/organization.htm).

85. *Tenet* v. *Doe*, 544 U.S. 1, 11 (2005).

86. Ibid. at 11 (Stevens, J., concurring).

87. The *Tenet* Court likewise distinguished a 1988 case, *Webster* v. *Doe*, in which the Court permitted judicial review of a CIA employee's constitutional discrimination claim. As the Court explained in *Tenet*, "there is an obvious difference, for purposes of *Totten*, between a suit brought by an acknowledged (though covert) employee of the CIA and one filed by an alleged former spy. . . . Only in the latter scenario is *Totten*'s core concern implicated: preventing the existence of the plaintiff's relationship with the government from being revealed." *Tenet* v. *Doe*, 544 U.S. at 10, discussing *Webster* v. *Doe*, 486 U.S. 592 (1988).

88. The government may be able to dampen that effect, in part, by filing spurious state secrets privilege claims. The absence of information on a topic may also be a state secret and so properly privileged.

89. We note that even were Congress to pass legislation clearly overturning the *Totten* justiciability doctrine in all circumstances, the government could still prevent the disclosure of state secrets through the (more expensive) option of settling cases at an early stage. To avoid revealing information through which cases it settles, the government could always oversettle. Our suggestions are designed to protect national security, even at the occasional expense of justice, and that will often leave private parties who have been harmed by the government without redress. We believe that such sacrifices are merited in order to protect the security of the whole. Likewise, if the government chooses to settle a range of cases, including some that are meritless, in order to avoid disclosing information, that too is for the benefit of the whole.

90. *In re* United States, 872 F.2d 472, 477 (D.C. Cir. 1989). Note that internal citations and quotation marks are omitted.

91. Note also that any public admission by Congress that the United States should compensate a particular person would also tend to confirm any allegations in the same way as a judicial holding.

92. See, for example, Jack Goldsmith and Neal Katyal, "The Terrorists' Court," *New York Times,* July 11, 2007.

93. See Chesney, *supra,* note 6, at 1313.

94. See D. A. Jeremy Telman, "Our Very Privileged Executive: Why The Judiciary Can (and Should) Fix the State Secrets Privilege," *Temple Law Review* 80, no. 2 (2007), pp. 499, 509–10.

STUART TAYLOR JR. *and* BENJAMIN WITTES

9

Looking Forward, Not Backward: Refining U.S. Interrogation Law

The worldwide scandal arising from the abuse of prisoners in Abu Ghraib, Guantánamo, Afghanistan, and secret CIA prisons during the Bush administration has been a stain on the honor of the United States and a catastrophe for its national image. Understandably eager to save innocent lives by breaking the resistance of a few al Qaeda leaders, Bush and his aides went way overboard. Instead of crafting special rules to allow for exceptionally tough interrogations of those few leaders and maintaining strict limits to ensure that those interrogations stopped short of torture, the Bush team chose to gut the laws, rules, and customs restraining coercive interrogation. They did so with a public bravado and an ostentatious disregard for international law that both scandalized world opinion and sent dangerous signals down through the ranks. Those signals contributed to lawlessness and to confusion about what the rules were supposed to be. They helped open the floodgates both to CIA excesses widely seen as torture and to brutal treatment by the military of hundreds of low-level and mistakenly arrested innocent individuals in Iraq and Afghanistan and of an unknown number of prisoners at Guantánamo. All that inspired widespread international and domestic revulsion and gravely undermined the political and moral standing of the United States and its ability to work with some allied governments.

The policies that led to the scandal were largely abandoned long ago by the Bush administration itself. Years before President Obama took power, the former president's lawyers stopped claiming for Bush the power to nullify, in

On August 24, 2009, as this volume was going to press, the Obama administration confirmed as its settled policy the ban on all forms of coercive interrogation that it had tentatively adopted in January. It also released a redacted version of a 2004 CIA inspector general's report and other documents including new details about the agency's brutal interrogations under President Bush and the information obtained. We have inserted brief mentions of these events where appropriate.

effect, the federal law that makes torture a crime. While the administration did not concede that certain highly coercive methods—including waterboarding, an infamous form of simulated drowning—are banned under current law, the CIA had discontinued use of that method after employing it to help break three al Qaeda figures in 2002 and 2003. And, in the Detainee Treatment Act in 2005 and in the Military Commissions Act of 2006, Congress adopted new restrictions on interrogation. The military, with sharp prodding from Congress and the Supreme Court, got out of the coercive interrogation business entirely in 2006.

But Congress, the media, and other critics have continued to focus so intensely on the sins of the past, particularly in light of President Obama's release of the prior administration's formal legal opinions on coercive interrogation, as to neglect serious analysis of what is today a far more important question: What rules should govern future interrogations? In particular, what should the U.S. government do the next time that it captures known terrorist leaders who are likely to possess information that could save lives but who are fiercely determined not to divulge that information? Should the law prohibit CIA interrogators from using any coercion at all, as the Democratic-led Congress voted to do in 2008, and thereby reclaim some international good will by disavowing what may prove to be an important safeguard against terrorist mass murders? If not, then exactly how much coercion should Congress allow, using what interrogation methods, on what kinds of prisoners, and with what high-level approvals and congressional oversight?

The new administration has so far offered answers to those questions that are at once bold and tentative. They are bold in the sense that they represent a virtually complete repudiation of what remained of the Bush administration's policies. The prior administration still permitted the CIA to hold detainees in secret sites away from the prying eyes of the International Committee of the Red Cross (ICRC) and to subject them to interrogation tactics not authorized by the military and—in some cases—in violation of, or at least in grave tension with, extant law. The Obama administration, by contrast, has revoked the CIA's standing detention authority and required that it comply with military interrogation policies, including an instruction not to "threaten or coerce" detainees. It has required ICRC access for all detainees. Whereas Bush spoke proudly and publicly of the "tough" interrogations that he authorized, Obama emphasized in his inaugural address that "we reject as false the choice between our safety and our ideals" and stressed in his first address to Congress that "living our values doesn't make us weaker, it makes us safer and it makes us stronger. And that is why I can stand here tonight and say without exception or equivocation that the United States of America does not torture."[1] He also stressed in a press conference in April 2009 that he did not regard coercive interrogation as having netted the United States intelligence benefits. "I put an end to these practices," he said. "I am absolutely convinced that it was the right thing to do, not because there might not have been information that was yielded by these various detainees who were subjected to this treatment, but because we could have gotten this information in other ways, in ways that were consistent with our values, in ways that were consistent with who we are."[2]

On the other hand, Obama's new policies are tentative both in the sense that they are nonstatutory—accomplished through an executive order, not changes in the law itself—and in the sense that they may prove temporary. While Obama has created a hard-line anti-coercion policy for now, nothing prevents him—or his successor—from giving the CIA more flexibility in new interrogation rules down the road. And Obama is free to make secret exceptions to his order if a crisis arises in which he, like Bush, may consider coercion necessary.

This chapter deals fundamentally with the prospective question of how to amend U.S. interrogation law to balance the need to avoid Bush-like excesses against the need to get intelligence from captured terrorists. It begins by examining some of the deceptions and evasions that frustrate candid discussion of coercive interrogation and torture. It then reviews the post–September 11 evolution of Bush administration policies on interrogation, the experiences of the CIA and the military, and the lessons to be learned from those experiences. It focuses, in particular, on two questions: Has coercive interrogation saved lives that could not have been saved through conventional questioning, either in the post–September 11 context or earlier in history? And is it inevitable that coercive methods, once allowed, will spin out of control? It then turns to a discussion of why, in our judgment, it is essential for Congress and the president to craft decent, effective, democratically legitimate, internationally respectable interrogation laws for the future; of what those rules should forbid and authorize; and of how to handle exceptionally exigent circumstances that may call for violating the usual rules.

There is no one best legal regime. Each possible approach to the questions raised has real costs. But the United States should be able to improve on the legacy of Bush. It should also be able to improve on the approach of human rights groups such as the American Civil Liberties Union, Amnesty International, and Human Rights Watch—and of Congress and the Obama administration to date. Congress has moved from a what-me-worry passivity about coercive practices, to passing in December 2005 a law imposing virtuous-sounding but vague restrictions on interrogators without giving them clear guidance, to voting in 2008 for far more stringent restrictions (a bill that Bush vetoed) without serious discussion of the costs and benefits of any of the possible approaches. And while the Obama administration has not embraced such legislation, the policies that the new president has adopted do, in effect, the same thing.

We, by contrast, favor a regime characterized by relatively stringent baseline rules but with flexibility built in for the most wrenching, highest-stakes cases. Until the public record offers a firmer sense than it now does of the effectiveness of both mildly and highly coercive interrogation techniques, any responsible policy proposal will necessarily be somewhat tentative. And our proposal could shift in a more or less restrictive direction in response to changes in the understanding of what "works" in interrogation. That said, in our view, it is essential that U.S. interrogation policy be anchored in law. And, at least as the record currently stands, that law should have the following contours:

—The military should continue to ban all coercive interrogation, and the CIA should avoid it except in extraordinary circumstances, with vigorous congressional oversight to ensure compliance.

—The CIA should retain the option of using mildly coercive methods such as threats, isolation, and disruption of normal sleep patterns for carefully limited periods of time, on high-value prisoners who defy standard interrogation methods.

—Highly coercive interrogation that falls short of torture should be off limits even for the CIA, with an important exception: Congress should reserve to the president and the attorney general the power to authorize the CIA to use highly coercive methods such as sleep deprivation and forced standing on a very small number of high-value prisoners if, and only if, the president and attorney general comply with detailed procedures to ensure restraint and accountability.[3]

—Torture should remain a crime in all circumstances, and the definition of torture should be tightened to reflect a more commonsense understanding of morally unacceptable coercion. If an emergency so dire should arise that the president or a subordinate feels compelled to cross (or arguably cross) the line into authorizing illegal torture, his only option should be to violate (or arguably violate) the law and chance the consequences.

Deceptions and Evasions

It's not easy to have an honest conversation about this subject. The main reason is that many people are deeply conflicted, in part as a matter of morality and in part because very little is known about how likely it is that coercion, up to and including torture, could elicit otherwise unobtainable, potentially life-saving information.

The idea of torturing or brutalizing any fellow human being fills civilized people with visceral horror—even more horror, for many, than the idea of dropping bombs from on high that will bring a torturous, agonizing death to countless innocent people. Torture is condemned by the moral codes of all civilized societies. It degrades and can do severe psychological damage to the torturers as well as those tortured. The natural human impulse is to say "never." But many people also have heard of or can imagine dire circumstances involving so urgent a need to extract lifesaving information from individuals who refuse to give it that they might say, "In this case, anything goes." Indeed, when Americans were asked in an October 2005 Pew poll about whether "the use of torture against suspected terrorists in order to gain important information" could be justified, only 27 percent said "never."[4] And in an April 2009 CNN/Opinion Research Corporation poll of 2,019 Americans—at a time of vast and sometimes blood-curdling publicity about harsh interrogations by the Bush administration—50 percent approved the Bush approach while 46 percent disapproved, even though 60 percent said that some of the Bush procedures were a "form of torture."[5] Moral absolutes tend to founder in the turbulent seas of real life. Many people therefore try to have it both ways by resorting to various deceptions, including self-deceptions, and evasions.

President Bush's deceptions were especially large. He insisted not only that "we do not torture" but also that his policies treated all prisoners "humanely,"[6] even as his top aides with his knowledge secretly approved such clearly inhumane, highly coercive interrogation methods as waterboarding to break suspected al Qaeda operatives.[7] Vice President Cheney trivialized waterboarding, versions of which were known at least since the Spanish Inquisition as an agonizing and terrifying ordeal, as a mere "dunk in the water."[8]

Human rights activists and many in the media and elsewhere resort to various deceptions and evasions of their own to depict as virtually cost-free their position that U.S. forces should never use coercive interrogation.[9] Many absolutists seek to preempt candid, fact-based analysis of costs and benefits by glibly declaring that even apart from moral scruples, coercive interrogation is never—or almost never—the most effective way to obtain lifesaving information. Many label as "torture" even interrogation methods that inflict only mild discomfort, not severe pain, on high-level terrorists against whom the government has a mountain of evidence. Many who accuse Bush and his top aides of war crimes also gloss over the difficulty of the choices that they faced, while misleadingly pretending that highly coercive interrogations are virtually unprecedented in U.S. history and that they have long been clearly illegal under both domestic and international law.

Congress also has been less than forthright. Its leaders and members raised no serious complaints about coercive interrogation for years after September 11, despite CIA briefings of leading figures in both parties. When Senator John McCain and others then pushed through legislation in December 2005 banning the CIA from using "cruel, inhuman and degrading treatment" of prisoners under interrogation, they defined those terms far more narrowly than their colloquial meaning would suggest, even as they tacitly reserved the right to trash the CIA if it failed to squeeze detained terrorists hard enough to prevent attacks. Worse, when the Democratic congressional leadership pushed through in February 2008, over McCain's objection, a provision that would effectively prohibit the CIA from using even mild forms of coercion, almost all supporters of the ban grossly misled the public by concealing its unprecedented sweep.[10]

The media have misled the public too. Almost without exception, the major news organs misrepresented the no-coercion-at-all provision as banning only the use of waterboarding, beatings, frigid cells, sexual humiliation, and other extremely coercive methods.[11] In fact, the ban would also have extended even to interrogation methods such as angry yelling, denying or threatening to deny hot food rations, and any and all other methods that "threaten or coerce" prisoners in any way—no matter how dire and urgent the calamities that might be averted. Bush's veto of the bill drew widespread denunciation in the media, almost all of which again concealed the radical scope and novelty of the proposed ban.[12] When Obama in effect implemented that sweeping prohibition through his executive order, the press once again largely ignored the magnitude of the policy change, treating it as a rejection of extreme interrogation techniques rather than a requirement that the CIA use the Army Field Manual, as revised in 2006, to make interrogations gentler than ever before.

Those of us who come down somewhere between the Bush administration and the human rights activists are tempted to slip into evasions of our own. We abhor torture but want some latitude for the CIA to use highly coercive methods if necessary to squeeze timely, lifesaving information out of the few prisoners most likely to have it. One temptation is to disavow "torture," which is a federal crime, while gravitating toward very narrow definitions of it so as to leave room for highly coercive interrogations in the most dire and urgent emergencies. (That was carried to extremes in the infamous August 1, 2002, Bush Justice Department "torture memo" that leaked in 2004.) A second temptation is to cling to the perhaps unrealistic hope that a limited dose of coercion might break the resistance of and extract lifesaving information from hardened terrorists without crossing the line by inflicting pain so severe as to constitute torture. A third temptation is to gloss over the difficulty of drawing clear lines between the theoretically small number of prisoners who seem *most likely* to have lifesaving information and the many who *just might* have it.

The hypothetical ticking–time bomb scenario, in which a terrorist is known in advance to have information that could stop an imminent attack, is dismissed by many human rights activists and academics as an "intellectual fraud," as one put it.[13] In fact, coercive interrogation has at times prevented bombs from going off. But those occasions have been so rare as to be a dangerous model for policymakers to follow.[14] To avoid any kind of deceptions or evasions, we begin by defining our terms precisely. For the purposes of this chapter,

—"Torture" refers only to government use of interrogation methods that fit the narrow definition in a 1994 U.S. law criminalizing any "act . . . specifically intended to inflict severe physical or mental pain or suffering . . . upon another person within [an agent's] custody or physical control." It is not torture under U.S. or international law to inflict pain that is not quite "severe." Also, in an important narrowing of both international and popular definitions, the 1994 U.S. law defines "severe mental pain or suffering" as "the prolonged mental harm" caused by methods including "the threat of imminent death" and "procedures calculated to disrupt profoundly the senses or personality."[15] The definition in the United Nations Convention against Torture and Other Cruel, Inhuman, or Degrading Treatment or Punishment, which governs the U.S. government's international law obligations, contains no such limitation on the meaning of "severe mental pain or suffering."[16] That means that some interrogation methods that amount to torture under international law and in the common understanding of the term are not criminally prosecutable as torture under U.S. law.

—"Cruel, inhuman, or degrading" treatment (often abbreviated to CID and in this chapter also referred to as "near-torture") refers to highly coercive methods that are not so painful as to be torture. CID is banned by the same UN convention that bans torture[17] and also by the 1949 Geneva Conventions. But U.S. domestic law—although not the Obama policy—allows the CIA sometimes to use methods that many would call cruel, inhuman, or degrading.

—"Highly coercive" and "brutal" refer generally to methods that might reasonably be classified by some as torture and by others as CID.

—"Mildly coercive" refers to threats, isolation, mild sleep deprivation, and other interrogation methods that do not amount to CID or torture.

There is much room for argument about which of those definitions best fits a particular interrogation method or combination of methods. Sleep deprivation, for example, might amount to mild coercion, near-torture, or even torture depending upon how long the prisoner is kept awake and what else is being done to him or her at the same time. These definitions, however, are intended for the purpose of discussion in this chapter of different gradations of coercion that law and policy—if not always the public debate—treat differently.

A Brief History of Post–9/11 Prisoner Abuse

We do not intend here to reprise the entire history of the Bush administration's approach to coercive interrogation. A brief overview, however, helps frame the contours of the current policy debate.

Five days after the September 11 attacks, Vice President Cheney said on NBC's *Meet the Press*: "We also have to work the dark side, if you will, the shadows, in the intelligence world. . . . It is a mean, nasty, dangerous and dirty business, and we have to operate in that area."[18] Looking back a year later, Cofer Black, former chief of the CIA's counterterrorism center, said in testimony to the congressional intelligence committees, "After 9/11, the gloves came off."[19] Neither man referred specifically to interrogation, but that was a big part of their war plan. And they were not the only ones. It was a climate of extreme fear, in the context of which many people, even prominent liberals, were openly contemplating the perceived need for coercive interrogation.[20]

In our judgment, the administration was quite right to think about what degree of coercion was appropriate under the circumstances. But there was a right way and a wrong way to go about it. The administration could have urged Congress to enact judicious modifications of the criminal justice and military interrogation rules to allow for a period of incommunicado and, if necessary, aggressive interrogation of suspected terrorists held overseas. Instead, Cheney, Bush, and others began laying the groundwork for circumventing all domestic and international restrictions on tough interrogations and overriding even the 1994 federal law that made it a crime to torture prisoners.

The story of the path that they took is now familiar. It started with the decision to deny the protections of the Geneva Conventions to al Qaeda and Taliban detainees. That may well have been an accurate interpretation of the original understanding of the 1949 Geneva Conventions, but it was at odds with the views of human rights groups and many international law experts and drew strenuous objections from the State Department.[21] (As discussed below, it also was rejected by the Supreme Court in June 2006.) It also departed from the prior U.S. policy of complying with Geneva even when compliance was not legally required. The decision concerning Geneva was the legal and rhetorical foundation for the Bush program of highly coercive interrogations. Common Article 3 of the Geneva Conventions requires that prisoners protected by it "shall in all circumstances be treated humanely" and bans "violence to life and person, in particular . . . cruel treatment and torture; [and] outrages upon personal dignity, in particular humiliating and degrading treatment"—a ban that can be read as encompassing most or all coercive interrogation methods. All violations of Common Article 3 were then—and some are still—prosecutable under the federal War Crimes Act of 1996.[22] But Bush's decision, codified in an order of February 7, 2002, swept away those legal impediments for more than four years.[23]

By eviscerating the rules instead of recognizing the need for occasional deviations from them, the administration ended up with highly implausible definitions of both torture and inhuman treatment that left ample room for abuse of *all* detainees, not merely those few whose seniority and immediate importance to terrorist operations may actually have justified a measure of coercion. The result was to brutalize some small fry and innocent detainees mistakenly seized as terrorists while violating all legal restraints on excess.

Events on the ground were also pushing in that direction—a combination of normal battlefield stress, post–September 11 desire for revenge, and intense pressure to gather intelligence that might save American lives. By late 2001, U.S. soldiers in Afghanistan had begun brutalizing substantial numbers of detained Afghans and others in prisons at the Bagram and Kandahar air force bases. Much of that prisoner abuse was freelancing by troops in the field, not part of any official policy. But some of it probably reflected in part the signals sent by the administration's rhetoric, such as Cheney's talk of "the dark side," and by the administration's apparent lack of interest in putting a stop to the abuse. Some prisoners appear to have been murdered in custody.[24]

There was, in short, a convergence going on between high-altitude policymakers keen to facilitate intelligence gathering by relaxing the rules that restrain abuse, interrogators in the field who felt encumbered by those rules, and some soldiers in the field with sadistic impulses of precisely the type that such rules are intended to restrain.

The CIA's Coercive Interrogation Program

The capture in late March 2002 of Abu Zubaydah, a senior al Qaeda logistics man, focused high-level attention on specific interrogation methods. Abu

Zubaydah had been shot three times and severely wounded during the battle that ended in his capture. After the United States flew in doctors to ensure his recovery, he was questioned gently by FBI and CIA agents at a secret detention facility in Thailand. That questioning elicited some useful information, at least in the view of the FBI.[25] But the CIA officers thought that he was providing disinformation and hiding important secrets that could save many lives. They wanted to get rougher. They also wanted legal cover so that interrogators and their superiors would not end up getting prosecuted or hung out to dry for trying to protect their country, as had occurred to CIA officials in the 1970s.[26]

What the Bush team should have done in late 2001, when it was already anticipating a need for coercive interrogations, or in 2002, when that need became apparent, was to ask Congress to resolve legal uncertainty. It should have sought more detailed legislative rules specifying—among other things—what interrogation techniques should be allowed, with one set of rules for the ordinary run of cases and a separate set of special rules for the highest-value prisoners. Congress might not have given Bush and Cheney everything that they wanted, but the nation would have been better off had Bush and Congress come as close as possible to crystallizing a national consensus on whether and when to use coercive interrogation. Instead, the administration exploited legal uncertainty. In a series of high-level meetings, the president's top security aides discussed and approved tough interrogations methods proposed by the CIA, including waterboarding.

And the CIA got the legal cover that it wanted in the form of two secret, August 1, 2002, memos from the Justice Department's Office of Legal Counsel (OLC). Some called them "get out of jail free cards"[27] because they provided a seemingly ironclad defense against any prosecution for torture: good-faith reliance on advice of the Justice Department office seen as the authoritative source of legal guidance for executive branch officials. The first "torture memo," as it has been called since it leaked in June 2004, went to astonishing extremes to tell the CIA that it could legally do just about anything, including torture, to get information out of suspected terrorists. That memo was signed by Assistant Attorney General Jay Bybee, but John Yoo, Bybee's deputy, was the principal draftsman, and the powerful vice presidential counsel David Addington was very much involved.[28] Among other things, the Yoo-Bybee memo strained for a reading of the 1994 anti-torture statute that was so narrow that it attracted widespread condemnation when it was made public, advising that only the intentional infliction of pain that was so severe as to be "equivalent in intensity to the pain accompanying serious physical injury such as organ failure, impairment of bodily functions, or death" amounted to torture. The memo also claimed that as commander in chief, the president could, if he chose, effectively nullify criminal statutes such as the anti-torture law and authorize interrogation methods that would amount to torture by any definition. Not even burning prisoners' flesh, yanking off their fingernails, or cutting off their fingers one by one were ruled out. The memo's sweeping language sought to strip the law's protections not only from terror kingpins but also from Taliban foot soldiers, innocent bystanders, and anyone else in the world that U.S. forces might choose to brutalize.

The second August 2002 memo was considerably more careful, although its authors strained to bless the legality of some repugnant practices. It approved ten specific interrogation methods, including the "attention grasp," in which the interrogator grabs the detainee's collar with both hands in an effort to shock him; slamming detainees into a flexible wall to instill shock and fear (but taking precautions to prevent injury); slapping a detainee's face; confining a detainee in a dark box for up to eighteen hours or in a smaller box for up to two hours; forcing a detainee to stand "about four to five feet from a wall" with arms "stretched out" and "fingers resting on the wall" supporting "all of his body weight"; forcing a detainee to maintain a variety of "stress positions," including "sitting on the floor with legs extended straight out" and "arms raised above [the] head" and "kneeling on the floor while leaning back at a 45 degree angle"; depriving a detainee of sleep for extended periods; exploiting a detainee's phobias by—in Zubaydah's case—putting a harmless insect with him in a confinement box while telling him falsely that it could sting him (a technique that the agency never ended up trying); and waterboarding.[29]

Later memos by Bybee's and Yoo's successors describe additional procedures: manipulating detainees' diets by giving them "commercial liquid meal replacements [instead of] normal food"; forced nudity; slapping detainees' abdomens; and dousing detainees with cold water.[30] And they make clear that those techniques could be used in combination with one another. One memo, in fact, is specifically devoted to analyzing the "combined use of certain techniques."[31]

The general impression of the program the memos offer is one of highly controlled and regulated brutality. The CIA clearly did not use its coercive techniques wantonly. They were, rather, "generally used in an escalating fashion, with milder techniques used first" and harsher ones used only when milder ones failed. They were subject to various limits and under constant medical monitoring.[32] Moreover, the number of detainees subjected to enhanced interrogation techniques of any kind was quite small. Of the ninety-four detainees who passed through the CIA's detention program, only twenty-eight were interrogated with any of the enhanced techniques. And only three detainees were waterboarded.[33]

At the same time, there is no way to make those techniques seem humane, as some of the program's defenders have sought to do. The memos make clear that waterboarding, for example, constitutes a "threat of imminent death" and that it was used repeatedly on both Abu Zubaydah and Khalid Sheikh Mohammed. Exactly how many times remains unclear. One of the memos quotes a CIA inspector general's report to the effect that the CIA waterboarded Abu Zubaydah 83 times and Mohammed 183 times, but that appears to be the number of specific instances of pouring water onto their faces, not the number of waterboarding sessions.[34] In any event, the memos make clear that the "CIA used the waterboard extensively" in those cases.[35] What's more, detainees were deprived of sleep for extraordinary periods of time: "more than a dozen detainees have been subjected to sleep deprivation of more than 48 hours, and three detainees have been subjected to sleep deprivation of more than 96 hours; the longest period of time for which any detainee has been deprived of sleep by the CIA is 180 hours," one memo recounts.[36]

And both the memos and the leaked ICRC report on interrogation tactics in the program—which is based on interviews with the detainees after their transfer to Guantánamo and is broadly consistent with most of the facts recited in the Justice Department memos—describe the specific methods of sleep deprivation as horrifying. "Ten of the fourteen [detainees interviewed] alleged that they were subjected to prolonged stress standing positions, during which their wrists were shackled to a bar or hook in the ceiling above the head for periods ranging from two or three days continuously, and for up to two or three months intermittently," the ICRC reports—a tactic the OLC memos describe as designed to prevent sleep. Both describe detainees subject to this technique being forced to wear diapers and not being allowed to use the toilet.[37] It is hard to read the material without a deep sense of revulsion.

And yet critics of the program often elide too quickly the question of what the agency or the administration should have done instead. The March 2003 capture in Pakistan of Khalid Shaikh Mohammed (KSM, in official shorthand), in part based on Abu Zubaydah's disclosures, is as close to a ticking time bomb as U.S. interrogators have come in the real world. KSM was the architect of the September 11 attacks and al Qaeda's chief of operations. As such, he probably knew more than anyone else alive about any planned attacks and where to find other key terrorists. The CIA therefore had good reason to believe that unlocking the secrets in his head might save dozens or hundreds of lives—perhaps many, many more, in the unlikely but at the time entirely conceivable event that al Qaeda was preparing a nuclear or biological attack on a major U.S. city.

The CIA also had reason to believe that the only chance of saving the many lives that might depend on learning KSM's secrets was to use highly coercive methods amounting to near-torture or worse. If interrogators stuck to the kid-glove interrogation rules that were demanded by human rights groups and that they routinely tried before resorting to coercion, this tough, committed jihadist was not about to betray his cohorts to his hated enemies. Nor was there much chance that mildly coercive interrogation methods—such as yelling, threatening violence, or slapping his face—would break his resistance.

So the choice facing the interrogators and their bosses—at least as they perceived it—was either to risk seeing preventable mass murders unfold and to be blamed for failing to stop them, or to risk professional ruin by subjecting KSM to near-torture or torture. People disposed to criticize what the CIA did or to assert that highly coercive interrogation should never be used, can claim to have a fully considered opinion only if they are prepared to say exactly what they would have done with KSM.

The CIA has contended that the interrogations in the program were dramatically effective, leading to a chain of captures of al Qaeda leaders and thereby disrupting specific plots. That claim is disputed, and the Obama administration apparently was not impressed. FBI agents involved in the Abu Zubaydah case, for example, have given dramatically different accounts, describing him as a mentally troubled al Qaeda hanger-on who provided CIA interrogators with increasingly dubious information as his treatment became more and more coercive and gave up his important information before the rough stuff ever began.[38] The CIA made hundreds of hours of videotapes of the interrogation that could help resolve the disputes as well as provide evidence for investigation of the interrogators and their bosses. But the CIA destroyed the tapes in November 2005.[39] The public now knows a great deal about what the CIA did to get information. Without knowing more about what it obtained and how much of it was obtainable by other means, a rigorous cost-benefit analysis is impossible.

The Military: From al-Qahtani to Abu Ghraib

The same alarmed intelligence reports about major impending attacks in the summer and fall of 2002 that helped spur the brutalizing of Abu Zubaydah also focused attention on Mohammad al-Qahtani. Al-Qahtani became known as the "20th hijacker" after the government figured out in July 2002 that, shortly before September 11, he had been en route to meet Mohammed Atta, who was waiting for him at the Orlando airport when al-Qahtani was refused entry to the United States.[40] That made al-Qahtani an obvious candidate for intensive interrogation.

But important as he was, al-Qahtani was no KSM. Seized in Afghanistan in November 2001 and sent to the military's Guantánamo prison camp in February 2002, he had already been in captivity for almost a year by the time the coercive phase of his interrogation began. His knowledge might have been of some value to intelligence analysts assembling a mosaic of al Qaeda's operations and in identifying other detainees at the base. But it was probably too stale to be a plausible bet to stop any particular attack, let alone an imminent attack.[41]

The Pentagon's most fundamental error was its decision that al-Qahtani was an appropriate candidate for the kind of highly coercive interrogation that can be justified— if at all—only for prisoners likely to have information that could prevent imminent or already planned attacks. The rationale underlying the decision to use highly coercive methods on al-Qahtani could be stretched to justify the wholesale tormenting of dozens or even hundreds of other prisoners as well. A conceptual door had been swung open that would not easily be shut.

Al-Qahtani had received resistance training in an al Qaeda camp and predictably stood fast through weeks of traditional, noncoercive military interrogation, concocting the preposterous story that his reason for trying to enter the United States had been to deal in used cars and that his reason for going to Afghanistan had been an interest in falconry.[42] With Defense Secretary Donald Rumsfeld impatiently demanding better intelligence from Guantánamo, al-Qahtani's handlers put him in strict isolation for many weeks and sought permission to get rougher to "enhance our efforts to extract additional information." The handlers proposed a list of eighteen methods.[43]

Acting on the advice of Pentagon general counsel William J. Haynes II, Rumsfeld approved most of the methods on December 2, 2002. The Rumsfeld-approved methods included isolation for up to thirty days; interrogation for twenty hours at a time, in unfamiliar settings; forced nakedness; forced grooming and shaving of beards; depriving detainees of light and sound; hooding them; denying them hot rations and comfort items; "mild, non-injurious physical contact such as grabbing, poking in the chest with the finger, and light pushing"; using "individual phobias (such as fear of dogs) to induce stress"; and "the use of stress positions (like standing) for a maximum of four hours."[44] Haynes and Rumsfeld did not approve requests for permission to use the three harshest of the suggested techniques: exposure to cold weather or water; implied threats of severe pain or imminent death for the detainee or his family; and waterboarding, which by then the CIA had used on Abu Zubaydah with Justice Department approval. Haynes advised that those methods, too, "might be legally available" but that "as matter of policy, a blanket approval of [those] techniques is not warranted at this time. Our armed forces are trained to a standard of interrogation that reflects a tradition of restraint."[45] Rumsfeld and Haynes included no guidance on how long or in what combinations the methods that they approved could be used.

In contrast with the CIA's program, which was carefully regimented and seems to have stayed—certain notorious incidents aside—within the bounds of the guidance that it received, things in the military spun out of control. According to a subsequent 2005 Southern Command report and leaked daily logs of the interrogation that appeared in *Time* magazine, al-Qahtani's interrogators pushed the approved methods past the limit, often using several at once over long periods of time and adding others that were not on the list of approved methods. The prisoner was isolated from other detainees for 160 days; interrogated for 18 to 20 hours a day for 48 of 54 consecutive days; manacled in painful stress positions for hours; and forced to wear a woman's bra and thong on his head during interrogation, to dance with a male interrogator, to stand naked in front of a female interrogator, to be straddled by a female interrogator, and to perform dog tricks on a leash. He was pumped full of intravenous fluid until he had to urinate on himself; he had water poured on his head; he was menaced by a snarling, unmuzzled dog; and he was told that his mother and sister were whores, in addition to other kinds of abuse.[46]

An official military investigation found in 2005 that al-Qahtani's interrogation had been abusive and that some actions had been unauthorized. But it stopped short of calling them torture.[47] Al-Qahtani's lawyers have claimed that the interrogation so ravaged him that he was still a broken man almost six years later, unable to communicate meaningfully even with those who would help him.[48] In any event, al-Qahtani did eventually begin to cooperate, providing information that interrogators have regarded as critical and that his lawyers and attorneys for other detainees have derided as unreliably implicating numerous other detainees.

How many Guantánamo prisoners besides al-Qahtani were also subjected to highly coercive interrogation is in dispute. Many of those who have been released have alleged that they were tortured, but al Qaeda operatives were trained to make such claims whether true or false. The use of coercive methods at Guantánamo drew strenuous objections from FBI officials who were there and from some in the military, including the Pentagon's Criminal Investigative

Task Force. They complained that the methods were inhumane, possibly ille-gal, and ineffective.[49] By the end of 2002 similar complaints at high levels of the Pentagon led to withdrawal of Rumsfeld's approval for some of the coer-cive methods.

The Bush administration clearly helped unleash forces that it could or would not control, in Afghanistan and Iraq as well as at Guantánamo, when in the cases of al-Qahtani and others it jettisoned the restraints that had long been imposed by the Army Field Manual and the Geneva Conventions with-out putting any other clear rules in their place. The rules in the 1992 edition of the Army Field Manual theoretically remained in force. But those were vague and easily overridden by the need to obtain information to prevent planned attacks, by the president's disparagement of the Geneva Conventions, and by other high-level pronouncements such as Cofer Black's "after 9/11 the gloves came off." Such high-level signals to get tough combined with freelance brutalization by troops in the field to produce widespread abuse of prisoners.[50]

Indeed, at least to some extent, the tolerance of brutality in the few instances in which officials overtly countenanced it seems to have migrated to cases in which senior officials never intended to promote abuse. Several offi-cial investigations of abusive treatment of military prisoners concluded that the high-level approvals of the methods used to torment al-Qahtani had con-tributed to a culture of confusion about what the rules were, helping to fos-ter the abuse of prisoners in Afghanistan and Iraq. Rumsfeld, who was con-cerned about improving intelligence in a deteriorating Iraq theater, had sent his Guantánamo commander, Lieutenant General Geoffrey Miller, to "Gitmo-ize" interrogations in Iraq.[51] And while the abuses at Abu Ghraib were never authorized by policy, military intelligence officials do appear to have encour-aged guards to abuse detainees by way of softening them up for interrogation. Many and perhaps most of the prisoners brutalized had little or no useful intelligence to impart. Indeed, in most instances, abuse bore little relation to intelligence gathering efforts; much of the disgusting conduct by MPs on the night shift at Abu Ghraib in the fall of 2003 was done for sport, not for any purpose related to interrogation.[52] Still, the Bush administration forgave itself too much when it claimed that the abuses at Abu Ghraib were utterly unre-lated to its policy choices. The "augmented techniques for Guantánamo migrated to Afghanistan and Iraq where they were neither limited nor safe-guarded," concluded one official report on prisoner abuse.[53] Another report said: "Confusion about what interrogation techniques were authorized resulted from the proliferation of guidance and information from other the-aters of operation; individual interrogator experiences in other theaters; and the failure to distinguish between interrogation operations in other theaters and Iraq. This confusion contributed to the occurrence of some of the non-violent and non-sexual abuses."[54]

Some judgments have been harsher. The Senate Armed Services Committee, in a lengthy report, concluded: "Interrogation policies endorsed by senior military and civilian officials authorizing the use of harsh interrogation techniques were a major cause of the abuse of detainees in U.S. custody."[55] While the report is flawed in a number of respects and this conclusion is significantly overstated, the notion that what happened at Guantánamo didn't stay at Guantánamo is clearly corroborated by other findings.[56]

The Bush Era Reforms

As noted above, Rumsfeld started yielding to internal dissent about coercive interrogations in December 2002, just a month after he had authorized the coercive methods that military interrogators used to torment al-Qahtani. After a forceful complaint by Alberto Mora, the Navy's general counsel, about the al-Qahtani interrogation, Rumsfeld withdrew his authorization for most of the coercive methods in January 2003. He said that other coercive methods could be used only with his personal approval. Rumsfeld also had Haynes convene a "working group" to study interrogation methods. It recommended a list of thirty-five methods, some of them mildly but not highly coercive,[57] and Rumsfeld approved twenty-four of them in part in an April 2003 memo.

The list of twenty-four included the seventeen methods already described in the Army Field Manual plus subjecting detainees to a sort of "good cop, bad cop" routine, denying them hot rations and limiting them to the Meals Ready to Eat given to soldiers in the field, putting them in isolation, changing their sleep schedules, making temperature adjustments to disorient them and other environmental manipulations designed to induce discomfort, and using so-called "false-flag" interrogations meant to trick detainees into talking by convincing them that the interrogator is from another country. Rumsfeld disapproved the use of blindfolds and even mild, non-injurious physical contact.[58]

But the partial Pentagon pullback from approving highly coercive interrogation methods did not immediately put an end to abuse of prisoners on the ground in Afghanistan and Iraq. General Miller's summer 2003 trip to Iraq and the infamous Abu Ghraib photos—mostly taken in October 2003—dramatized the extent of the abuse still to come.[59]

Additional cautionary notes were sounded throughout 2003 and into 2004. In December 2003, Jack Goldsmith, the new head of the Justice Department's

OLC, advised top Pentagon officials that the Fourth Geneva Convention, pertaining to occupied territories, prohibited coercive interrogations of any Iraqis, even Iraqi terrorists.[60] Then, in March 2004, Goldsmith wrote to Haynes that the Pentagon could no longer rely on a March 2003 OLC memo by John Yoo, who had given the Pentagon much the same almost-anything-goes advice that the infamous August 2002 "torture memo" had given the CIA.[61] Then the Abu Ghraib scandal broke in April 2004. By mid-2004, the military's coercive interrogations were largely past.

What's more, in 2006 Congress and the Supreme Court helped slam the door shut on any future coercive interrogations by the military. First, in December 2005, the so-called McCain amendment to the Detainee Treatment Act banned subjecting any person in the military's custody or control "to any treatment or technique of interrogation not authorized by and listed in the United States Army Field Manual on Intelligence Interrogation."[62] Second, in June 2006 the Supreme Court ruled in *Hamdan* v. *Rumsfeld* that Common Article 3 of the Geneva Conventions protects even al Qaeda terrorists, contrary to the February 7, 2002, Bush order and underlying OLC memorandum.[63] While the decision did not immediately involve interrogation and the justices did not even mention the subject, their decision had the effect of rendering all U.S. interrogations subject to the broad ban under Common Article 3 on inhumane, "cruel," or "humiliating and degrading" treatment of prisoners.

Given the fact that violations of Common Article 3 were then prosecutable under the federal War Crimes Act, the decision seemed to many experts to knock the legal props out from under the administration's interrogation program. Indeed, the *Hamdan* decision meant that notwithstanding the Justice Department's still-quite-narrow reading of the anti-torture statute, the highly coercive interrogations of Abu Zubaydah, KSM, al-Qahtani and some others could very plausibly be called war crimes. That came as an extremely unpleasant surprise to the officials at the highest level of the administration who had explicitly approved the methods used on those prisoners.

Finally, in September 2006, after detailed internal debate, the Pentagon adopted major revisions to the Army Field Manual, which had acquired the force of law as a consequence of the McCain amendment.[64] The new rules allow some new noncoercive methods, including forms of trickery, but ban a list of eight specified harsh methods.[65] More remarkably, and in contrast with the 1992 edition of the Army Field Manual—which listed as Geneva-compliant a method called "Fear Up (Harsh)," defined as exploiting a prisoner's fears by behaving in an overpowering manner with a loud and threatening voice—the September 2006 edition bans *all* coercion and threats.[66] The revised rules include enough detail to provide clear notice to military interrogators of what they can and cannot do. They comply with the Geneva Conventions. And since they were adopted, there have been few complaints about military interrogations.

The McCain amendment also gave the CIA new legal guidance—albeit much vaguer guidance than it gave the military. It granted the agency more latitude to use coercive methods than it gave the military, imposing a high-altitude ban on "cruel, inhuman, or degrading" treatment of prisoners. Critically, it defined those terms with reference to federal case law that allows the use of coercive interrogation methods if the need for information is sufficiently dire and urgent.[67]

But the *Hamdan* decision subjected the CIA, as well as military interrogations, to the strict requirements of Common Article 3 of the Geneva Conventions and of the War Crimes Act, prompting the CIA to suspend temporarily its "enhanced interrogation program." Then, in October 2006, the administration and Congress blunted the impact of the *Hamdan* decision on CIA interrogators by rushing through a new interrogation law, enacted as part of the Military Commissions Act (MCA).

While the MCA's chief purpose was to reconstitute the military commissions that the Court had struck down, section 6 of the new law effectively immunized administration officials from any prosecution under the War Crimes Act for most pre-MCA conduct violating Common Article 3 unless it had inflicted such severe pain as to violate the anti-torture law, too.[68] (Previously, the Detainee Treatment Act had immunized officials who relied reasonably and in good faith on Justice Department advice that specified that the interrogation methods used were legal.[69]) Looking to future interrogations, the MCA also specified that only "grave breaches" of Common Article 3 could be prosecuted under the War Crimes Act, and it defined "grave breaches" narrowly enough to exclude much conduct that could be considered "humiliating or degrading." Only murder, maiming, sexual abuse, biological experiments, hostage taking, violations of the narrowly drafted torture statute, and "cruel or inhuman treatment" would qualify as prosecutable "grave breaches."

The MCA delegated to the president the authority to define the parameters of Common Article 3 short of the grave breaches that the statute itself outlined. President Bush did so in an executive order in July 2007, which interpreted Common Article 3 and the MCA in ways that allow room for some highly coercive interrogation methods so long as the purpose is to gain intelligence rather than to humiliate or degrade the prisoner.[70] Justice Department officials opined that interrogation methods "undertaken to prevent a threatened terrorist attack" might be permitted even if the same methods would be illegal if done "for the purpose of humiliation or abuse."[71] When it became public in 2008, that logic was attacked by some experts as at best strained. Still, any use of waterboarding (to pick one example) after the effective date of the MCA might violate the War Crimes Act as "cruel or inhuman treatment," if the resulting "mental harm" is "serious and non-transitory"; it did not need to be prolonged enough to fall within the definition of "torture."[72] Indeed, while the Justice Department continued to maintain that the CIA's use of waterboarding with "strict limitations and safeguards" did not violate the anti-torture statute, it conceded that *Hamdan* and the MCA "would make it much more difficult to conclude that the practice was lawful" than it had been before.[73]

Whatever the precise limits placed on future interrogations by the MCA, it is clear that the McCain amendment and the September 2006 revision of the Army Field Manual mean that if and when any president again wants suspected terrorists squeezed hard for information, the CIA will have to do the dirty work.

And unless one wishes to see coercive interrogation banned entirely, that division of labor makes a great deal of sense. It was a mistake, as many military lawyers argued at the time, for the Bush administration to allow military interrogators to use highly coercive methods. The military has held tens of thousands of prisoners in occupied Iraq and in Afghanistan. Most are small fry with little or no useful information. Most also qualify—as a matter of U.S. policy, if not strict legal right—for the kid-glove treatment required by the Fourth Geneva Convention for citizens of occupied countries. In addition, thousands of military interrogations are conducted by low-ranking personnel with much less professional training and supervision than CIA interrogators, as illustrated by the catastrophic breakdown of discipline at Abu Ghraib. These are among the reasons why the military has traditionally imposed strict restraints on its interrogators and why the Pentagon made the restraints more exacting than ever in the September 2006 revision of the Army Field Manual.

The CIA, on the other hand, has since September 11 assembled a small cadre of highly trained professional interrogators operating far from combat zones and under close supervision and only in cases involving people who they believe to be the highest-value detainees. Those conditions provide some insurance against the grave danger that individuals will get carried away in seeking to break a prisoner and thereby violate the law or policy limits—as some apparently did despite the CIA's safeguards.

The Obama Reforms to Date

Banning coercive interrogation entirely is exactly what the Obama administration has sought to do. The new president's executive order concerning CIA interrogation and detention authorities came within forty-eight hours of his inaugural oath, and it made quite clear that, at least for the immediate term, Obama—unlike his predecessor—was not going to hide rough interrogations behind words like "humane." The order took strong policy stands on all of the key questions—and it marked a significant shift.[74]

To begin, the order revoked a great deal of the legal guidance the Bush administration had given the CIA on the subject of interrogation and replaced it with a requirement that CIA interrogations comply with the Army Field Manual—a requirement that Obama appears to be making permanent as this book goes to press. That step, long sought by human rights groups and other critics of the Bush administration's harsh interrogation policies, effectively accomplished with a stroke of the presidential pen what Congress had sought but failed to do the previous year, stymied by President Bush's veto.

Obama's order contained one loophole of indeterminate significance. The passage allowing reliance on the Army Field Manual and forbidding reliance "upon any interpretation of the law governing interrogation issued by the Department of Justice between September 11, 2001, and January 20, 2009" begins with the following caveat: "unless the Attorney General with appropriate consultation provides further guidance." That seems to permit, in the event of an exigent circumstance, the CIA to go to the attorney general for additional legal guidance, but it in no way guarantees a permissive result. In other words, the agency cannot count on the availability of any technique other than the specific set of approved noncoercive procedures to which the military is already bound by law. The order eliminated not merely the latitude to conduct highly coercive interrogations, *but also the latitude to use indubitably legal techniques that do not happen to be approved by the Army for use by its interrogators.* That was a tremendous change—albeit one that, with the CIA's secret prisons already depopulated and their occupants moved to Guantánamo Bay, had little capacity to impact many detainees in the short term.

Obama's order did contain another important nod to the possibility that the CIA may have legitimate needs for techniques that the military does not authorize. It came in the form of a "special task force"—to be led by the attorney general and composed of several cabinet members, intelligence leaders, and the chairman of the Joint Chiefs of Staff—that was charged with reporting to the president in 180 days. The executive order tasked the group with studying "whether the interrogation practices and techniques in [the Army Field Manual], when employed by departments or agencies outside the military, provide an appropriate means of acquiring the intelligence necessary to protect the Nation, and, if warranted, to recommend any additional or different guidance for other departments or agencies." It was possible, in other words, that as a result of the study the CIA would regain some measure of flexibility. But that has not happened. In August 2009, the task force recommended the creation of an interagency interrogation team for high-value detainees—housed at the FBI, not the CIA—and concluded that "the Army Field Manual provides appropriate guidance on interrogation for military interrogators and that no additional or different guidance was necessary for other agencies."

The only other latitude that the Obama administration leaves the CIA is that it does not prohibit the continued use of renditions—which have sometimes in the past served to let ugly interrogations take place under the auspices of foreign governments. While the Obama administration's emerging rendition policy may be marginally more restrictive than the Bush administration's, it is possible that it too could serve as a back door through which the CIA could regain—though foreign government subcontractors—some interrogation flexibility.

With the CIA now subject to the same interrogation rules as the military, there was no longer any reason to allow it to retain its detention authority—other than, perhaps, in order to hold people in a transient fashion before turning them over to other agencies or countries. Accordingly, Obama's order also revoked the CIA's detention power, requiring the agency to "close as expeditiously as possible any detention facilities that it currently operates" and clarifying that it "shall not operate any such detention facility in the future." (The document's definition of "detention facilities" excludes "facilities used only to hold people on a short-term, transitory basis.") In the future, it goes on, the International Committee of the Red Cross must be notified of and given "timely access to any individual detained in any armed conflict in the custody or under the effective control of . . . the United States Government, consistent with Department of Defense regulations and policies." In other words, no more secret prisons.

For as long as the current policy remains in effect, the human rights community has won virtually everything that it asked for concerning interrogation—except durability. The new policy, after all, can vanish as quickly as it appeared.

Did Post–9/11 Coercive Interrogations Save Lives?

To many Americans, the new policy will seem like an unqualified good—unless and until the country suffers another mass-casualty attack. But the question of whether coercive interrogation should continue under any circumstances depends, to a great degree, on the extent to which it may produce lifesaving intelligence unobtainable by other means. The public record is littered with contradictory claims about this fundamental empirical question, on which the media have shed remarkably little light. In general, Bush administration officials and CIA officers who have participated in coercive interrogations, with certain notable exceptions, have asserted that coercion has saved lives, as have some Pentagon reports on coercive interrogations in the military. By contrast, most FBI officials, military interrogators, non-CIA lawyers, and journalists contradict the CIA-Bush claims and assert that the rapport-building approach that they have long favored is not only more moral and more consistent with American values but also far more effective at eliciting accurate information.

Neither side in the dispute brings a lot of hard evidence to the table. Consider, for example, the weakness of the Bush administration's public claims that coercion extracted valuable information from Mohammed al-Qahtani, the Guantánamo detainee alleged to have flown to the United States to meet Mohammed Atta. In the words of a 2005 military report, he "ultimately provided extremely valuable intelligence,"[75] but its claims to that effect have been so vague as to inspire little confidence. The 2005 report, for example, could have been a reference to al-Qahtani's less-than-reliable statements fingering about thirty of Osama bin Laden's supposed bodyguards among his fellow detainees.[76] Southern Command's General Bantz Craddock also testified in congressional hearings that the once-defiant prisoner had "provided insights" into al Qaeda's planning for the September 11 attacks.[77] But that could mean only that al-Qahtani had confirmed that he had been en route to meet Atta when he flew to Orlando in August 2001. The Schlesinger Report said that al-Qahtani and another coercively interrogated Guantánamo prisoner gave up "important and time-urgent information."[78] That stops short of saying that the information saved lives and does not make clear what it was. And al-Qahtani, for his part, said in 2006 that all of his statements under coercive interrogation had been falsehoods adopting "the story that the interrogators wanted to hear."[79]

The countervailing claims by FBI and military intelligence officials that the coercive interrogations of al-Qahtani and others at Guantánamo produced no useful intelligence have also been heavier on generalities than on specifics.[80] Some stress the fact that in May 2008, Susan Crawford, the Pentagon official in charge of trials of Guantánamo prisoners, dismissed war crimes charges against al-Qahtani. Crawford later stated that al-Qahtani had been tortured and the evidence against him was tainted.[81] But that does not negate the possibility that al-Qahtani provided good information about al Qaeda.

One of the more persuasive accounts of successful use of the kind of mildly coercive interrogation that we favor allowing the CIA to use came from a former Army interrogator in Afghanistan. Using the pseudonym Chris Mackey, he wrote with a co-author Greg Miller:

> The early story of the war in Afghanistan was one of frustration and failure for us. Many Al-Qaeda prisoners had been trained to resist, and our schoolhouse methods were woefully out-of-date. . . . [Later] our experience in Afghanistan showed that the harsher the method we used—though they never contravened the [Geneva] Conventions, let alone crossed over into torture—the better the information we got and the sooner we got it.

Mackey said that he and his colleagues "never touched anyone." Rather, their main methods were to threaten to hand over prisoners to their home countries' brutal intelligence services and to deprive them of sleep. The latter approach was limited by the rule that the interrogator had to stay awake as long as the prisoner.[82]

Another account of coercive interrogation that "worked," although it clearly violated both military law and policy, came in 2003, when Army Lieutenant Colonel Allen B. West, a battalion commander in Iraq, threatened an unresponsive detainee with death by twice firing his pistol during an interrogation while demanding to know the whereabouts of his accomplices. The detainee, an Iraqi policeman who allegedly was part of a plot to kill West and his soldiers, revealed his cohorts' names and plans for a sniper attack the next day. That may well have saved the lives of U.S. soldiers.[83] It is far from clear that a noncoercive interrogation could have obtained the same information.

As noted above, CIA officials have argued that the waterboarding of Abu Zubaydah saved lives, perhaps many lives. But FBI officials involved in interrogating the same man minimized his importance. "The problem is they didn't realize he didn't know all that much," Daniel Coleman, a retired FBI agent who worked on the case, told reporters.[84] Again, different witnesses to the same interrogation came away with radically different perceptions of the value of coercion.

KSM, on the other hand, clearly knew a lot, and the evidence that coercion in his case netted valuable information is fairly compelling. Yet even concerning KSM no consensus exists. He confessed to a role in more than thirty criminal plots, including the videotaped beheading in Pakistan of *Wall Street Journal* reporter Daniel Pearl.[85] The reliability of some of his statements has been questioned, including his claimed role in Pearl's death.[86] "Some intelligence officers say that many of Mr. Mohammed's statements proved exaggerated or false," an October 4, 2007, *New York Times* article reported. It quoted a former senior agency official as saying that "many C.I.A. professionals now believe patient, repeated questioning by well-informed experts is more effective than harsh physical pressure." Even a former CIA executive director, A. B. Krongard, told author Ron Suskind that KSM and other al Qaeda captives "went through hell, and gave up very, very little."[87]

On the other hand, a subsequent *Times* article reported that after the waterboarding and other brutalization of KSM, he became "quite compliant" in the course of rapport-building efforts by a CIA interrogator. The article's description of the interrogation process leaves some doubt as to whether the reason that the prisoner became compliant was the brutalization by the tough guys or the gentler questioning by the interrogators who followed up: A "paramilitary team put on the pressure . . . to force a prisoner to talk. When the prisoner signaled assent, the tormenters stepped aside. After a break that could be a day or longer, [an] interrogator took up the questioning."[88]

Whatever the reason, KSM discussed his "fellow extremists' goals, ideology and tradecraft" and "provided more and more detail on Al Qaeda's structure, its past plots and its aspirations."[89] As for the Pearl murder, KSM "pointed out to [an interrogator] details of the hand and arm of the masked killer in a videotape of the murder that appeared to show it was him."[90]

Former national intelligence director Mike McConnell, former president Bush, former CIA directors George Tenet and Michael Hayden, and former attorney general Michael Mukasey have all claimed that the interrogations of KSM and others saved many lives. Tenet said, "I know that this program has saved lives. I know we've disrupted plots. I know that this program alone is worth more than [what] the FBI, the Central Intelligence Agency and the National Security Agency put together have been able to tell us."[91] According to Jack Goldsmith, that view "permeated the executive branch during my time in office."[92] McConnell told the *New Yorker*: "Have we gotten meaningful information? You betcha. Tons! Does it save lives? Tons! We've gotten incredible information. . . . We have people walking around in this country that are alive today because this process happened."[93]

Even the 2004 CIA inspector general's report, which was famously critical of the program, acknowledged that CIA interrogations had led to key terrorist captures and disrupted plots, and it suggested that key detainees ultimately gave intelligence under coercive interrogations that they had held back under standard interrogations. President Bush himself provided the most detailed account claiming big successes for the CIA's "enhanced" interrogation program in September 2006. If Bush—whose information came from the CIA—was telling the truth, coercive interrogation has indeed saved many innocent lives since September 11. Bush said that the initially "defiant and evasive" Abu

Zubaydah—after being subjected to tough methods that were later revealed to include waterboarding— disclosed information in 2002 that helped lead to the capture of other accomplices in the September 11 attacks, including Ramzi Binalshibh; that those two provided information that helped lead to the capture of KSM; and that he in turn gave up "information that helped us stop another planned attack on the United States" and described "many details of other plots to kill innocent Americans." KSM's disclosures helped U.S. agents find other terrorist leaders including Hambali, the leader of Jemaah Islamiyah (al Qaeda's Southeast Asian affiliate), and Hambali's brother in Pakistan, which in turn "led us to a cell of 17 Southeast Asian . . . operatives," who Hambali admitted "were being groomed at KSM's request for attacks inside the United States—probably using airplanes."[94]

Later Bush speeches and articles by his former speech writer Marc Thiessen added details: KSM was initially defiant but, after being tormented and waterboarded, gave up information leading to the capture of a terrorist named Zubair, then to the capture of Hambali, and then to his brother "Gun Gun" in Pakistan, whose information led to a cell of seventeen Southeast Asian terrorists. That chain of events, the CIA insists, unraveled the dangerous "Second Wave" plot, planned by KSM and Hambali, which called for the Southeast Asian terrorists to crash a hijacked airliner into the tallest building in Los Angeles, the Library Tower. Bush critics have claimed to find various holes in that account.[95]

Most chillingly, perhaps, Bush said that

> KSM also provided vital information on Al Qaeda's efforts to obtain biological weapons. During questioning, KSM admitted that he had met three individuals involved in Al Qaeda's efforts to produce anthrax, a deadly biological agent—and he identified one of the individuals as a terrorist named Yazid. KSM apparently believed we already had this information, because Yazid had been captured and taken into foreign custody before KSM's arrest. In fact, we did not know about Yazid's role in Al Qaeda's anthrax program. Information from Yazid then helped lead to the capture of his two principal assistants in the anthrax program. Without the information provided by KSM and Yazid, we might not have uncovered this Al Qaeda biological weapons program, or stopped this Al Qaeda cell from developing anthrax for attacks against the United States.[96]

Of course, Bush does not have much credibility on intelligence matters, and the CIA may have misled him; moreover, both Bush and the CIA had a big stake in justifying the brutal interrogations. President Obama, for his part, came to the conclusion after grilling CIA officials, including Hayden, that the information that the CIA obtained could have been had by other means, and some FBI officials have scoffed at the CIA-Bush claims. It is also true, however, that the FBI—locked in a perpetual turf war with the CIA and eager to recapture the lead in terrorism investigations—had a big stake in selling the notion that its own noncoercive interrogation methods work and that the CIA's methods do not.

News reports of the September 2006 Bush speech focused on his contemporaneous announcement that KSM and thirteen other "high-value terrorist detainees" had been moved from secret prisons abroad to Guantánamo to face military trial and his request for the legislation that would ultimately become the MCA.[97] Remarkably, not one major newspaper or magazine reported at the time the details of the president's claims about the output from the coercive interrogation program. That pattern of ignoring the best available evidence that coercive interrogation may have saved lives, combined with the vast media attention to the arguments by human rights activists and FBI officials that coercive interrogation does not work and can yield false or unreliable information, has provided the public with a misleading and unbalanced picture. And, of course, as many in the media tend to forget when seeking to dramatize the flaws of coercive interrogation, it is hardly the only type of intelligence gathering that can yield false and unreliable information. Consider how Ahmed Chalabi and other Iraqis with agendas of their own helped mislead the administration into believing that Saddam Hussein had weapons of mass destruction.

There is, of course, countervailing evidence. FBI director Robert Mueller, for example, told *Vanity Fair* in 2008 that he did not believe that any attacks had been disrupted because of intelligence obtained through the coercive methods.[98] A recent book by a military interrogator writing under the pseudonym Matthew Alexander describes the great successes that the military had in breaking terrorists after abandoning coercion—and specifically how it managed to locate and kill Abu Musab al Zarqawi using smart, not brutal, interrogations.[99]

Our point is not that it is clear that brutality works, much less that it clearly works better than nonbrutal alternatives. Our point is, rather, that the bottom-line lessons of the post–September 11 experience are that coercion is often useless or counterproductive, especially when used indiscriminately against people who have little or no information to divulge; that there is no conclusive proof that it has saved lives; but that the claims that it has saved lives are too numerous and plausible to dismiss. For that reason, no president who takes seriously his or her responsibility to protect the American people should want to be bound in all circumstances by a flat criminal law ban denying the president the option of authorizing even mild coercion.

Historical Evidence that Coercion Can Work

While the competing agendas of various participants complicate the debate about whether the administration's post–September 11 coercive interrogations have saved lives, a body of historical evidence shows fairly conclusively that such coercion has sometimes saved lives—though not that it is a good bet to save lives in any particular emergency. History does not support the confident claims by ideologically driven opponents of coercion that "torture never works" because prisoners will give false confessions and make up false stories to stop the pain being inflicted on them.[100] Nor does it support corollary claims that milder forms of coercive interrogation do not work either.

Most experienced military and FBI interrogators emphatically agree that coercion is generally ineffective and vow that they would never try it. And it is probably true that, as most veteran interrogators, psychologists, and other experts say, less coercive methods are equally or more effective most of the time. It's also true that there is little or no empirical evidence that coercive interrogation "works" —or that it does not. That is the main message of a 2006 report of the Intelligence Science Board, a collection of papers entitled *Educing Information: Interrogation: Science and Art.* The first paper baldly states: "We do not know what systems, methods, or processes of interrogation best protect the nation's security."[101] Another paper says that "virtually none" of the authorized techniques used by U.S. personnel over the past fifty years "are based on scientific research or have ever been subjected to scientific or systematic inquiry or evaluation." It adds: "There is little or no research to indicate whether [coercive] techniques succeed in the manner and contexts in which they are applied. Anecdotal accounts and opinions based on personal experiences are mixed, but the preponderance of reports seems to weigh against their effectiveness."[102]

But how many people really believe that coercive methods are *never* effective? How many people doubt that they personally could be coerced or tortured into revealing secrets, especially if their tormentors had ways to check the accuracy of what they said immediately? If you were arrested near a crowded train station in which you had hidden a bomb, and an interrogator brandished a red-hot poker an inch from your eyes while demanding, "Where's the bomb?" would you refuse to answer? Concoct a lie that would be likely to crumble under further pressure? After your lie was exposed and the interrogator began torturing you with that red-hot poker, would you hold fast? We suspect that we would blurt out the truth before it came to that. We also suspect, on the other hand, that we might hold our tongues if subjected only to mild coercion.

Of course, if you do not know of any hidden bomb even though the interrogator thinks that you do, no amount of torture will get its location out of you, and you will indeed concoct false stories to stop the pain. That is why there are countless examples of suspects confessing under pressure to crimes that they did not commit. Moreover, if the interrogator's goal is not to get to the truth but to force a confession or simply to humiliate you, the results of the interrogation may be a great deal more noise than signal. Coercion is thus at best a crude and imperfect means of obtaining intelligence.

But in a case like KSM's, it may also be the only hope of learning what a terrorist mastermind knows in time to save the innocent people whom he is conspiring to murder. Interrogators are not looking for a confession to use at trial but for information that could prevent mass murders. They also have strong incentives and, in many cases, opportunities to check the accuracy of a prisoner's statements: they can interview co-conspirators, use polygraph tests, find out whether people or things are where the prisoner said that they would be, and more.

Indeed, a substantial body of recent and not-so-recent historical evidence supports the proposition that both mild coercion and harsher methods, including torture, have indeed extracted important information, probably saving lives. Examples, beginning in 1946, include the following:

—In 1946, British forces found and detained the wife of Rudolph Hoess, the commandant of Auschwitz. Through several days of interrogation, she claimed that Hoess was dead. The British then told her that unless she wrote down her husband's whereabouts quickly, they would put her three sons on a train to the Soviet Union, where it was understood that the KGB would kill them. She gave the British the information that they wanted. They caught Hoess that evening, disguised as a farm worker.[103]

—In 1978, in a decision finding coercive British interrogations of suspected Irish Republican Army terrorists to be unlawful but not severe enough to constitute torture, the European Court of Human Rights nonetheless found that they had been effective in obtaining "a considerable amount of intelligence information, including the identification of 700 members of both IRA factions and the discovery of individual responsibility for about 85 previously unexplained criminal incidents."[104]

—A 1984 federal appeals court decision recited the following findings of fact: Two kidnappers seized a taxi driver and held him for ransom. One was caught while collecting the ransom. He refused to tell police where the cabbie was held. Several officers "threatened him and physically abused him by twisting his arm and choking him until he revealed where [the cab driver] was being held." The court found that the officers had acted "in a reasonable manner to obtain information they needed in order to protect another individual from bodily harm or death."[105]

—A Sri Lankan army officer told terrorism scholar Bruce Hoffman a personal story, apparently from sometime in the 1990s but impossible to verify, as an example of the need for ruthlessness to defeat terrorists such as the Tamil Tigers. The officer's unit caught three hardened Tamil Tigers suspected of having recently planted in the city of Colombo "a bomb that was then ticking away, the minutes counting down to catastrophe." The officer asked the three where the bomb was. They were silent. He asked again, adding that if they did not answer, he would kill them. They remained silent. He pulled his pistol from his gun belt, pointed it at one man's forehead and shot him dead. The other two talked immediately. The bomb, hidden in a crowded railway station and set to explode during evening rush hour, was found and defused.[106]

—In 1995, Philippine intelligence agents caught an al Qaeda member named Abdul Hakim Murad in a Manila bomb factory. Murad was defiant through sixty-seven days of savage torture, including beatings that broke his ribs and lighted cigarettes crushed into his genitals. He finally broke when agents disguised as Mossad agents threatened to take him to Israel. He then revealed a plot to assassinate Pope John Paul II, crash eleven U.S. airliners carrying some 4,000 people into the Pacific Ocean, and fly a private Cessna loaded with explosives into the CIA's headquarters. Philippine authorities finally turned him over to the United States.[107]

—Israel's secret services have broken up terrorist cells while planned bombings were in the operational stage, as Israel's High Court of Justice detailed in the very same 1999 decision in which it declared unlawful, absent legislative authorization, the coercive methods that the security services called "a moderate degree of physical pressure." Indeed, it said that such coercion "has led to the thwarting of murderous attacks" and cited several cases in which interrogators had obtained lifesaving intelligence. For example, an applicant who complained of Israeli torture had admitted under interrogation "that he was involved in numerous terrorist activities in the course of which many Israeli citizens were killed," including the bombing of the café "Appropo" in Tel Aviv, in which three women were murdered and 30 people were injured. . . . A powerful explosive device, identical to the one detonated at the Café "Appropo" in Tel Aviv, was found in the applicant's village (Tzurif) subsequent to the dismantling and interrogation of the terrorist cell to which he belonged. Uncovering this explosive device thwarted an attack similar to the one at Café "Appropo."[108]

—An al Qaeda terrorist named Jamal Beghal was arrested in the Dubai airport in October 2001. His lawyer later charged that he had been "tossed into a darkened cell, handcuffed to a chair, blindfolded and beaten and that his family was threatened." After some weeks, he suddenly decided to cooperate and revealed secrets that thwarted a planned bombing of the U.S. embassy in Paris and that could possibly—had he been caught and interrogated sooner—have prevented the September 11 attacks.[109]

Some of these cases are disputed, and none is by itself dispositive. Our point is not to defend the sometimes savage tactics described in these examples—or in the countless others that point in the same direction. It is, rather, to emphasize that it will not do to pretend that the United States can ban coercion without cost. While it remains very much an open question how often and under what circumstances coercion generates useful intelligence, the correct answer clearly is not "never." As Philip Bobbitt puts it,

> There is a reason why, in the very teeth of explicit and pervasive law to the contrary—domestic and international— . . . the U.S., the UK, France, and Israel have repeatedly engaged in highly coercive techniques of interrogating terrorists. That reason has more to do with the moral imperatives of [protecting their people] than it does with the depravity of officials.[110]

The Arguments for Banning All Coercion and their Flaws

The fact that coercive interrogation has probably saved many lives, at least on rare occasions, does not disarm those who say that torture or less severe forms of coercion are always wrong. One of the more candid arguments for that proposition comes from Michael Ignatieff:

> Those of us who oppose torture should also be honest enough to admit that we may have to pay a price for our own convictions. *Ex ante,* of course, I cannot tell how high this price must be. *Ex post* following

another terrorist attack that might have been prevented through the exercise of coercive interrogation—the price of my scruple might simply seem too high. This is a risk I am prepared to take, but frankly, a majority of fellow citizens is unlikely to concur.[111]

The following, in roughly ascending order of persuasiveness, are the nine principal arguments that torture and near-torture—some would say any kind of coercion—should *never* be used, and the reasons we regard "never" as an unpersuasive and indeed morally flawed stance.

—First, absolutist opponents say that torture or near-torture is simply immoral in all circumstances, no matter how strong the evidence that the prisoner was involved in planning an imminent mass murder and no matter how many lives that it might save.[112] That is a weak argument on its own terms. By choosing to allow the massacre of innocents in order to avoid inflicting pain on would-be mass murderers, it embraces the greater of two moral evils. Bobbitt takes the moral offensive against this kind of absolutism. Positing a hypothetical ticking-bomb case, he asserts: "In such a situation, only a self-absorbed monster would say, sweetly, 'Oh no, I mustn't (even if I wish I could), sorry,' thus deliberately sentencing unnumbered innocents to death and dismemberment in order to protect the manifestly guilty."[113]

—Second, one of the most common arguments against brutal interrogation is that if the United States abuses its prisoners, it will expose U.S. prisoners to abuse as well. That makes sense in the context for which the Geneva Conventions were originally designed: wars between states in which the belligerents capture enemy soldiers and are willing to provide reciprocal assurances that prisoners of war will be treated well as honorable, lawful combatants. The reciprocity argument carries less weight when the prisoners being detained are stateless terrorists committed to torturing and murdering as many American soldiers and civilians alike as they can. Reciprocity presumes a degree of enemy commitment to the treaties—a commitment that is simply counterfactual in the case of global terrorists.

—Third, one clear cost of the highly coercive CIA and military interrogations of al Qaeda terrorists has been and will continue to be that it makes it far more difficult, if not impossible, to prosecute major terrorist suspects with any semblance of legitimacy unless none of the essential evidence derives from the coercive interrogations. The fruits of those interrogations will and should be inadmissible in civilian courts in almost all cases and also in military commissions. That helps account for why—seven years after Bush ordered the creation of a system of military commissions to prosecute al

Qaeda terrorists for war crimes—so few prosecutions have proceeded before them and no defendant has been convicted of any role in the September 11 attacks or other murderous crimes. Indeed, the proceedings at Guantánamo have generated far more publicity about what was done by the United States to extract information from the defendants than about their alleged crimes.

The inability to use evidence in court is a high price to pay for whatever intelligence was gained through coercive interrogations, but the price may have been worth paying if the intelligence gained has saved lives. Holding "enemy combatants" for the duration of the war either under the laws of war or under some other administrative detention regime presents a plausible— if suboptimal—legal alternative to prosecuting them. While establishing the guilt of these mass murderers beyond a reasonable doubt at public trials represents an abiding policy objective, it is not the only policy objective. It may sometimes be more important to get intelligence that might thwart future attacks than to publicly prove the guilt of and punish those responsible for past attacks.

—Fourth, opponents of any coercion argue that any use of interrogation methods that can reasonably be called "torture" either violates the 1994 law making torture a crime or invites disrespect for that law. Moreover, they argue that any use of near-torture or even mildly coercive interrogation violates international law, including the Geneva Conventions and the U.N. Convention against Torture and Other Cruel, Humiliating, or Degrading Treatment or Punishment. It follows that even far more judicious use of coercive interrogation than that practiced by the Bush administration opens the United States to charges of violating international law, including its treaty obligations.

The trouble with this argument is that while the use of torture and near-torture surely violates international law, the use of mildly coercive interrogation on stateless terrorists does not clearly violate Geneva or any other international agreement, at least not as ratified by the United States. In addition, not all use of near-torture violates U.S. law. Finally, while the United States should strive to comply with international law when possible, neither it nor any other nation has shrunk from violating international law when necessary to protect its vital interests.

—Fifth, opponents of coercive interrogation argue that even if it does sometimes "work," it so infrequently offers the most effective approach that it leads to a net loss in the amount of good intelligence obtained. This point is probably true in most circumstances. Our view, outlined above, that coercive interrogation *can* prove effective in obtaining lifesaving information under certain circumstances does not negate the argument that it happens so

rarely and unpredictably that the large costs of a coercive interrogation program to effective intelligence collection outweigh any of its benefits. Indeed,
apart from the fact that the Bush administration could point to no conclusive
public evidence that its coercive interrogations were effective, there are stacks
of books and articles from the past few years reciting dozens and even hundreds of examples of coercive interrogations of small fry and mistakenly suspected innocents that yielded little or no useful information. There also are
cases in which prisoners responded to torture or near-torture by misleading
the Bush administration into disastrous misjudgments and blunders. It also
might well be true that because of rampant excesses, the Bush administration's
coercive interrogation policy generated more costs than benefits—though
that is impossible to assess rigorously without a firm sense of how many lives,
if any, it saved. But even if one assumes that the costs to intelligence gathering of the Bush interrogation program vastly exceeded its benefits to intelligence gathering, the same would not necessarily be true if the current administration and Congress were to adopt interrogation laws and policies
authorizing more judicious use of more limited forms of coercion.

—Sixth and seventh, opponents contend that coercive interrogation, once
begun, tends to send its practitioners and advocates hurtling down two slippery slopes. The first leads to the use of ever more extreme methods on prisoners who are not easily broken, such as Abu Zubaydah and KSM, or who
have no useful information. The first August 1, 2002, "torture memo" greased
the path down this slope by effectively telling the interrogators that just about
anything that they might want to do was legal and that the president's word
was the law. Perhaps the easily broken sort of prisoner who can be forced to
spill his guts by mild coercion is not likely to know very much; perhaps the
hardened terrorist leaders who are most likely to have lifesaving information
will not reveal it unless put through out-and-out torture. If it can be established with confidence that those propositions are true, it is proper to ban all
coercive interrogation, since the law has long banned pushing the prisoner's
pain to the point of torture.

The trouble is that those propositions cannot be established with confidence. Nobody knows the set of tactics that optimizes the ratio of the valuable
intelligence extracted in emergency situations to the coercive force exerted—
which seems, to us anyway, to be the morally essential ratio. The Israelis appear
to have obtained a considerable amount of lifesaving intelligence by highly
coercive methods that stopped short of torture. Chris Mackey's book cites
similar successes with milder coercion in Afghanistan. And a case can be made
that the moral imperative to prevent terrorist mass murders may justify—as

a matter of right and wrong, although not as a matter of law—the suffering of a few terrorists such as Abu Zubaydah, KSM, and al-Qahtani.

The other slippery slope leads toward brutalizing large numbers of small fry and innocent detainees. Harsh methods initially designed for use against only the worst of the worst, who presumably have the most lifesaving information, tend to spread to less important cell leaders; then to individual foot soldiers; then to their siblings, parents, children, and neighbors; and then to many innocents who are wrongly suspected of being terrorists. That certainly occurred in the military (though not the CIA) under Bush.

A *Washington Post* editorial drew a broader lesson. Speaking of the dismissal of the war crimes charges against al-Qahtani, it asserted, "His case is testament to the fact that extreme tactics, even when used to prevent violence, almost always backfire."[114] But "almost always"—with its implication of inevitability—probably overstates the matter. The brutal methods used on al-Qahtani migrated overseas because of avoidable Bush administration blunders and arrogance. Bush did not have to toss the Geneva Conventions aside and throw the military into a state of confusion about what law, if any, interrogators had to obey. The Justice Department did not have to give the White House and CIA memos that so drastically narrowed the anti-torture law and asserted the president's power to order wholesale torture. Rumsfeld did not have to give al-Qahtani's handlers such an open-ended authorization to work him over or take so little care to prevent the spread of techniques intended only for use at Guantánamo. General Miller did not have to advise that prisoners be treated like dogs. The military did not have to circulate a confusing succession of inconsistent rules at Abu Ghraib. Indeed, the administration did not have to permit coercive interrogation in the military—which holds the most and lowest-level detainees—at all. Confining the use of such methods to the CIA's small corps of highly trained interrogators and to its especially high-value group of detainees greatly limited the number of prisoners subjected to them.

In other words, in the future, with better laws and better leaders, the United States might be able to save lives by using coercive—and in dire emergencies highly coercive—interrogation methods only on the few prisoners who seem especially likely to have lifesaving information and to do so without crossing the line into torture and without again brutalizing large numbers of small fry and innocents.

—Eighth, opponents argue that coercive interrogation represents a betrayal of American values and traditions. Since the Revolutionary War, the United States has taken pride in its renunciation of torture and abuse of helpless prisoners. While the British brutalized captured members of George Washington's army, Washington ordered that British prisoners of war were to be treated "with humanity," to receive food and medical care, and to be housed in conditions comparable to those of their American captors.[115] From the Civil War through World Wars I and II, with the adoption of the Geneva Conventions and beyond, the United States took the lead in pushing for international rules to prevent mistreatment of prisoners of war. As Philip Zelikow, a former senior adviser to Condoleezza Rice, stressed in an April 2007 lecture, the high-level Bush administration approval of methods involving prolonged physical torment was unprecedented in U.S. history, even during World War II, which took hundreds of thousands of American lives. Nor did World War II–era leaders such as Henry Stimson, George Marshall, and Winston Churchill "rely on lawyers to tell them what was right and wrong," Zelikow said.[116]

That point has a great deal of merit. Coercion is an ugly thing; torture raises that ugliness to an especially high degree. But the high-minded ideals professed by U.S. leaders and expounded in the Geneva Conventions have often coexisted with some space in practice for the use of fairly tough coercive interrogation methods. In a carefully researched paper contradicting the conventional wisdom that the post–September 11 prisoner abuse was almost unprecedented in U.S. history, a scholar named William Levi has written: "Almost without exception, the techniques approved after 9/11 for military interrogations of unlawful combatants would have been understood to fall within the legal constraints of the Geneva Conventions for protected prisoners of war at one point or another pre-9/11."[117]

In a review of declassified Defense Department and CIA interrogation manuals, Levi found that even after ratification of the 1949 Geneva Conventions, both military and CIA interrogation techniques long remained much rougher than a literal reading of Geneva would have led one to expect. The military authorized and claimed as consistent with Geneva techniques including drugs, slaps, and other physical pressures short of torture to induce disorientation. And the CIA long maintained more permissive guidelines than the military. CIA manuals encouraged the use of sensory deprivation to soften up detainees for their interrogators. As the military's rules became tighter in the 1960s and early 1970s, the CIA began outsourcing some interrogations to foreign governments with much looser standards. U.S. forces trained Latin American governments how to use tactics that U.S. policy forbade and shared the information obtained.[118] In other words, the real history of U.S. interrogation has not taken place entirely on the high road; it has stepped off on the shoulder in exigent—and sometimes less than exigent—circumstances.

—Ninth and finally, opponents argue that coercive interrogation fans hatred of the United States and risks alienating allies. They are undoubtedly correct on that point. Perhaps the most powerful argument against coercive interrogation is that by abandoning the moral high ground, the United States forfeits international support, spurs anti-Americanism, and encourages more people to become terrorists than the nation can ever catch or kill. The evidence of the backlash against the United States is all around, in headlines and polls showing a deep drop in sympathy for the country all over the world since 2001. The brutal interrogations in Guantánamo, Afghanistan, and Iraq may also have done as much to alienate potential informants as to reap valuable intelligence. While that hypothesis is inherently untestable, it is sufficiently plausible to warrant firm repudiation of the Bush approach.

More broadly, the widespread view in Europe and elsewhere that the United States has systematically tortured prisoners has done incalculable damage to the international cooperation in fighting terrorists that is essential to success. In poll after poll, most people around the world say that the United States plays a negative role in world affairs.

The risk that alienating foreign opinion can contribute to military defeat is illustrated by the aftermath of the torture of Algerian revolutionaries by French forces during the 1957 Battle of Algiers. The French squeezed enough information out of the revolutionaries to win the immediate battle but lost the war, in part because their brutal tactics had swelled the ranks of the revolutionaries and their sympathizers as well as outraged public opinion in France and elsewhere.[119] All this adds up to a serious case that perhaps the only way to recapture the high ground in world opinion and to make a clean break with the Bush record would be to ban all coercive interrogation—even angry shouting—as Congress has voted to do and the new Obama policies do on at least a temporary basis.

A serious case—but ultimately an unpersuasive one, in our view. Polls and anecdotal evidence alike suggest that the image of the United States is not actually so bad in much of the world and that the anti-Americanism concentrated in the Muslim world and western Europe would not be greatly dissipated by a ban on coercive interrogation.[120] This anti-Americanism has numerous causes, including hatred of the U.S. alliance with Israel and the smugness and hypocrisy of Europeans who for decades have taken the U.S. security umbrella for granted. That is not to deny that a flat ban on coercive interrogation might improve the U.S. image abroad. But the same might be true if the new administration and Congress firmly repudiate the excesses and abuses of the Bush years while at the same time allowing limited, carefully controlled, coercive interrogation short of torture to meet dire emergencies and help unlock the secrets of important terrorist captives such as KSM.

Fixing the Law

We have seen the terrible consequences of allowing coercive interrogation to spin out of control. But the preceding discussion suggests that it is an over-reaction to ban *all* coercive interrogation—that is, to make permanent the current Obama policy, particularly by passing a statute of the type Congress would have enacted in February 2008 but for Bush's veto. A more clear-eyed consideration of long-term interrogation policy starts from a different, less comfortable premise—that the real question is not whether coercion is ever appropriate but how much coercion is appropriate, how rarely, and with what, if any, degree of legal sanction. We should also resist answering that question in simple terms, but acknowledge the need for different rules for different agencies that conduct interrogations. Threats and intimidation that are unacceptable in the military context and banned by the Army Field Manual may be routine and quite legal in, for example, the criminal justice context, where police officers and FBI agents regularly threaten suspects with lengthy prison terms—even the death penalty—to get them to cooperate. (Presumably for that reason, the Obama executive order specifically exempted the FBI from the requirement to follow the Army Field Manual.[121]) In the real world, there is no magic line between coercion and noncoercion. Even the line between physical coercion and psychological pressure is not altogether sharp.

Humility is critical in this policymaking exercise. In the absence of more rigorous study of how coercion has worked in practice, society can only guess at answers to the questions of when and how much coercion is appropriate. It follows, then, that any policy proposal that has not been predetermined by ideology must be tentative—subject to revision in a more permissive direction if evidence develops that coercion saves lives and in a less permissive direction if evidence develops that it produces results that are either too confounded with noise or obtainable by less ugly means. While we await more empirical evidence of what works and what does not, we believe that U.S. laws and policies should be guided by the following principal lessons of the post–September 11 experience:

—Rapport-building methods such as those used by military interrogators under the Army Field Manual should be the preferred approach for interrogating suspected terrorists. They not only present fewer legal and moral problems, they also often offer the most effective means of obtaining the largest volume of useful information. What's more, they certainly facilitate eventual criminal prosecution more readily than do coercive methods. They do not alienate our allies—though the noncriminal detentions that enable them may still do so—nor do they rally world opinion against the U.S. fight against terrorism.

—When noncoercive methods seem unavailing, it will often—although not always—be because the prisoner has little or no information to give up. One cannot assume that every prisoner is going to tell all if interrogators only keep on him long and hard enough to "break" him. Sometimes, they don't tell all because they don't know much.

—Coercive methods may well spur such prisoners to mislead interrogators by fabricating stories to stop the pain inflicted on them. That claim is often repeated by those for whom it ineluctably counsels abstention from all coercive methods all the time. While it does not lead us to that conclusion, it should induce a great deal of caution about authorizing highly coercive practices and a skepticism about the intelligence gotten from detainees subjected to those practices without strong corroborating information.

—Any use of coercive methods also poses a grave danger that the interrogators will be tempted to ratchet up the pressure to the point of near-torture or torture if mild coercion does not produce results. Again, this point does not necessarily counsel abstention from all coercion, but it should induce especially clear and rigorous regulatory constraints on escalation.

—Vague definitions of what is and is not lawful are doubly dangerous. On the one hand, they may tempt some officials to twist the law to allow extreme methods, giving latitude to people like Yoo, who wanted to beat the law until it confessed. On the other hand, vagueness can also induce undue risk aversion. When the law does not offer clarity about what methods are legal, it can deter officials from using even perfectly defensible techniques that should be lawful and might save lives. The current reliance on the Army Field Manual, which stops far short of the legal lines—wherever they reside—is an example of that danger. Unsure of where the legal lines actually lay, the military set its regulatory limits extremely conservatively.

—High-level approval of coercive interrogation can ripple down through the ranks, leading to wholesale brutalization of small-fry detainees who know little or nothing of value, as well as of wrongly suspected innocent people. It is, therefore, critical not to have a *general policy* of authorizing harsh interrogations. To minimize the danger of the contagion's spreading and diffusing throughout the government, any coercive methods should be administered only by well-trained personnel in an isolated program. Those interrogators must be carefully screened to filter out people who might be tempted to abuse prisoners as a form of retribution or as a source of sadistic pleasure.

Most of the major elements of a policy based on the foregoing principles are already in place, the product of the reforms of the late Bush years and the early Obama months. The Bush administration already reduced the risks of brutalizing small-fry detainees and of using unfit or badly trained interrogators by ending the military's use of coercive interrogation methods. By late 2006, coercion was already segregated to the tiny CIA program, which had been emptied of subjects. The Obama policy, while eliminating the program, keeps in place the principle that high-value detainees should face interrogation by an elite cadre of interrogators. That means that the small number of the highest-value prisoners will still be handled by a small number of carefully chosen and specially trained interrogators.

Meanwhile, the *Hamdan* decision and the MCA's revision of the War Crimes Act, both of which took place in 2006, have fortified the case that it is a war crime to use waterboarding and perhaps some other highly coercive methods that the CIA had previously employed on the basis of the Justice Department's opinion that they were lawful. In addition, waterboarding was already barred by the CIA's classified interrogation rules when Obama shut down the agency's program. And both Obama in a press conference and Attorney General Eric Holder in his confirmation hearings made clear that they regard waterboarding as torture.[122]

What's more, the McCain amendment codified a series of important judgments that reflect a kind of consensus about military interrogation policy—a consensus that could plausibly inform future policymaking about CIA interrogations, too. The first of the judgments is that Congress is not well-suited to write the granular rules of interrogation policy. The McCain amendment says nothing about the details of what military interrogators may and may not do. Rather, it delegates to the military itself the authority to write the rules and merely requires as a matter of law that the military then follow those rules. It therefore leaves the military with great policy latitude both to set the boundaries and, if circumstances change, to alter them. If the military tomorrow decided that it needed to use more coercion and could justify it under the high-altitude principles Congress has set, it could rewrite the Army Field Manual to ramp up the permissible pressure at least to some degree—all without going to Congress.

The second judgment reflected in the McCain amendment is that the legal restraints on interrogation should not be enforced by adding new criminal laws to those banning torture (which we would tighten as detailed below) and war crimes. Even if a tactic violates the Army Field Manual or, more fundamentally, the ban on cruel, inhuman, or degrading treatment, it remains an administrative matter under the MCA unless it is sufficiently violent to constitute a "grave breach" of the Geneva Conventions. In other words, Congress has recognized that not every violation of the interrogation rules or of international law should be criminally prosecutable.

The result of those policy judgments and their wide acceptance is that the residual policy dispute is quite narrow. A near consensus has developed that military detainees should not be coercively interrogated at all and the CIA should rarely use coercion. The only real dispute is over that tiny handful of nonmilitary detainees who are both high-value enough to have access to prospective terrorist planning information and who stubbornly resist noncoercive interrogation.

While President Obama's policy makes a clean break with the Bush record, it actually does not effectively answer the question of how best to handle this group. Indeed, the new policy seems likely to fail on both a substantive and a procedural level. First, it goes too far by banning all coercion all the time. Second, the rule is unstable because it can so easily be changed at the whim of the president, whether Obama or, perhaps, a successor more like Bush. An administration down the road that wanted to resume waterboarding could rescind the current order and adopt legal positions like those of the prior administration. Unless the Obama administration and Congress hammer out rules that provide interrogators with clear guidance about what is and is not allowed and write those rules into statute, the United States risks vacillating under the vagaries of current law between overly permissive and overly restrictive guidance.

The general goals of new legislation should be threefold:

—To make it a crime beyond cavil to use interrogation methods considered by reasonable people to be torture. The torture statute already does that to some degree, but the fact that it arguably permitted techniques as severe as waterboarding suggests that it may require some tightening. The key here is that the statute should cover *all* techniques the use of which ought to prompt criminal prosecution.

—To subject CIA interrogators in almost all cases to rules that, without relaxing current law's ban on cruel, inhuman, and degrading treatment, permit relatively mild forms of coercion that are properly off limits to military interrogators.

—To allow the president, subject to strict safeguards, to authorize use of harsher methods short of torture (as defined in the revised criminal statute) in true emergencies or on extraordinarily high-value captives such as KSM.

Only Congress can provide the democratic legitimacy and the fine-tuning of criminal laws that can deliver such a regime. Only Congress can, for example, pass a new law making it clear that waterboarding—or any other technique of comparable severity—will henceforth be a federal crime. Only Congress can offer clear assurances to operatives in the field that there exists a safe harbor against prosecution for conduct ordered by higher-ups in a crisis in the genuine belief that an attack may be around the corner. Only Congress, in other words, can create a regime that plausibly turns away from the past without giving up what the United States will need in the future.

Refining the Torture Statute

Congress could accomplish the first of the three objectives most simply by adopting a definition of torture for purposes of the anti-torture statute that is more specific and detailed—and therefore less amenable to interpretative manipulation—than current law and that bans a somewhat wider range of brutality. The goal here should not be to pass a narrow anti-waterboarding law, since it requires no particular creativity to imagine inflicting some equivalent suffering by means that would not fit the terms of such a statute. Rather, the legislature should aim to define and ban the *category of techniques* that induces discomfort of such enormity that any reasonable person would regard them as torture.

As described earlier, federal law currently defines torture as "an act committed by a person acting under the color of law specifically intended to inflict severe physical or mental pain or suffering . . . upon another person within his custody or physical control." And it defines "severe mental pain and suffering" to include "the prolonged mental harm caused by or resulting from" any of four distinct behaviors: "the intentional infliction or threatened infliction of severe physical pain or suffering," "the administration or application, or threatened administration or application, of mind-altering substances or other procedures calculated to disrupt profoundly the senses or the personality," "the threat of imminent death," and "the threat that another person will imminently be subjected to" the other harms listed.[123]

There are two problems with this definition. First, "severe" is almost infinitely malleable. The statute does very little to tell an interrogator—or a president—how much pain will trigger criminal liability. Does it have to be "equivalent in intensity to the pain accompanying serious physical injury such as organ failure," as John Yoo suggested, or will discomfort beyond the scratches and bruises of day-to-day life suffice? What about techniques—such as waterboarding, for example—that leave no permanent mark or damage yet cause excruciating suffering and panic?

Second, the requirement that "mental harm" be "prolonged" introduces an analytical circularity. How can the interrogator know before he performs a technique whether it will cause *prolonged* mental harm or just temporary mental harm? And how could a jury possibly ascertain his intent? Indeed, why would any interrogator other than a sadist *ever* intend to cause prolonged mental harm?

To correct those problems, Congress should both give texture to the word "severe" and remove the requirement that mental harm be "prolonged," replacing it with a definition based on intensity and the more textured understanding of severity. Congress might define "severe physical pain or suffering" as, for example, "physical discomfort of such intensity and duration as to be unendurable by an average person." And it might define "severe mental pain or suffering" as "the mental harm caused by or resulting from" the four currently listed tortures as well as a more generalized fifth category: "the infliction of any other techniques of mental or psychological manipulation that are of sufficient intensity and duration as to be unendurable by an average person." Not every technique of coercion hurts enough to render a person willing to do anything to make it stop. Those that do are the ones that deserve the special opprobrium of the criminal law. Such a rule will not by any means make completely clear where along the spectrum coercion crosses the line into torture. It will, however, both offer more guidance than current law does and clarify that certain specific techniques whose status is now arguable fall clearly on the criminal side of the line.

For additional clarity, Congress might follow the Army's lead and identify a specific set of off-limits tactics—not as a comprehensive list but as a representative sample. The Army Field Manual both identifies the techniques that it authorizes *and* specifically proscribes techniques to be avoided. The relevant language reads:

> If used in conjunction with intelligence interrogations, prohibited actions include, but are not limited to,
>
> —Forcing the detainee to be naked, perform sexual acts, or pose in a sexual manner.
>
> —Placing hoods or sacks over the head of a detainee; using duct tape over the eyes.

—Applying beatings, electric shock, burns, or other forms of physical pain.

—"Waterboarding."

—Using military working dogs.

—Inducing hypothermia or heat injury.

—Conducting mock executions.

—Depriving the detainee of necessary food, water, or medical care.[124]

A similar approach for CIA interrogations might well specify different techniques, but laying out examples in statute would offer executive branch lawyers guidance regarding the sort of coercive intensity that Congress means to ban.

CIA Flexibility under the McCain Amendment

Even if Congress were to tighten the torture statute to reflect a more intuitive understanding of torture, a considerable gap would remain between the prohibitions in the revised statute and those in the Army Field Manual, which forbids even mild coercion or intimidation. A smaller but still substantial gap also exists between methods that "shock the conscience" and are thus banned by the McCain amendment and the Army Field Manual. Thus, a second key goal of legislative policy should be to both authorize and set strict limits on CIA interrogations in this legal space—that is, space forbidden to the military as a matter of policy but not precluded by any statute. Congress should, in other words, make clear that CIA interrogations need not follow the Army Field Manual but must by law follow a parallel code developed for the agency's own use.

Specifically, Congress should require the administration to adopt and submit to the congressional intelligence committees a detailed CIA interrogation manual, subject to revision by legislation. Like the Army Field Manual, the CIA manual should prohibit the use of any interrogation methods other than those it specifies, subject to the emergency exception described below; it should carry the force of law for those whose behavior it governs; and it should be enforced though administrative discipline, not by criminal sanction, except to the extent that violations involve highly coercive methods that amount to either torture under the definition as revised above or a violation of the War Crimes Act.

Unlike the Army Field Manual, however, the CIA manual should permit the agency far greater latitude—subject to the existing legal prohibitions on cruel, degrading, and inhuman treatment and the criminal prohibitions discussed above—both to put pressure on detainees to cooperate and to give

them benefits in exchange for cooperation. The CIA manual should authorize a range of mildly coercive methods. For example, the CIA should retain the
options of yelling, making threats, disrupting sleep patterns in a carefully limited manner, denying hot rations and comfort items, and perhaps forcing prisoners to stand for long enough to make them uncomfortable but not so long
as to put them in agony. The rules should forbid any violent physical contact.

The basic principle is that for a limited group of detainees (the highest-
value, most dangerous terrorist suspects in U.S. custody) and a limited group
of interrogators (the most highly skilled and best-trained personnel in the
government), the government should take advantage of every technique that
it can reasonably defend as lawful. Such interrogation might make it more difficult to prosecute the prisoners, whose coerced statements would be inadmissible in federal court. But that cost would be justified by the hope of
obtaining potentially lifesaving information. And any statements made before
coercion was used would still be admissible.

The CIA manual should be made public to the maximum extent possible.
The agency's interrogation rules have long been classified, on the theory that
captured terrorists should not know the limits of what might be done to them
in advance lest they be encouraged to hold out. Indeed, al Qaeda trains its terrorists in what interrogation methods to expect and how to resist. So it might
be necessary to keep some details under wraps. But perhaps not. The emergency exception described below would have the benefit of signaling to high-
value captured terrorists that they might be subjected to methods tougher
than those listed in the public manual. While the emergency exception would
also have the cost of signaling the same to the rest of the world, the world
would know that the tougher methods were reserved for the direst emergencies. In any event, it is essential for the broad contours of the manual and its
techniques to be public—and debated in public—so that it does not appear
that the United States is secretly authorizing interrogation practices more
brutal than it admits to its own people and the world at large.

An Emergency Exception

The combination of military interrogations under the Army Field Manual
and CIA interrogations under a more permissive CIA manual should provide
adequate flexibility for almost all interrogations U. S. personnel will have to
conduct. There likely will be exceptions, however—those rare captives who
seem especially likely to have lifesaving information yet prove resistant to the
usual interrogation methods—and both Congress and the executive branch
must take account of this group. In such situations, the executive branch will

face an excruciating dilemma: give up on obtaining information on which large numbers of innocent lives may depend or exceed the baseline rules for interrogations. It is reasonable to anticipate the executive branch's choice in such situations. Restraint will not appeal to officials who fear that it will sacrifice innocent lives. The question Congress must confront, therefore, is whether it wants to regulate the choice or force executive branch officials to choose between obeying the law and saving lives. In our view, the widespread acknowledgment—often quite backhanded—that in such situations coercive tactics that are otherwise unacceptable may be justified warrants congressional recognition.

Congress should, therefore, create an emergency exception to the rule against using any interrogation method not specified in the CIA manual. The exception should authorize the CIA to deviate from its interrogation manual only on personal order of the president, on a case-by-case basis, to use otherwise banned, highly coercive methods short of torture. To prevent interrogators from going too far—and to protect those using authorized methods from subsequent accusations that they did go too far—any such order should detail in writing why extraordinary methods are needed, what methods can be used, for how long, and in what combinations. It should also be accompanied by a Justice Department opinion finding that the proposed interrogation plan violates neither the prohibition against torture nor the War Crimes Act. There should, however, be no requirement that such emergency orders comply with international law, which is thought by many experts to ban all highly coercive interrogation methods—a ban that no president would or should recognize as sacrosanct when innocent lives are at stake.

The emergency exception should immunize personnel acting within the four corners of such an order from any subsequent prosecution or civil liability. For such orders, in other words, the president alone should be accountable, through the political process, including impeachment.

To provide political accountability, the orders should be valid only if signed by the president personally and shared promptly with the intelligence committees, much as presidents have long shared "findings" authorizing covert actions. The president should also be required to disclose on a regular basis the number of such orders that have been issued. That would ensure that the president does not slough such decisions off on mid-level career officials who might either resort too readily to near-torture or face years of investigation and insinuations of criminality for reasonable field judgments that appear too aggressive with the comfortable benefit of hindsight. It would also ensure that

Congress is kept informed and has appropriate recourse if the president misuses this power.[125]

Congress should, in our judgment, retain the principle that there are no exceptions to the criminal prohibitions in the anti-torture statute or the War Crimes Act. That is not to deny the possibility that torture—and nothing less than torture—might save lives in some imaginable scenario. But it will rarely, if ever, be knowable in advance that a prisoner has information that can avert imminent catastrophe and that the information can be elicited by torture and only torture. Because of that and because the costs of authorizing torture are so high, the law must regard anyone who resorts to torture, including the president, as a criminal. If such a lawbreaker acts honorably, based on a good-faith conviction that his actions were necessary to avert imminent danger to innocent lives, his protection should lie in prosecutorial judgment, public opinion, a defense of necessity, the common sense of jurors, the president's pardon power, and the judgment of history.

Anything less than a rule allowing no legal exceptions would amount to a formal endorsement of torture by the U.S. government, for the first time in history. And that would be an invitation to abuse and another disaster for the image of the United States. Senator John McCain, a victim of torture and a leading critic of waterboarding and other harsh practices, gave the right answer when presented in 2005 with a hypothetical situation involving a nuclear bomb hidden in New York. Citing President Lincoln's probably unconstitutional suspension of habeas corpus to save the union, McCain responded: "You do what you have to do, but you take responsibility for it."[126]

Conclusion

Amid the long, painful, and bruising political battle over interrogation policy, the United States has made enormous progress. The country has solved the problem of military interrogations and narrowed the problem of the highest-stakes CIA interrogations. Given that U.S. forces worldwide hold many thousands of people, it is notable that the government has reached near-consensus on how to treat all of them except a tiny group that, in all probability, currently numbers zero.

That said, Congress's work is not done. As long as it leaves the definition of torture as narrow as it is and as long as such a wide gap persists between what is lawful in the highest-stakes interrogations and what the Army Field Manual permits, its guidance will remain at once overly permissive and overly restrictive—overly permissive in that the law will not criminalize conduct that reasonable people will intuitively understand to be torture and overly restrictive in that the rules will prohibit coercions that, under certain circumstances, are altogether reasonable. A better balance is possible—one that would protect the security of the United States without staining its honor.

Notes

1. Barack Obama, Inaugural Address, Washington, January 20, 2009; Barack Obama, Address to Joint Session of Congress, Washington, February 24, 2009.

2. Barack Obama, News Conference by the President, Washington, April 29, 2009.

3. CIA director Michael Hayden has said that since 2001, the agency used "enhanced techniques" on only about one-third of the fewer than 100 suspected al Qaeda terrorists of whom it has had custody. U.S. Senate Select Committee on Intelligence, *Open Hearing: Current and Projected National Security Threats,* 110th Cong., 2nd sess., February 5, 2008. As subsequent releases made clear, ninety-four detainees passed through the CIA's detention program, of whom twenty-eight were interrogated with any of the enhanced techniques. See Steven G. Bradbury to John A Rizzo, memorandum, "Re: Application of United States Obligations under Article 16 of the Convention against Torture to Certain Techniques that May Be Used in the Interrogation of High-Value Al Qaeda Detainees," May 30, 2005, p. 29 (hereafter "Convention against Torture" memo).

4. Fifteen percent said "often"; 30 percent, "sometimes"; 24 percent, "rarely"; and 4 percent, "don't know/refused." See the Pew Research Center for the People and the Press, *Beyond Red vs. Blue* (http://people-press.org/report/?pageid=953/).

5. See Paul Steinhauser, "Poll: Don't Investigate Torture Techniques," *CNN,* May 6, 2009 (http://politicalticker.blogs.cnn.com/2009/05/06/poll-dont-investigate-torture-techniques/).

6. See, for example, Eric Schmitt and Tim Golden, "Pentagon Plans Tighter Control of Questioning," *New York Times,* November 8, 2005, p. A1.

7. See Jan Crawford Greenburg and others, "Sources: Top Bush Advisors Approved 'Enhanced Interrogation,'" *ABC News,* April 9, 2008 (http://abcnews.go.com/TheLaw/LawPolitics/story?id=4583256&page=1/); Dick Cheney, interview by Jonathan Karl, *ABC News,* December 15, 2008. Here, "humane" is used in the colloquial sense. The Senate, in reservations to treaties, and Congress and the president, in interpretations or modifications of treaties, have sometimes defined "inhuman" more narrowly than dictionary definitions of "inhumane."

8. See Dan Eggen, "Cheney Defends 'Dunk in the Water' Remark," *Washington Post,* October 28, 2006.

9. Some, when pressed, turn out not to be such moral absolutists after all. See Benjamin Wittes, *Law and the Long War* (New York: Penguin Press, 2008), pp. 183–84,

discussing the retreat from absolutism by retired *New York Times* columnist Anthony Lewis when pressed on "ticking time bomb" question.

10. This provision, section 327 of the proposed Intelligence Authorization Act for Fiscal Year 2008, would have barred the CIA from using any interrogation method not authorized by the Army Field Manual for military interrogators, whose rules had been revised in September 2006 to make them far more restrictive than before and to ban *all* coercion and threats. Department of the Army, Field Manual 2-22.3, *Human Intelligence Collector Operations* (Department of the Army, 2006), § 8-35. See Stuart Taylor Jr., "Interrogation: Anti-Bush Overreaction," *National Journal,* December 15, 2007; Stuart Taylor Jr., "What to Do about Waterboarding," *National Journal,* March 1, 2008.

11. See, for example, David Herszenhorn, "Bill Curbing Terror Interrogators Is Sent to Bush, Who Has Vowed to Veto It," *New York Times,* February 14, 2008, p. A24; Dan Eggen, "Bush Poised to Veto Waterboarding Ban," *Washington Post,* March 8, 2008, p. A2.

12. See, for example, Editorial, "Horrifying and Unnecessary," *New York Times,* March 2, 2008, p. A10; Editorial, "Moral Barrier: The President Stands in the Way of a Ban on Torture," *Washington Post,* February 15, 2008.

13. See David Luban, quoted in Wittes, *Law and the Long War,* 185.

14. Phillip Bobbitt lists the improbable circumstances that must coincide for interrogators to know that a bomb is ticking and that their prisoner has information that could prevent it from going off. See Phillip Bobbitt, *Terror and Consent: The Wars for the Twenty-First Century* (New York: Alfred A. Knopf, 2008), p. 362.

15. See 18 U.S.C. § 2340, which reads:

(1) "Torture" means an act committed by a person acting under the color of law specifically intended to inflict severe physical or mental pain or suffering (other than pain or suffering incidental to lawful sanctions) upon another person within his custody or physical control;

(2) "Severe mental pain or suffering" means the prolonged mental harm caused by or resulting from—

(A) the intentional infliction or threatened infliction of severe physical pain or suffering;

(B) the administration or application, or threatened administration or application, of mind-altering substances or other procedures calculated to disrupt profoundly the senses or the personality;

(C) the threat of imminent death; or

(D) the threat that another person will imminently be subjected to death, severe physical pain or suffering, or the administration or application of mind-altering substances or other procedures calculated to disrupt profoundly the senses or personality.

Examples might include pulling off fingernails, cutting off fingers, applying scalding pokers or electric shock to genitals and other body parts, severe beatings, and (subject to the "prolonged mental harm" provision) holding a gun to the prisoner's head while threatening to shoot him.

16. "Convention against Torture and Other Cruel, Inhuman, or Degrading Treatment or Punishment," December 10, 1984, *United States Treaties and Other International Agreements.* See Committee against Torture, *Conclusions and Recommendations of the Committee against Torture (advance unedited version),* 36th sess., CAT/C./U.S.A./CO/2 (Geneva, 2006), at 3 (acts that cause severe mental suffering are torture "irrespective of their prolongation or its duration"); Philippe Sands, *Torture Team: Rumsfeld's Memo and the Betrayal of American Values* (New York: Palgrave Macmillan, 2008), pp. 169–70 and nn. 6–7. The United States specified its narrower definition of "severe" mental suffering in understandings lodged when it ratified the Convention. Ibid; *Reservations, Understandings, and Declarations, Convention against Torture and Other Cruel, Inhuman, or Degrading Treatment or Punishment,* S17486-92, Amendment No. 3200-3203, 101st Cong., 2nd sess., *Congressional Record* 136 (October 27, 1990).

17. Examples might include prolonged sleep deprivation that stops short of torturous extremes, forcing prisoners into uncomfortable but less-than-torturous "stress positions," and slaps or pokes in the chest that are not very painful. Some experts suggest that some methods that would not constitute CID for people of Western cultures might amount to CID for some others; devout Muslims, for example, might feel degraded if straddled by naked women.

18. Dick Cheney, interview by Tim Russert, *Meet the Press,* NBC, September 16, 2001.

19. See Frank Davies, "'Americans Are Going to Die,' CIA Warned," *Miami Herald,* September 27, 2002.

20. See, for example, Sanford Levinson, "The Debate on Torture: War against Virtual States," *Dissent* (Summer 2003), p. 79; Alan Dershowitz, *Why Terrorism Works: Understanding the Threat, Responding to the Challenge* (Yale University Press, 2003); Philip B. Heymann and Juliette N. Kayyem, *Protecting Liberty in an Age of Terror* (MIT Press, 2005), p. 31; Richard Posner, "The Best Offense," review of *Why Terrorism Works,* by Alan Dershowitz, *New Republic* 28 (September 2002).

21. See Stuart Taylor Jr., "We Don't Need to Be Scofflaws to Attack Terror," *National Journal,* February 2, 2002; Jane Mayer, *The Dark Side: The Inside Story of How the War on Terror Turned Into a War on American Ideals* (Doubleday Books, 2008), pp. 122–25.

22. 18 U.S.C. § 2441.

23. President George W. Bush to the Vice President and others, memorandum, "Humane Treatment of Al Qaeda and Taliban Detainees," February 7, 2002, in *The Torture Papers,* edited by Karen J. Greenberg and Joshua L. Dratel (New York: Cambridge University Press, 2005), pp. 134–35.

24. Tim Golden, "In U.S. Report, Brutal Details of 2 Afghan Inmates' Deaths," *New York Times,* May 20, 2005, p. A1; Human Rights Watch, *"Enduring Freedom:" Abuses by U.S. Forces in Afghanistan,* March 7, 2004, pt. III.

25. Dan Eggen and Walter Pincus, "FBI, CIA Debate Significance of Terror Suspect," *Washington Post*, December 18, 2007, p. A1; see Ron Suskind, *The One Percent Doctrine: Deep Inside America's Pursuit of Its Enemies since 9/11* (New York: Simon and Schuster, 2006), pp. 99–101, 111, 115–18.

26. Eggen and Pincus, note 25 above; Jack Goldsmith, *The Terror Presidency: Law and Judgment inside the Bush Administration* (New York: W.W. Norton, 2007), pp. 90–97.

27. Goldsmith, *The Terror Presidency*, p. 97.

28. This memo, formally titled "Standards of Conduct for Interrogation under 18 U.S.C. §§ 2340-2340A," has been published in Greenberg and Dratel, *The Torture Papers*, pp.172–217.

29. Jay S. Bybee to John Rizzo, memorandum, "Interrogation of Al Qaeda Operative," August 1, 2002, pp. 10–12.

30. Steven G. Bradbury to John A. Rizzo, memorandum, "Re: Application of 18 U.S.C §§ 2340-2340A to Certain Techniques that May Be Used in the Interrogation of a High-Value Al Qaeda Detainee," May 10, 2005, pp. 7–10 (hereafter "Certain Techniques" memo).

31. Steven G. Bradbury to John A. Rizzo, memorandum, "Re: Application of 18 U.S.C. §§ 2340-2340A to the Combined Use of Certain Techniques in the Interrogation of High-Value Al Qaeda Detainees," May 10, 2005 (hereafter "Combined Effects" memo).

32. Bradbury to Rizzo, "Certain Techniques" memo, p. 5.

33. Bradbury to Rizzo, "Convention against Torture" memo.

34. Ibid., p. 37.

35. Ibid., p. 8.

36. Bradbury to Rizzo, "Certain Techniques" memo, p. 12.

37. International Committee of the Red Cross, *ICRC Report on the Treatment of Fourteen "High Value Detainees" in CIA Custody,* February 2007. See also Bradbury to Rizzo, "Certain Techniques" memo, p. 14.

38. Suskind, *The One Percent Doctrine*, pp.114–15; Mayer, *The Dark Side*, pp. 155–57; Ali Soufan, "My Tortured Decision," *New York Times*, April 23, 2009, p. A27.

39. See Mark Mazzetti, "CIA Destroyed Tapes of Interrogations," *New York Times*, December 6, 2007.

40. The National Commission on Terrorist Attacks upon the United States, *The 9/11 Commission Report*, July 22, 2004, p. 248.

41. See, for example, Sands, *Torture Team*, pp. 128, 144–48, 225.

42. Adam Zagorin and Michael Duffy, "Inside the Interrogation of Detainee 063," *Time*, June 20, 2005, p. 26; Evan Thomas and Michael Hirsch, "The Debate over Torture," *Newsweek*, November 21, 2005; Lieutenant General Mark Schmidt and Brigadier General John Furlow, U.S. Department of Defense, *Final Report, Investigation into FBI Allegations of Detainee Abuse at Guantaùnamo Bay, Cuba Detention Facility,* June 9, 2005 (hereafter Schmidt Report), p. 14.

43. See General James T. Hill to the chairman of the Joint Chiefs of Staff, memorandum, "Counter-Resistance Techniques," October 25, 2002, in *The Torture Papers,*

edited by Greenberg and Dratel, p. 223. The memo forwards a request from Major General Michael E. Dunleavey, commanding general of Joint Task Force 170 at Guantánamo. See pp. 225–35.

44. William J. Haynes II to Secretary of Defense, memorandum, "Counter-Resistance Techniques," November 25, 2002, in *The Torture Papers,* edited by Greenberg and Dratel, pp. 236–37. See also related memoranda of General James T. Hill, Major General Michael E. Dunleavy, Lieutenant Colonel Diane E. Beaver, and Lieutenant Colonel Jerald Phifer, pp. 223–35.

45. Ibid.

46. Schmidt Report, p. 20; Zagorin and Duffy, note 42 above.

47. Schmidt Report, pp. 20, 26.

48. Editorial, "Torture's Blowback," *Washington Post,* May 16, 2008, p. A18; Sands, *Torture Team,* pp. 206–08.

49. See Human Rights First, *Tortured Justice: Using Coerced Evidence to Prosecute Terrorist Suspects,* May 2008 (hereafter cited as Tortured Justice Report), p. 29, and sources collected therein; Sands, *Torture Team,* pp.112–20.

50. See Raymond Bonner, "Questioning Terror Suspects in a Dark and Surreal World," *New York Times,* March 9, 2003.

51. See, for example, Josh White, "Top Officer Ordered to Testify on Abuse: Use of Dogs to Scare Detainees at Issue," *Washington Post,* April 9, 2006, p. A14.

52. See, for example, Schlesinger Report, in *The Torture Papers,* edited by Greenberg and Dratel, pp. 908–75. See particularly p. 914.

53. Ibid., pp. 914–15.

54. *Investigation of Intelligence Activities at Abu Ghraib,* special report prepared at the request of the Department of Defense, August 2004, in *The Torture Papers,* edited by Greenberg and Dratel, pp. 987–1131. The quoted language appears on p. 989.

55. Carl Levin, Senate Armed Services Committee, *Report of an Inquiry into the Alternative Analysis of the Issue of an Iraq-Al Qaeda Relationship,* October 21, 2004, p. xxvi.

56. For one reason to be skeptical of the Senate Armed Services Committee report on factual questions, see Stuart Taylor Jr., "Inconvenient Facts and Detainee Abuse," *National Journal,* January 10, 2009.

57. *Working Group Report on Detainee Interrogations in the Global War on Terrorism; Assessment of Legal, Historical, Policy, and Operational Considerations,* April 4, 2003, in *The Torture Papers,* edited by Greenberg and Dratel, pp. 286–359, especially pp. 340–47.

58. Memorandum of Donald Rumsfeld for the commander, U.S. Southern Command, "Counter-Resistance Techniques in the War on Terrorism," April 16, 2003, in *The Torture Papers,* edited by Greenberg and Dratel, pp. 360–63.

59. See Sands, *Torture Team,* pp. 150–54; Inspector General Glen Fine, *A Review of the FBI's Involvement in and Observations of Detainee Interrogations in Guantanamo Bay,* special report prepared at the request of the Department of Justice, May 2008 (hereafter cited as Fine Report), pp. viii-ix, xxii: "FBI observations confirm that prolonged short-shackling [continued] for at least a year after" the April 2003 Rumsfeld order took effect barring this and some other coercive practices.

60. Goldsmith, *The Terror Presidency,* pp. 40–42.

61. Ibid., pp. 152–55.

62. *Detainee Treatment Act of 2005,* Public Law 109-148, 109th Cong., 1st sess., October 5, 2005, § 1002.

63. *Hamdan* v. *Rumsfeld,* 548 U.S. 557 (2006).

64. Department of the Army, Field Manual 2-22.3, *Human Intelligence Collector Operations* (2006).

65. These eight methods include waterboarding, beatings and other physical pain, induced hypothermia or heat injuries, forced nakedness, and deprivation of food, water, or medical care. Ibid., §§ 5-75, 8-18.

66. Department of the Army, Field Manual 2-22.3, *Human Intelligence Collector Operations,* § 8-35: the interrogator "must be extremely careful that he does not threaten or coerce" a detainee or "act as if he is out of control or set himself up as the object or focal point of the [detainee's] fear"; see Taylor, "Interrogation: Anti-Bush Overrreaction."

67. *Detainee Treatment Act,* §§ 1003, 1004. Section 1004(d) specifies that "the term 'cruel, inhuman, or degrading treatment or punishment' means the cruel, unusual, and inhumane treatment or punishment prohibited by the Fifth, Eighth, and Fourteenth Amendments to the Constitution of the United States, as defined in the United States Reservations, Declarations and Understandings to the United Nations Convention against Torture and Other Forms of Cruel, Inhuman or Degrading Treatment or Punishment done at New York, December 10, 1984." The relevant federal case law under those constitutional amendments boils down to a balancing test in which the court decides whether the methods used to get information out of the prisoner were far harsher than can be justified by the importance and urgency of the information sought. Specifically, the Supreme Court has ruled that suspects have a substantive due process right to be free from police practices "so brutal and so offensive to human dignity" that they "shock the conscience." *Rochin* v. *California,* 342 U.S. 165, 174 (1952): pumping a suspect's stomach merely to get evidence for drug prosecution shocks the conscience. The Court has suggested that the test calls for balancing the harshness of the methods used against the urgency of the need for information. See *County of Sacramento* v. *Lewis,* 523 U.S. 833, 849 (1998): "conduct intended to injure in some way *unjustifiable by any government interest* [emphasis added] is the sort of official action most likely to rise to the conscience-shocking level." If the information sought could avert an imminent killing, for example, the balancing test might allow use of very harsh methods indeed. See *Leon* v. *Wainwright,* 734 F. 2d 770, 772-73 (11th Cir. 1984). Indeed, Justice Antonin Scalia said in an interview broadcast by BBC in Britain that in the unlikely event of a "ticking time bomb" scenario, "It would be absurd to say that you couldn't, I don't know, stick something under the fingernail, smack him in the face." Ralph Satter, "Scalia Says 'So-Called Torture' Cannot Be Ruled Out as Interrogation Method," *Associated Press,* February 14, 2008.

68. *Military Commissions Act of 2006,* Public Law 109-366, 109th Cong., 2nd sess., October 10, 2006, § 6 (amending 18 U.S.C. 2441); see especially provisions of 18

U.S.C. 2441(d)(2) retroactively and narrowly defining "severe" and "serious" physical and mental pain or suffering by reference to the torture statute, 18 U.S.C. 2340.

69. *Detainee Treatment Act,* § 1004(A).

70. Executive Order 13440, "Interpretation of the Geneva Conventions Common Article 3 as Applied to a Program of Detention and Interrogation Operated by the Central Intelligence Agency, July 20, 2007," *Federal Register,* title 72, no. 141, 40,705-09 (July 24, 2007). See Greg Miller, "Bush Signs New CIA Interrogation Rules," *Los Angeles Times,* July 21, 2007. See also General Michael Hayden, "Director's Statement on Executive Order on Detentions, Interrogations: Statement to Employees by Director of the Central Intelligence Agency, General Michael V. Hayden, on the Executive Order on Detentions and Interrogations," CIA press statement, July 20, 2007.

71. See Mark Mazzetti, "Letters Outline Legal Rationale for C.I.A. Tactics," *New York Times,* April 27, 2008.

72. See 18 U.S.C. § 2441(d)(2)(E)(2).

73. See House Committee on the Judiciary, Subcommittee on Constitution, Civil Rights, and Civil Liberties, *Oversight Hearing on the Justice Department's Office of Legal Counsel,* 110th Cong., 2nd sess., 2008; Dan Eggen, "Justice Official Defends Rough CIA Interrogations," *Washington Post,* February 17, 2008.

74. Executive Order, "Ensuring Lawful Interrogations" (January 22, 2009).

75. Schmidt Report, p. 20.

76. See Office of the Assistant Secretary of Defense (Public Affairs), "Guantánamo Provides Valuable Intelligence Information," U.S. Department of Defense news release, June 12, 2005; Daniel J. Dell'Orto, White House press briefing, June 22, 2004.

77. Senate Armed Services Committee, *Hearing on Guantanamo Bay Detainee Treatment,* 109th Cong., 1st sess., July 13, 2005.

78. Schlesinger Report, in *The Torture Papers,* edited by Greenberg and Dratel, pp. 908–75. The quoted language appears on p. 924.

79. See Sands, *Torture Team,* pp. 144–48, 159–60; Adam Zagorin, "'20th Hijacker' Claims that Torture Made Him Lie," *Time,* March 3, 2006.

80. See Tortured Justice Report, pp. 29–30, and sources collected therein—for example, former FBI agent Jack Cloonan told Human Rights First that the coercive interrogations at Guantánamo were "a complete and unmitigated failure" (p. 219). Dan Coleman, another former FBI agent, reportedly asserted: "Brutalization doesn't work; we know that. Besides, you lose your soul" (Mayer, *The Dark* Side, p. 119). And at a September 6, 2006, news briefing announcing the new Army Field Manual, Lieutenant General John Kimmons, deputy chief of staff for intelligence, asserted: "No good intelligence is going to come from abusive practices. I think history tells us that. I think the empirical evidence of the last five years, hard years, tells us that." Office of the Assistant Secretary of Defense (Public Affairs), "DoD News Briefing with Deputy Assistant Secretary Stimson and Lt. Gen. Kimmons from the Pentagon," U.S. Department of Defense news release, September 6, 2006.

81. Bob Woodward, "Detainee Tortured, Says U.S. Official: Trial Overseer Cites 'Abusive' Methods against 9/11 Suspect," *Washington Post,* January 14, 2009, p. A01.

82. Chris Mackey and Greg Miller, *The Interrogators: Task Force 500 and America's Secret War against Al Qaeda* (New York: Back Bay Books, 2005), pp. xxx, 285–89, 354–64, 468, 476, 477.

83. West's actions apparently violated the Uniform Code of Military Justice and would qualify as torture under international law, if not U.S. law. He was threatened with a court-martial for attempted assault and up to eight years imprisonment and was eventually forced to retire. See Audrey Hudson, "West Would Make 'Sacrifice' Again," *Washington Times,* December 19, 2003, p. 1.

84. Eggen and Pincus, note 25 above; see Suskind, *The One Percent Doctrine,* pp. 94–96, 100.

85. Scott Shane, "Inside the Interrogation of a 9/11 Mastermind," *New York Times,* June 22, 2008, p. A1.

86. Eggen and Pincus, note 25 above; Suskind, *The One Percent Doctrine,* pp. 229–230; Associated Press, "Khalid Sheikh Mohammed's Words Provide Glimpse into the Mind of a Terrorist," *USA Today,* March 16, 2007; see Elaine Shannon and Michael Weisskopf, "Khalid Sheikh Mohammed Names Names," *Time,* March 24, 2003: "Some officials remain skeptical that at least some of [KSM's statements were] intentionally misleading," but some were corroborated, and a counter-terrorism official said it was "valuable, credible, specific information."

87. Suskind, *The One Percent Doctrine,* pp. 228–30.

88. Shane, "Inside the Interrogation of a 9/11 Mastermind," note 85 above.

89. Ibid.

90. Ibid.

91. George Tenet, interview by Scott Pelley, *60 Minutes,* CBS, April 29, 2007; George Tenet, *At the Center of the Storm: My Years at the CIA* (HarperCollins, 2007), p. 256.

92. Goldsmith, *The Terror Presidency,* pp. 151–52.

93. Lawrence Wright, "The Spymaster," *New Yorker,* January 21, 2008, p. 52.

94. Speech of George W. Bush, Washington, September 6, 2006.

95. Timothy Noah, "More Library Tower Nonsense," *Slate,* April 27, 2009, contra Marc A. Thiessen, "The CIA's Questioning Worked," *Washington Post,* April 21, 2009, and Thiessen, "The West Coast Plot: An Inconvenient Truth," *National Review Online,* April 25, 2009 (http://corner.nationalreview.com/post/?q=ZDE5YTNmZTg5OWUy OTlkMGUxOTk3OGMxY2I4ZDQ4YWQ=).

96. Bush speech, note 94 above.

97. See, for example, Sheryl Gay Stolberg, "President Moves 16 Held in Secret to Guantanamo," *New York Times,* September 7, 2006, p. A1; R. Jeffrey Smith and Michael Fletcher, "Bush Says Detainees Will Be Tried," *Washington Post,* September 7, 2006, p. A1.

98. David Rose, "Tortured Reasoning," *Vanity Fair,* December 16, 2008, p. 4 (www.vanityfair.com/magazine/2008/12/torture200812?currentPage=1).

99. Matthew Alexander and John Bruning, *How to Break a Terrorist: The U.S. Interrogators Who Used Brains, Not Brutality, to Take Down the Deadliest Man in Iraq* (New York: Free Press, 2008).

100. See, for example, American Civil Liberties Union, "Safe and Free: Restore Our Constitutional Rights" (www.aclu.org/safefree/torture/index.html); Human Rights Watch, "Torture Doesn't Work" (http://www.hrw.org/en/news/2006/04/26/torture-doesnt-work); Amnesty International, "Counter Terror with Justice: No Justification for Torture" (www.amnesty.org/en/campaigns/counter-terror-with-justice/issues/no-justification-for-torture); Darius Rejali, *Torture and Democracy* (Princeton University Press, 2007). See also Thomas and Hirsch, "The Debate over Torture," p. 26: "Torture still works to extract the truth in the movies and on TV shows like the popular '24' but not in real life, say the experts. A prisoner who has his fingernails pulled out or his genitals shocked will say (and make up) anything to make the pain stop." The same article, however, also cites evidence that coercion *has* worked in real life: "In modern times, these tactics have been used by British intelligence to unravel the command structure of the IRA and by the Israelis to stop Palestinian suicide bombers."

101. Robert Coulam, "Approaches to Interrogation in the Struggle against Terrorism: Considerations of Cost and Benefit," in *Educing Information: Interrogation: Science and Art* (Washington: Center for Strategic Intelligence Research, 2006), pp. 7–16. The quoted language appears on p. 8.

102. Randy Borum, "Approaching Truth: Behavioral Science Lessons on Educing Information from Human Sources," in *Educing Information*, pp. 17–43. The quoted language appears on p. 35. See generally Tortured Justice Report, pp. 27–28, but see also sources cited at note 196: "The scientific community is not universal in its condemnation of these practices."

103. Laurence Rees, *Auschwitz: A New History* (New York: PublicAffairs, 2005), pp. 288–89.

104. *Ireland v. United Kingdom*, 25 Eur. Ct. H.R. (ser. A) 1978, at 42. The court ruled that a combination of harsh methods had violated the European Convention on Human Rights and qualified as cruel, inhuman, and degrading treatment. The methods, which the court stopped short of calling "torture," included forcing suspects to stand on their toes against the wall with fingers high above their heads; keeping dark hoods over their heads; assailing them with loud and hissing noises; and depriving them of sleep, food and drink.

105. *Leon v. Wainwright*, 734 F. 2d 770 (11th Cir. 1984).

106. Bruce Hoffman, "A Nasty Business," *Atlantic Monthly,* January 2002, p. 52.

107. Matthew Brzezinski, "Bust and Boom," *Washington Post,* December 30, 2001, p. W9; Steven Chapman, "No Tortured Dilemma," *Washington Times,* November 5, 2001, p. A18.

108. *Public Committee against Torture in Israel v. State of Israel,* 38 I.L.M. 1471 (1st H.C.J. 1999).

109. Jerome H. Skolnick, "American Interrogation: From Torture to Trickery," in *Torture: A Collection,* edited by Sanford Levinson (Oxford University Press, 2004), p. 111.

110. Bobbitt, *Terror and Consent,* p. 368.

111. Excerpted in Kenneth Roth and Minky Worden, *Torture: Does It Make Us Safer? Is It Ever OK?* (New York: New Press, 2005).

112. See, for example, Ariel Dorfman, "The Tyranny of Terror: Is Torture Inevitable in Our Century and Beyond?" in *Torture: A Collection,* edited by Levinson, p. 3; Henry Shue, "Torture," in *Torture: A Collection,* p. 47.

113. Bobbitt, *Terror and Consent,* p. 362. See also Michael Walzer, "Political Action: The Problem of Dirty Hands," in *Torture: A Collection,* pp. 61–75.

114. Editorial, "Torture's Blowback," note 48 above.

115. David Hackett Fisher, *Washington's Crossing: Pivotal Moments in American History* (Oxford University Press, 2004), p. 379; Mayer, *The Dark Side,* pp. 84–85.

116. Philip Zelikow, "Legal Policy for a Twilight War," lecture, Houston Journal of International Law, Houston, Texas, April 26, 2007.

117. William Ranney Levi, "Interrogation's Law," *Yale Law Journal* 118 (2009), p. 1434.

118. Ibid., pp. 144–149.

119. Hoffman, "A Nasty Business," pp. 50–51.

120. The Pew Global Attitudes Project, *Pew Global Attitudes Survey,* June 12, 2008, p. 2: "America's image has improved over the last year in many countries. . . . In most countries surveyed, however, views of the United States remain either mixed or negative. Among America's traditional allies in Western Europe, the U.S. continues to receive largely negative reviews. And in predominantly Muslim countries, highly unfavorable opinions prevail."

121. Executive Order, "Ensuring Lawful Interrogations," § 3(b).

122. See Barack Obama, News Conference by the President, April 29, 2009; Senate Committee on the Judiciary, *Executive Nomination,* 111th Cong., 1st sess., January 15, 2009, p. 19.

123. 18 U.S.C. § 2340.

124. Department of the Army, Field Manual 2-22.3, *Human Intelligence Collector Operations,* pp. 5–21.

125. This proposed approach elaborates on one detailed by Benjamin Wittes in *Law and the Long War,* pp. 209–18, and is somewhat similar to suggestions by scholars Philip Heymann and Juliette Kayyem in *Protecting Liberty in an Age of Terror* (MIT Press, 2005), chapter 1; and Phillip Bobbitt in *Terror and Consent,* pp. 388–93. See also Eric A. Posner and Adrian Vermeule, *Terror in the Balance: Security, Liberty, and the Courts* (New York: Oxford University Press, 2007); Michael J. Glennon, "Terrorism and the Limits of the Law," *Wilson Quarterly* 26, no. 2 (Spring 2002).

126. Thomas and Hirsch, "The Debate over Torture," p. 26; John McCain, "Torture's Terrible Toll," *Newsweek,* November 21, 2005, p. 34.

KENNETH ANDERSON

10

Targeted Killing in U.S. Counterterrorism Strategy and Law

It is a slight exaggeration to say that Barack Obama is the first president in U.S. history to have campaigned in part on a platform of targeted killing—but not much of one. During the campaign, he openly sought to one-up the Republican nominee, Senator John McCain, in his enthusiasm for the use of targeted strikes in Pakistan against al Qaeda figures. "You know," he said in his speech at the Democratic National Convention, "John McCain likes to say that he'll follow [Osama] Bin Laden to the Gates of Hell, but he won't even go to the cave where he lives."[1]

That Obama would, as president, follow Bin Laden to his cave, with or without the cooperation of the Pakistani government, he made perfectly clear. "If we have actionable intelligence about high-value terrorist targets and [then] President [Pervez] Musharraf won't act, we will," he said in another speech.[2] Indeed, while he criticized President Bush for being too aggressive in his approach to many aspects of counterterrorism operations, his criticism with respect to targeted killing was the polar opposite: "The Bush administration has not acted aggressively enough to go after Al Qaeda's leadership," he said. "I would be clear that if Pakistan cannot or will not take out Al Qaeda leadership when we have actionable intelligence about their whereabouts, we will act to protect the American people. There can be no safe haven for Al Qaeda terrorists who killed thousands of Americans and threaten our homeland today."[3]

Obama did not take long, on assuming office, to begin keeping his promise. On January 23, 2009, a mere three days into his presidency, strikes by Predator drones in the tribal areas of Pakistan destroyed two compounds and killed numerous people, reportedly including a high-value target.[4] Strikes have continued, even expanded, since then, and administration officials have made clear that they have no plans to curtail them—even as they reined in coercive interrogations and announced the closure of Guantánamo Bay.[5]

Obama was right as a candidate and he is correct as president to insist on the propriety of targeted killing—that is, the targeting of a specific individual to be killed, increasingly often by means of high-technology, remote-controlled Predator drone aircraft wielding missiles from a standoff position. The strategic logic that presses toward targeted standoff killing as a necessary, available, and technologically advancing part of counterterrorism is over-powering. So too is the moral and humanitarian logic behind its use. Just as crucial programs of Predator-centered targeted killing are under way now in Afghanistan and, accompanied by increasing international controversy, in Pakistan, such programs will be an essential element in U.S. counterterrorism operations into the future—against targets having little or nothing to do with today's iteration of the war on terror.[6] Future administrations, even if they naturally prefer to couch the matter in softer terms, will likely follow the same path. Even if the whole notion seems to some disturbingly close to arbitrary killing, not open combat, it is often the most expedient—and, despite the civilian casualties that do occur, the most discriminatingly humanitarian—manner to neutralize a terrorist without unduly jeopardizing either civilians or U.S. forces.

But there's a paradox in Obama's embrace of targeted killing. Even as the persuasiveness of the strategic and humanitarian logic for it increases, the legal space for it and the legal rationales on which it traditionally has been justified are in danger of shrinking. They are at risk of shrinking in ways that might surprise members of Congress and the Obama administration. And they are at risk of shrinking through seemingly innocuous, unrelated legal policy actions that the Obama administration and Congress might be inclined to take in support of various political constituencies, usually related to the broadly admirable goals of respecting human rights and international law.

U.S. domestic law—the law codifying the existence of the CIA and defining its functions—has long accepted, implicitly at least, some uses of force, including targeted killing, as self-defense to ensure the nation's security. Some of those uses do not necessarily fall within the strict terms of armed conflict in the sense intended by the Geneva Conventions and other international treaties on the conduct of armed conflict. Categories of the use of force short of armed conflict or war in a juridical sense (by intelligence services such as the CIA, for example) or by military agents in the defense of the nation and vital security interests date back in codified law to the founding of the CIA and, in state practice by the United States and other sovereigns, far further still.

Yet as a matter of legal justification, successive administrations have already begun to cede that ground. Even the Bush administration, with its unrivaled enthusiasm for executive power, always sought to cast its targeted killing as the killing of combatants in what it legally characterized as armed conflicts, governed by the laws of war known as "international humanitarian law" (IHL). That concession, however, if followed by the Obama administration and beyond, will likely reduce the practical utility of a policy and security tool of both long-standing provenance and proven current value. It will likely reduce the flexibility of the United States to respond to emerging threats before they ripen into yet another war with nonstate terrorists, and it will reduce the ability of the United Sates to address terrorist threats in the most discriminating fashion that advancing technology permits.

At this point, when many policymakers, members of Congress, and serious observers see primarily a need to roll back policies and assertions of authority made by the Bush administration, any call for the Obama administration and Congress to insist upon the power to authorize unilateral targeted killing—and to claim a zone of authority outside of armed conflict governed by IHL that even the Bush administration did not claim—must seem at once atavistic, eccentric, myopic, and perverse. Many will not much care that such legal authority already exists in international and U.S. domestic law. Yet the purpose of this chapter is to suggest that, on the contrary, the uses to which the Obama administration seeks to put targeted killing are proper, although they will require that the administration carefully preserve and defend legal authorities that it should not be taking for granted and that its predecessors, including the Bush administration, have not adequately preserved for their present-day uses.

People who threaten serious harm to the United States will not always be members of al Qaeda. Nor will they forever be those persons who, in the words of the Authorization for Use of Military Force (AUMF), "planned, authorized, committed or aided" the attacks of September 11.[7] As I will explain, it would have been better had the Bush and Clinton administrations, for their parts, formulated their legal justifications for the targeted use of force around the legal powers traditionally asserted by the United States: the right of self-defense, including the right to use force—even in circumstances not rising to the level of an "armed conflict"—in order to have firmly fixed in place the clear legal ability of the United States to respond as it traditionally has. Although the United States still has a long way to go to dismember al Qaeda and its affiliates and subsidiaries, although Osama bin Laden and key al Qaeda terrorist leaders remain at large, and although the president of the

United States still exercises sweeping powers, both inherent and granted by Congress, to use all national power against the perpetrators of the September 11 attacks, time moves on. New threats will emerge, some of them from states and others from nonstate actors, including terrorist organizations. Some of the new threats will be new forms of jihadist terrorism; others will champion new and different causes. Even now, Islamist terrorist organizations appear to be fragmenting into loose networks of shared ideology and aspiration rather than remaining tightly vertical organizations linked by command and control.[8] It will take successive feats of intellectual jujitsu to cast all of the targets that such developments can reasonably be expected to put in the cross hairs as, legally speaking, combatants.

Yet the problem is still deeper and more immediate than that, for the accepted space for targeted killing is eroding even *within* what a reasonable American might understand as the four corners of the U.S. conflict with al Qaeda. To some important actors—at the United Nations, among U.S. allies, among international law scholars, and among NGO activists—it is unclear as a matter of international law that a state of armed conflict would actually exist or that a targeted killing could qualify as an act of self-defense in many situations in which any U.S. president, Obama certainly included, would want to use targeted killing. The legal situation, therefore, threatens to become one in which, on the one hand, targeted killing outside of a juridical armed conflict is legally impermissible and, on the other hand, as a practical matter, no targeted killing even within the context of a "war" with al Qaeda is legally permissible.

Congress's role in this area is admittedly a peculiar one; it is mostly—though not entirely—politically defensive in nature. After all, the domestic legal authorities to conduct targeted killings and other "intelligence" uses of force have existed in statutory form at least since the legislation that established the Central Intelligence Agency in 1947 and in other forms long predating that.[9] The problem is that although domestic legal authority exists for the use of force against terrorists abroad, currents are stirring in international law and elsewhere that move to undermine that authority. Powerful trends and opinion-setting—so-called "soft law"—currents are developing in ways that, over time, promise to make the exercise of this option ever more difficult and to create the presumption, difficult to overcome, that targeted killing is in fact both illegitimate and, indeed, illegal per se, except in the narrowest of warlike conditions. The role of Congress therefore is to reassert, reaffirm, and reinvigorate the category as a matter of domestic law and policy and as the considered, official view of the United States as a matter of international law.

The Strategic and Moral Logic of Targeted Killing

U.S. counterterrorism operations are a hybrid employing distinct palettes of legal tools. One derives from criminal law; another from laws governing armed conflict.[10] Americans have been arguing about the two palettes—their relative uses, merits, and limitations—nonstop since September 11. Each occupies important ground in the legal and policy regulation of the use of force and violence in counterterrorism. As a matter of long-term counterterrorism strategy, each will continue to play an important role. Moreover, despite many now-familiar arguments, sometimes ferocious, over such issues as Guantánamo, habeas corpus, civilian versus military criminal trials, detention, rendition, and interrogation, both criminal law enforcement and armed conflict have well-established legal and policy protocols.

Criminal law is not about killing people as such; it is, rather, about arresting, literally stopping, their activities and punishing them for activities that violate the law. Resisting arrest can lead to deadly violence, but fundamentally law enforcement takes place within an ordered domestic society in which the government use of deadly force is incidental to the attempt to arrest alleged criminals. The virtue of law enforcement is that it takes place in a settled, ordered society with a legitimate government, but that also represents its limitation in dealing with terrorists, who are at once enemies of that society and criminals who often shelter beyond the reach of legitimate government institutions.[11]

Armed conflict accepts a willingness to kill people in the pursuit of political ends, and those killings are not limited merely to killings incident to attempted arrest. Its virtue is that it is addressed to enemies who come from outside a settled society to attack that society, but its limitation is that the use of military force in armed conflict succeeds by imposing its will on another party and does not benefit from the sense that its will is, in the first place, legitimate in the way that is true of the ordinary use of police forces within an ordered society. Policing and warmaking are two radically different deployments of violence by the state, the former being the exercise of a legitimate near-monopoly on the use of violence and the latter being the exercise of the level of violence dictated by military necessity in order to create a monopoly on the use of violence.[12] Yet core standards are reasonably clear for both criminal law and the law of war. To the extent that debate over the core standards arises, it normally does so on account of their uncertain application to an activity—for example, terrorism by transnational nonstate actors—that lies at the margins rather than the core of each.

Even before the September 11 era,[13] however, counterterrorism as practice, law, and policy has also consisted of activities that do not fall neatly under either of the two existing legal regimes.[14] The broadest policy description is "intelligence gathering," but that term encompasses an extraordinarily heterogeneous set of activities, among them classical intelligence-gathering functions such as surveillance—including telecommunications and Internet surveillance, human intelligence, satellite and observation intelligence, and analysis of material collected by whatever other means. Those activities also include coordination of intelligence community, law enforcement, military, and diplomatic efforts and exchange of information with friends and allies abroad. They include—of ever-increasing importance—the interdiction of terrorist financing and the investigation, seizure, and freezing of economic assets essential to terrorist organizations. In this discussion, I loosely refer to all these activities, despite their heterogeneity, as the third aspect of counterterrorism—following law enforcement and armed conflict—or as the third way of counterterrorism, or as intelligence activities in counterterrorism.[15] This third aspect of counterterrorism also includes the traditional intelligence function of the covert use of force.[16]

Within the wide range of intelligence functions, one naturally stands out as especially controversial: the use of, or the threat to use, deadly force. For while intelligence activities raise many thorny issues of domestic and international law, particularly when conducted on foreign territory and in violation of local law and sovereignty, none is so difficult as those that involve killing people.

Call it a "war on terror" or call it something else; it doesn't really matter.[17] A full response to terrorism, to al Qaeda and beyond, requires action across all three areas— criminal law, armed conflict, and intelligence functions, including covert deadly force and targeted killing. The Obama administration and the administrations that follow it will rely increasingly on intelligence-based use of force in counterterrorism operations undertaken outside the United States. Whether the activity is characterized as a legal matter or given some euphemistic label that improves its public acceptance, U.S. administrations will rely on targeted killing as a means of dealing with suspected terrorists—with al Qaeda; with its successors, imitators, and emulators; and with those who come after it, whether they share similar or dissimilar ideological causes. And administrations will do so whether or not Congress has passed a successor to the Authorization for Use of Military Force.[18] The Predator and Hellfire missiles were identified early on by candidate Obama as the weapons of the future,[19] and the Obama administration is not wrong to see the strategic advantages of the Predator, now and into the future, as the United States gradually seeks to ratchet down its full-on, overt wars.

This view is deeply embedded within the mainstream of President Obama's party. To cite only one example, note how unambiguously the Democratic international relations and intelligence *eminence grises* Graham Allison and John Deutch endorsed the Predator policy with regard to Pakistan:

> The counterterrorism strategy [of Predator strikes] in Pakistan that has emerged since last summer offers our best hope for regional stability and success in dealing a decisive blow against Al Qaeda and what Vice President Joe Biden calls "incorrigible" Taliban adherents. But implementing these operations requires light U.S. footprints *backed by drones and other technology that allows missile attacks on identified targets* [emphasis added].[20]

In response to the increasingly heard claim that the strategy of using drones and missiles for targeted killing backfires by inflaming Pakistani public opinion against the United States because of collateral civilian deaths,[21] Allison and Deutch offer a remarkably realpolitik answer. If "many Pakistanis see covert actions carried out inside their country as America 'invading an ally,'" the problem is not the drone campaign, they write; it is, rather, merely that "*the U.S. government no longer seems capable of conducting covert operations without having them reported in the press*" [emphasis added].[22]

There is a fundamental strategic and moral rationale behind both the policy trend toward targeted killing and toward the use of robotic and standoff platforms such as the drone Predator as the preferred means of effectuating it. The United States has found the limits of how extensively it can wage full-scale wars with its military; even if it wanted to take on more wars, it has logistical and political limits. In addition, the United States has discovered that full-on war is useful principally against *regimes*. Full-scale, large-scale warfare of the kind waged in Afghanistan and Iraq is useful primarily for bringing down a government that, for example, might harbor or support terrorists or might be believed to be willing to supply terrorists with material to create weapons of mass destruction. While this tool has a crucial strategic place in national counterterrorism policy, by its nature, it pertains to states and state-like groups. Large-scale military operations are less useful against transnational terrorists, who are few in number, dispersed across populations and often borders, disinclined to fight direct battles, and more efficiently targeted through narrower means. The fundamental role of overt warfare in counterterrorism is to eliminate the regimes that provide safe haven to terrorist groups. Terrorist groups themselves can be strategically understood as an extreme version of a guerrilla organization engaged in a strategy of logistical raiding—in which civilian morale and the resulting manipulation of political will is the logistical target.[23] Logistical raiders typically need a safe base to which to retreat, and full-scale war is most useful in eliminating such safe bases and convincing other regimes not to provide them.[24] But it is not usually an efficient way of going directly after the transnational terrorist groups themselves.[25]

Law enforcement applied outside the United States, on the other hand, has also discovered its outer limits. Many debates are still to be had over the rights of alleged terrorists once in U.S. custody, but whatever they are, few would argue that going out to "arrest" terrorists in, for example, Pakistan's tribal zones is a winning policy or a serious option. The same is true of Somalia and other places, and it will be true of other places in the world in the future.

Moreover, the political costs for any U.S. administration in taking and holding detainees are now enormous.[26] Once in custody, detainees are likely to be eventually accorded quasi-constitutional protections by the courts in some matters and to receive at least some version of habeas corpus. Politically, the most powerful institutional incentive today is to kill rather than capture terrorists. The intelligence losses of killing people, rather than capturing and interrogating them, are great.[27] But since the U.S. political and legal situation has made aggressive interrogation a questionable activity anyway, there is less reason to seek to capture rather than kill. And if one intends to kill, the incentive is to do so from a standoff position, because it avoids potentially messy questions of surrender.

All of this speaks to the advantages to the U.S. government of targeted killing of terrorists or persons seriously believed to be terrorists, and it also speaks to the advantages to the government of using standoff robotics technology to perform the attacks. But the humanitarian advantages of targeted killing also are enormously important, and they ought to be on the table. That is especially so given that targeted killing has come in for a barrage of criticism, legal and ethical, much of which seems perversely motivated by the fact that it can be more discriminate than full-scale military assault.[28] The fear seems to be that targeted killing using Predators and other robotics systems "lower[s] the threshold for violence."[29] It makes violence too easy to undertake.[30]

The same criticism is offered of evolving robotic technology that increasingly allows a party to target its use of force without having to risk its own personnel. Not using its own personnel allows the party to attack without the fear of counterassault, which might increase the need to use greater amounts of force and cause greater collateral damage. But it also, it is sometimes argued, reduces the inhibitions on the decision to use force.[31] For example, P.W. Singer, a theorist of military technology, says of robotic unmanned weapons systems: "When faced with a dispute or crisis, policymakers have typically regarded the use of force as the 'option of last resort.' Unmanned systems might now help that option move up the list, with each upward step making war more likely."[32]

Whatever the critics say, however, is unlikely to sway U.S. strategic policy, under the Obama administration or any that follows.[33] The humanitarian benefits of precision targeting are far more obvious than the more remote and abstract calculations of its humanitarian costs. The direct policy benefit of precision targeting is to introduce greater discrimination in targeting than full-scale military assault and large-scale war permit. The dozens and scores of civilian casualties caused by Predator missile strikes—against targets who deliberately surround themselves with civilians—are a step forward in the conduct of war from, for example, assault preceded by artillery barrage. Rights monitors can insist, with pious utopianism, that one must somehow "do it all"—exactly target without collateral damage—but that is merely to imagine, and demand, a world in which there are no trade-offs. Advancing technology allows for more discrete surveillance and, therefore, more precise targeting, which is better able to minimize collateral civilian damage—a good thing for those who do not want to kill innocent civilians. Indeed, humanitarians long called on advanced militaries to shift from designing more destructive weapons systems to designing more discriminating ones, and weapons designers have been seeking to comply over decades. There is something perverse about now criticizing their evolving efforts as making war so much less destructive and so discriminating as to be too easy to undertake.

The result is a strategic and moral incentive for targeted killing and for increasing the quality of technology to make targeted killing both more precise and more able to be done from a standoff position. Precision targeting and standoff delivery, each of which is independently desirable, considerably increase that incentive when combined.

None of this alters the equally impeccable strategic logic underlying the use of law enforcement mechanisms in some circumstances. Nor does it alter the logic behind other forms of intelligence activities, such as surveillance or financial interdiction or even the use of open, full-on war.[34] The United States can by no means rule out toppling a regime in pursuit of counterterrorism goals during the next ten or twelve years. But these are not disjunctive policies. Targeted killing is likely to increase as a policy preference as full-scale wars decrease in number and intensity and become less desirable as a means of effectuating counterterrorist objectives. Bush's Iraq adventure has surely reduced the U.S. appetite for invading the tribal regions of Pakistan, for example, and something has to fill the gap. That need is in part what has augmented the Predator's appeal, especially to the Obama administration. No doubt there will be political pushback—claims that the effect of the Predator campaigns in Pakistan are backfiring by mobilizing Pakistani anger over civilian casualties, for example. But given the political unreliability and military ineffectiveness of the Pakistani army and its preference for artillery barrages over focused counterinsurgency operations, those arguments are not likely to persuade.

The United States has long accepted a legal, political, and policy space for the use of force that takes place neither in the course of judicially supervised law enforcement operations nor in the context of large-scale, open armed conflicts that meet the treaty definitions or rise to a level of violence sufficient to be governed by IHL. That space of activity was accepted and considered to be vital to self-defense and national security throughout the long decades of the cold war. Only in certain times and places, after all, was the conflict with the Soviet Union and its allies a "hot" war, characterized by open and large-scale armed conflict, the sort of clashing of armies formally governed by IHL.[35] Political violence during the cold war was often covert and often denied, but it was authorized and endorsed by U.S. domestic law, dating back at least to the statutes that founded the CIA in 1947. That was so even though the activity in question frequently violated the law and sovereignty of states in which it took place and, unsurprisingly, was sometimes a source of grave diplomatic and other friction too. Following the revelation of abuses by the CIA in the 1970s, U.S. domestic law was tightened, "assassination" prohibited by executive order of President Ford in 1976, and congressional oversight mechanisms strengthened. But, as discussed below, far from eliminating this category of violence by limiting such uses of force solely to "armed conflict" in the meaning governed by IHL, U.S. domestic law quietly and intentionally preserved the category while strengthening the oversight.

This category of force is now an obvious means by which to confront non-state transnational terrorists outside the territorial United States. The United States is no longer in the cold war. But the legal and political regimes that it (and other states, both friend and foe) elaborated through state practice, allowing uses of covert and discrete force as a matter of self-defense, are, if anything, more relevant in confronting transnational terrorism today. Yet as matters now stand, great pressures will be brought to bear against the very existence of this legal and political category—great precisely because they are idealistic and morally well-intended. Should those pressures prevail, they will bind the hands of the president and Congress, preventing them from taking what is paradoxically the most discrete and most precisely targeted lethal measure available against terrorists. The result would be to throw the United States into the much more difficult policy dilemma of using larger-scale military activity against terrorists or taking no very meaningful action at all.[36]

Targeted Killing and Armed Conflict

Targeted killing is not a generally defined legal term in domestic or international law.[37] I take it here to mean the intentional, direct targeting of a person with lethal force intended to cause his death. It is not an unintended collateral killing. Targeted killing can sometimes occur in law enforcement—for example, the killing of a hostage taker in order to save the hostage or, for that matter, the legal execution of a convicted criminal. Likewise, it frequently and without particular controversy takes place as part of overt, open armed conflict—circumstances in which IHL is unquestionably the paradigm of law in force. While there are some important questions about the application of the rules of targeted killing during unquestioned, open, large-scale armed conflict, the pattern of rules under IHL is relatively clear.[38]

The trouble for the United States arises because, as the war on terror migrates away from the most overt of armed conflicts, the question of whether a given targeted killing takes place in a legally cognizable armed conflict becomes open to debate. That might seem surprising, given the importance of targeted killing as part of armed conflict in U.S. military doctrine and its importance in both the Afghanistan and Iraq wars and in the extension of the Afghanistan operation into Pakistan. Predator strikes have been important in all of those operations, and other kinds of "covert," unacknowledged operations involving both military and CIA personnel have been taking place in Pakistan and elsewhere.[39] But—at least if armed conflict means as a matter of law anything more than the mere fact that a party has undertaken to use lethal force—it is not always clear that those killings have taken place within, rather than outside of, an armed conflict.

That anomaly reflects different legal meanings and standards, pursuant to different legal instruments and regimes, for the term "armed conflict." The problem is not merely that terms have one meaning in ordinary parlance and another in precise legal contexts. One scholar points out that the recent massive, three-volume, four-thousand-plus-page study by the International Committee of the Red Cross of the customary law of international humanitarian law "included nothing on the definition of the term, because it remains much disputed . . . [and] terminological disputes are rife; several commentators express doubt, for instance, that attacks even by well-organized terrorist groups like Al Qaeda can constitute 'armed attacks' within the meaning" of the UN Charter and, by implication, the international law of self-defense.[40]

International lawyers argue over the meaning of "armed conflict," starting with the most basic question: is "armed conflict" governed by the law of "resort to force" or the rules of warfare (IHL)—or both? Eminent legal scholar and former West Point law professor Gary Solis states flatly, for example, that for a targeted killing to be lawful, "an international or noninternational conflict must be in progress. Without an ongoing armed conflict the targeted killing of a civilian, terrorist or not, would be assassination—a homicide and a domestic crime."[41] But that only raises the question of what constitutes an "armed conflict" in the first place.

Does the prohibition to which Solis alludes refer to armed conflict in the sense of a resort to force in self-defense? Or to armed conflict within the meaning of IHL, which governs not the decision to resort to force but how force is used during hostilities? If the former, then the long-existing structure of civilian CIA authority to act in accordance with domestic law makes sense. If the latter (or both), then the lawful authority of the CIA to use force becomes unclear at best, because it is a civilian agency with authority to act, as discussed below, outside the scope of armed conflict conducted and governed under IHL.

The stakes on this question are high, because the international legal standards that must be satisfied are radically, conceptually different. They answer sharply different questions. International law governing the resort to force deals fundamentally with separating legitimate self-defense from illegitimate aggression. IHL, by contrast, does not address the *legitimacy* of the resort to force but the conduct of any party in an armed conflict. It is concerned, at bottom, with the conduct of the parties in hostilities, with separating combatants from noncombatants. It does not apply to every resort to force—only those that meet particular treaty requirements or rise to a certain level of violence constituting "armed conflict" under IHL. Yet if legally it's really simple murder, as Solis suggests, to engage in targeted killing outside of such armed conflict—even if in lawful self-defense—then the United States has a big problem.

In the lay understanding of the term "armed conflict," at least, it is obvious that the United States is engaged in one in Pakistan; its aircraft and missiles are engaged against targets there, and it also sends in special forces and other personnel to engage in fighting. Again, in the common understanding of the term, it was only a little less obvious that a Predator strike against an al Qaeda figure fleeing in a vehicle across the desert in Yemen was part of the U.S. "armed conflict," the U.S. war, against al Qaeda. For that matter, in that same common understanding—if not, perhaps surprisingly, in the views of all legal commentators—the events of September 11 itself constituted an armed attack in an armed conflict initiated by al Qaeda. Even if al Qaeda is a nonstate actor using criminal means, September 11 was an act that was both a crime and part of an armed conflict.

But as a question of IHL, whether something is an "armed conflict" to which the rules of warfare apply is not settled simply by saying that a party— the United States—has undertaken a targeted killing and therefore it is engaged in armed conflict governed by IHL. The U.S. government, after all, might simply have engaged in murder. The same is true for an al Qaeda attack. The fact that both al Qaeda, a nonstate actor, and the United States regard themselves as being in a state of war with one another also is peculiarly immaterial to the question of whether IHL applies. The answer to the question of whether a "resort to force" in any particular circumstance triggers the application of IHL depends instead on a specific set of triggers contained in applicable IHL treaties, starting with the Geneva Conventions and the Hague Regulations. Those triggers depend first on the language of the relevant IHL treaty defining the application of IHL and next on whether the fighting between the parties has reached some factually determined threshold.[42] Very roughly, that requires either hostilities between two states or else, in the case of nonstate actors—such as in a civil war—fighting that is ongoing, persistent, widespread, and organized. A resort to force might well raise an international law question of whether it constitutes, on the one hand, an act of aggression or, on the other, a lawful resort to self-defense. But that question is separate from the question of whether a particular resort to force also invokes IHL as the law governing the conduct of that resort to force. Running the two questions together leads to serious problems. The most serious is that what the United States regards as lawful armed conflict, much of the rest of the world might well regard as something close to simple murder.

The overall point for present purposes is that the targeted killing of a nonstate actor by either the armed forces of a state or its civilian agents (such as the CIA) does not automatically, *by reason of the use of force alone*, trigger the application of IHL. Nor does the fact that since the African embassy bombings in the 1990s the United States has seen itself as being in a state of armed conflict with al Qaeda and in addition, under the AUMF and domestic court rulings, in an armed conflict with all those responsible for the September 11 attacks.

At the moment, few in the United States seem much to care about this problem. After all, the struggle with al Qaeda intuitively seems to be covered as an armed conflict under IHL, so the distinction that I'm making here and the concern that I'm raising about the resulting legal jeopardy for those engaged in carrying out or authorizing targeted killings must be a kind of paper tiger, a remote law school hypothetical with no bearing on actual policy. But for an administration committed to this strategic instrument, to view the problem thus would be a significant mistake. As the war extends to Pakistan, to targets beyond al Qaeda "combatants" (whatever that means, precisely), and to places such as Yemen or Somalia, then the question of whether targeted killing outside of legally cognizable armed conflicts can be legal reemerges, in sometimes surprising ways. It emerges even more acutely if—when—at some point in the future, threats to the United States do not come from al Qaeda at all but from some other group against whom Congress has not passed an authorization for force buttressed by resolutions of the UN Security Council.[43]

The Stakes in Targeted Killing

Even accepting that there are two quite different meanings of "armed conflict," is anything actually at stake here? I have suggested rather ominously that if the United States does not move to reassert and protect its long-held legal positions on targeting killing, it stands to lose them. But is there any good reason to think that that is true? After all, the Obama administration does not appear to see a problem with its legal rationales. Neither did the Bush or Clinton administrations before it. The war on terror, they all have contended, is armed conflict in some theory or another.

But there are two problems here. The first is the long-term issue to which I alluded earlier: whether, in some future conflict unrelated to al Qaeda, situations might arise that do not meet all the definitions of armed conflict. The second is a more immediate problem: a close look at the way international law is formulated and interpreted and the manner in which it is developing suggests that even the Obama administration's current targeted killing policies are likely to come under much greater pressure than recent administrations have understood.

Let's start with what is now the standard view among the leading academic experts on the subject of targeted killing. The scholarly community, as Mark Osiel accurately says, "is almost entirely hostile to the practice, sanctioning it only under the most restrictive conditions, of a sort than can virtually never be satisfied in practice."[44] Nils Melzer's formidable treatise, *Targeted Killing in International Law*,[45] for example, starts from the premise that the *only* two possible paradigms for addressing even the concept of targeted killing are judicially monitored law enforcement and armed conflict under IHL. "[O]utside the conduct of hostilities," he writes, "the extra-custodial killing of an individual cannot be the actual purpose, but must remain the undesired and inevitable consequence, of an operation absolutely necessary to achieve a different, legitimate aim."[46]

By "hostilities" here, Melzer does not mean armed conflict in some colloquial sense—nor in the sense of military action in a country's self-defense. He means in the technical sense of armed conflict in IHL. That this is the premise of the leading legal treatise, rather than its conclusion, gives some sense of how far U.S. domestic political views at the center of the political spectrum are from the views of the "international law community," of which Melzer's views are representative. That view alone, if adopted by the International Criminal Court or a European magistrate with broad jurisdiction in human rights matters, could make murderers and war criminals out of President Obama and any of the people working for him on targeted killing. Farfetched? A forthcoming Naval War College "Bluebook" article remarks in passing that cross-border operations in Pakistan might potentially expose "U.S. military personnel to international criminal liability."[47]

But the argument goes further and deeper. Indeed, the most insistently offered objections are not simply definitional arguments about the term "armed conflict." They also involve human rights law and arise from the human rights claims of the individuals targeted, generally under the International Covenant on Civil and Political Rights (ICCPR).[48]

The ICCPR is a core UN treaty on the protection of human rights, rooted in the same process that led to the Universal Declaration of Human Rights.[49] It is a broad statement of civil and political rights in international law, and it establishes a long series of important guarantees related to physical and personal integrity—including guarantees against arbitrary killing and extrajudicial execution.[50] Although the ICCPR is not the only international human rights treaty that poses a challenge to the practice of targeted killing, the challenge that it poses is fundamental because, under the readings of the treaty offered by many international lawyers, at least, such killing would be extrajudicial execution or something similar. As of this writing it has been ratified by at least 164 nations.

The United States ratified the ICCPR in 1992 but, like many countries, entered a number of treaty reservations, understandings, and declarations that limit its application in U.S. conduct and law.[51] The United States has taken much criticism for taking those steps as well as for the fact that the Senate ratified the treaty with the express understanding that it created no private right of action to enforce its terms judicially.[52] Most important for the purposes of targeted killing, the United States has never accepted that the ICCPR applies extraterritorially—that is, that it regulates U.S. actions beyond U.S. borders[53]—and it has always flatly rejected the application of the ICCPR in the setting of armed conflict. Legal protection for the U.S. ability to use Predators depends in no small part on preserving the U.S. insistence, first, that the ICCPR does not apply extraterritorially and, second, that it does not apply in IHL armed conflicts, in which IHL substitutes as the legal regime in force, superseding ordinary human rights law.

Were the ICCPR conceded to apply extraterritorially, the difficulties of the U.S. counterterrorism effort would be compounded immeasurably by the growing belief that human rights law, and the ICCPR in particular, continues to apply in some fashion *even during hostilities*. As with the definition of armed conflict, here too, the U.S. position is an increasingly alienated one. The Organization of American States Inter-American Commission on Human Rights, for example, advanced the contrary position in recent years in a report on U.S. counterterrorism.[54] Whether the United States will continue to hold the line—and whether policymakers understand the stakes in holding the line with respect to the Predator campaign in Pakistan and any other recourse to targeted killing in the future—is far from clear. It is also unclear—even among rights advocates themselves—how human rights standards are supposed to be interpreted and applied in armed conflicts. But from the standpoint of NGO advocates, that lack of clarity is itself a virtue, allowing for a game of post hoc bait-and-switch involving the legal rules on nearly any topic in armed conflict and serving as a way to always reach a result that one likes.

Congress and the Obama administration will come under considerable pressure to cede ground, because from the standpoint of advocates, access to the ICCPR, whether extraterritorially or within the United States, particularly in judicial proceedings, offers human rights advocates an opportunity to achieve their much-sought-after dream of making an end-run around inconvenient (if democratically enacted) U.S. domestic law. Those advocates, it bears emphasis, are not marginal individuals. For example, in 2008 Harold Koh, recently confirmed as State Department legal adviser, signed a letter issued by a group of legal scholars stating that the ICCPR applies to armed conflict and implying that it must apply extraterritorially as well.[55] And in the confirmation proceedings following his nomination to the State Department, he conspicuously did not retract his view of extraterritorial application, stating merely that he looked forward to reviewing the U.S. position in the interagency process.[56]

Response to U.S. practice from human rights groups and international organizations has largely tracked the scholarly theoretical consensus. In response to the killing of Haitham al-Yemeni by a CIA Predator strike in Pakistan in 2005, Amnesty International said that, assuming the facts as it described them, the "USA has carried out an extrajudicial execution, in violation of international law." Amnesty believes that the governments of the "USA and Pakistan should have cooperated to arrest Haitham al-Yemeni rather than kill him." The fundamental reason that it gave was that whether or not the killing was part of an armed conflict, international human rights law continued to apply in that situation.[57] Amnesty takes the position, in other words, that human rights law—including broad rights against arbitrary killing and the guarantee of due process—should have applied in that instance *irrespective of whether it was an armed conflict or not.* It is hard to see the circumstances in which a targeted killing could be permissible under such a standard, which is precisely Amnesty's point.

Very few people in the United States, regardless of political persuasion, would regard the Predator strike in Yemen on November 3, 2002—which killed six people, including a senior member of al Qaeda, Qaed Salim Sinan al-Harethi, in a vehicle on the open road—as anything other than a good thing, regardless of how one characterizes it legally. Yet the UN special rapporteur on extrajudicial, summary, or arbitrary executions described it as a "clear case of extrajudicial killing."[58] The legal analysis presented concurred with that of Amnesty International and many others: it does not matter whether the targeted killing takes place during armed conflict, nor does it matter how the United States justifies it legally; international human rights law continues to apply no matter what and to require governments to seek to arrest rather than to kill targeted persons.

A subsequent UN special rapporteur on extrajudicial, summary, or arbitrary executions summarized his office's view in 2004: "Empowering Governments to identify and kill 'known terrorists' places no verifiable obligation upon them to demonstrate in any way that those against whom lethal force is used are indeed terrorists, or to demonstrate that every other alternative had been exhausted."[59] Once again, it is hard to see how targeted killing as a policy could survive in any form with such a legal characterization.

Various European allies of the United States have been extremely hostile toward the practice. Swedish foreign minister Anna Lindh was among the most outspoken critics of the U.S. targeting of al-Harethi in November 2002. She described the operation as "a summary execution that violated human rights. . . . Even terrorists must be treated according to international law. Otherwise any country can start executing those whom they consider terrorists."[60] The criticism is even stronger when the actor is Israel—which undertakes targeted killing in keeping with the peculiarly long-term, "mixed" war–national security and intelligence–law enforcement nature of its struggle—and, incidentally, with far more procedural protections than the United States uses, including judicial review. Then the gloves come off completely in expressions of international hostility to the practice.[61]

To be clear, under the standards that these groups are articulating, such practices are regarded as *crimes* by a sizable and influential part of the international community. That is the case whether or not these acts are currently reachable under the jurisdiction of any particular national or international tribunal. As the coercive interrogation debate shows, with Spain and other countries considering prosecutions in their own courts, the trend is toward expansion of courts' jurisdiction. And the U.S. claim that the killings are of combatants in an armed conflict governed by either self-defense or IHL does not cut much ice against the views of those who either reject the armed conflict claim outright or else claim that even in armed conflict, human rights standards apply.

U.S. officials seem to believe that by adhering to IHL's formal, technical definition of "combatant" to select a lawful target, they have done an especially good and rigorous parsing of the legal requirements. As far as the international law community is concerned, however, following the combatancy standard is not an especially rigorous approach that demonstrates a party's concern for international law. To the contrary, it is by definition a relaxation of the ordinary standard of international human rights law, including prohibitions on murder and extrajudicial killing—and it can be justified only by the existence of an armed conflict that meets the definitions of IHL treaties.

At times it appears that the government of the United States has little idea how much its concession to the formal requirements of combatancy concedes. Yet when the United States argues that it's okay to target someone because he is a combatant, it effectively concedes that the conflict must meet the definition of an IHL conflict for such an attack to be legitimate. By contrast, what the United States needs—and what its historic position has asserted—is a claim that self-defense exists as a doctrine apart from that of IHL armed conflict that can justify the use of force against an individual. In 1989 Abraham Sofaer, then the legal adviser to the State Department, stated that the United

States has long assumed that the "inherent right of self-defense potentially applies against any illegal use of force, and that it extends to any group or State that can properly be regarded as responsible for such activities."[62]

To put the matter simply, the international law community does not accept targeted killing, even against al Qaeda, even in a struggle directly devolving from September 11, even when that struggle is backed by UN Security Council resolutions authorizing force, even in the presence of a near-declaration of war by Congress in the form of the AUMF, and even given the widespread agreement that the United States had both an inherent right and legal authorization to undertake military action against the perpetrators of the attacks. If targeted killing in the course of an armed conflict that the international community had agreed so completely was a lawful and appropriate military response to terrorism now constitutes extrajudicial execution, how will it be seen in situations down the road, after and beyond al Qaeda, when it does not take place under the obvious condition of an IHL armed conflict and lacks all those legitimating authorities?

In the view of much of the international law community, a targeted killing can be something other than an extrajudicial execution—that is, murder—only under the following conditions:

—It takes place in an armed conflict.

—The armed conflict is an act of self-defense within the meaning of the UN Charter.

—The armed conflict is also an armed conflict within the meaning of IHL.

—Even in an armed conflict under IHL, the circumstances must not permit application of international human rights law, which would require that a government attempt to arrest rather than kill its target.

As a practical matter, those conditions would forbid all real-world targeted killings.

The United States, for its part, has never accepted those criteria. The result is that a strategic centerpiece of U.S. counterterrorism policy rests on legal grounds regarded by large and influential parts of the international community as deeply illegal—extrajudicial killing is one of the most serious violations of international human rights, after all, as well it should be. The change of administration from Bush to Obama gives some protection to the policy, but it is not likely to last for all of the Obama term, and it is even less likely to last beyond it. The discussion turns now from how the international law community sees targeted killing to U.S. views of the subject under both international and domestic law.

The U.S. View of Targeted Killing

How does the United States legally justify its targeted killing practices today? That is not an easy question to answer definitively, because much of the legal analysis and background has not been made public. Even when one gets hints, through publicly available Justice Department opinions, for example, one does not know whether the entire record is on the table and what facts, still under wraps, lawyers might have relied on in their legal analyses. Drawing on publicly available information and some informal, anecdotal discussions with former government officials, however, one might hazard some assumptions about current legal policy.

Since the intelligence community first became aware of the threat from al Qaeda, apparently during the Clinton administration, the United States has seemed to justify at least some of its targeted killings by treating them as acts of armed conflict by dint of their being acts of self-defense but then also asserting that the person in question is a lawful target under IHL. The legal rationale appears to conflate the questions of resort to force and armed conflict under IHL. The determination thus appears to become whether the target qualifies as a "combatant" who may be targeted under IHL. The fundamental difficulty with that approach is that it conflates the general customary obligations of necessity and proportionality under the international law of self-defense with the treaty-specific definition of a combatant under IHL. As I have explained, those obligations share certain roots but are not the same.

For example, the 9/11 Commission reported that the Clinton administration justified legally an (ultimately abortive) operation to kill bin Laden in Afghanistan in 2000 on grounds that "under the law of armed conflict, killing a person who posed an imminent threat to the United States would be an act of self-defense, not an assassination."[63] During that period, of course, the United States was clearly *not* in a state of armed conflict in Afghanistan, and the incident predated the AUMF as well. While the rationale here invokes self-defense, it then turns to invoke the "law of armed conflict" without, however, specifying whether it is the law of resort to force or the IHL law regarding conduct of hostilities. Indeed, it is not clear whether the rationale treats a person who poses an "imminent threat" as a combatant who may be targeted per se—IHL would impose a more exacting analysis of combatancy and "direct participation in hostilities"—but certainly the framework runs the risk of rationale by circular fiat: if one regards a person as an imminent threat, the person becomes, by that fact alone, a combatant.

Discussions with former officials suggest that successive administrations have not considered that to be a problem. The method of legal rationale appears to have been, from the 1990s until today, as follows: "We know we have been in a state of armed conflict with al Qaeda, whether under self-defense *or* IHL, so it does not really matter which one. Developments since September 11 have confirmed all that through the AUMF and Security Council resolutions and much else besides. So the question of whether the applicable law is the law of resort to force and self-defense or instead IHL and standards of combatancy is really moot. We have an armed conflict, so why worry about the question of whether it is based on one body of law or another?"

The real issue—one emphasized in informal conversations—seems to be that unless the target is a duly designated "combatant," the targeted killing would become an "assassination." As discussed below, assassinations are specifically prohibited by U.S. domestic regulations; assassination, however, is a U.S. domestic law category, legally separate from the international law question of extrajudicial execution. But if this were the proper way of interpreting assassination under U.S. domestic law, then the effect would be to force the United States into a legal analysis based on combatancy.

This framework for legally analyzing targeted killing decisions has the virtue of taking advantage of the fact of broad—although far from universal—agreement that in some sense the United States is at war with al Qaeda. Although discomfort with that paradigm might eventually grow to the point that individuals may become liable for authorizing extrajudicial executions under the guise of the laws of armed conflict, that point has not yet been reached. So the path of least resistance taken over the past fifteen years still works to some degree for now. But it will not work if the international law community's view of the subject gains further traction, particularly in the context of states or tribunals that claim universal jurisdiction over human rights violations, or if the United States feels compelled to take on targets with whom it is not as clearly at war as it is with al Qaeda.

Targeted Killing as Self-Defense?

As I have already indicated, the proper international legal rationale for targeted killing is self-defense, not the target's combatant status under IHL. Unfortunately, self-defense is one of the most contested issues in all of public international law. The UN Charter says, at Article 2 (4), that all member states shall "refrain in their international relations from the threat or use of force against the territorial integrity or political independence of any state."

It also goes on to say, at Article 51, that nothing in the present charter shall "impair the inherent right of individual . . . self-defence if an armed attack occurs against a Member of the United Nations." As readers are likely well aware, whole libraries are filled with commentary on the potential conflicts between the two articles (as well as the potential conflicts and interpretive issues with respect especially to the meaning of "armed attack" and the "inherent" right of self-defense under customary law, which long predates the charter). In this discussion, I confine myself strictly to the question of how a targeted killing might be viewed with respect to self-defense.[64] Even so, the question remains alarmingly broad because targeted killing is an activity on the cusp of perhaps the most difficult practical issue of self-defense: preemption and prevention and anticipatory self-defense.[65]

There are many views on this question and nearly endless controversies. But in the long-standing U.S. view, self-defense encompasses at least three categories:

— self-defense against an actual use of force or hostile act
— "preemptive self-defense against an imminent use of force"
— "self-defense against a continuing threat."

These categories are not new.[66] Hays Parks, the senior Department of Defense law-of-war attorney, noted them, for example, in a memorandum on assassinations back in 1989, long before the emergence of al Qaeda or the circumstances of September 11.[67] Broadly speaking, the United States grounds its customary law views concerning anticipatory self-defense on the so-called Caroline Doctrine, which permits such actions but also limits them to circumstances in which the "necessity of self-defense is instant, overwhelming, leaving no choice of means, and no moment for deliberation."[68] Despite the apparent restrictiveness of the Caroline language and despite the fact that many international law commentators regard it as having been superseded or at least severely curtailed by the UN Charter, it as served as a source of evolving state practice for the United States since before the Civil War to the present day. It also has been seen as a source of legal justification for preemptive and preventive self-defense. One corollary of the long-standing U.S. interpretation of self-defense (but one that is widely reflected in the views and state practice of other states since 1945) is that, notwithstanding the apparently literal language of Article 51, no "armed attack" need have occurred "before a state may use force to counter a threat."[69]

Moreover, as Parks also noted, the United States has always interpreted international law (including the Caroline Doctrine) in a manner that allows it to respond to the emergence of new kinds of threats.[70] Those interpretations include the self-defense right to respond to nonstate actors, such as al Qaeda (indeed, the Caroline Doctrine originally concerned a nonstate actor at the U.S.-Canadian border in 1837). And the United States also accepts some evolving version of what has sometimes been called the "accumulation of events" or "active defense" view of anticipatory self-defense—a variation of the category of "self-defense against a continuing threat." One scholar describes the "active defense" view as follows:

> A state may use past practices of terrorist groups and past instances of aggression as evidence of a recurring threat. In light of this threat, a state may invoke [the right of self defense] . . . if there is sufficient reason to believe that a pattern of aggression exists. What may appear to be retaliation is quite often an "active defense" in which a state uses past terrorist acts to justify launching preemptive strikes. Advocates of this theory believe that it offers a much more practical response to a terrorist threat; in effect, a state will no longer need to wait until it is attacked before it may use force.[71]

Not surprisingly, the prestige of this theory suffered somewhat when Saddam Hussein's Iraq turned out not to have weapons of mass destruction. Nonetheless, it remains the legal view of the United States, particularly with regard to terrorist nonstate actors. It almost unquestionably remains the view of the Obama administration, which has been notably slow to formally relinquish the legal powers of counterterrorism exercised under the Bush administration. The legal policy of the United States has remained remarkably stable on this topic; as Hays Parks stated in 1989, the right of self-defense would support direct attack on—and one can add, targeted killing of—terrorist leaders when "their actions pose a continuing threat to U.S. citizens or the national security of the United States."[72] That is not narrow language, and it was not devised post–September 11 or by the Bush administration; it was an accurate statement of U.S. policy in the 1980s. Through the Clinton administration, the Bush administration, and into the Obama administration today, some version of self-defense has remained the true, if sometimes obfuscated, underlying legal rationale for targeted killing.

What do these long-standing U.S. views mean for targeted killing under international law? Three things primarily: First, the United States accepts as a matter of international law that targeted killing requires justification in some fashion as self-defense in order to be a legal resort to force. Second, however, the U.S. view of international law governing self-defense is pragmatic and flexible and it changes over time to meet new circumstances. Third—and crucially from the standpoint of protecting the U.S. legal position—the question of whether something plausibly constitutes self-defense is debated by many different "communities of interpretation" of international law, including states, congeries of states, academics and nongovernmental organizations, the Security Council, the General Assembly, and the International Court of Justice. That said, the United States is entitled to assert its own interpretation of international law should it choose to make the effort to do so—and provided that it is willing to bear possible substantial international diplomatic costs. That requires, however, being willing to assert and reassert its interpretation over time, to announce its view and to act on that view.

The trouble, once again, is that much of the world sees the U.S. right of self-defense far more narrowly. Important actors in the community of international law do not even accept that the situations in which the United States has undertaken targeted killing in, for example, Pakistan constitute legitimate self-defense under the UN Charter. For example, the eminent international law scholar Sean D. Murphy has a forthcoming article in *International Law Studies,* the influential journal of the U.S. Naval War College,[73] expressing grave and careful concern that, in the absence of meaningful consent by the government of Pakistan, a broad "right of self-defense against al Qaeda targets in Pakistan based on the attacks of 9/11, however, is . . . problematic, since the requirements of necessity and proportionality likely preclude unilateral uses of force against a third State that was not implicated in those attacks."

The gap between U.S. needs and consequent views of self-defense and the views of the international law community is probably unbridgeable. But this is not a case of the United States versus the rest of the world. There are a sizable number of states that have to worry about the possibility of enemies using third countries as havens, shielded by claims of the third country's sovereignty. It is a delicate dance in international law; no one wants to say too much one way or the other. When states do act, discreet silence is very often the reaction. Thus, leaving aside the United States and Israel, Murphy notes that Turkey has undertaken "various cross-border operations against the Kurdish separatist guerrilla organization . . . without being condemned by the Security Council, General Assembly, or [the] International Court."[74] When, in 2008, Colombia attacked FARC guerrilla camps across the border in Ecuador, none of the "principal organizations of the United Nations criticized the action; while the Organization of American States adopted a resolution declaring the Colombian raid to be a violation of Ecuador's sovereignty, the OAS stopped short of expressly condemning Colombia."[75] Two judges of the International Court of Justice (ICJ) each stated in separate opinions in the

2005 case *Armed Activities on the Territory of the Congo* that if the ICJ still endorses a literal reading of Article 51, limiting self-defense to attacks by another state, then the ICJ is no longer consistent with either state practice or the practice of the Security Council.[76]

In other words, it is important not to see the United States as some solitary outlier on this point, far removed from other states. The gap, rather, lies with the influential, loose body of "soft-law" opinion makers, activists, academics, and commentators. And the tension here is neither surprising nor necessarily unhealthy. The United States will always have a need to make flexible decisions about national security. And the dynamic will always and forever be that middling state powers, emerging great powers, outright enemies, idealistic NGOs, UN functionaries, law professors and intellectuals, and other such actors will seek to leverage their influence by using the rhetoric of international law to constrain U.S. flexibility in exactly this regard.

With respect to international law, therefore, the U.S. justification for the legality of a particular targeted killing should be based on self-defense, irrespective of whether an armed conflict under IHL that might provide a further justification is also under way. Conceding over time that targeted killing can be distinguished from extrajudicial execution only if it is part of an armed conflict under IHL will subject the United States to requirements that it has not traditionally accepted as a matter of international law but that it will find difficult to dismiss when the IHL standard of armed conflict has not been met. In this area, the United States will receive plenty of pushback just on the question of what constitutes its legitimate self-defense under international law. It buys itself only additional constraints if it also allows the international law of self-defense to run together with the law governing the conduct of hostilities.

U.S. Domestic Regulation of Targeted Killing

Modern U.S. statutory authority for non–law enforcement exercises of force by "intelligence" actors begins with the National Security Act of 1947, which created the CIA and granted it authority to engage in a wide variety of intelligence activities. The 1947 act also authorized the performance of "additional services of common concern" and "such other functions and duties related to intelligence affecting the national security as the President or the National Security Council may direct."[77]

The reference to "other functions and duties"—commonly termed the "Fifth Function"—is deliberately obscure. But as foreign relations legal scholar Philip Trimble observes, the breadth of known incidents under the Fifth Function is sufficient to suggest that "the executive branch has interpreted the legislative mandate broadly and Congress has regularly acquiesced."[78] During the 1960s, for example, functions included assisting in overthrowing governments in Iran and Guatemala; assisting in attempts to "assassinate leaders in Cuba, Chile, and Zaire"; supporting "civil wars in Iraq and Laos"; and attempting an "invasion of Cuba."[79] Although one might characterize a number of those activities as having taken place as part of armed conflicts, the characterization would not apply to all. In any case, the United States was not participating as a party to the conflicts, where they existed. Whether rightly or wrongly, justly or unjustly, the United States has often used force, not under color of law enforcement or in the context of IHL armed conflicts to which the United States was a party but under domestic statutory authority.

The point, for the purposes of this discussion, is that legal or not, under the international law of self-defense, those earlier cold war interventions were undertaken on the understanding that there was a valid basis in international and domestic law for uses of force apart from, and short of, war in the IHL sense. And, moreover, that force might be used by civilian agents, rather than regular armed forces, of the United States. Notwithstanding the reforms that have strengthened congressional oversight and other watchdog functions over the past several decades, nothing in the basic statutory arrangement challenges the fundamental assumption that U.S. domestic law permits in certain circumstances the use of force, including targeted killing, by civilian agents of the government in circumstances that implicate self-defense under international law but do not necessarily constitute an IHL armed conflict.

The domestic law governing the "intelligence community" changed dramatically in the 1970s, largely because covert uses of force came to light and were found by many to be wrong, imprudent, unjust, or unjustified under claims of self-defense or imperative national security. Watergate-era congressional hearings in 1974 resulted, among other things, in funding restrictions on intelligence activities under the Hughes-Ryan Amendment to the Foreign Assistance Act of 1974.[80] That amendment, combined with the Intelligence Oversight Act of 1980, laid down the basic pattern of post-Watergate domestic law restrictions on "covert" actions, including those that involve the use or the threat of use of force:[81]

—Intelligence agencies had to seek and receive a presidential finding before undertaking any such operation.

—The president had to be informed of the operation.

—The substantive standard for such actions was that "each such operation is important to the national security of the United States."

—The president had to report on each operation "in a timely fashion," although not necessarily in advance, to the intelligence committee of each house of Congress.

—Congress could express its will in current or future funding.[82]

In this statutory and regulatory arrangement for the conduct of intelligence activities, Congress left deliberately vague what constitutes an operation covered by the statute. The use of force is not explicitly mentioned at all, although it is unquestionably understood. The statute glosses over thorny U.S. domestic law issues of separation of powers. But while the fundamental constitutional issues, Michael Reisman notes, remain inconclusively resolved, there is no ambiguity on the authority to engage in covert action. "[I]f there was any doubt regarding the statutory basis for covert action, the Hughes-Ryan Amendment . . . and Intelligence Oversight Act of 1980 removed it."[83]

The statutory regime contains no suggestion that such operations, insofar as they use force, legally can take place only as part of an armed conflict within the meaning of international humanitarian law. Indeed, the first statutory definition of "covert action," offered in 1991 in the Intelligence Authorization Act for Fiscal Year 1991, refers very obliquely to covert uses of force. "Covert action," under the statute, means activities to "influence political, economic, or military conditions abroad, where it is intended that the role of the United States Government will not be apparent or acknowledged publicly." It specifically does not include activities the "primary purpose of which is to acquire intelligence."[84] Moreover, covert action is defined not to include either "traditional diplomatic or military activities or routine support to those activities [or] traditional law enforcement activities conducted by United States Government law enforcement agencies or routine support to such activities."[85] It is an attempt to regulate and require oversight of covert actions—even by allowing Congress to refuse to fund them—not to legislate them out of existence. Actions covered included the 1984 mining of Nicaraguan harbors.

Moreover, reforms of intelligence actions in the past three decades have been overwhelmingly concerned with the oversight of *peacetime* covert uses of force (that is, uses outside an IHL armed conflict) in particular—presumably because Congress was most concerned that peacetime operations would be less scrutinized than operations conducted as part of an acknowledged armed conflict in which the existence of the conflict was plain and the application of law-of-war standards was clear. Hence the exception in the statute for "traditional" military activities, such as open, overt war. Currently an important internal government debate is under way with respect to whether various Predator strikes in Pakistan constitute "covert" activities that, notwithstanding their connection to the ongoing war, are nonetheless covered by the statute or whether they are instead part of the "traditional" activities of the military in conducting war. Whatever the correct answer, no one engaged in that debate is questioning that the fundamental category is covert operations that might take place either in the context of an IHL armed conflict or as part of an operation justified by the doctrine of self-defense.

The U.S. Assassination Ban

The U.S. law that most closely addresses targeted killing outside of armed conflict is not a statute. In the Church committee hearings in Congress in the mid-1970s, the CIA's role in various assassination attempts in earlier years was revealed and became a matter of widespread public outrage. In the wake of that uproar, the Ford administration issued an executive order banning U.S. government employees from engaging in or conspiring to engage in political assassination.[86] The order was repeated in slightly varying language by President Carter[87]—who unaccountably dropped the word "political" —and was finally reissued by President Reagan in the form still in force today, Executive Order 12333. The pertinent section reads: "No person employed by or acting on behalf of the United States Government shall engage in, or conspire to engage in, assassination."[88]

This brief sentence has occasioned considerable scholarship and other commentary, much of it learned and ingenious, intended to interpret and reinterpret the provision. The executive order, after all, provides no definition of assassination, and the materials collateral to the three versions of the order shed little if any authoritative light on what it is supposed to mean. The issue has been repeatedly on the table for the obvious reason that, interpreted as widely as it might be, executive order 12333 would appear to preclude the targeting of the head of a hostile state who was, for example, the commander in chief of enemy armed forces and otherwise a legal target. The order does not distinguish between wartime and peacetime or between armed conflict governed by IHL targeting standards and anything else.

Commentators have suggested various ways of reading the ban. The Church committee was focused on the shocking revelations of CIA participation in plots against foreign leaders in peacetime; "peacetime" was specifically mentioned by President Ford in his contemporaneous suggestion of support for legislation banning assassination of foreign officials. A Congressional Research Service report suggests that "assassination may be viewed as an intentional killing of a targeted individual for political purposes." Many others, however, have argued, in part based on the focus of the Church committee hearings, that assassination as understood in U.S. usage connotes attacks directed at political leaders and that terrorists are not political leaders. Still others have noted that the term carries a sense of covertness and treachery, not merely surprise. And still others have argued that acts of self-defense—including armed conflict undertaken within the legal meaning of self-defense and surprise attacks as part of self-defense—are outside the scope of the assassination ban. The U.S. government has expressed its official views, however. Abraham Sofaer, the Reagan administration's legal adviser to the State Department, for example, stated as the policy of the U.S. government that assassination was to be understood not merely as killing with a political motive or aimed against a political leader but that it also had to be, independently, a "murder" in the first place. Sofaer noted that "virtually all available definitions of 'assassination' include the word 'murder' . . . a crime [and] that element is the most fundamental aspect of the assassination prohibition"; thus, under "no circumstances" should assassination be defined to include any otherwise "lawful homicide."[89] The view of the State Department of the 1980s, which apparently was not contravened by later pronouncements, was that unlawfulness is a necessary prior element of an assassination.

Actual U.S. state practice since the issuance of the Reagan order strongly supports a narrow reading of it, including the view that to violate the executive order, the homicide must have been independently unlawful. After all, in 1986, not long after the issuance of the order, President Reagan ordered a retaliatory air strike against Libya. According to press accounts and seemingly eschewing locutions about attacking a military target that might merely collaterally include the Libyan president, Muammar Qadaffi, the president said that the attack was aimed at Qadaffi personally, in order to try to kill him.[90] The First Gulf War and the more recent Iraq and Afghanistan wars all saw efforts at "decapitation" strikes aimed at the leadership of enemy regimes, for impeccable military but also humanitarian reasons: killing a regime's leaders—a legitimate target in war—might bring a war to a close without great loss of life among nonleaders.[91] Such actions were all in the course of armed conflict governed by IHL since they constituted state-to-state hostilities covered by the formal terms of Article 2 common to the Geneva Conventions and in each case the political leadership was regarded without controversy as a legitimate target of attack. Predator strikes in Pakistan, Yemen, and other places where IHL might or might not apply to the use of force have not been considered by the former Bush administration or the Obama administration to contravene the order or to require its modification or revocation, supporting the view that they see it as narrow in the ways that Sofaer indicated when he announced it in 1989 as U.S. policy.

The best reading of the executive order at this point is to say that, without further definition, it is a ban coextensive with preexisting U.S. obligations under international law. Sofaer suggests as much when he says that examination of international "laws of war *also* supports limiting the assassination prohibition to illegal killing"—but then carefully makes clear that illegal killing does not include the lawful exercise of the right of self-defense under international law.[92] And, with respect to domestic law, assassination is a term of art referring to a form of already illegal murder[93] but not something that should be construed "in a manner that inhibits the lawful exercises of lethal force."[94]

That said, the assassination ban operates as a principal analytic constraint on targeted killing outside the context of IHL armed conflict, though on its formal terms it can apply within it as well. When government lawyers worry about the lawfulness of a proposed targeted killing, their concern seems not to be about the IHL definition of armed conflict; it appears to focus instead on whether the killing qualifies as an assassination or not. Recourse to the position of the State Department in 1989 urges that this focus is the wrong one. Moreover, by embracing extra and unnecessary justifications to avoid the possibility that an exercise of lethal force might be characterized as an assassination under criteria that are far wider than the State Department's view of an already illegal killing, the position of the United States on targeting in self-defense is gradually weakened.

Pressure on the U.S. Position

To all of this, the Obama administration might ask a resounding "So what?" The human rights and other issues raised might exist in some hypothetical counterterrorism campaign far in the future if some administration were prepared to sign on to readings of international law that the United States has always rejected. But for now, in the fight against al Qaeda, the United States has the AUMF and does not accede to the more extravagant arguments of the international human rights community. The result is that targeted killing is governed by IHL, and the United States uses it only when the conditions of self-defense have all been met. Those facts, conveniently, also get around the assassination ban. Perhaps some legal issues might be raised over operating in parts of Pakistan and over targeting parties who are not clearly related to al Qaeda. But practically, it all seems like the same "armed conflict," so whatever legal problems might exist tomorrow, the United States does not have a legal difficulty today.

That even the Bush administration always treated its targeted killings as the targeting of combatants covered by the AUMF in a war covered by IHL says something about the pressures the U.S. legal structure faces from actors in the international legal community. Those pressures are unlikely to abate. The current U.S. view of the nation's authority to conduct targeted killings, as described above, is barely more palatable to key elements of the international community than the one that I advocate. What's more, seemingly innocuous changes in and acquiescence to various legal regimes and rules could end up undermining the U.S. legal rationale for targeted killing. The United States, to cite only one example, would like to have a more productive engagement with the International Criminal Court; that would put a considerable premium on the future definition of the crime of "aggression" in that tribunal because the United States might thereby finally accept a definition of aggression that subjects its own soldiers, agents, and officials to the court's interpretations as a matter of individual criminal liability.

Some of the long-term international legal pressure turns on a fundamental difference in understanding of how international law works—a difference that sometimes has a strong effect on its interpretation. In the long-held U.S. view, international law classically binds sovereign states through their consent, either contractually through explicit treaties or implicitly through their assent to gradually evolving customary law. By contrast, those seeking to constrain states or alter their behavior without their consent have an incentive to expand the canon of what is implicitly agreed to by states—and generally binding on all of them—in the form of this body of customary international law.[95] Since custom is not limited to the explicit terms of a ratified treaty, it is open to expansive restatement, interpretation, and invention by a wide variety of both government and nongovernment actors. Classically, customary law has been evidenced principally by the actual behavior of states—functioning to ensure that international law does not over time become a purely paper enterprise whose terms depart further and further from what states actually do. What is not prohibited to states, however, is generally permissible for them. So in that view, the question of targeted killing is not whether it is affirmatively allowed but whether some treaty provision or some genuinely accepted customary rule prohibits it.

The traditional underpinnings of international law are, however, contested in the contemporary world because the "ownership" of international law—who sets its terms, interprets its rules, and determines its content and meaning—is no longer entirely in the hands of sovereign states. Other actors—international advocacy organizations, international tribunals, international organizations and their functionaries, professors and academics, middle-weight states that see international law as a means to constrain more powerful states—play a significant role in defining and interpreting international law and setting its terms. And while it is easy now for the U.S. administration to pretend that those currents of influence do not exist, they have a way of seeping in as real constraints on U.S. practice.

The stakes are higher than U.S. policymakers appear to realize, as even a cursory look over the past few years should make plain. At the most overt level, there is the possibility of prosecution abroad based on a consensus view of international law that the United States rejects. No one who has watched the European eagerness to initiate criminal and civil proceedings against Israeli and U.S. officials in ever-proliferating judicial forums can be entirely sanguine about a giant gulf between U.S. and international understanding of a practice that the international law community regards as murder.[96] The more aggressively the United States uses targeted killing, the more glaring the gulf will become—until, in some jurisdiction, someone decides to assert the consensus view as operative law. Absent some aggressive effort to defend the U.S. position, that magistrate or prosecutor will have the overwhelming weight of international legal opinion behind him.

But the problem for the United States is not limited to the possibility of criminal proceedings abroad. U.S. courts themselves are far from immune to the influence of developments in soft law. Consider only the manner in which U.S. detention policy has been affected by parallel currents of opinion on international law imported into U.S. law through Supreme Court opinions. Only seven years ago, a U.S. administration took a "so what" attitude toward the ferment in international law over detention that was similar to the current consensus on targeted killing. International legal scholars, NGOs, international organizations, and most countries took a far more restrictive view of the detention authority residing in IHL—specifically with respect to the protections due unlawful enemy combatants—than did the United States, which had quietly preserved but not fought aggressively for a different approach over the preceding decades. The Supreme Court, however, has now gone a considerable distance to bridge the gulf by insisting that at least a portion of the Geneva Conventions covers all detainees. Whatever one thinks of that judgment, it is a striking example of the capacity to affect U.S. law of the sort of international legal developments that are now appearing with respect to targeted killing.

More broadly, there are hidden but important costs when the United States is perceived by the rest of the world to be acting illegally. For one thing, it limits the willingness and capacity of other countries to assist U.S. efforts. Detention here again offers a striking example: virtually no other country has assisted openly in U.S. detention operations outside active war zones since September 11 in large part because of concerns over its legality. The more heavily and aggressively the United States banks on holding to a policy merely because it has always done so, when a strong consensus outside the United States regards that policy as criminal per se, the more tension it can expect in efforts to garner the cooperation of other countries and organizations in counterterrorism efforts. Absent a strong effort to establish the legitimacy of current U.S. practice, that too will, over time, push the United States away from targeted killing as a lawful practice. Legitimacy is created by the assertion of the legitimacy and lawfulness of the practice, not by the mere fact of state practice alone.

The Obama foreign policy team may assume that the world's goodwill toward the new administration means world acceptance over time of such actions. That assumption is surely mistaken. The admirable, if mistaken, views of international law scholars and the international law community on how, specifically and in this circumstance, human rights law should apply universally did not develop because Obama's predecessor was named Bush—and they will not melt in the face of affection for a popular new president. Over the long run, if the Obama administration wants to continue to fight using more discriminating, precisely targeted weapons instead of full-scale combat, it is going to have to confront this problem while it still has intellectual and legal maneuvering space.

Legitimate Concerns

The concerns that underlie all of this ferment in international law—chiefly, targeting mistakes and excessive collateral damage—are real and substantial. A wholly justified worry about arguments for targeted killing, particularly as offered here, is that they defend the practice without offering anything in the way of standards for its effective regulation. If Congress and the administration wish to maintain and defend the legitimacy of this category of violence and to demonstrate that it is not unlimited or unregulated and that it does exist within bounds, the question of visible domestic standards requires attention. Indeed, the reach to situate this activity under the law of IHL armed conflict is, in substance, a reach to standards of proportionality, discrimination in targeting, and minimization of collateral damage.

It would be a profound mistake, as I have argued, to formally adopt such standards on the mistaken view that they *must* apply as a matter of a particular regime of international law that has its own triggers regarding when it applies. Treating these standards as binding law in their own right rather than as useful and appropriate policy standards would be an unwelcome additional invitation to war crimes prosecutions by other states and international tribunals against those engaged in key missions.

The standards that do apply as a matter of binding customary law of self-defense are, as noted, necessity and proportionality, and they apply even to the conduct of self-defense operations. In seeking ways to operationalize those two legal requirements, it is highly relevant to look to IHL standards, even if they do not apply as law as such. For example, the minimum calculation of proportionality with respect to collateral damage should begin with the classic IHL formulation weighing military advantage against harm to innocent third parties and certainly should not drop below that. These are areas in which existing standards developed in IHL *are* highly persuasive as a policy matter and important in informing the content of customary law of the conduct of self defense operations. Congress and the administration should move to address valid concerns about substantive standards without taking steps that imply that international bodies or other states are being invited to treat U.S. activities as potential war crimes under their jurisdiction. The U.S. government also should recognize that its ability to sustain such programs over the long term depends in considerable part on continuing efforts to develop technologies that afford greater discrimination in targeting—and that doing so requires research and development.

However, the elephant in the room, so to speak, is the standard by which U.S. forces select targets in the first place. That is the core objection to the whole practice, raised by UN special rapporteurs and many others: on what basis does the United States conclude that a person is a terrorist? While the substantive standard governing the evaluation of a potential targeted killing in relation to collateral damage to innocent third parties is best drawn from the law of IHL armed conflict, target selection in targeted killing is an intelligence matter. And although military intelligence has much to offer in the way of methodology, military law has much less. Yet the intelligence community, for many reasons, has had only limited success in picking targets since 9/11— although the quality of target selection in the current campaign of Predator strikes by the CIA in Pakistan has clearly gone up. Congress can require that more information be given to the intelligence committees and require greater monitoring of target selection either before or after an attack, but it faces great limits in doing more than that. Congress cannot make intelligence judgments—not to mention that it seems quite unable to keep secrets.

The concerns over targeted killing are not, of course, limited to targeting and collateral damage. Other states, particularly friendly and allied states, have excellent reason to view the practice with political alarm—quite apart from their abstract legal assessments of it. Britain, for example, has a certain number of radical imams who appear to influence their followers directly to, among other things, take up jihad in Pakistan and Afghanistan against Britain's U.S. and NATO allies.[97] In *purely* hypothetical terms, the United States might do well to target and kill those imams in Britain. While the United States obviously is not going to do that, it will target al Qaeda with Yemen's consent in Yemen, and there are circumstances in which it will target terrorist suspects in some other sovereign's territory without that sovereign's consent.

What the United States should seek, that being the case, are policy standards that distinguish between two distinct, prototypical situations. On the one hand, policy should unashamedly permit the use of Predators and Hellfire missiles against the leadership of a terrorist organization under, for example, the following conditions:

—The group poses a grave threat to the United States.

—The group's leadership is safely ensconced in a failed state somewhere.

—A state of armed conflict within the meaning of IHL may or may not exist.

—Seeking to obtain custody or extradition or to take other "ordinary" measures will not only be unavailing, it will tip off the targets.

—The administration has concluded that it cannot undertake another full-scale military assault, least of all for the purpose of killing a discrete, small group of terrorists.

That describes Afghanistan under the Taliban, of course, but it even more accurately captures Pakistan and its trajectory today (as the Obama campaign correctly recognized), with all the policy unpleasantness that it implies.

On the other hand, the United States certainly would want a rule that prohibits such acts as the 1978 poisoned–umbrella tip killing of Bulgarian defector Georgi Markov by Bulgarian state security agents on the streets of London[98] or the 2006 poisoning of former Russian FSB agent Alexander Litvinenko, also in London, allegedly by Russian government agents.[99] The latter actions would surely be covered by the assassination ban if they were proposed as U.S. operations; they were not remotely cases of "self-defense," although such actions in the case of radical imams who are operationally part of al Qaeda conceivably might be. The distinction has to be more meaningful, obviously, than the mere assertion that "it's different when our guys do it." The United States, moreover, presumably wants it known that its agents will not undertake targeted killings in the United Kingdom under any circumstances, even if they might in Somalia; there will also be a category of states for which strategic ambiguity is preferred. Here a rule of *international* law will necessarily not avail; because of the formal equality of states, international law will have great trouble separating the Britains from the Somalias. Yet that is precisely what policy as a practical, substantive matter requires.

But what, then, does separate them—besides the not irrelevant factors of power, friendship, and alliance with the United States and its community of allies? The most obvious factor is that a failed state creates ungoverned territory in which terrorists can find a haven. However, while that factor is the most obvious, the truly ungoverned territory of a truly failed state probably is not the most dangerous with respect to the harboring of terrorist organizations. Precisely because it is obviously ungoverned, objections to intervening there, even by those who would ordinarily object, would be fewer. The most dangerous safe havens are not entirely failed states but states that are functioning sufficiently to offer the levers of the state to terrorist organizations, either because the state is a fully functioning one that shares the ideological or tactical aims of the terrorists or because the state is functioning sufficiently to provide both a buffer against outside pressure and a launching pad but not functioning sufficiently well to prevent terrorists and their supporters from exercising important powers. The latter description captures at least part of the complex situation of al Qaeda and the Taliban in Pakistan. These situations mark the most important category of places in which the United States might see value in targeted killing.

At the other extreme are liberal democracies functioning under the rule of law that permit the adjudication of legal claims such as the question of Russian agent involvement in the London incident. It is sometimes suggested that a genuinely "neutral" way of dividing places in which some form of forcible covert activity (usually speaking of abduction of an alleged terrorist) is acceptable from those in which it is not is the presence, first, of a functioning state. The difficulty with stopping there is that Iran is a functioning state and for that very reason a successful sponsor of terrorist groups. Next, then, it is suggested that it must be a functioning state governed by *the rule of law*, by which extradition and other such claims can be openly and neutrally adjudicated. The difficulty is that it is possible to have a state with a reasonably neutral rule of law that is part of a system that is neither liberal nor democratic and that is entirely sympathetic to the aims and open to the means of terrorism.

At some point, in other words, however much one might point to neutral criteria such as the rule of law or to widely (though by no means universally) held criteria such as "liberal democracy," in the end they do not quite describe the dispositive factors. When it comes to the specific issue of terrorism, it comes down to whether a state (or a sufficiently powerful and independent part of it) is willing to give haven to enemies of the United States—to that and to the costs and risks of using covert force, including the risk of its becoming known, versus the benefits.[100] There are indeed overwhelmingly principled reasons why the United States would not carry out such attacks in London, but those principles are not completely neutral; they also have very much to do with the ideals and interests that the United States and the United Kingdom share.

Comity, therefore, is a powerful—if non-legal, non–law-based—argument against violent covert action, targeted killing, abduction, and similar acts. Indeed, it might well be the most powerful—or at least the most *accurate*— argument in choosing a policy response. But it is a calibrated argument, not a categorical one—an argument that operates on a sliding scale with respect to the community of nations: friends, allies, those who might cooperate under a carrot or stick scheme, enemies, and territory that is only nominally governed. It also should be noted that this matter implicates not only state sovereignty—which is directly challenged when targeted killing is undertaken without the host state's consent—but also human rights. All things being equal, the best and proper way to proceed is through mechanisms of the rule of law: presentation of evidence to a neutral tribunal and transparent operation of the mechanisms of justice. That is preferred for both principled reasons and practical ones—intelligence methods are very far from infallible. But things are not always equal when it comes to preventing terrorism, and in that regard not all states are equal, either.

But it would lead the reader astray not to acknowledge that of anything in this chapter, the proposal of a rule of comity for sovereign states in which the United States would undertake targeted killing and sovereign states in which it would not is purely a policy proposal—and the least compatible with widely held assumptions of the international law community in that it contravenes the basic assumption of the sovereign equality of states. On the other hand, it has the virtue of realist clarity, how the United States behaves, and how other states behave. But, to reiterate, this is all hypothesizing about policy, not law.

What Should Congress Do?

Does the analysis presented here offer any practical policy prescriptions for Congress and the administration? The problem is not so much a need for new legislation to create new structures or new policies; the legislative category in which many instances of targeted killing might take place in the future already exists. The task for Congress and the administration, rather, is instead to *preserve* a category that is likely to be put under pressure in the future and, indeed, is already seen by many as a legal nonstarter under international law.

Before addressing what Congress should do, one might ask from a strictly strategic political standpoint whether, given that the Obama administration is committed to this policy anyway, it is politically prudent to draw public attention to the issue at all. Israeli officials might be threatened with legal action in Spain, but so far no important actor has shown an appetite for taking on the Obama administration. Perhaps it is better to let sleeping political dogs lie.

Answering that question requires making difficult political calculations. However, the sources cited above suggest that even if no one is quite prepared at the moment to take on the Obama administration over targeted killing, the intellectual and legal pieces of the challenge are already set up and on the table. With certain positions concerning human rights law and its application having been asserted and the United States having unthinkingly abandoned its self-defense rationale for its policy, the play can be made at any time—at some later time in the Obama administration or in the next Republican administration, prying apart the "U.S." position to create a de facto alliance among Democrats and Europeans and thereby undermining the ability of the United States to craft a unified national security strategy.[101] The United States would be best served if the Obama administration did that exceedingly rare thing in international law and diplomacy: getting the United States out in front of the issue by making the U.S. position plain rather than merely reacting in surprise when its sovereign prerogatives are challenged by the international soft-law community.

The deeper issue here is not merely a strategic and political one about targeted killing and drones; it goes to the very grave policy question of whether it is time to move beyond the careful ambiguity of the CIA's authorizing statute in referring to covert uses of force under the doctrines of vital national interest and self-defense. Is it time to abandon strategic ambiguity with regard to the Fifth Function and to assert the right to use force in self-defense and yet in "peacetime"—that is, outside of the specific context of an armed conflict within the meaning of international humanitarian law? It is quite possible that in a world in which secrecy is more and more difficult and there is a general fragmentation of voice and ownership with respect to international law, strategic ambiguity has lost its raison d'être. That question is larger than the one addressed here, but on a range of issues including covert action, interrogation techniques, detention policy, and others, a general approach of overt legislation that removes ambiguity is to be preferred.

The single most important role for Congress to play in addressing targeted killing, therefore, is to assert openly, unapologetically, and plainly that the U.S. understanding of international law on this issue of self-defense is legitimate. To assert, that is, that the United States sees its conduct as permissible for itself and for others and to put the weight of the legislative branch behind the official statements of the executive branch as the *opinio juris* of the United States, its authoritative view of what international law is on this subject. If this statement seems peculiar, that is because the task—as fundamental as it is—remains, unfortunately, poorly understood.

If whether targeted killing is to be a tool of choice for the United States in confronting its nonstate enemies is really a matter of political consensus between left and right, then this is an essential task for Congress to play in supporting the Obama administration as it seeks to speak with a single voice for the United States to the rest of the world. Congress needs to backstop the administration in asserting to the rest of the world—including to its own judiciary—how the United States understands international law regarding targeted killing. And it needs to make an unapologetic assertion that its views, while not dispositive or binding on others, carry international authority to an extent that relatively few others do—even in today's emerging multipolar world. After all, international law traditionally accepts that states with particular interests, power, and impact in the world carry more weight in particular matters than other states. The U.S. view of maritime law matters more than does landlocked Bolivia's. The views on international security law of the United States, the core provider of global security, matter more than do those of Argentina, Germany or, for that matter, NGOs or academic commentators. But the United States has to speak—and speak loudly—if it wishes to be heard. It is an enormously important instance of the need for the United States to reclaim "ownership" of international law—not as its arbiter nor as the superpower alone, but as a very powerful, very important, and very legitimate sovereign state.

Intellectually, continuing to squeeze and force all forms and instances of targeted killing by standoff platform within the law of IHL armed conflict is probably not the most analytically compelling way to proceed. It is certainly not a practical long-term approach. Not everyone who is an intuitively legitimate target from the standpoint of self-defense or vital national security will already be a party in an armed conflict or a combatant in the strict IHL sense. Requiring use of such IHL concepts for a quite different category is likely to have the deleterious effect of deforming the laws of war, over the long term—starting, for example, with the idea of a "global war," which is itself a certain deformation of the IHL concept of hostilities and armed conflict.

The most intellectually honest approach would be to begin from the category of self-defense as the United States has traditionally understood it in international law and then defend the category as it currently exists in U.S. domestic statutory law for the intelligence community—that as long as a targeted killing legitimately meets the legal criteria of self-defense, it can be lawful to target people who might not be, under the strict law of IHL armed conflict, combatants. Needless to say, that for the moment appears to be a political nonstarter—as evidenced by the fact that even the Bush administration seems never to have engaged in a targeted killing of someone who it conceded was not, legally speaking, a combatant under IHL. In practical terms, the space Congress needs to defend is targeted killing within the broad vision of armed conflict as defined by the traditional U.S. interpretations of the inherent right of self-defense.

Specifically, Congress and the Obama administration should find ways, formal and informal, of asserting that as long as targeted killing satisfies standards of self-defense, the United States regards it as lawful in the sense of not being per se illegal and that it can and will be carried out as part of essential counterterrorism operations under existing domestic legal authority granted to the intelligence community and the CIA. One way to do that is by adding language to the basic CIA statute that explicitly provides for what is already implicit: that the power to carry out its "other" functions applies in peacetime and is not limited to circumstances of internationally recognized IHL armed conflict.[102] In so doing, Congress should refer in the statute to the exercise of vital national security interests as including the inherent right of self-defense as the United States interprets that legal concept. There is value in tying such uses of force under domestic law directly to the assertion of the right of self-defense under international law in order to make their basis clear and to establish that they are different from IHL armed conflict.

The independent legal existence of the category of intelligence agency uses of force, including targeted killing, as lawful self-defense should also be stated—frequently—in hearings, in official statements of the administration, and by the CIA, the Justice Department, and the State Department as the *opinio juris* of the United States. This policy can be expressed by Congress in statements accompanying appropriations bills and other legislative pronouncements. Given the extent to which such issues increasingly appear in U.S. domestic litigation, such as cases brought under the Alien Tort Statute, the Department of Justice needs a standing policy of defending this position vigorously as the foreign policy of the United States, assented to by the political branches, to which the judiciary should pay due deference.

Most important, Congress should reiterate and endorse two positions regarding the International Covenant on Civil and Political Rights. The first is the long-standing U.S. position that the ICCPR does not apply extraterritorially. The second is that IHL substitutes for—and displaces—any more general human rights regimes, including the ICCPR, in armed conflict within the meaning of IHL. That is important because so much of the international law community now takes it as a matter of course both that the ICCPR does apply extraterritorially and that it continues to apply in the course of an IHL armed conflict. As a consequence, as mentioned previously, virtually any targeted killing can be easily characterized as an extrajudicial execution—and the agents who carry it out, whether civilian or military, might at some point be threatened with indictment in some jurisdiction or international tribunal for an international crime. If Congress does not want that to happen, it needs to push back against the premise that the ICCPR has anything to say about U.S. conduct of such operations.

Even as they defend targeted killing against those who would simply treat the category as having all but entirely disappeared under international law, Congress and the administration need to establish standards to regulate the practice. That is hard. With respect to domestic law, proposals to create a comprehensive charter for the CIA have come and gone without fruition with regularity over the decades.[103] They do not succeed because discretion is at the heart of the intelligence agency action agenda. Likewise, both strategic deniability and the tacit agreement among the great powers to acquiesce in this category so long as it is not celebrated as such and remains within a set of loose and unstated bounds conspire to keep the rules unstated or, at least, stated vaguely. The same is true with respect to the specific question of targeted killing—no comprehensive charter can be both written and effective.

There are, however, areas in which a regulatory structure can be imposed—and should be, so that the law is more than a blank check—starting with necessity and proportionality in the conduct of self-defense operations. None of that will satisfy those for whom the category is morally wrong and legally impermissible as such—but for those for whom approval is possible in principle but who look for the devil in the details, important aspects of regulatory control would include the two basic issues in targeted killing: identification of the target (is the individual who he is said to be?) and minimization of collateral damage to innocent third parties. Congress should therefore instruct the administration and the CIA to brief the intelligence committees on the mechanisms that it uses to make targeting selection decisions—not just in the case of Predator campaigns undertaken as part of the ongoing conflict in Afghanistan extending over to Pakistan but also with respect to its protocols for determining targets outside of existing conflict zones and armed conflict at all, which is to say, any targeted killing. In the same vein, Congress can instruct the CIA in hearings, in briefings to the intelligence committees, and in other forums that it expects to be informed of protocols that the CIA would apply to targeted killing outside of armed conflict zones to ensure minimal collateral damage, respect for proportionality, and discrimination in targeting—and to ensure that the CIA is committed to applying the substance of the standard law of war regarding the protection of innocents when seeking its target. At a minimum, those collateral damage protocols should adopt those used in IHL—although in many instances, the appropriate level of caution to protect innocent civilians might well be higher than that required on the conventional battlefield. Standards drawn from IHL should be a policy minimum, not a maximum.

Congress should also consider instructing the CIA to develop criteria, secret or otherwise, for determining—perhaps subject to revision by Congress—what countries among U.S. friends and allies would *not* be places where the United States would consider undertaking targeted killing under any circumstances. Of anything said in this chapter, perhaps the most jarring to the international lawyer is the claim that as a matter of informal policy the United States might need to distinguish among states in which it would never contemplate a targeted killing and the states in which circumstances might make it necessary, with or without the state's consent. Of course, such a distinction lies behind every political calculation of targeted killing, the same realist calculation that lies behind the political actions of U.S. friends and foes and those in between. Yet this proposition cannot really be expressed as a matter of international law as such, because international law begins from the sovereign equality of states. This proposal takes a distinctly realist tack, breaking states down into friends and enemies, differentiating between places where the rule of law obtains and places where it does not, and applying other such distinguishing criteria.

Congress could engage in this thoroughly political exercise by, for example, asking for hearings in which the administration would be invited to offer the criteria under which state sovereignty might be ignored and a targeted killing undertaken. Congress could instruct the administration to provide private assurances as to what places, regimes, and countries would or would not be exempt and could make the discussion of who and why a matter of intelligence oversight briefings. It is an idea that has costs and benefits, to be sure, and it is recommended, if by anything, by virtue of its realism.

Finally, Congress should greatly beef up the level of briefings and information provided to the intelligence committees and should review the issue of oversight of covert and clandestine operations to determine whether existing oversight mechanisms are sufficiently robust and contemporaneous. Given the controversies now emerging over briefings to congressional oversight committees regarding interrogation, they almost certainly are not sufficient. The point about briefings to Congress is partly to allow it to exercise its democratic role as the people's representative; just as important, however, is that such mechanisms ensure, if properly and thoroughly carried out and documented, that Congress has either acquiesced in an executive decision or taken steps to object positively. Any administration should want to ensure that it has plainly and fully informed the intelligence committees so that the accountability and burden of making very difficult decisions about targeted killing are shared across the political branches of government. So there's a mutual advantage here. Moreover, there is room to consider public reporting, after the fact, of some form and in some fashion to ensure that the public can know what actions have been taken. A regime of violent covert action based around pure secrecy and executive discretion is a recipe for indictment. The political branches should be forced into joint accountability. If targeted killing is really to become a tool of choice for certain types of counterterrorism operations, U.S. oversight mechanisms need to reflect its new importance.

Conclusion

The ultimate lesson for Congress and the Obama administration about targeted killing is "Use it or lose it." That is as true of its legal rationale as it is of the tool itself. Targeted killing conducted from a standoff platform, with improving technologies in surveillance and targeting, is a vital strategic, but also humanitarian, tool in long-term counterterrorism efforts. War will always be an important option; so will the tools of law enforcement, as well as all the other nonforce aspects of intelligence work, diplomacy, and coordination with friends and allies. But the long-standing legal authority to use force covertly, as part of the writ of the intelligence community, remains a crucial tool—one that the new administration will need and evidently knows that it will need. So will administrations beyond it.

Although the United States is in a war, in its view, with al Qaeda, much of the world does not accept that premise; in any event, the threat from transnational terrorism will not forever come from al Qaeda. Even within the world of jihadist transnational violence, al Qaeda is gradually becoming a notional enemy. For some, that is a meme by which to announce that the threat is past or overrated, but that is not my intent here at all. Rather, I want to ensure that the United States does not tie its hands needlessly tomorrow by assuming that the nature of the threat and the specific legal rationale offered to address it will always be the same. Transnational jihadist networks are indeed becoming more diffuse, less and less directly tied in a "corporate" sense to al Qaeda. They are inspired by it, perhaps, and driven by a shared ideology, but they are not under its command, control, active direction, or other ordinary indicia of affiliation.[104] Terrorism by ideological affinity and loose network is likely to become more, rather than less, the norm into the future. The death of Osama bin Laden and his top aides by Predator strike tomorrow would alter national security counterterrorism calculations rather less than might be hoped. As new terrorist enemies emerge, so long as they are "jihadist" in character, some might continue referring to them as "affiliated" with al Qaeda and therefore as co-belligerents. But the label will eventually become a mere legalism in order to bring them under the umbrella of the AUMF passed after September 11. Looking even further into the future, terrorism will not always be about something plausibly tied to September 11 or to al Qaeda at all. Circumstances alone, in other words, will put enormous pressure on—and ultimately render obsolete—the legal framework currently employed to justify targeted killing operations.

What the United States can do is to insist on defining armed conflict self-defense broadly enough and human rights law narrowly enough—as it has traditionally done—to avoid exacerbating the problem and making it acute sooner or even immediately.

Ideology and ideas matter in shaping policy, especially at the intersection of international realpolitik, diplomacy, and law. Thus, I have made frequent reference to a loose community of interpretation, formation, deployment, and, really, "ownership" of international law. Such "ownership" matters too. The United States stands at a curious moment in which the U.S. *strategic* trend is toward reliance on targeted killing and the U.S. *political* trend is toward legitimization, even across party lines, but the international *legal* trend is toward severely and sharply containing the practice within a narrow conception of either the law of armed conflict under IHL or of human rights and law enforcement, although traditionally it has been considered self-defense under international law and has been regulated as covert action under domestic intelligence law. Many in the world of ideas and policy have already concluded that targeted killing as a category, even if proffered as self-defense, is unacceptable and indeed all but per se illegal. If the United States wishes to preserve its traditional powers and practices in this area, it had better assert them. If it does not, it will find that as a practical matter they have dissipated through desuetude.

Notes

1. Barack Obama, "The American Promise," speech, Democratic National Convention, Denver, August 28, 2008.

2. Barack Obama, "The War We Need to Win," speech, Woodrow Wilson International Center for Scholars, Washington, August 1, 2007.

3. Karen DeYoung, "Obama Tends toward Mainstream on Foreign Policy," *Washington Post*, March 3, 2008, p. A07; full text of questionnaire responses is available at www.themorningleader.lk/20080611/interviews.html.

4. R. Jeffrey Smith, Candace Rondeaux and Joby Warrick, "2 U.S. Airstrikes Offer a Concrete Sign of Obama's Pakistan Policy," *Washington Post*, January 24, 2009, p. A01.

5. See Mark Mazzetti and David E. Sanger, "Obama Expands Missile Strikes inside Pakistan," *New York Times*, February 21, 2009, p. A1; Karen DeYoung and Joby Warrick, "Drone Attacks inside Pakistan Will Continue, CIA Chief Says," *Washington Post*, February 26, 2009, p. A10; David E. Sanger and Eric Schmitt, "U.S. Weighs Taliban Strike into Pakistan," *New York Times*, March 18, 2009, p. A1; Pir Zubair Shah, "Missile Strike Kills 4 in Pakistan," *New York Times*, March 16, 2009; Jay Solomon, Siobhan Gorman, and Matthew Rosenberg, "U.S. Plans New Drone Attacks in Pakistan," *Wall Street Journal*, March 26, 2009; Pir Zubair Shah and Alan Cowell, "Missile Strike Said to Kill 10 in Pakistan," *New York Times*, April 1, 2009, p. A10; Robert Birsel, "U.S. Missile Kills 13 in Pakistan," *Reuters*, April 4, 2009; Eric Schmitt and Christopher Drew, "More Drone Attacks in Pakistan Planned," *New York Times*, April 6, 2009, p. A15; Nahal Toosi, "Suspected U.S. Missile Kills 3 in Northwest Pakistan," *Associated Press*, April 8, 2009; Jane Perlez, "Pakistan Rehearses Its Two-Step on Airstrikes," *New York Times*, April 16, 2009, p. A10.

6. See Habibullah Khan and Nick Schifrin, "Allegations that CIA Predator Drones Have Bases in Pakistan," *ABC News*, February 23, 2009 (http://abcnews.go.com/International/story?id=6938365&page=1). See also Pir Zubair Shah, "U.S. Airstrike Kills 21 in Pakistan," *New York Times*, March 14, 2009, p. A8; Simon Cameron-Moore, "U.S. Missile Strike in Pakistan Hit al Qaeda Nest," *Reuters*, January 31, 2008.

7. *Authorization for Use of Military Force,* Public Law 107-40, 107th Cong., 1st sess., September 18, 2001, §2(a).

8. See, for example, Mark Sageman, *Leaderless Jihad: Terror Networks in the Twenty-First Century* (University of Pennsylvania Press, 2008).

9. *National Security Act of 1947,* 50 U.S.C. 401.

10. See Monica Hakimi, "International Standards for Detaining Terrorism Suspects: Moving beyond the Armed Conflict-Criminal Divide," *Case Western Reserve Journal of International Law* 40 (2009), pp. 593, 601–10, addressing the debate of criminal law or armed conflict law within the treatment of suspected terrorists; Davis Brown, "Use of Force against Terrorism after September 11th: State Responsibility, Self-Defense, and Other Responses," *Cardozo Journal of International and Comparative Law* 11 (2003), pp. 18–26; Derek Jinks, "September 11 and the Laws of War," *Yale Journal of International Law* 28 (2003), p. 1.

11. The implications of terrorists who are at once "criminals" and "enemies" is discussed in Kenneth Anderson, "What Do We Do with bin Laden and al Qaeda Terrorists? A Qualified Defense of Military Commissions and the United States Policy on Detainees at Guantanamo Bay Naval Base," *Harvard Journal of Law and Public Policy* 25 (2002), p. 593.

12. The differences between police work and war is discussed in Kenneth Anderson, "Law, Language, and Terror: Policemen or Soldiers? The Dangers of Misunderstanding the Threat to America (Commentary on 9-11)," *Times Literary Supplement,* September 21, 2001; Kenneth Anderson, "Remarks on Literature and International Law," remarks, American Society of International Law, Washington, DC, April 10, 1997.

13. See Richard A. Clarke, *Against All Enemies: Inside America's War on Terror* (New York: Free Press, 2004), pp. 54–61. See also Derek Chollet and James Goldgeier, *America between the Wars: From 11/9 to 9/11* (New York: PublicAffairs, 2008), pp. 8–13.

14. Philip Bobbitt, *Terror and Consent: The Wars of the Twenty-First Century* (New York: Penguin Books, 2008).

15. Talk of a "third way" in counterterrorism risks conveying a deeply erroneous impression, however, in two regards. One is that it is a sort of "kinder, gentler" counterterrorism, whereas (as intended here) it fully embraces use of force as part of its methods. A second is that it replaces the other two, whereas instead it completes the picture of counterterrorism, with intelligence activities taking place alongside large-scale, overt war and criminal law enforcement, as appropriate to the circumstances. See Kenneth Anderson and Elisa Massimino, "The Cost of Confusion: Resolving Ambiguities in Detainee Treatment," in *Bridging the Foreign Policy Divide,* edited by Derek Chollet, Tod Lindberg, and David Shorr (New York: Routledge, 2008).

16. "Covert" activities has a statutory definition that sets it apart from the ordinary usage intended in this statement; that definition appears later in the discussion, but in general it includes not only officially unacknowledged use of force but also any unacknowledged activity by the government or its agents to attempt to influence the policies of a foreign government—including, for example, unacknowledged propaganda

or public relations, information campaigns, and other activities that are entirely unrelated to use of force.

17. Jack L. Goldsmith, *The Terror Presidency: Law and Judgment inside the Bush Administration* (New York: W.W. Norton and Company, 2007), pp. 177–83. Under the Obama administration, the terms "global war on terror," "the long war," and others are to be replaced by "overseas contingency operation," at least for the moment. See, for example, Al Kamen, "End of the Global War on Terror," in "44: The Obama Presidency," *Washington Post*, March 23, 2009 (http://voices.washingtonpost.com/44/2009/03/23/the_end_of_the_global_war_on_t.html?hpid=news-col-blog).

18. See, for example, Solomon, Gorman, and Rosenberg, "New Drone Attacks," note 5 above.

19. Barack Obama, "A New Strategy for a New World," speech, Ronald Regan Building, Washington, July 28, 2008, indicating a need for "more Predator drones" in the U.S. fight against al Qaeda.

20. Graham Allison and John Deutch, "The Real Afghan Issue Is Pakistan," *Wall Street Journal*, March 30, 2009, p. A23.

21. Most recently, for example, from Australian countersinsurgency expert David Kilcullen, who appealed in congressional testimony to "call off the drones." Doyle McManus, "U.S. Drone Attacks in Pakistan Backfiring, Congress Told," *Los Angeles Times*, May 3, 2009.

22. Allison and Deutch, "The Real Afghan Issue Is Pakistan."

23. See Archer Jones, *The Art of War in the Western World* (University of Illinois Press, 2000), pp. 83–86.

24. U.S. Department of the Army, *U.S. Army/Marine Corps Counterinsurgency Field Manual: U.S. Army Field Manual no. 3-24: Marine Corps Warfighting Publication no. 3-33-5* (University of Chicago Press, 2007), I-85 through I-90.

25. I emphasize here transnational terrorists, such as the leadership of al Qaeda—bin Laden and those at the top of his organization—rather than groups that organize and undertake fighting directly in theaters of war, such as al Qaeda in Iraq.

26. Matthew C. Waxman, "Detention as Targeting: Standards of Certainty and Detention of Suspected Terrorists," *Columbia Law Review* 108 (2008), pp. 1365, 1401–02.

27. Benjamin Wittes, *Law and the Long War: The Future of Justice in the Age of Terror* (New York: Penguin Press, 2008), p. 183.

28. Much of this criticism is summed up in P. W. Singer, *Wired for War: The Robotics Revolution and Conflict in the 21st Century* (New York: Penguin Press, 2009).

29. James Der Derian, quoted in P. W. Singer, "Robots at War," *Wilson Quarterly* (Winter 2009), p. 47.

30. Saeed Shah, "Anger in Pakistan at U.S. Plan to Expand Drone Attacks," *The Guardian*, March 19, 2009. See also Jane Perlez, "Pakistan's Military Chief Criticizes U.S. over a Raid," *New York Times*, September 10, 2008.

31. The objection is actually a very old one, stretching back at least to the founding of the International Committee of the Red Cross in the mid-nineteenth century. Florence Nightingale, for example—though she later became a firm supporter of the Red Cross movement—wrote in response to the call for a Red Cross Society that "such a Society . . . would relieve governments of responsibilities which really belong to them . . . and being relieved of which would make war more easy." Kenneth Anderson, "First in the Field: The Unique Mission and Legitimacy of the Red Cross," *Times Literary Supplement* (July 31, 1998).

32. Singer, "Robots at War," p. 47.

33. P. W. Singer was also an adviser to the Obama campaign on military and security matters, so perhaps the critique offered by his book will have greater sway than here suggested.

34. Political scientist Charli Carpenter correctly points out that this analysis creates an artificial binary between what is termed here full-scale war and targeted killing, whereas the menu for the use of force offers many choices in between. Charli Carpenter, e-mail message to author, March 19, 2009. That is true and important, but as a pure policy matter at this point in the Obama administration—and for whatever it is worth, my personal conversations with Obama staffers suggest that it is today a binary choice—the administration, for many obvious reasons, wants to avoid any possible on-the-ground engagements to which the United States is not already committed. Circumstances can always force an administration's hand, of course, and it is never inconceivable that events could do so with respect to Iran or North Korea. But my informal conversations suggest, entirely unsurprisingly, that the administration seeks to avoid any new engagements. The only one that was suggested as a new form of engagement was stronger activity as part of the multilateral, Security Council–authorized, anti-piracy measures off the coast of Somalia—and even there only on the clear understanding that there would not be a U.S. presence on the ground. In that case, simply as a matter of practical policy, the choices are binary, and drone air strikes look appealing when force must be used. My thanks to Carpenter for this comment and others; she is not responsible for anything said here, particularly given her strong disagreement with the normative thrust of this entire discussion.

35. Referring, of course, to overt clashes between the Soviet and NATO armies and leaving aside the many proxy wars that each fostered instead.

36. The strategic situation in that case is somewhat akin to the problem of the United States in the early cold war, when over-reliance on nuclear deterrence and lack of tools for intermediate non-nuclear responses tied the hands of the United States: although the actual confrontations were serious, they were not serious enough to warrant nuclear war.

37. Various writers have proposed different definitions—for example, "Targeted killing: the intentional slaying of a specific individual or group of individuals undertaken with explicit governmental approval." Major Matthew J. Machon, *Targeted*

Killing as an Element of U.S. Foreign Policy in the War on Terror (Fort Leavenworth, Kans.: School of Advanced Military Studies, 2006), 20.

38. The standard reference work on targeted killing and law is Nils Melzer, *Targeted Killing in International Law* (Oxford University Press, 2008). It is a marvelous work of scholarship, more comprehensive than any existing source, by a senior ICRC legal adviser. Despite its depth of scholarship and unpolemical language, it is something of an advocacy brief, however. It is difficult to see any circumstances under which Melzer would accept outcomes not congenial to his prior legal views, and, indeed, there is very little in the book that does more than note U.S. legal objections to some of the book's core positions and then reject them, without ever suggesting that they might have merit or at least constitute a defensible alternative view. It is in this sense the indispensable book on the subject, one which no researcher on this subject can do without, and yet, under the surface of the extraordinary scholarship, it relentlessly advocates a particular end. Melzer discusses all aspects of the topic, including law enforcement uses of targeted killing, a subject that is usually skipped over, just as I do here. See ibid., pp. 222–39.

39. See, for example, Micah Zenko, "Predator Strikes Are Not the Answer," *The Guardian*, March 19, 2009.

40. Mark Osiel, *The End of Reciprocity: Terror, Torture, and the Law of War* (Cambridge University Press, 2009), p. 586, n. 102; these commentators include, for example, Rosa Ehrenreich Brooks, currently a senior adviser in the Department of Defense. See Rosa Ehrenreich Brooks, "War Everywhere: Rights, National Security Law, and the Law of Armed Conflict in the Age of Terror," *University of Pennsylvania Law Review* 153 (2003), pp. 675, 756.

41. Gary Solis, "Targeted Killing and the Law of Armed Conflict," *Naval War College Review* 60 (Spring 2007), pp. 127, 135.

42. Analysis begins with Article 2 common to the Geneva Conventions. It has sometimes been summarized as saying that international humanitarian law is applicable in international armed conflicts "whenever any difference arises leading to the use of armed forces between the militaries of two states." Derek Jinks, "The Temporal Scope of Application of International Humanitarian Law in Contemporary Conflicts," background paper, *International Humanitarian Law Research Initiative*, Harvard Program on Humanitarian Policy and Conflict Research, January 2003, p. 3. However, it bears emphasizing that "use" of armed forces in interstate armed conflict is more than, for example, merely their appearance at the border in a time of tension—it refers to actual engagements between the armed forces of states. The Tadic decision of the ICTY Trial Chamber (*Prosecutor v. Dusko Tadic*, no. IT-94-1-T, Opinion and Judgment, May 7, 1998) thus expresses a standard that is overly broad in stating that an "armed conflict exists whenever there is a resort to armed forces between States," because according to that standard a resort to armed force might occur without actual armed engagement between armed forces. The lack of a common definition of armed

conflicts makes the threshold for application of international humanitarian law to internal conflicts much more difficult to resolve and highly fact-dependent. Jinks, "Temporal Scope," pp. 3–4.

43. To use slightly more technical language, although still not as fully as a lawyer would put it: one therefore distinguishes the *jus in bello* meaning of armed conflict from that under *jus ad bellum,* the legal question of the resort to force. Discussion comes later of "self-defense" under international law and its connection to targeted killing, but for now I note that "armed conflict" is often used in the sense of the legal regime governing resort to force—viz. the UN Charter and customary international law. The charter does not actually use the term "armed conflict," referring instead to "international peace and security," "aggression," "self-defense," and "armed attack." The emphasis of the charter terms is what one would expect in provisions focused on the resort to force—the beginning of conflict. Armed conflict, by contrast, is a term that conveys a greater sense of ongoing conflict, which is what one would expect in connection with the conduct of fighting. "Armed conflict" is thus a term somewhat more closely associated with *jus in bello* and conducts questions of international humanitarian law; the charter does not use traditional terms associated with the customary law of *jus ad bellum,* such as belligerency.

However, "armed conflict" is also a term used frequently with respect to each body of law, without necessarily a precise legal genealogy attached. Why does this issue, which apparently is one of mere nomenclature, matter? Because the standards for armed conflict that trigger application of the treaty—and thereafter, the operational rules—are different under each regime. International humanitarian law makes one kind of assessment; the charter, looking to resort-to-force rules, refers to breaches of international peace and security, aggression, and violations of territorial integrity of a state, among other things. Self-defense, under the charter and customary international law, has it own standards—many of which are highly contested. The term "armed conflict" is often used for one or another, but the standards and legal consequences can differ. In traditional state-to-state conflicts, the distinction typically might not make very much difference—but precisely in circumstances involving nonstate fighters acting transnationally, the distinctions might indeed matter.

44. Osiel, *The End of Reciprocity,* p. 407, n. 4.

45. Melzer, *Targeted Killing,* note 38 above.

46. Ibid., p. 243. It is clear from the book's text that Melzer intends "hostilities" in the sense of an armed conflict under international humanitarian law.

47. Sean D. Murphy, "The International Legality of U.S. Military Cross-Border Operations from Afghanistan into Pakistan," *U.S. Naval War College International Law Studies* 85 (forthcoming 2009), p. 2 (manuscript on file with author). I am grateful to Murphy for sharing an advance draft of his paper with me and allowing me to cite it.

48. "International Covenant on Civil and Political Rights," 999 U.N.T.S. 171, March 23, 1976, *United States Treaties and Other International Agreements.*

49. John Quigley, "The International Covenant on Civil and Political Rights and the Supremacy Clause," *DePaul Law Review* 42 (1993), pp. 1287, 1287-88, describing the background and history of the ICCPR.

50. "International Covenant on Civil and Political Rights," p. 171, Article 6.

51. See, for example, Chrissy Fox, "Implications of the United States Reservations and Non-Self-Executing Declaration to the ICCPR for Capital Offenders and Foreign Relations," *Tulane Journal of Comparative and International Law* 11 (2003), p. 303.

52. Ibid., pp. 322–23, expressing international criticism on U.S. refusal to budge on certain ICCPR provisions.

53. See U.S. Department of State, *Second and Third Periodic Report of the United States of America to the UN Committee on Human Rights Concerning the International Covenant on Civil and Political Rights, Annex I,* October 21, 2005; Matthew Waxman, statement before the UN Human Rights Committee, July 17, 2006: "In addition, it is the long-standing view of the United States that the Covenant by its very terms does not apply outside of the territory of a State Party."

54. See Inter-American Commission on Human Rights, "Report Colombia 1999," chapter IV, §11; Inter-American Commission on Human Rights, "Guantanamo Detainees Case (Precautionary Measures); Juan E. Mendez to attorneys for those requesting provisional measures, letter, March 13, 2002, quoting letter notifying the United States of the imposition of provisional measures, available at www.ccr-ny.org/v2/legal/september_11th/docs/3-13-02%20IACHRAdoptionofPrecautionary Measures.pdf. But see U.S. Department of State, *Response of the U.S. Government of 15 April 2002 to the IACHR with regard to the Commission's Decision to Order Precautionary Measures in the Guantanamo Detainees Case,* April 15, 2002.

55. See Senate Committee on the Judiciary, Subcommittee on the Constitution, *Restoring the Rule of Law,* prepared testimony, Diane Marie Amann and others, 110th Cong., 2nd sess., September 16, 2008, n. 29. The letter directly states that international human rights law "applies in time of war." It refrains from directly stating that the ICCPR applies extraterritorially. Instead, it states that "U.S. treaty obligations regulate U.S. operations even when conducted outside the United States" and then follows up with a series of provisions from the ICCPR, in the context of detention, but equally applicable to targeted killing. It seems evident that this statement is intended to be about the extraterritorial application of the ICCPR as well as other treaties.

56. See Harold Hongju Koh, "Written Responses to Pre-Hearing Questions Submitted to Legal Advisor-Designate Harold Hongju Koh by Senator Richard Lugar, Senate Foreign Relations Committee," 2009, available at http://lugar.senate.gov/sfrc/pdf/KohQFR.pdf, 1.

57. Amnesty International USA, "An Extrajudicial Execution by the CIA?" (www.amnesty.org/en/library/asset/AMR51/079/2005/en/bcffa8d8-d4ea-11dd-8a23-d58a49c0d652/amr510792005en.html).

58. UN Economic and Social Council, Commission on Human Rights, *Report of the Special Rapporteur on Extrajudicial, Summary, or Arbitrary Executions, Asma Jahangi,*

Addendum: Summary of Cases Transmitted to Governments and Replies Received, March 24, 2004, pars. 611-12, UN Doc. 2004/7/Add.1; UN Economic and Social Council, Commission on Human Rights, *Extrajudicial, Summary, or Arbitrary Executions, Report of the Special Rapporteur, Asma Jahangi, Submitted Pursuant to Commission on Human Rights Resolution 2002/36,* January 13, 2003, par. 37, UN Doc. E/CN.4/2003/3.

59. Cited in United Nations, Office of High Commissioner for Human Rights (www2.ohchr.org/english/bodies/chr/special/counter-terrorism.htm).

60. "Remote-Controlled Spy Planes," *CBSNews.com,* November 6, 2002 (www.cbs news.com/stories/2002/11/06/attack/main528396.shtml).

61. For a tiny sample, see notes to Amos N. Guiora, "Targeted Killing as Active Self-Defense," *Case Western Reserve Journal of International Law* 36 (2004), p. 319. In this chapter I have not devoted attention to Israel, although it has a far more developed jurisprudence regarding targeted killing than the United States has. The reason is that the long-term nature of the conflict, the fact that the conflict takes place in a confined geographic space, the special role of the Israeli Supreme Court in Israeli society, and other factors make me believe that the Israeli experience is actually less instructive for the United States than one might think. It seems to me quite inappropriate in the U.S. context to discuss judicial review of targeting killing, for example.

62. Abraham D. Sofaer, "Sixth Annual Waldemar A. Solf Lecture in International Law: Terrorism, the Law, and the National Defense," *Military Law Review* 126 (Fall 1989), pp. 117–18. In an important sense, most of what is advocated in this chapter is a restatement, endorsement, and updating of what Sofaer announced as U.S. policy in that address. It bears careful scrutiny today as the best statement of U.S. views of international law regarding U.S. rights and duties in responding to terrorism abroad. This chapter quite deliberately treads virtually no new ground not already laid out in this address.

63. The National Commission on Terrorist Attacks upon the United States, *The 9/11 Commission Report,* July 22, 2004, p. 132.

64. For example, Joel Westra, *International Law and the Use of Armed Force* (New York: Routledge, 2007); Yoram Dinstein, *War, Aggression, and Self-Defense* (Cambridge University Press, 2001); Volker Franke, *Terrorism and Peacekeeping: New Security Challenges* (Westport, Conn.: Greenwood Publishing Group, 2005). The literature is voluminous, to say the least.

65. See, for example, William Walton Keller and Gordon R. Mitchell, *Hitting First: Preventive Force in U.S. Security Strategy* (University of Pittsburgh Press, 2006); George P. Fletcher and Jens David Ohlin, *Defending Humanity: When Force is Justified and Why* (Oxford University Press, 2008); Alan M. Dershowitz, *Preemption: A Knife That Cuts Both Ways* (New York: W.W. Norton and Company, 2007).

66. For a robust assertion of them as *opinio juris* of the United States government—and a formulation to which the United States government would do well to return today—see Abraham D. Sofaer, "Terrorism, the Law, and the National Defense."

67. Hays Parks, "Memorandum of Law: Executive Order 12333 and Assassination," memorandum, December 1989, pp. 4, 7.

68. See, for example, Mayur Patel, "Israel's Targeted Killings of Hamas Leaders," *ASIL Insights,* May 2004. It should be noted that the U.S. interpretation of the Caroline Doctrine does not read Webster's apparently confining words as much of a restriction—it would be more accurate, perhaps, to say that the United States uses the Caroline Doctrine less as a constraint than as a recognition of the customary right of anticipatory self-defense.

69. Matthew C. Wiebe, "Comment, Assassination in Domestic and International Law: The Central Intelligence Agency, State-Sponsored Terrorism, and the Right of Self-Defense," *Tulsa Journal of Comparative International Law* 11 (2003), p. 363, citing Nathan Canestaro, "American Law and Policy on Assassinations of Foreign Leaders: The Practicality of Maintaining the Status Quo," *Boston College International and Comparative Law Review* 26 (2003), pp. 1, 16–17.

70. Parks, "Memorandum of Law," p. 7.

71. Howard A. Wachtel, "Targeting Osama bin Laden: Examining the Legality of Assassination as a Tool of U.S. Foreign Policy," *Duke Law Journal* 55 (2005), pp. 677, 692.

72. Parks, "Memorandum of Law," p. 7, n. 8.

73. Murphy, "Cross-Border Operations," p. 25.

74. Ibid., p. 18.

75. Ibid., p. 18.

76. *Armed Activities on the Territory of the Congo (Dem. Rep. Congo* v. *Uganda),* 2005 I.C.J. 168, 223 (December 19, 2005).

77. See 50 U.S.C. 403-3(d)(5).

78. Phillip R. Trimble, *International Law: United States Foreign Relations Law* (New York: Foundation Press, 2002), p. 250.

79. Ibid.

80. Ibid., p. 321.

81. *Foreign Assistance Act of 1974,* Public Law 93-559, 93rd Cong., 2nd sess. (1974).

82. A good short summary of these requirements is found in Alfred Cumming, "Covert Action: Legislative Background and Possible Policy Questions," Congressional Research Service, February 9, 2009.

83. W. Michael Reisman and James E. Baker, *Regulating Covert Action: Practices, Contexts, and Policies of Covert Coercion Abroad in International and American Law* (Yale University Press, 1992), p. 118.

84. 50 U.S.C.A. 413b(e).

85. Ibid., p. 124, citing *Intelligence Authorization Act for FY 1991,* Public Law 102-88, 102nd Cong., 1st sess. (1991), p. 105, stat. 429. See also "1991 Acts Senate Report," no. 102-85; "House Conference Report," no. 102-66; "1991 U.S. Code, Congressional and Administrative News," p. 193.

86. Nathan Canestaro, "American Law and Policy on Assassinations of Foreign Leaders: The Practicality of Maintaining the Status Quo," *Boston College International and Comparative Law Review* 26 (2003), pp. 1, 22.

87. Ibid.

88. Boyd M. Johnson III, "Executive Order 12,333: The Permissibility of an American Assassination of a Foreign Leader," *Cornell International Law Journal* 25 (1992), pp. 401, 408–09.

89. Abraham D. Sofaer, "Terrorism, the Law, and the National Defense," at 117–18.

90. See Seymour M. Hersh, "Target Qaddafi," *New York Times,* February 22, 1987 (www.nytimes.com/1987/02/22/magazine/target-qaddafi.html?sec=&spon=&page wanted=1), reporting that the bombing raid on Libya was understood by the Reagan administration to be an attempt to kill Qaddafi. Hersh's account has been sharply disputed by military lawyers and other who were involved with the planning of the mission. See, for example, W. Hays Parks, "Definition of Assassination," Memorandum of International Law Branch, International Affairs Division, Office of the Judge Advocate General, Department of the Army, November 2, 1989.

91. See Robert F. Turner, "Intentional Targeting of Regime Elites: The Legal and Policy Debate," *New England Law Review* 36 (2002), p. 785; Thomas Wingfield, "Taking Aim at Regime Elites: Assassination, Tyrannicide, and the Clancy Doctrine," *Maryland Journal of International Law and Trade* 22 (1999), p. 287.

92. Abraham D. Sofaer, "Terrorism, the Law, and the National Defense," at 122.

93. See, for example, Craig R. Whitney, "War on Terror Alters U.S. Qualms about Assassination," *International Herald Tribune,* March 29, 2004, p. 2.

94. Abraham D. Sofaer, "Terrorism, the Law, and the National Defense," at 122.

95. See, for example, Curtis Bradley and Jack Goldsmith, "Customary International Law as Federal Common Law: A Critique of the Modern Position," *Harvard Law Review* 110 (1997), p. 4; Jack Goldsmith and Eric Posner, "The New International Law Scholarship," *Georgia Journal of International and Comparative Law* 34 (2006), p. 463, highlighting the limitations of customary law.

96. The Israeli targeted killing of Salah Shehadeh in Gaza in 2002 illustrates where things would be likely to go. Shehadeh was head of the military wing of Hamas, and on the night of July 22, 2002, an Israeli F-16 dropped a bomb on his Gaza residence, killing him but also his wife, three of their children, and eleven others, mostly children. Legal proceedings were initiated in Britain and Spain against the Israeli commanders, and an Alien Tort Statute suit was filed in the United States. It would be a mistake to have any illusion that that will not be the trajectory of legal actions against the United States and its officials down the road.

97. Kim Sengupta, "Army Is Fighting British Jihadists in Afghanistan," *The Independent,* February 25, 2009.

98. See W. Hays Parks, "Memorandum of Law: Executive Order 12333 and Assassination," memorandum, DAJA-1A (27-1a), December 1989.

99. Guy Faulconbridge, "Russian Laughs Off Threat of Poisoning Extradition," *Washington Post,* January 26, 2007; Associated Press, "Russia Refuses British Request to Extradite Suspect in Poisoned Spy Case," *International Herald Tribune,* July 5, 2007; Associated Press, "Putin Says British Calls for Lugovoi Extradition 'Stupidity,'" *International Herald Tribune,* June 4, 2007.

100. See Eric A. Posner and Adrian Vermuele, *Terror in the Balance: Security, Liberty, and the Courts* (Oxford University Press, 2007) for a discussion of cost-benefit analysis in the counterterrorism context.

101. This strategic political question is discussed at Kenneth Anderson, "Gaming Spain and Universal Jurisdiction," Opinio Juris Blog, May 15, 2009 (http://opinio juris.org/2009/05/15/gaming-spain-and-universal-jurisdiction/).

102. For example, as an amendment to the *National Security Act of 1947,* 50 U.S.C. 401 (2005).

103. Trimble, *International Law,* p. 252. The proposal for a charter dating to the 1970s "would have established extensive substantive standards for covert operations, prohibited a number of acts like assassinations of foreign leaders, and created elaborate procedures for decision-making. At one point the proposed legislation was 263 pages long. It fell of its own weight." Ibid., p. 252. Unfettered discretion is not the right approach—but neither is the attempt at comprehensive managerial legislation.

104. Marc Sageman, *Leaderless Jihad: Terror Networks in the Twenty-First Century* (University of Pennsylvania Press, 2008); Marc Sageman, *Understanding Terror Networks* (University of Pennsylvania Press, 2004).

Contributors

Kenneth Anderson is a professor at Washington College of Law at American University and a research fellow at the Hoover Institution. He is also a member of the Hoover Institution's Task Force on National Security and Law. He has published extensively on human rights, the laws of war, global civil society, and international law. Formerly general counsel of the Open Society Institute and director of the Human Rights Watch arms division, he is political science editor of the *Revista de Libros* (Madrid), editorial board member of the *Journal of Terrorism and Political Violence,* and a frequent contributor to the *Times Literary Supplement* and other publications. He is author of the forthcoming book *Returning to Earth: Abiding Principles for Relations between the United States and the United Nations.*

Wells C. Bennett is an associate in the international arbitration and litigation practices at Arnold and Porter LLP. He previously served as law clerk to the Honorable Terrence W. Boyle at the U.S. District Court for the Eastern District of North Carolina. He holds a JD and an LLM in international law from Duke University School of Law.

Robert M. Chesney is a professor at the University of Texas School of Law and a nonresident senior fellow at the Brookings Institution. He is also a member of the American Law Institute, a term member of the Council on Foreign Relations, a senior editor of the *Journal of National Security Law and Policy,* and former chair of the national security law section of the Association of American Law Schools. Subsequent to preparation of his chapter in this volume, Chesney served with the Detainee Policy Task Force, a body established by President Obama to examine the full range of options relating to capture, detention, trial, and disposition in the context of armed conflict and counter-terrorism operations.

Justin Florence is an associate with the law firm O'Melveny and Myers and a nonresident fellow at the Georgetown Center on National Security and the Law. He previously served as law clerk to the Honorable Diana Gribbon Motz at the U.S. Court of Appeals for the Fourth Circuit. His writings on national security law have appeared in the *Yale Law Journal, Harvard Law and Policy Review, Legal Times,* and *Slate.* He graduated from Yale Law School, where he was executive editor of the *Yale Law Journal,* and he holds a master's degree in American history from Harvard University.

Matthew Gerke is a fellow at the Georgetown Center on National Security and the Law. He previously worked at the Pentagon and in Baghdad, dealing with rule-of-law issues in the reconstruction of Iraq. Before that, he was in private practice litigation. He holds a BA from Princeton University, a JD from the University of Michigan Law School, and a master's degree in international public policy from the University of Michigan.

Mark Gitenstein has practiced law in Washington, D.C., since 1989. He served on the staff of the Senate Intelligence Committee from 1975 to 1978 and as lead Democratic counsel, and then chief counsel, of the Senate Judiciary Committee from 1981 to 1989. He also served as chair for the vice presidential transition from November 2008 to February 2009. He is currently serving as U.S. ambassador to Romania.

Jack Goldsmith is Henry L. Shattuck Professor of Law at Harvard Law School. He is the author of *The Terror Presidency: Law and Judgment inside the Bush Administration* (2007). He also served as assistant attorney general for the Office of Legal Counsel at the Department of Justice from October 2003 through July 2004 and as special counsel to the general counsel of the Department of Defense from September 2002 through June 2003.

David Kris is the author or coauthor of several works on national security law, including the treatise *National Security Investigations and Prosecutions* (2007). He was previously deputy general counsel and chief compliance officer at Time Warner, adjunct professor of law at Georgetown University, and a nonresident senior fellow at the Brookings Institution. Kris is currently serving as the assistant attorney general, National Security Division, at the Department of Justice.

Robert S. Litt headed the white-collar criminal defense practice at Arnold and Porter LLP. Before joining the firm, he served for five years as principal associate deputy attorney general and as deputy assistant attorney general in the Criminal Division of the Department of Justice; before that, he was a federal prosecutor. Subsequent to the preparation of his chapter in this volume, he became general counsel to the Office of the Director of National Intelligence.

David Martin is Warner-Booker Distinguished Professor of International Law at the University of Virginia. He was general counsel of the Immigration and Naturalization Service from 1995 to 1998 and took leave from the University in January 2009 to serve as principal deputy general counsel of the Department of Homeland Security.

Stuart Taylor Jr. is a columnist for *National Journal* and a contributing editor for *Newsweek*. He is also a nonresident senior fellow in Governance Studies at the Brookings Institution.

Matthew C. Waxman is an associate professor of law at Columbia Law School. He is also adjunct senior fellow for law and foreign policy at the Council on Foreign Relations and a member of the Hoover Institution's Task Force on National Security and Law. He served in several senior national security positions within the executive branch from 2001 to 2007, including as deputy assistant secretary of defense for detainee affairs from 2004 to 2005.

Benjamin Wittes is a senior fellow and research director in public law at the Brookings Institution. He is the author of *Law and the Long War: The Future of Justice in the Age of Terror* (2008). He is also a member of the Hoover Institution's Task Force on National Security and Law.

Index